WHAT'S NATURE WORTH?

WHAT'S NATURE WORTH?

Narrative Expressions of Environmental Values

◆

Edited by

TERRE SATTERFIELD

and

SCOTT SLOVIC

◆

THE UNIVERSITY OF UTAH PRESS

Salt Lake City

Printed on acid-free paper

08 07 06 05 04
5 4 3 2 1

The Defiance House Man colophon is a registered trademark of The University of Utah Press. It is based upon a four-foot-tall Ancient Puebloan pictograph (late PIII) near Glen Canyon, Utah.

LIBRARY OF CONGRESS CATALOGING-IN-PUBLICATION DATA

What's nature worth? : narrative expressions of environmental values /
edited by Terre Satterfield and Scott Slovic.
p. cm.
Includes bibliographical references (p.) and index.
ISBN 0-87480-790-5 (pbk. : alk. paper)
1. American literature—20th century—History and criticism—Theory, etc.
2. Nature in literature. 3. Authors, American—20th century—Interviews.
4. Natural history literature—Authorship. 5. Environmental literature—Authorship.
6. Environmental policy—United States. 7. American literature—20th century.
8. Natural history—United States. 9. Nature—Literary collections.
10. Natural history—Authorship. 11. Narration (Rhetoric) 12. Storytelling.
I. Satterfield, Terre, 1960– II. Slovic, Scott, 1960–
PS163.W46 2004
810.9'36—dc22

2003020987

CONTENTS

ACKNOWLEDGMENTS

This project is the product not only of a unique cross-disciplinary collaboration between the two editors but also of layer upon layer of support and collaboration among family, friends, colleagues, agencies, and institutions. We are acutely conscious of how much we have benefited from many other people and groups while working on *What's Nature Worth?* during the past seven years.

First, invaluable financial support was provided by grants SBR9602155 and SES0080720 from the U.S. National Science Foundation under the Ethics and Values program. Any opinions, findings, conclusions, or recommendations expressed here are our responsibility and do not necessarily reflect the views of the funding agency.

Second, we might never have met each other and begun our work together had it not been for our connections with Decision Research in Eugene, Oregon. We are grateful to Paul Slovic for putting us in touch with each other, to many DR colleagues for helpful commentary on grant proposals, and particularly to Leisha Wharfield for skilled and generous assistance in preparing the manuscript.

Third, this project would be nonexistent were it not for the insights, eloquence, and good will of the twelve participating writers. We deeply appreciate the time and energy all have contributed to the interviews that constitute the core of this book, and we greatly value the contributions to society these extraordinary people have made. Particular thanks go to John Daniel who, on top of all else, helped prepare an interview protocol that was engaging and appropriate for the diversity of authors reflected here.

Fourth, in addition to Decision Research, two other institutions—the University of Nevada, Reno, and the University of British Columbia—have provided excellent professional homes for us as we've pulled this manuscript together. And the University of Utah Press has expressed keen interest in this work from the beginning—we are particularly grateful to Dawn Marano for her patience and for applying just the right amount of pressure.

Finally, Scott would like to express his gratitude to Susan Bender and Jacinto Slovic for taking such an interest in this work. Terre, equally, would like to extend her deep appreciation to Sherri Burns for her constant good humor and support.

INTRODUCTION: WHAT'S NATURE WORTH?

TERRE SATTERFIELD AND SCOTT SLOVIC

EXPLORING "ENVIRONMENTAL VALUES" IN THE CONTEXT OF NARRATIVE

The study of environmental values is both familiar and unfamiliar territory for students of nature writing. It is familiar in the sense that writers have long used various literary modes, especially narrative nonfiction, to portray their sense of how a person comes to value certain kinds of landscapes, or to know the particular microcosms that constitute one's immediate physical surroundings. But the study of environmental values is unfamiliar territory in the sense that most students of nature writing, and most nature writers themselves, are unaware of the effort spent in philosophical, economic, social science, and policy circles on the elicitation and articulation of environmental values. These scholars and policy practitioners are concerned with questions of how to elicit and represent values from different members of the public so as to initiate a democratic dialogue about environmental policy; less attention has been paid, to date, to the modes of discourse—the forms of expression—that might best enable the public to communicate value information to decision makers and policy officials.

In *Environmental Values in American Culture*, Kempton, Boster, and Hartley use the term "values" to refer to people's "guiding principles of what is moral, desirable, or just." They argue that "values are crucial, especially in the area of global environmental change, because the worst consequences of global change will be experienced in the future. If all people intently pursued their individual economic self-interest, based on their own past experience, nothing would be done to improve the situation. Cultural values are a necessary basis for environmental action, even if they may not be sufficient by themselves" (1995, 12). However, the predominant interpretation of the construct "environmental values" focuses less on the moral or philosophical aspect of the term than on the translation of places and natural phenomena into purely economic worth. This perspective posits a hypothetical market for environmental (i.e., nonmarket) goods and calls for public stakeholders to assign monetary value to an improvement of such things as spotted-owl habitat, riparian areas, or Alaska's oil-soiled Prince William Sound. These pricings are then aggregated to guide policy analysts' cost-benefit equations.

Many have found this approach to values lacking and have argued that people do not ordinarily think in terms of the monetary equivalent of improved landscapes or more bald eagles. Values, these critics argue, are instead about moral conviction and emotional attachments—not simply market pricing.[1] Until quite recently, scholars have defined the process of determining values as a way of thinking external to emotions and have disparaged emotions as bodily states lacking in conceptual complexity or content. Stocker and Hegeman (1996), among others, have countered this assumption by arguing that values may be internal to and even inseparable from emotions. Emotions, they write, "provide evidence for or symptoms of value . . . are expressions of [value] and may even be [a form of] evaluative knowledge" (1).

This book aims to take a first step toward bridging the gap between a literary community that, in subtle and intuitive ways, has thought deeply about the value of nature and a policy-oriented group of scholars that seeks to develop better tools for representing and discussing environmental values. Our project is derived from a set of twelve exchanges (by personal interview or by questionnaire) over a three-year period with prominent nature writers. We think of these writers as lay ethicists, important voices for articulating the multidimensional worth (spiritual, aesthetic, economic, and so forth) of nature. In particular, we have sought out these writers and asked them to explain what they see to be the connection between the language of story (or "narrative") and the way many people comprehend the value of nature (a point we elaborate on more fully below). These conversations have emphasized the philosophical and psychological aspects of the intersection between narrative and values, and in many cases the authors have commented as well on what they take to be the efficacy of particular narrative techniques in communicating or exploring subtle ideas about environmental values. The importance of narrative to expressions of value was recently acknowledged by psychologists interested in theories of communication, a good example being Timothy Earle and George T. Cvetkovich's *Social Trust: Toward a Cosmopolitan Society* (1995), which points to the relationship between narratives and moral development. This idea is less well appreciated in the realm of environmental values and policy research at this time—and one of the central purposes of this book is to find a way to bring the concept "narrative expressions of value" into the realm of stakeholder discussions of value and policy. Already it is clear that there is a cautious interest in this idea. When the subject of narrative is approached at professional meetings, ears invariably perk up, precisely because cost-benefit equations strike so many as an ill-suited medium for thinking about human "assessments" of nature. Robert W. Kates, in his editorial for the March 1999 issue of *Environment*, "Part and Apart," states: "We who study and write of nature, often in the sterile language of science or policy, are also bedeviled by [Robinson Jeffers's phrase] 'Love that, not man apart from that.' Most of us share with writers their love of nature and we delight in their eloquence. But we too are constantly torn between being part of and apart from our studies and policies. Our human-centered focus is enshrined in our language." Kates here implies that certain world views, especially non-anthropocentric perspectives, are simply inexpressible in the relatively "sterile language of science or policy"—that the language itself inhibits certain ways of thinking. The fact that the editorial board of *Environment*, a journal devoted to environmental science and policy, should choose to publish a lengthy introduction to environmental literature in 1999 suggests a new open-mindedness toward the relevance of literary discourse (including narrative) to policy research.

The writers we invited to participate in this study were encouraged in the interview context to examine why they used narrative forms to express notions of value and whether they found such forms better or worse than traditional approaches to thinking about values. We use this interview-based evidence to provide readers of this volume with the opportunity to consider what is conventionally meant by environmental values (material that is covered in this introduction) and to compare (and we hope expand) that definition via authors' very different (and sometimes entirely dissident) conceptions of value. This is not a typical scholarly text in that it does not seek a theoretical or analytic breakdown of the primary "value" or "narrative" themes raised by the authors. Rather, we use the chapter introductions to orient the reader to the author's insights and literary background and thereafter allow the author to articulate his or her own conclusions on the subjects at hand.

Nine of these interviews were conducted face to face with important figures in the contemporary renaissance of environmental writing in the United States, and the other three took place via written correspondence. The authors we interviewed work in a variety of literary genres—chiefly, the nonfiction essay, the short story, and poetry—and have branched out into such media as the journalistic essay, on-line book reviews, and didactic newspaper editorials. Linguist and poet Ofelia Zepeda, the editor of the University of Arizona Press's Sun Tracks Series, and prolific poet, fiction writer, and editor Simon J. Ortiz have helped to illuminate the importance of cultural background in this discussion of how and when narrative is important. William Kittredge and Richard Shelton, of the University of Montana and the University of Arizona, respectively, are two of the most distinguished creative-writing teachers in the American West—and eminent essayists, storytellers, and poets in their own right. Stephen Trimble and Gregory McNamee work in an eclectic range of media, from photography to the on-line book review, as well as in more conventional nonfiction nature essays, and their comments offer a broad understanding of the practical impact of environmental narratives and images. Gary Paul Nabhan and Robert Michael Pyle are two of the country's major practitioners of the subcategory of environmental writing known as "natural-history writing," a form noted for its bringing together of scientific information and narrative flair—and for this reason their comments on the tensions and compatibilities between these seemingly contrasting modes of thought are particularly important. Bruce Berger, John Daniel, Alison Deming, and Terry Tempest Williams are distinguished poet-essayists, noted for their use of highly aestheticized language and their at once clear-headed and passionate approaches to environmental controversies in the West, ranging from sea-turtle hunting in the Gulf of California to logging disputes in the Pacific Northwest and wilderness preservation in southern Utah.

What Is Conventionally Meant by "Environmental Values"?

We begin here with a brief and necessary introduction to the strategies policy researchers use in defining and researching environmental values (EV). Though most EV scholars are by definition multi-disciplinary thinkers, we rely upon disciplinary distinctions here to some extent in order to clarify several of the more common approaches. In offering only one or two examples of each scholarly approach, we can present a glimpse of each, if not a fully comprehensive survey. The book's bibliography offers a fuller representation of applied and theoretical research for readers who are interested in further pursuing the nuances of the field.

"Environmental values" is a complicated term involving myriad distinctions. Regardless, most researchers in policy contexts agree that a primary goal of values research is to represent public thinking about the importance of natural goods (biologically significant systems, ecosystem services, treasured landscapes, and/or threatened species). These value-laden expressions constitute the chief means through which the diverse groups of people that make up the amorphous thing we call "the public" are included in policy decisions about land management. Thus, when the National Estuary Project (NEP) set up research stations in several key U.S. states (such as Tillamook Bay in the state of Oregon, Galveston Bay in Texas, and Chesapeake Bay in Maryland), one component of their mandate was the establishment of estuary management and remediation programs that were ecologically and socially defen-sible. In Tillamook, Oregon, for example, the NEP's goal was to develop ascience-based, community-supported management plan. Achieving this meant that the NEP staff had to both understand and communicate the range of ecological impacts attached to potential management plans (for instance, restoring critical fish habitat by limiting livestock access to streams and thus mitigating high fecal coliform counts in the estuary, or altering upstream forest practices in order to reduce sedimentation in the estuary). Value positions were thus elicited from a committee of Tillamook citizens; once identified, their values were used to weigh the pros and cons of different resource-management actions. By way of this process, the management plans ultimately reflected both the value-orientations of local citizens and the knowledge of expert scientists. Working with citizens revealed strong support for actions to protect and restore tidal wetlands and an endorsement of high-intensity—even if more costly for taxpayers—initiatives including anti-erosion improvements in forest roads and the construction of additional cattle-restrictive fencing along streams as long as the loss of productive farmland was limited. An explanation of this case can be seen in Gregory and Wellman's "Bringing Stakeholder Values into Environmental Policy Choices" (2001).

For much of the last decade, resource economists and more recently ecological economists have interpreted the construct "environmental values" to mean that monetary prices should be assigned to different environmental goods or services. This effort has taken two forms. The first focuses on estimating the dollar-value of the services provided by the world's ecological systems, as part of the total "economic value of the planet" (see especially Costanza et al. 1998). Toward this end, the current economic value of seventeen ecosystem services (services such as climate regulation, nutrient cycling, gas regulation such as CO_2/O_2 balance, or water supply and regulation) for the entire biosphere is estimated to be in the range of U.S. $16–54 trillion per year (Costanza et al. 1998, 3–5). Most of these services are outside the market—that is, they are not normally considered items to be bought or sold by consumers.

A second, related form of valuation studies also uses dollar estimates to represent the interest of lay stakeholders. This approach is explained particularly well in R. C. Mitchell and R. T. Carson's *Using Surveys to Value Public Goods: The Contingent Valuation Method* (1989). Values are elicited from individual participants (citizens) in the form of statements about the amount in dollars individual citizens would be "willing to pay" (WTP) to protect, for example, a rare species or, less frequently, the amount an individual would be "willing to accept" (WTA) in compensation for damage to habitat or loss of that species. Gregory offers a hypothetical scenario to explain this concept:

> If a person is willing to pay $10, for example, to enjoy a day of fishing, then the experience is valued at this much or more because the individual is willing to give up the other things that this $10 could buy to acquire one day's angling. Similarly, if a person would take no less than $20 to accept the loss of access to a park, then he or she would be willing to give up what this $20 could buy; this willingness to accept compensation is a measure of the person's economic valuation of the park. (Gregory 1999, 37)

Responses to tasks such as these from many groups or individuals are sometimes further aggregated into a summary assessment of the average "market" value of the goods in question. Thereafter, these estimates are pitted in a benefit-cost analysis against the "costed interests" (the summing up in dollar figures) of other stakeholders who could include industry, regulatory agencies, different citizen groups, environmental nongovernmental organizations (NGOs), and so forth. These economic valuation or "utilitarian" approaches are rooted in welfare economics and assume that individuals are rational actors who evaluate situations and select desired outcomes on the basis of what benefits them as individuals. For recent instruction on this approach, see A. M. Freeman's *The Measurement of Environmental and Resource Values: Theory and Methods* (1993). For a critical review of its assumptions, see Mark Sagoff's "Aggregation and Deliberation in Valuing Public Goods: A Look Beyond Contingent Pricing" (1998).[2]

Economic value figures heavily in many ecologically important decisions, and the attribution of monetary worth to ecosystem services can serve to highlight ecological functions otherwise taken for granted. Nonetheless, ethicists and social scientists are more centrally concerned with public conceptions of species or ecosystem worth, with the complex, multidimensional, and often nonmonetary value-orientations and positions that underlie conceptions of nature. Paul Stern and Thomas Dietz offer a good expression of alternatives to CV methods in their 1994 article "The Value Basis of Environmental Concern."

One concern with CV methods is that the very language of cost-benefit analysis (its monetary focus and rationalistic tone) seems to determine the outcome of the discussion or at least point the discussion away from nonmonetary values, that is, deeply held social, moral, spiritual, ecological, or ethical concerns. Scholars such as John Foster, Ilana Ritov, Daniel Kahneman, David Schkade, and Cass R. Sunstein have argued that we cannot think about or easily offer a consistent price for nonmarket goods and tend instead to use the pricing opportunity to say something else, to express "support for public intervention, anticipated moral satisfaction from a [monetary] contribution, and . . . the intensity of [one's] attitudes to the issue at hand" (Ritov and Kahneman 1997, 37). Further, some members of the public consider the mere request to price a threatened species habitat as socially taboo or morally offensive; we find this response, for instance, in Fiske and Tetlock's study of "Taboo Tradeoffs: Reactions to Transactions that Transgress Spheres of Justice" (1997) and Baron and Spranca's "Protected Values" (1997; see also Baron and Leshner 2000). Critics find the act of pricing abhorrent because it assumes that one is willing to trade off, given the right dollar amount, something one holds dear, such as the protection of a rare species. The trade-off is avoided or resisted, argue Baron and Spranca, because it reflects back to the respondent-pricer the message that they are indeed *willing to pay* or substitute cash for an endangered species and are thus morally compromised.

Ethicists, representing the discipline of philosophy, have led the effort to counter the trend toward monetary expressions of value by defining both anthropocentric and ecocentric theories of worth. They have helped develop the language now used across disciplines to discuss such things as the instrumental, historic, symbolic, intrinsic, and existence value of nature; influential works in this area include J. Baird Callicott's "Non-anthropocentric Value Theory and Environmental Ethics" (1984) and "On the Intrinsic Value of Nonhuman Species" (1986), Mark Sagoff's *The Economy of the Earth* (1988), Bryan Norton's "Thoreau's Insect Analogies: Or, Why Environmentalists Hate Mainstream Economists" (1991), and Holmes Rolston III's *Conserving Natural Value* (1994). These scholars, and others, as historian Roderick Nash has summarized in his history of environmental ethics, *The Rights of Nature* (1989), have articulated a value-based defense of the rights of biotic communities and have countered the exclusion of important dimensions of value that results from excessively monetary approaches. Holmes Rolston

(1999) notes that environmental ethics was unknown in Western philosophy until the mid-1970s, yet today thousands of works have been published on the "theory and practice about appropriate concern for, values in, and duties to the natural world" (407).

While philosophers, particularly ethicists, are concerned with public education and the need for people to recognize the many reasons why natural systems are morally and ecologically indispensable, psychologists, sociologists, and anthropologists tend instead to consider the construct "values" from a more neutral or relativistic position. The focus for this latter group of social scientists is not on such things as more or less important ("good" or "bad") values, but on values, attitudes, or world views that are held by humans and guide behavior. Examples of this work include Stephen Kellert's study "Attitudes, Knowledge, and Behavior toward Wildlife among the Industrial Superpowers: United States, Japan, and Germany" (1993), which uses surveys to define nine attitudinal perspectives on wildlife (naturalistic, scientistic, moralistic, aesthetic, etc.). Kellert has also produced a detailed analysis of value differences based on nationality, gender, class, and economic status, published as *The Value of Life: Biological Diversity and Human Society* (1996). Other studies separate values into a tripartite system: egocentric, sociocentric, and biocentric values (see again Paul Stern and Thomas Dietz's "The Value Basis of Environmental Concern," 1994) or economic, social, and universal (as in Lawrence Axelrod's "Balancing Personal Needs with Environmental Preservation," 1994), and/or make clear distinctions between individual, scientific, and process/democratic interests (see especially John M. Foster's *Valuing Nature? Ethics, Economics and the Environment*, 1997; and Timothy O'Riordan's "Frameworks for Choice: Core Beliefs and the Environment," 1995). Others still have documented the escalation of environmental concern over time and demonstrated that values or attitudes once thought extremely radical are held by a broad variety of individuals and groups; this has been demonstrated in Riley Dunlap and colleagues' studies adapting an attitude or "New Environmental Paradigm" scale (Dunlap et al. 2000); and Appendix C in Kempton, Boster, and Hartley, *Environmental Values in American Culture* (1995).

Further, work such as that cited above by Kempton, Boster, and Hartley has proved extremely effective for defining lay mental and cultural models or "theories of cause." These models or cognitions include individuals' "simplified representations of the world, [representations] that allow one to interpret observations, generate novel inferences, and solve problems" (1995, 10). Kempton and his colleagues demonstrate that lay models can be effectively compared with expert-scientific models of such things as the root causes of global warming. This in turn reveals both the gaps in lay knowledge and the different value positions that permeate widely held assumptions about natural systems. Finally, many have worked with traditional ecological knowledge, sometimes called local knowledge or aboriginal science, to consider the influence of this knowledge on sustainable agricultural practices (See Scott Atran and Douglas Medin's "Knowledge and Action: Cultural Models of Nature and Resource Management in Mesoamerica," 1997). Atran and Medin have examined Itzaj Maya, Yucatec Maya, and Ladino understandings of inter-species interactions among those living in Guatemala's neotropical forests (the latter two groups are immigrants to the area). These researchers tie "the sudden turn from sustainable to unsustainable forest use [to] . . . differences in how native Maya and immigrant communities conceive of and manage forest resource systems in the same area" (1997, 171).

Despite these advances and alternative, non-economistic methods for the study of values, the field remains impeded by several basic concerns. Most valuation procedures have stripped their value-elicitation tasks of many of the affective qualities that are the hallmark of a deep value commitment to such things as environmental causes. Tasks may be met with resistance or indifference precisely because one is expected to de-animate—take the literal and symbolic life out of—oneself and the good in question via the act of converting one's zeal for salmon swimming valiantly upstream into a dollar metric or a flat statement about the merits of salmon. Such "flatness" or oddness of metric only increases the abstractness of the task from the respondent's point of view. Even *radically green* survey items such as "I am willing to sacrifice my standard of living in order to ensure that nature is preserved" or "All species, including human species, have an equal right to co-exist" can ring true and yet remain disembodied or depersonalized. The respondents who agree with these statements vary considerably in their agreement with the suggestion that "timber harvests should be reduced" (Satterfield and Gregory 1998, 632–34). This happens because such statements lack a context that allows respondents to link, and researchers to predict, actions on the basis of elicited value responses. This can also happen because there is a poor fit between valuation tools and the conversational, narrated, and storied way in which lay stakeholders talk to one another about their values. The crisp declarative sentences of WTP formulas and survey tools—I am willing to pay "x"; I believe "y"—can deny respondents a means for realistic engagement in the task and thus leave them struggling to conjure up a scenario to which a set of values might apply. (See especially Satterfield 2001 for elaboration on these above points.)

A final conundrum for values researchers couples the nuances of question-elicitation wording (the way in which a question is posed) with the basic democratic query—what constitutes an informed choice or, in this case, value? The value analyst's goal is to set up a value-elicitation task regime in which it is appropriate, indeed cognitively easy, for participants to think about their values. And yet students of judgment and decision making have long noted that very subtle changes in wording or phrasing can influence the elicited response (Tversky and Kahneman's 1981 article "The Framing of Decision and the Psychology of Choice"). That is, when presented with a survey question or simple dollar-elicitation task, participants are easily influenced. Their responses are not the product of stable opinions; instead they are constructed during the process of inquiry.[3] Equally, in a famous set of experiments by Tversky and Kahneman in the early 1980s, participants were shown to resist an outcome represented as a loss more strongly than an equivalent outcome represented as a gain. They demonstrated that we are more averse to a gamble that involves a 25 percent chance of loss than one involving a 75 percent chance of a gain or win even though, technically, they are the same.

This poses a challenge to the very idea of effective value-elicitation efforts because the researcher is caught between the need for informed choice (thus, the need for substantive background material about the biological features of a wetland or local residents' commitment to a place) and the knowledge that relatively subtle cues can influence responses. Background information or reading material that accompanies a value-elicitation process cannot be assumed to be a neutral "just the facts" preparatory course. Yet it is equally futile to avoid such material so as to avoid influencing respondents. This conundrum has produced some of the most exciting new work in valuation contexts, generally known as constructive valuation processes; see, for instance, John W. Payne, J. Bettman, and E. Johnson, "Behavioral Decision Research: A Constructive Processing Perspective" (1992); David A. Schkade and John W. Payne, "How People Respond to Contingent Valuation Questions: A Verbal Protocol Analysis of Willingness to Pay for an Environmental Regulation" (1994); and Robin Gregory, Sarah Lichtenstein, and Paul Slovic, "Valuing Environmental Resources: A Constructive Approach" (1993; see also Gregory and Slovic 1997).

These newer approaches posit that discussion with public stakeholders about values must be an actively constructive process. Value elicitation efforts should thus be set up so that the value problem can be de-composed into its component parts and thereafter addressed in a sequential ("constructed") manner; the dialogic exchange should be arranged so as to help people think deeply about their values without simultaneously placing unrealistic cognitive demands on participants. In short, participants need a user-friendly context in which relevant value information is rendered salient, enabling participants to be able to think about their values and thereafter provide the policy researcher with a good quality (i.e., informed and thoughtful) response.

The above delineation of value deliberation practices illuminates, we believe, four central problems. First, values must be constructed in the process of inquiry because many values do not conform to dollar expressions and are often ill-formed (and difficult to articulate); respondents thus need help to both clarify and tease out good-quality value information. Second, background information (be that technical, ethical, or ecological) must be framed in such a way that it facilitates learning, thereby rendering possible an informed judgment. Third, elicitation tasks must facilitate stakeholder participation by using a language or discursive frame that is meaningful and relevant to the stakeholder. Finally, many declarative-statement-based and monetary expressions of value suffer from a kind of emotional poverty that should be avoided or resisted as unrepresentative of human thought and behavior. Such expressions are unnecessarily de-animated or stripped of their moral and affective qualities.

Why Narrative? Why Nature Writers?

All of this brings us to the questions central to this volume: Why—amidst this larger struggle over how to elicit what constitutes an environmental value—might narrative expressions of value matter? Why should we consider writers' insights on these questions pertinent? In this next section, we offer a few thoughts on both questions, doing so via a brief reference to the social-science literature on narrative information frames and via a few excerpts from the interviews contained in this volume.

First, what *is* narrative? Literary scholars tend to use the terms "narrative" and "story" almost interchangeably. Often these concepts are defined rather broadly to encompass not only artfully crafted "literature" or "film," but even informal or *internal* tales we tell our friends or ourselves. In his essay "Narrative" for the volume *Critical Terms for Literary Study* (1995), J. Hillis Miller explains: "As adults, we hear, read, see, and tell stories all day long—for example, in the newspaper, on television, in encounters with co-workers or family members. In a continuous silent internal activity, we tell stories to ourselves all day long. Jokes are one form of narration. Advertising is another. . . . At night we sleep, and our unconscious minds tell us more stories in our dreams, often exceedingly strange ones. Even within 'literature proper' the range of narrative is wide and diverse. It includes not only short stories and novels but also dramas, epics, Platonic dialogues, narrative poems, and so on" (66). When we focus on "narrative" in this book, we mean the term to include not only the telling of stories of particular events, but the use of various forms of non-discursive language or the hybrid use of discursive analysis and more emotive and experiential modes of expression, including sensory imagery, characters, and scenes. Information can be carried and framed just as fully through narrative as it can be in more formal didactic forms of language. Our hope in this book is to pursue an understanding of the particular connections between narrative discourse and environmental values. As Lawrence Buell states in *Writing for an Endangered World: Literature, Culture, and Environment in the U.S. and Beyond* (2001), "Argument can state, but narrative can actually dramatize [e.g., ethical dilemmas at the situational level]. . . . Does [literary narrative] supply a conceptual template of practical value in adjudicating real-life controversies? No, not if what you want is a blueprint: a set of guidelines or procedures. But that is not something literature was necessarily supposed to furnish in the first place" (240–41). Nonetheless, narrative expression can carry subtle statements of authors'/tellers' values and can probe and elicit values-related thoughts from readers/listeners.

Consider the idea that values should be constructed during the elicitation process in part because many valuation problems are exceedingly complex and because certainty about one's value position is not always readily available to consciousness. A good value-facilitator must, given these problems, do two things. First, provide thought-provoking and even introspective opportunities for the reader-participant so that he or she can gain some clarity with regard to a value position. And, second, simplify the problem for the reader; the problem (perhaps an issue about stream health or habitat preservation) must be broken down into its component parts so as to render those parts salient and therefore available for deliberate examination.

Narrative modes of expression often function in precisely these ways. Many stories offer readers or listeners an opportunity for introspection or reflection, a process through which the audience comes to know (i.e., construct) something about their world view though the act of monitoring or observing their reactions to the story. "Storytelling," notes William Kittredge in this volume, "invites readers to make up a story of their own, to use the story they're being told as a mirror in which to view their own responses to their own concerns." This process is true not only for the reader but for the writer as well. Gary Paul Nabhan, in his interview for this project, finds that he teases out his own sense of value in the act of storytelling: "The more story-driven the essay is, the less likely I am to know or be conscious of the values I'm talking about. I can see it afterwards, with hindsight, but I seldom know about it in advance." For Terry Tempest Williams the point is somewhat different. Storytelling, she notes, is akin to setting up a trance: "When a story is told everything quiets down, the body language changes and one is brought into the story." This story or trance offers a place to retreat to for reflection, without the tyranny of a fixed conclusion.

The value-facilitator might also come to find that narratives, by definition, suit the need for structures that help simplify decision tasks by decomposing the problem. This is because narratives are built around plot or event structures (as Shlomith Rimmon-Kenan explains in the 1983 book *Narrative Fiction: Contemporary Poetics*) that can be analogously used in valuation contexts to outline the attributes of a problem (say, stream-water quality, current and historical salmon populations, aboriginal fishing rights, or dam impacts). Attributes such as these can be clearly stated as features of the plot and are also more memorable because plot structure provides something of an overall cognitive map of the problem, as Anne R. Kearney suggests in her article "Understanding Global Change: A Cognitive Perspective on Communicating through Stories" (1994). Further, the more clearly available readers or participants find the features of a problem to be, the more they are able to reserve their cognitive or contemplative energies for value deliberation.

Narrative qualities may help to satisfy the need for value *tools* that facilitate informed judgments given that most valuation contexts require participants to process or assimilate new technical and social information before offering a (value-based) judgment. Embedding social and technical detail (as is common in the work of many well-known nature writers such as Wendell Berry and Barry Lopez) within a narrative may be optimal because it triggers or relies upon dual modes of information processing (a rationalistic mode and a narrative-experiential mode). Theories of dual modes of processing can be traced to Aristotle's *Nicomachaean Ethics* but are best expressed contemporarily by Jerome Bruner's *Actual Minds, Possible Worlds* (1986) and as the central feature of Seymour Epstein's "Cognitive-Experiential Self Theory" (CEST), described in "Integration of Cognitive and Psychodynamic Unconscious" (1994). Bruner has proposed that human cognition relies upon two modes of thought: "a paradigmatic or logico-scientific [mode that] attempts to fulfill the ideal of a formal, mathematical system of description and explanation" (12) and a narrative mode that deals instead with good and believable stories infused with human "intention and action and the vicissitudes and consequences that mark their course" (13). More importantly, Bruner claims that "efforts to reduce one mode to the other or to ignore one at the expense of the other inevitably fail to capture the rich diversity of thought" (11).

Finally, valuation scholars are likely to be responsive to the capacity for narratives to engage their readers and reintroduce affect (even in its most subtle forms) to problems of judgment and valuation. Satterfield, Slovic, and Gregory (2000) have found that narrative and morally meaningful valuation frames, versus techno-rationalist ones, can improve people's ability to cognitively manage, analyze, and evaluate complex decision problems. Shanahan, Pelstring, and McComas (1999) have similarly concluded, when comparing the efficacy of survey statements to narrative passages, that "narratives are a distinct communication context that may provoke different thoughts and feelings than simple belief statements" and that "narrative measures can tap into different constructs [as compared to] typical attitude measurements" (412, 416). The potential efficacy of narratives in valuation contexts may stem from their ability to facilitate task engagement and operationalize an emotively and morally rich language that is consistent with *lay* talk of values. J. Baird Callicott has argued in the essay "Non-Anthropocentric Value Theory and Environmental Ethics" that value in nature is "grounded in human feelings" and "projected" onto the natural object that "excites" the value held (1984, 305). Engagement, others have noted, can be achieved by employing emotion to add meaning to otherwise abstract information (see Melissa L. Finucane, Ali Alhakami, Paul Slovic, and Stephen M. Johnson, "The Affect Heuristic in Judgments of Risks and Benefits" [2000]; and T. Kida and J. F. Smith, "The Encoding and Retrieval of Numerical Data for Decision Making in Accounting Contexts" [1995]) and by concretizing information through the use of imagery and anecdote. We have already noted Epstein's and Bruner's defense of the importance of affect to experiential levels of processing. Further, Antonio Damasio has argued in *Descartes' Error: Emotion, Reason, and the Human Brain* (1994) that emotion is essential to rational thought because it provides a basis for cognitive investment in judgment and decision making. Finally, Keith Oatley, in his 1994 study "A Taxonomy of the Emotions of Literary Response and a Theory of Identification in Fictional Narrative," has developed a categorization of emotional response to literature with the aim of demonstrating that it is through affectively engaging devices that we enter into the world of the narrative. By seeing the problem through the narrator's point of view, we take the problem on as our own and endeavor to solve it from a less distanced perspective than might be typical of cost-benefit or survey practices.

Writers featured in this volume also talk of engagement and the use of a living, breathing narrator (a kind of affective presence) to enhance a story's capacity to include the reader in the told experience. For John Daniel, "to listen to a story is to be inside the story." As well, in following the narrator, he finds that "one gives oneself to be led but not passively. You may take part of the insights as your own or you may reject them outright." But to follow, as we put it, the living, breathing narrator is not necessarily to be emotionally overpowered by that voice. Kittredge finds that he appreciates narrative because it restrains coercive inclinations by "stepping on [his] desire to preach," while Terry Tempest Williams suggests that stories permit the reader to "enter through the back door," to consider values in their own good time. In the end, much of the value content is left implicit; the reader is given cues and provocations, and then is expected to build on these. This is part of the dynamic interaction between text and reader. Highly skilled authors respect their readers' imaginative power, providing triggers but otherwise leaving the readers themselves to draw their own conclusions.

In 1986, National Book Award–winning nature writer Barry Lopez made an assertion that has since been widely circulated; he expressed his belief that nature writing "will not only one day produce a major and lasting body of American literature, but . . . might also provide the foundation for a reorganization of American political thought" (297). Daniel G. Payne, in his 1996 book called *Voices in the Wilderness: American Nature Writing and Environmental Politics*, has examined the influence of specific writers—particularly Ralph Waldo Emerson, Henry David Thoreau, George Perkins Marsh, John Burroughs, John Muir, Theodore Roosevelt, Aldo Leopold, Rachel Carson, and Edward Abbey—on the conservation movement and environmental policy in the United States from the mid-nineteenth century to the present. The complexities of environmental rhetoric—including the rhetorical practices of nature writers—have been examined in the 1996 collection *Green Culture: Rhetorical Analyses of Environmental Discourse*, edited by Stuart C. Brown and Carl G. Herndl. The present volume probes many of the issues of political efficacy and literary rhetoric explored in the above-mentioned studies; however, in this case, a dozen distinguished authors respond, directly and indirectly, to a broad range of questions about language, values, and politics. We are hopeful that the insights provided here will prove useful to future scholars studying many aspects of environmental writing and to social scientists, resource managers, and politicians interested in understanding new approaches for receiving public input for policy-making.

The Interview Outline

Although we could conceivably build a rich academic defense of the utility of narratives for valuation contexts (indeed we are guilty of a little of this already), the more important point for this collection is to permit authors to speak for themselves. Only some of those interviewed here were aware of the applied and scholarly values of literature in the social and economic sciences. Whether or not this was the case, we were careful to introduce these ideas to the writers in a manner that was merely sufficient to contextualize our interview questions. The basic outline for the interviews was the product of several conversations between writer John Daniel and the editors of this collection. Based upon those conversations, Daniel made a list of questions that he believed would be meaningful to most writers and would serve our own investigative ends. We regard his efforts toward this end as exemplary and thus the full list is reproduced in the written questionnaire responses herein prepared by William Kittredge, Richard Shelton, and Bruce Berger. Key questions in Daniel's questionnaire include the following:

- Do you see your work as an attempt to articulate the value(s) of nature?
- Do you feel that a responsive reader learns natural values from your work, or that your work alerts the reader to values already held?
- What do you see as the strengths and limitations of narrative as a carrier/elicitor of natural values?
- Can natural values be fully and accurately expressed in purely rational terms, or is there inevitably an emotive content?
- In your opinion or experience, what would be the best ways to elicit these values and identify them in people who may harbor them but find them difficult to articulate?
- What piece of your work best expresses your sense of the value of nature?

Three of the interviews were conducted via mail, but most were completed in person at the writers' homes, at the University of Arizona Poetry Center, or at the offices of Decision Research in Eugene, Oregon. Some of the interviews followed the written questionnaire closely, while others deviated dramatically. At times, authors resisted the very idea of environmental values and produced fascinating commentary born of that resistance. The transcribed text of each interview was edited and ordered so as to cull out the most important pieces of conversations that at times lasted several hours. We consider this volume, in a sense, to be an extension of Edward Lueders's influential 1989 volume of transcribed public dialogues between eight prominent nature writers, *Writing Natural History: Dialogues with Authors*. However, this new collection includes brief samples of each author's work relevant to the values context established in this introduction and in the interviews. Also, the discussions presented here focus more explicitly on the language of environmental values and on the social and political efficacy of environmental writing than is the case with the dialogues published in *Writing Natural History*.

Each chapter comprises a biographical sketch of the author and his or her work, followed by an edited representation of the interview proper. After each of the interviews, we have included a value-related selection of the author's work, demonstrating how the author who has just explained his or her notions of the relation between narrative or imagistic language and the communication of values actually goes about achieving this connection in a literary text.

As we stated above, this book aims to take a first step toward associating a literary community that has made significant progress in refining the language of environmental values with scholars who themselves seek to develop better tools for representing and discussing these values. We believe that the contextualizing introductions to each conversation, the interview transcripts, and the selected examples of values-oriented environmental writing will inspire members of the literary community to appreciate the potential significance of their work for the formulation of public policy, while scholars approaching this topic from the social and natural sciences will be compelled to rethink current elicitation methods in order to encompass crucial dimensions of human thinking and expression that have hitherto been left out of mainstream valuation practices.

1

INCITING STORY: NARRATIVE AS THE MIRROR OF AUDIENCE VALUES

Born in Portland, Oregon, in 1932, William "Bill" Kittredge grew up on a cattle ranch and farm in the remote Warner Valley of southeastern Oregon, some three hundred miles from Eugene. The Kittredge family owned thirty-three square miles of farmland and controlled grazing rights to another fifteen hundred acres. Eventually, after he had watched his grandfather and father oversee the process of working the land, responsibility for the MC Ranch passed into Kittredge's own hands. He did this work for eight years, before realizing his heart was not in it. During the years when he was growing up in the Warner Valley and later when he came to manage the MC Ranch, things were changing—the progress of industrial agriculture meant the diminishment of the place itself, the gradual, subtle disappearance of birds and the decreasing fertility of the soil. In the title essay of his 1987 book *Owning It All*, Kittredge recalls the image of vast numbers of waterbirds in the Warner Valley of his childhood, an image that was "wonder-filled and magical" and that gave him the feeling of being "enclosed in a living place" (62).

Kittredge attended high school in nearby Klamath Falls, then left the Warner Valley to major in agriculture at Oregon State College in Corvallis, graduating in 1953. Married, with two young children, he served in the Air Force for three years before returning to the Warner Valley to supervise the demise of the ranch for eight years. The fate of the ranch paralleled (and perhaps contributed to) the author's own psychological stress. Kittredge's first marriage dissolved in 1967, and the ranch was sold. A year later, remarried, he made his way to the Iowa Writers' Workshop and embarked on a literary career. He joined the creative-writing faculty at the University of Montana in 1969 and remained in that position until his retirement in 1997. Although his second marriage failed in 1974, Kittredge was beginning to straighten himself out and forge a new vision of himself as a writer and re-framer of the mythology of life in the rural West. His relationship with author and filmmaker Annick Smith began in 1977, and this signaled an important phase of emotional stability and literary productivity in Kittredge's life, which has continued to the present.

After he had published a few dozen scattered stories and essays in the mid-1970s, Kittredge's literary career took off in 1977 when he established his partnership with Steven M. Krauzer. The two edited a series of books, including *Great Action Stories*, *The Great American Detective*, and *Fiction into Film*, between 1977 and 1979, and under the pseudonym "Owen Rountree" began publishing what would become a nine-book series of western adventure novels called "Cord." In 1978, Kittredge came out with the first collection of his own stories, *The Van Gogh Field and Other Stories*, followed by *We Are Not in This Together* in 1984. His first major book of nonfiction, *Owning It All*, appeared three years later, launching what has become a series of efforts to rethink and rearticulate the mythology, the big story, of how human beings interact with the landscape of the American West. The memoir *Hole in the Sky* continued this process in 1992, as did *Who Owns the West?* in 1996. He reworked these issues yet again in *Taking Care: Thoughts on Storytelling and Belief* (1999) and *The Nature of Generosity* (2000). In his written responses to the questions on narrative and values for this interview, Kittredge stated that "Writers always want to think each restatement of belief is a step forward, toward coherency. So I like to think . . . my work in progress . . . [is] where it's at for me right now, at the moment." Always restlessly straining to formulate the ideas just a little better, to get them right, Kittredge has developed an almost ritualistic process of telling and retelling similar stories, rephrasing and restructuring his narratives but retaining essential content, in order to make the issues freshly potent in his own imagination.

Perhaps Kittredge's major concern as an author is the telling of stories that go beyond momentary, entertaining tales and represent, instead, efforts to reform and reimagine society and our relationship to the land we live on. In the essay "Owning It All," he writes, "In the American West we are struggling to revise our dominant mythology, and to find a new story to inhabit. Laws control our lives, and they are designed to preserve a model of society based on values learned from mythology. Only after re-imagining our myths can we coherently remodel our laws, and hope to keep our society in a realistic relationship to what is actual" (64). This statement suggests that what we think of as the imaginative musings of individual writers and artists working in other media has the potential power to define how audiences think of themselves, of society as a whole, and of the very planet. This is very like the ideas some social scientists profess, in which story is often construed as a primary behavior-organizing mechanism. "Story," as invented by an individual mind, is directly associated with "mythology," the vast, deterministic cultural narrative that shapes identity and guides behavior.

Having devoted much of his life as a writer to recanting the agricultural practices that his family tried in the Warner Valley between the 1930s and the 1960s, Kittredge might be expected to provide a vitriolic critique of the culture of which he was once a part. Although there is certainly a strong measure of criticism in his work, and particularly self-criticism, what's more noticeable is his effort to evoke self-examination on the part of his readers. The goal of his writing, in other words, has been to get his readers to look inward, to ask questions of themselves and their lifestyles, not merely to express his personal misgivings and castigate his own family and neighbors. As he explains in the following discussion, one of the chief values of narrative discourse is that it invites readers or listeners to participate emotionally in the events and processes they're learning about, and this in turn inspires audiences to invent their own stories. Storytelling and story-hearing are active forms of intellectual experience—and to the extent that they impinge on participants' notions of what's meaningful and valuable in the world, both presenter and receiver are engaged in this process. Unlike other forms of values processing that call for readers to assess importance in an artificially detached, disengaged way, story offers a way to imagine value with its full emotional valence. And the way to encourage people who are not natural storytellers to begin participating in this process is simply to begin telling stories.

In the Epilogue to *Who Owns the West?*, entitled "Doing Good Work Together: The Politics of Storytelling," Kittredge recalls a time when the poet C. K. Williams came to Missoula "and spoke of 'narrative dysfunction' as a prime part of mental illness in our time. Many of us, he said, lose track of the story of ourselves, the story that tells us who we are supposed to be and how we are supposed to act" (157–58). This belief in the central importance of story in human life permeates much that Kittredge himself states, in his literary work and in the following discussion. What's radical about this is that he identifies story as a vital phenomenon even in a society that has, in some ways, attempted to remove itself from the narrative structure of information in favor of quantitative, decontextualized modes of presenting ideas and information. Using an encompassing pronoun ("we") that suggests the universality of this need for story, Kittredge claims, "We live in stories. What we are is stories. We do things because of what is called *character,* and our character is formed by the stories we learn to live in" (1996, 158).

In the discussion that follows, William Kittredge explores his sense of the role of story in our culture, particularly as a medium for formulating and expressing values and beliefs. The two brief stories that are collected here, one a section from *Who Owns the West?* and the other an article from *Outside* magazine that was later adapted for the same book, offer examples of how the author himself seeks to use narrative formats as a way of determining the importance of certain places, people, seasons, and landscapes in his own life, and as a way of expressing the meaning of these things. The first, untitled selection highlights the process by which Kittredge came to love the place where he grew up, the Warner Valley, emphasizing with intricate detail the sensory experience of that landscape. At the same time, with delicate irony, the narrative reveals how his childhood exposure to the agricultural style of his father was "an initiation into the values of distance and order": although the story focuses on the family side of detachment and precision, the rest of Kittredge's writings on industrial ranching and agriculture make it clear that this story is exploring in an intimate, familial context the very aloofness and obsession with control that would eventually lead to the ecological degradation of the valley and, in turn, to his own disenchantment with that lifestyle. The second text, called "A Saving Light" in the *Outside* version, extends the theme of the childhood story to focus on how Kittredge responds to the natural world—the autumn light, the quality of air, an encounter with a badger—as an aging adult, thinking back to his earlier, contrasting attitude, particularly toward badgers (symbols of obstacles to his agricultural goals). This narrative, in particular, makes explicit the author's conversion from self-centered, unappreciative abuser of nature to sensitive, attentive observer. Unlike the earlier self who wore rubber gloves while dropping strychnine-laced carrots in badger holes, the speaker in the narrative—the author's contemporary persona—has adopted the habit of "Going Out," merely seeking contact with "reality." The author criticizes himself for past wrongdoings and warns of similar misdeeds (cyanide mining) slated to occur, but the bulk of the essay focuses on his annual, autumnal quest to achieve sensory contact with the physical world as a form of imaginative "sustenance," a way of supporting and vivifying his mind during the coming winter. Each of these stories, though rooted in the powerful specifics of Kittredge's life, offers evocative emotional and physical content that seems likely to prompt readers to think of comparable aspects of their own lives—experiences that might well emerge as stories during class discussions, letters to old friends or family members, or conversations with co-workers.

Several of the points raised in the following questionnaire responses express some of the new, emerging definitions of values. Kittredge refers to values in terms very close to those used by scholars working with cognitive models. He suggests that stories are closely associated with the cultural narratives that shape identity and guide action. This resembles the claims about story made by some social scientists in which story is construed as a primary behavior-organizing mechanism and can be a compelling means through which values are encoded.

But to say one has a cultural model that is value-infused is not to say that such models or the values embedded in them are static phenomena. Kittredge seems to sense this dilemma about the changing face of values. For value-elicitation researchers the problem is not a simple matter because it means that elicitation tools may capture a rather ephemeral value moment when in fact they pretend to be fixing on something much more stable. Kittredge touches on this very idea when he notes that writers are seeking coherency but that narratives of self are also a work in progress. Our narratives and the values they express change over time and place. If values researchers begin to ask participants for their value-infused stories, they must also recognize that stories are not merely an accounting of value-driven experience but an effort, in the act of telling the story, to make sense of and find meaning in those events.

Kittredge refers to a certain "narrative dysfunction" by which he means that people have lost the ability to clarify and structure information through the use of narrative forms. This is a claim that psychologists and students of judgment and decision making have begun to attend to; that is, they are beginning to appreciate the wisdom of presenting technical information in narrative form. Recently, Terre Satterfield, Robin Gregory, Paul Slovic, and other social scientists have experimented with the presentation of value and technical information in narrative form versus a plain, expository prose. They wondered whether participants in either condition would be better able to absorb information and then use that information while evaluating a policy. Interestingly, participants followed conventional wisdom by rating the expository text as better suited than the narrative text to the relaying of technical information. And yet when making policy judgments, the participants in the narrative condition proved to be more sensitized to value and technical information and more likely to use that information when evaluating a policy. Policy judgments made by participants in the non-narrative condition offered only random responses and did not appear to have paid attention to the pre-judgment information.

♦

QUESTIONNAIRE RESPONSES FROM WILLIAM KITTREDGE

William Kittredge returned his responses to the narrative-values questionnaire by fax from his home in Missoula, Montana.

Q1: How do you think you became a nature writer?

Kittredge: I'm not sure I'm a "nature writer." I'm not by training or any particular inclination a naturalist of the sort who pays detailed attention to the intricate processes, evolving energies, of what we call "nature." But I am utterly convinced that those processes—in totality, as they work out on earth—constitute our only possible physical and psychic home, and that the kind of creature we are cannot exist for long anywhere else. We are made of such processes. I think human cultures (the accumulation of so-called "memes") are disrupting them at a speed genetic evolution cannot begin to keep pace with. If not self-aware and careful, we will destroy our only home.

Humans, I believe, are genetically driven to make a positive effect in the world (produce offspring and what at least at the time are understood as coherencies). I've dedicated much of my writing to urging the preservation of the integrity of so-called "life processes" because I understand such work to be the most powerfully positive political action that I, within my personal limitations, can take.

Q2: Do you see your work as an attempt to articulate the value(s) of nature?

Kittredge: Yes, see above.

Q3: Which statement is closer to the truth in your case, or are both true?

A. You write in order to express your sense of nature's value.

B. You derive a sense of nature's value from the process of writing.

Kittredge: Both are true, I think. Most writers work to explore and express a sense of what they take to be true in both cautionary tales and celebrations. We are continually forced to reevaluate our beliefs when we expose them to the properly corrosive and unforgiving processes of work. (Only in the typing do we tumble to the chance that the great ideas we thought up while gazing out the window are mostly horse-shit.)

Q4: What mode(s) of expression work(s) best for you in articulating the values of nature: Exposition? Argument? Description? Narrative? A combination? Please explain.

Kittredge: The so-called personal essay, a combination of emblematic anecdotes and abstract conjecture, an investigative process with the storyteller functioning as a detective going into some secret place (underworld) and reporting back to the reader, his conjecturing keyed to the anecdotes, ending in a classically Aristotelian recognition scene and some sense of the consequences of that recognition, works best for me. It's a form that forces me to step on my desire to preach and invite the reader to share in the processes of discovery and thus come to emotionally possess some version of what I mean to say.

My initiation in understanding these processes began with a 1979 telephone call from Terry McDonnel, who was starting a magazine called *Rocky Mountain*. Terry wanted me to write an essay for the first issue; I said I didn't know how, and Terry said, "I'll tell you." Then he did, on the telephone. He described this simple formula I just described, which works in imitation of the common, endlessly repeated human decision-making process—quest, insight, consequences.

Q5: Why is this mode the most successful? How does it appeal to/elicit understanding in the reader or listener?

Kittredge: The form leads readers into emotional participation in the processes of coming to understand. The storytelling invites readers to make up stories of their own, to use the story they're being told as a mirror in which to view their own responses to their own concerns. E. M. Forster says something to the effect that the medium we work in is the reader's imagination. Working with the language of story, we are in effect working with readers' imagination at the same time.

Q6: Do you feel that a responsive reader learns natural values from your work, or that your work alerts the reader to values already held?

Kittredge: Both.

Q7: What do you see as the strengths and limitations of narrative as a carrier/elicitor of natural values?

Kittredge: We are an animal evolved to be at home among animals, in the rain and out. Places, to the degree that we can know them, are essentially locations for stories about the significances we've found there. Carl Sagan once wrote that "Electricity is the way nature behaves." The so-called natural world is something humans—all humans—create in their imaginations, out of sensory experience filtered through language. It is also our only residence.

Fully imagined and precisely rendered storytelling about creatures (including humans) in the natural world can lead readers to the once commonplace but now rarer pleasure of inhabiting what we can call the "ecological imagination," a sense that we are irrevocably wedded to "natural" processes, that we are participants in a system of energies that we call "sacred" because we are part of it, where we feel whole and intuit that we are part of holiness. I think the recent popularity of the novel *Cold Mountain* [by Charles Frazier] is a symptom of a vast hunger for this feeling. The character who makes the book work is Ruby, ecological imagination personified. That, I think, the likelihood of helping readers imagine holiness, is the great strength of narrative.

Q8: Has your sense of the importance of narrative changed over the course of your writing life to date? If so, how? If you didn't begin as a writer of narrative, how did it happen that you became one?

Kittredge: In the beginning I had nothing but stories, attempts at reverence. Later I came to theories, politics, intentions toward reforming the world. And now I'm heading back toward stories. We writers should think of our work as a gift, a set of mirrors rather than a set of instructions. It's how teaching should work.

Questions 9 and 10: Are there values that can *only* be told in and learned from narrative? Can natural values be fully and accurately expressed in purely rational terms, or is there inevitably an emotive content?

Kittredge: Values can usually be intellectually understood. But narrative helps readers internalize values, make them their own, emotionally, as necessary to life rather than simply interesting or distracting, as platforms from which to act.

Q11: Is there inevitably an ethical or moral content to these values?

Kittredge: Depends on what you mean by moral and ethical. It's important to take care of people and places we've learned to value—most often because they are necessary to our survival. This is what I mean by values. Values make our lives physically and psychically possible. Beyond that we tend to talk about fuzzily defined cultural abstractions. Who is the more important moral artist, Mozart or Hank Williams? An answer to that question depends pretty much on cultural context.

Q12: Why are these values difficult for many people to express?

Kittredge: Naming is an attempt to fix processes in place, to hold them static. Ezra Pound said only verbs are real, not nouns. Processes won't hold still. We have to falsify incessantly in order to sift processes through the scrim of subject-verb-object language. Narrative as a technique tries at least partway to avoid this problem by inciting readers toward making up their own complex, constantly re-forming stories out of what has been written or told. The audience is invited to form their own value systems out of their responses to experience. In this way narrative attempts to be less coercive than other forms of language.

Q13: In your opinion or experience, what would be the best ways to elicit these values and identify them in people who may harbor them but find them difficult to articulate?

Kittredge: The $64 question. Begin by impressing people with the practical political importance of formulating their own values. Impress them with the idea that their values live in their own stories, not in stories artists drop on them. Encourage storytelling, and thus moral and ethical thinking, at all levels.

Q14: In your opinion, are these values "held," so to speak, or are they more closely integrated with one's being? Are they learned or are they innate?

Kittredge: Values are clearly the result of our response to innate impulses coded into our genes. Whatever we may think of our mothers, we have no choice but to respond to them emotionally. We sucked sustenance from their bodies, once, or wished we could. We also are driven to think well of ourselves, continually moved to make a positive effect in the world, perhaps as a way to help us down the road toward psychic survival. (See John Bowlby on patterns in animal and infant behavior, and Gerald Edelman on the human brain—"The most complex object we know about, with more possible synaptic connections than there are atoms in the known universe.") While that's determinism (anti-freedom), we are seldom forced to realize that we aren't free, at least inside our minds. And anyway, even then, we can take solace in the thought that we're like the weather. The complexity of the forces driving us makes our actions sort of impossible to predict in any long-range way. At least until we get way better computers (for openers, one as complex as a brain).

Q15: Do you believe that environmentally responsible behavior flows from having a conscious sense of the values of nature? From an unconscious sense? Or is there no reliable causal relationship between values and behavior?

Kittredge: Cultural forces obviously color our ideas about what to do in response to our innate impulses. Advocates of simple answers to complex questions often end up endorsing some version of fascism. It's a clear danger for the environmental movement.

Q16: Has your own sense of the values of nature changed over time? If so, how? Can you identify particular experiences that contributed to the change(s)?

Kittredge: Yes. A detailed answer would take a lot of pages. I tried to write about it in *The Nature of Generosity.*

Q17: Do you consider beauty a value of nature? If so, please hazard a definition of natural beauty.

Kittredge: Of course. Beauty in nature is that which encourages us to feel at home in the weave of energies, and not isolated. It is connected, obviously, to solace and religious feelings.

Q18: Do you find more value (non-utilitarian) in some things and creatures of nature than you do in others? If so, what do you think accounts for the differences?

Kittredge: No. Some creatures and places make me feel at ease, others are threatening, even demonic, reminding me of my own mortality, but the entire run of things is interconnected in a larger thing. Thus the parts are not really parts at all, and are of equal value.

Q19: Do rocks have rights? Trees? Whales? Planets? Is there a concept other than "rights" by which you prefer to identify the worthiness of natural things and creatures?

Kittredge: I doubt that we are ultimately capable of operating on the basis of equal rights to rocks, or even houseflies. We use and kill in order to exist. See Richard Nelson on hunting. And we take care in order to ensure the continued existence of our kind. So I don't worry myself with theories about the rights of rocks. This can be taken as an excuse for various exploitations, but I don't see any other way of proceeding (even Jainists have to use the world or cease to exist—it's our unavoidable situation).

Q20: Does wilderness have value in and of itself? To what extent is wilderness an objectively identifiable thing, and to what extent is it a category of mind projected onto natural surroundings?

Kittredge: Wilderness is a cultural construct which changes meaning in various contexts. What we can know is an ever-flexing matrix of metaphor, which is determined by what we experience, and in turn acts as a filter determining what we can experience.

Wilderness is commonly understood as a place humans have not physically influenced, an invaluable genetic warehouse, and, psychologically, a location where humans can experience the ancient psychic situation of the species. At the same time, it's clear there is little on earth that's not been influenced by our presence. The pure thing, whatever that would be, untouched, by definition, may not have existed for millennia. Again, what do we mean? Wilderness?

Q21: How important is direct sensory experience of nature to having a sense of natural values and being conscious of those values?

Kittredge: For me, the psychic value of experiencing "nature" arises from the way it brings me to re-experience my sense of being part of necessary and thus invaluable energies.

Q22: Aldo Leopold wrote: "A thing is right when it tends to preserve the integrity, stability, and beauty of the biotic community. It is wrong when it tends otherwise." Do you agree? How would you modify his definition to better reflect your own view?

Kittredge: There's always a lot wrong with abstract statements about values. Abstractions are like that. Leopold's notion of what's right assumes a lot of things that derive from his apparent sense that the survival of "life" is the main or only purpose of whatever it is we think of as reality. A biotic community is intricately organized electricity. Why is it more sacred than a star?

Q23: Leopold wrote of the land community, by which he meant the entire biota in a place. Is community in some sense a natural value of your own? How so?

Kittredge: Community and communiality are natural values. Our need for them is built into our genetic organization. Without our social life, alienated and isolated, we as a creature go crazy.

Q24: What is the most important value of nature, if you believe there is one?
Kittredge: Psychic community.

Q25: What is the least understood or appreciated value of nature? Why is it poorly understood or appreciated?
Kittredge: Psychic community. In our society we're loathe to talk or even think about loneliness. Instead we act as if we can cure ourselves by conquering and by owning. Television ads tell us we're incomplete, and thus sad. And it's mostly true. TV ads advocate buying something, an addition to the self, which will help us feel complete if still isolated, happy or at least distracted. Thus, shopping. As a substitute for psychic community.

Q26: Do you believe that we have made progress toward a generally held land ethic—an ethical sense that values the things and creatures and systems of nature—since Leopold called for one in the 1940s? What do you see as the chief obstacles to such an ethic? How optimistic or pessimistic are you about our chances of realizing a land ethic?
Kittredge: I've never understood what a so-called "land ethic" would be. Perhaps it is the word "ethic." I don't know what it means in this usage. Again, the thinking behind its use seems pretty fuzzy.

On the other hand, it's clear to me that taking care of our only place to live is a version of taking care of ourselves, and that we'd better get on with it. If that's a land ethic, then sure, I believe in a land ethic.

As for the question of hopelessness, it's obvious that a vast sea-change in public consciousness is under way, world-wide. John Cobb tells us that controlling paradigms in European (world ruling class) thought evolved from Catholicism to Nationalism to so-called "Economism" (belief that economic growth is progress) after World War II. And now there's an upsurge of belief in the coalescing system of thought Cobb labels "Earthism" (belief that taking care is progress).

Polls reported in the *Utne Reader* claim there are about forty million citizens who could be called "Earthists" in the United States at present. (Many of us began thinking about "Earthism" when we read the invaluable work of Rachel Carson in the 1960s.)

The dialogue, battle, contest, whatever you want to call it, between the belief systems Cobb calls "Economism" and "Earthism" is being fought all over the world. Confrontations are reported on the front page of every newspaper we see. I want to believe that Earthism is clearly winning. Humans, no matter the degree to which their genes and cultures encourage them to be selfish, are nevertheless creatures evolved to cooperate and take care of one another. Another vast shift in human belief systems is under way.

Q27: Is it a land ethic in Leopold's sense that we most need, or is it something else?

Kittredge: We need to understand that taking care of our only place to live, inside the system of life on earth, is our only way to take care of ourselves and our progeny. It's pretty simple.

Q28: What piece of your work best expresses your sense of the value of nature?

Kittredge: Writers always want to think each restatement of belief is a step forward, toward coherency. So I like to think my most recent work and my work in progress are where it's at for me right now, at the moment. [When he responded to this questionnaire, Kittredge was working on the manuscripts that became *Taking Care: Thoughts on Storytelling and Belief* (1999) and *The Nature of Generosity* (2000).]

♦

Excerpt from *Who Owns the West?*[1]

Our ideas of paradise, it is said, originate in childhood. Mine connect to a great valley out in the deserts of southeastern Oregon, just at the time World War II was beginning. We moved to a huge new ranch, and my father built us a house that was fresh and clean and smelled of sawdust. From the screened veranda we could see out over the wild-hay meadows and willow-lined sloughs of the Thompson Field and beyond to swamplands my father was draining to farm. But fields and farming did not interest me then.

In mid-May, when the old homesteader's apple orchard back of our house was blossoming and thick with mystery, it was time for my father to plant his garden. This was an important venture, meant to help feed his harvest crew. A hired man dumped a horse-drawn plow and a disc and a harrow out of a pickup truck, and the next morning showed up leading a harnessed team of bay geldings. When the soil was worked to a perfect tilth, at least in this memory, my father showed up with stakes and a roll of white twine and began laying out the long precise crop rows.

We were all out there in that vivid spring light—my brother and I, and my mother with my brand-new sister wrapped in blankets. But my father didn't pay us much attention. This was business. He was intent on accuracy, sighting down the strings, setting out six one-hundred-foot rows of strawberries (enough to keep us in crates of strawberries through a long run of summers), onion sets, and corn in hills, as well as peas, pole beans, and squash, all in prelude to the communality of bunkhouse meals. We loved him and one another, but we were spectators. Don't go running through the rows of planted spinach and chard or you will get your butt paddled. It is possible to think of that time as an initiation into the values of distance and order.

The times I recall as sacred came later in the summer. They were sacred because they were useful, encouraging me to love my life, the wonders of the place where I lived, and the possibility in the creature that I was. Our irrigation ditch wove through a couple of miles of sandy hills from a low dam in Deep Creek Canyon. A long row of old Lombardy poplar creaked and rustled in the afternoon winds while I sat on my heels and studied the water flowing through the miniature redwood weirs (called boxes) my father had built in the little ditches across the head end of the garden. The water turned rainbows in the light and muddied in the dry ditch rows and went where it had to go, soaking and seeping. I watched longlegged spiders walk on water. The squash blossomed, yellow-jackets hummed at their business, the corn grew until it was taller than I was, I stole strawberries from under the leaves and stepped on the stink-bug beetles, crushing them and enjoying their stench.

But things had changed by the time I was enrolled up at the one-room Adel School. My brother and sister and cousins and I built play-time ditches and levee banks around little bare-dirt square fields we laid out with what we saw as grown-up precision beneath the apple trees outside the back door to our house. We farmed with toys in the place of the D-7 Caterpillar tractors my father used in his operations out on the far side of the valley. We were preparing for life, imitating what we understood as real.

I was on my way to becoming a little agribusiness farmer.

♦

A Saving Light[2]

In the northern Rockies we usually have a week or so of rain around the autumnal equinox. The nights go to freezing. The air seems cleansed. We walk into distances turned faintly golden, implying connection to paradise and eternity.

The days ring with the intimation that it is almost time to get indoors to what I think of as the carpentered life, living in rooms in artificial light, focusing eyes down to indoor work. But not yet.

Western larches are dropping their golden needles on the mountain slopes above the Big Blackfoot River. Translucent yellow aspen leaves flutter in the touch of a breeze I cannot feel, then quiet themselves. The sky is perfect doll-baby blue, and cool.

The part of the world I most revere is at its most beautiful, and it's time for the fall ritual I think of as Going Out, the point of which is to forget yourself and fall away into moments of intimacy with the holiness of things. It's not some soft-headed option; if we get too far out of touch with the feel and smell and taste and look of things we can go abstract and delusional.

People like me are particularly vulnerable. I will be 59 this autumn. Friends are beginning to die from the wear of their lives (not necessarily natural causes). It could happen to me. I could die before I taste the autumn air again. It is a crazy-making notion.

Every fall, contact comes in some different way. Last year it was the badger, outside its burrow under the rotting foundation of an old log barn. I remember it exactly still, entirely too close, squat and poised, a fierce and fearless creature, and nothing I expected to see. I have a history of bad killer-karma with badgers.

When I was a rancher, badgers dug their burrows in my levee banks. Carrots soaked in strychnine turned a luminous orange, and I dropped them in the burrows. I went at that work with rubber gloves.

I found a badger in the open and wounded him with a .22 pistol. He did the thing I never imagined an animal doing, angry and wounded or not. He charged. I ran for my pickup and dived into the box, just ahead of his rage. He hissed, and I raised the pistol but didn't shoot again.

It is a memory I despise. In the confusion of that moment I began to turn away from agriculture and the idea that I was fit to own some of the earth. I wonder if the badger died in its burrow of the wound I inflicted. I like to think it healed and lived to an ancient badger age.

Upstream on the Big Blackfoot, men have discovered gold. They control 44 square miles of mineral rights and say the deposits are worth close to $175 million. Someday they may pile up the marginal ore and spray it with cyanide to leach out the last precious remnants, like they do down in Nevada. Maybe some of the poison will find its way into the river and drift downstream to the badger and me.

The light comes in slants from everywhere, like the sky might be scattered with mirrors and prisms. It shimmers with a clarity so absolute that everything seems on the verge of going grainy and dissolving. Paintings in the caves at Lascaux and Altamira, made by artists over 400 generations ago, are grainy in the same pointillist way. One of my reasons for living in Montana is the light in October. I was not raised to pay much attention to notions of the sacred, but I think of this light as holy.

Part of the impulse toward Going Out is a remnant of our primal drive toward hunting and gathering. Another part, more important for me, has to do with contacting the living world in a way I am never able to really bring off.

If I could manage it I might truly realize that the western larches have the same life that I do, only longer. It is a religious impulse, but actually healing back to nature seems impossible to me. Maybe I find it so because I understand that everything is built of stories, which are to some degree imaginary.

Maybe we have all become too many selves. Maybe that's the main point of Going Out, trying to get back to the ancient single-minded child (animal) inside us, which we imagine as wedded to reality.

The badger turns and vanishes down his burrow, and I am alone in the ringing light on this bluff above the Big Blackfoot. I have to think we have overdone it with our endless cyanide and strychnine and such.

I have been engaged in another version of hunting and gathering, stocking my imagination for the long nights of winter. My moment with the badger, poised and motionless in memory, is a form of sustenance. It feeds my imagination. What I have been seeking, most centrally, is a way to imagine myself healed to the glory of things in this light.

2

ADVICE AND COUNSEL: RESPECTING THE SOURCES OF WISDOM

Simon J. Ortiz was born in Albuquerque, New Mexico, in 1941 and raised in the nearby Acoma Pueblo community of McCartys (called "Deetseyamah" in the Acoma language). He attended elementary school at the Bureau of Indian Affairs school on the Acoma reservation, and later attended Fort Lewis College in Colorado and the University of New Mexico, eventually earning his M.F.A. in creative writing at the University of Iowa. He is the author of numerous books of poetry and several collections of his own short stories, and has edited volumes of stories and essays by Native American authors. He began his literary career with the poetry chapbook *Naked in the Wind* (1971). His other publications include *Going for the Rain* (1976), *A Good Journey* (1977), and *Fight Back: For the Sake of the People, For the Sake of the Land* (1980)—all three of which were re-published together in the volume *Woven Stone* (1992). In 1981, he published a mixed collection of prose and poetry, *From Sand Creek*, and a second chapbook, *A Poem Is a Journey*. His short stories have appeared in *Howbah Indians* (1976), *Fightin': New and Collected Stories* (1983), and *Men on the Moon: Collected Short Stories* (1999). Other volumes of his poetry include *After and Before the Lightning* (1994) and *Out There Somewhere* (2002). He has taught at many institutions throughout the United States, including the Institute of American Indian Arts, Navajo Community College, Sinte Gleska College, San Diego State University, Marin College, Lewis and Clark College, and Colorado College, among others. After spending most of the 1990s living in Tucson, Arizona, he moved in 2001 to take a five-year position as a professor of English and Native American studies at the University of Toronto. That same year, he received a special Western States Book Award for lifetime achievement.

Ortiz's work demonstrates his interest in adapting the structures and themes of his native oral tradition to the printed, literary format. He frequently uses personal anecdotes and historical contexts in both poetry (indicated by short lines, repetitive phrasing, and tightened syntax) and short fiction. Often he will base a piece of writing on a fragment of conversation between two ordinary characters, sometimes an interaction between native and non-native people. His poetry will occasionally borrow the parallel, repetitive structure of a song or ceremonial chant, and when he reads this work aloud, it has an incantatory effect. Throughout Ortiz's long career, he has emphasized that a person's identity, his or her deepest sense of self, comes from a combination of paying attention to the physical landscape and respecting and remembering the stories (the cultural values encoded in oral tradition) learned while young. Just as Gary Nabhan's "Hornworm's Home Ground" shows that the "sources of wisdom" are not always the scientists who record technical findings in respected journals, Ortiz often shows in his work that there is powerful wisdom about human nature and about the physical world in the words of ordinary people, even down-and-out wanderers and frail, elderly neighbors and relatives.

One of the most significant features of Ortiz's writing, a communicative tendency evident as well in his responses to the questions directed to him in the following interview, is the mode of indirectness, sometimes indicated by digression. Indirectness is presented as an implicitly valuable way of communicating important ideas—it's not meant as evasiveness or vagueness, but as a form of respect. In the interview, he immediately asserts a distinction between "advice" and "counsel," suggesting that story often functions as one or the other, sometimes as both. "Advice" means ordinary, practical suggestions about how to do something, how to behave; "counsel," on the other hand, is a way of offering deeper, more fundamental wisdom about survival, about preserving self and community and land. It is common for advice and counsel to be embedded in the concrete details of story rather than communicated in abstract, analytical language. Story may seem, to the unfamiliar listener, like an oblique, evasive style of communication, when in actuality it's an especially concrete and specific approach to communication.

There is a tendency in mainstream American culture, and in industrialized societies more generally, to privilege written forms of communication and oral presentations that mirror the syntax and vocabulary of written language. However, as Ortiz argues in the interview, it's also possible to discern advantages in oral language—and some of the values of orality, such as openness and indeterminacy, seem much like the advantages writers throughout this set of interviews are attributing to the language of story (both written and spoken story). Ortiz states, "The risk with the written form, even when it's an extension of the oral tradition or an effort to document the oral tradition, is that there's always the danger of things being left out in the process of being recorded, written in stone. The stone has only so much space. And lived life has no limitations, no borders, no boundaries." It is also common in rationalist cultures to assume that essential information can be objectified and passed from one person to another like a physical thing, with no personal change occurring on the part of either the giver or the receiver. Ortiz offers a strikingly different perspective on the nature of give and take with stories, pointing out that "The story makes no sense until it brings us into being, into existence, into the reality of that existence. Otherwise, it's just information—otherwise, it's just facts." When we allow "story" to "bring us into being," we are allowing it to change us, to alter our relationship to the social and natural world (reality). Increasingly, in the era of postmodern textual and cultural studies, we have become sensitive to the idea that there is no such thing as fixed, objective truth—to the contingency and subjectivity of meaning. Ortiz's concern about language that merely aims to pass "information" or "facts" from one party to another, based upon his background in a native community that privileges the oral tradition and narrative communication, provides eloquent insight into the widely accepted contemporary view of how language functions.

The two samples of Ortiz's writing included here are the title story from the 1999 collection *Men on the Moon* and the poem "Yuusthiwa" from *Woven Stone*. The story "Men on the Moon" presents, with gentle humor, the responses of a Native American family to the television broadcast of American astronauts landing on the moon. Grandfather Faustin is bemused by and concerned about the news of the moon landing, sensing something ridiculous about people traveling all the way to the moon to collect rocks "for knowledge" that will "better mankind." The story is, in various ways, about where we turn for knowledge and wisdom. Faustin and his grandson Amarosho watch television for amusement (preferring wrestling to the space reports), but not for deep knowledge of the world; Faustin, though unfamiliar with the aims of modern science, imparts wisdom to his grandson through his questions about space exploration; and the space scientists themselves are searching far and wide for vital knowledge, apparently not realizing that the knowledge they seek could be found much closer to home. "Yuusthiwa," the poem Ortiz discusses during one section of the interview, is also, in part, about knowing where to look for knowledge. And knowing how to ask the right questions. The poet's father, when he finally has the opportunity to talk with the old man Yuusthiwa, asks about the secret of his good health at age 114—and in a simple sentence receives vital "counsel."

♦

A Conversation with Simon J. Ortiz

Terre Satterfield and Scott Slovic conducted this interview in the guest cottage at the University of Arizona Poetry Center.

Slovic: We're here to explore how different authors think about the connection between language—in particular, the language of story—and environmental values, how they use narratives and verbal images in order to communicate what is important or meaningful to them in relation to the natural world. We'd like to compare writers' insights to practices in the professional world of values research, which tend to rely on purely economic definitions of value and/or quantitative approaches for understanding values.

Satterfield: Yes, and one of the reasons we're interested in this is because we believe that not all values can be articulated by expressing material worth. Certain kinds of meanings, certain values, might be better suited to other forms of expression, perhaps expression through stories. This gets us to the question: How do writers and poets use language and narrative to get certain environmental values across to their readers so that the readers can reflect upon those ideas for themselves?

Ortiz: Well, I know that stories are very important. Story is really kind of an affirmation of ourselves, the reason why we live. I often use the phrase "advice and counsel." I guess you could say, in one sense, that story is advice and counsel. There is often a concrete, non-abstract, or direct way of saying something. Part of the concept of story is that it includes us and makes certain that we know that it's important, that there's value in the story that is behind or is inclusive of this advice and counsel. Sometimes this information, this message, comes through indirectly.

It's just like [pause] Joy Harjo says to her daughter, who is my daughter too, you were born and I held you and you unfolded like a butterfly. You were born from the chrysalis. At the end, she says: I breathe with you as you breathe, as you breathed your first breath, there was your promise to take this on, like the rest of us, this journey from now on. The poet is saying to the new child, you know, one rainy dawn twenty-four years ago there was a baby. The poem is a way of expressing love for that child, for that self really. It's like a prayer.[1]

I go out every morning. I try to run, almost every morning, when I'm not lazy. I go down to the little river north of here. El Niño has made this little river run all winter long and well into the spring. It's not running now, except maybe out by the mountain. But the point is to say thank you, to say I'm alive, to say hey, it's a great morning, even if I don't feel that great. If I were speaking to my nephews, to my younger relatives, and telling them this is what I do, it would be a form of advice and counsel. This is the story that we tell.

Slovic: When you receive advice and counsel from another person's writing, how do you respond to that information?

Ortiz: I identify with it. I identify with certain reactions that the writer may be expressing—the concerns that Edward Abbey or Gary Snyder may have. If I identify with them, this means that I understand what they are talking about and I've been in that situation. I know what the feeling is.

Slovic: Are there some kinds of writing, kinds of stories, that you're more likely to identify with, or others that alienate you, make you say, "I disagree"?

Ortiz: Well, if I go back some years to when I really began, say, when I was in high school, I was often moved by two particular kinds of writing. One was the American Jewish story—set in the cities in living conditions that were not always the best. I liked that urban kind of setting. I identify with that as an Indian, as a Native American. The other kind of story that I liked was literature of the Southern tradition. Erskine Caldwell, William Faulkner, Jesse Hill Ford, and so on. There were some similarities there between the urban ghetto story and the poor white agrarian farmer. I liked that. And I also liked Black, or the African American writers, you know. Richard Wright. I liked his work.

Slovic: Was it the subject that appealed to you or the way these people told their stories?

Ortiz: I don't know. I don't think it was an ethnic sort of thing. I was just really curious and hungry for something different.

Satterfield: Or is it because the content of those works came closer to your advice and counsel notion of where story and values meet?

Ortiz: Well, advice is when you're being told something that might be technically helpful, that is, the best way to go somewhere, directions. Counsel has to do with how—how you should behave.

Satterfield: A way of living or being?

Ortiz: Yes. The best way to conduct oneself. For example, I can hear people say, in the Acoma language, "Teh neh nieu shru, kudrahnaiya eh kurahnaishtiya. Kudraa-mah ehmiihtse kutrah-haatse": *Respect your mother and father. Your home is your land.* That is counsel, but there's some advice in there as well as counsel. It suggests behavior: mentally, emotionally, spiritually, this is the way we should be.

Slovic: Are there some people in Acoma society, or in society in general, who have the unique privilege of offering advice and counsel?

Ortiz: I think that elders are always expected to. For example, I was just talking to my son this morning on the phone. I love my son. I love all my kids. I don't know certain things about their professional lives, but as a father, as a parent, I try to be protective and hopefully not authoritarian. There's a certain kind of communication that is not unique to Native culture or Indian culture. Two weeks ago, my son wanted me to go with him to Acoma, to McCartys, because there was going to be a television interview, part of a documentary a friend of mine was doing. My son wanted me to be there with him.

I truly had other things to do. But I also wanted to say: You can handle this yourself. So, as any elder, older person, I have that role to play—to be available as an advisor. And also, in my culture, I have another role too, a formal role as an uncle to my sister's children, my nieces and nephews.

Slovic: When you began your career, when you were younger, did you view your work as a form of advice and counsel?

Satterfield: Or has that evolved over time? Have you become more comfortable with that role in time?

Ortiz: Well, America does funny things to you. It wants you to be Indian. And you are Indian, not necessarily because it tells you to be, but because of your own inherent Native sense of self, your identity. You have your own culture. Yet there's a certain image that America requires. They want to make sure that you are Indian in their image, that you fit their own conception of that image. This is why I bring up the point about elders. When I was growing up, I was expected to respect my elders. That was just the way it was. Listen to your grandfather and grandmother, listen to your aunts and uncles, listen to your mother and father. You know, those are givens. It's accepted.

And so as a younger person, writing, I wasn't necessarily expecting that I would eventually be an elder. I didn't think that what I wrote down was going to be regarded as advice and counsel. Far from it. My writing, like that done by others, was simply [pause] a force from within, and it came to be out there by the act of writing. It's almost like leaving a mark on the trails, on the roads that you've walked, maybe even graffiti on the walls. Later, when people come up to me and say, "Hey, I really like what you wrote in that book or poem," I'm appreciative of that. But I also believe that unconsciously, or self-consciously, I think *that's an old poem.* I want to sort of dismiss it and say, I don't know how that came about. You get self-conscious about it.

It's not that I question myself or put myself down, as an elder. But I know that part of what's taking place is that I'm being seen as an elder when it's not what I had in mind at the time of writing. I see my own role, more formally, as a figure in American Indian literature, as one of the first, the generation of the 1960s, who began to get published and who began to assert themselves, on the written page, as having an oral tradition.

Satterfield: Is it somehow easier to offer advice and counsel when writing as compared to telling a story out loud? Are the two forms different in some way when it comes to articulating counsel? Advice?

Ortiz: Advice and counsel includes one's behavior, one's lifestyle. It's not just telling, it's not just talking about it. It's actually living it, I think.

Satterfield: Demonstrating it?

Ortiz: Yes, through behavior. Demonstrating it by being the model, the role model, for those who are watching. You *are* a role model. And so it is harder. It's also more complete, more inclusive. It's not just so much writing down. Writing is technically definitive. When you write something down, in the Western culture, it's like a documentation.

Satterfield: Written in stone, in that sense?

Ortiz: It's documentation that establishes something as fact. I was just writing a letter about this to a friend of mine who's contributed to an essay anthology that I'm now doing. I was trying to get her to expand her paragraphs to record and establish fact. This sense of being precise, supposedly objective, is a very Western cultural-intellectual tradition, whereas in the oral tradition of the Native American, despite the inclusivity I mentioned, you don't have to worry about how a certain thing is defined and recorded and established.

The risk with the written form, even when it's an extension of the oral tradition or an effort to document the oral tradition, is that there's always the danger of things being left out in the process of being recorded, written in stone. The stone has only so much space. And lived life has no limitations, no borders, no boundaries.

Satterfield: In that sense, should we think of the oral tradition as a form of dialogue? If I'm following you, the written form is manifested as a piece of paper. It's hard, it's fast, it's there, whereas there's a space when telling a story—because it isn't necessarily precise or material—that allows the people listening to do something with the story themselves, to think it through, and even adapt it, in their own minds?

Ortiz: Yes, yes. I've always loved that. Holden Caulfield, in Salinger's book, has this tendency to digress. He likes to digress. The oral tradition is its own digression, and it is lovely! Oral tradition is digression. And in that digression, there's an opening up. Salinger knew he couldn't tell that whole story. He needed to have Holden Caulfield make it real, make it his own story through digression. So yes, the oral tradition is much more encompassing. That's why story is so important.

Slovic: What you are talking about has rather profound implications for the effort to identify and articulate values in a research context meant to elicit the public's values. The situation you're describing, this openness to narrative digression, requires time and patience to enable digressors to move and shape their stories into forms appropriate to them. And yet what most values-elicitation tasks (such as public hearings or surveys) aim for is efficiency. The question is how can one cut to the chase, collect, write, and convert values to numerical form as quickly as possible. Digression is, at best, extra noise in this context. So, what is lost there? Could it also be that digression is central to the communication of important feelings and ideas?

Ortiz: Yes, because culture is not necessarily only little measurements, calculations. Concrete analysis, studies, and so forth are necessary. But culture, really, is what we had and how we respond to something. Recently, I gave a talk at a Grand Canyon Trust symposium. But I met a person from Salt Lake City, I think she was from Salt Lake City—she's part of a movement to release the Grand Canyon dam, I mean, she and her group. I think that the Grand Canyon dam has never worked out—it's costly, it's not efficient, and they should let the water out and just let it be natural. Just yesterday on the phone I was talking to somebody else about this. This is part of the process of cultural change, part of the cultural context, the cultural dynamics, that we as people of this Earth, of this particular part of the Earth, participate in. I think that obviously there can be studies, there can be research, there can be facts and figures to support this one or the other argument, you know, but I think that it is important that the story, whatever the story may be, be expressed. I mean when the Grand Canyon dam was constructed, the idea of it, there was some sort of story that was taking place at that time. Well, the story continues, and we're a part of that story.

I think that one of the things that really makes America a vital and vigorous nation is the sense of participating in the story—we realize that we have a role in this story taking place, and we can even say that we are the story itself. We are the story of what's happening, you know. Here in the Southwest, or anyplace really, throughout the country—the story of America. I think I said this up in Nevada—I said the story, the real and true story of America, has never been told. And one of the reasons why it has never been told is because the Native American is, in a sense, not included in the story. And yet, we are the story of America. The Native American culture and its values and its philosophy are the story of America, although facts and figures can be cited that dismiss that idea.

Satterfield: I'm reading into this, fairly or not, a little sort of sub-plot there that says that there are dangerous stories and not dangerous stories. And one form of a dangerous story is the one that looks good, but excludes the broader story or the whole picture. Any thoughts on that, on story and the way it includes or excludes?

Ortiz: No, I think if anything is dangerous about a story it's when it's not told, when a person's story is not told.

Satterfield: So the danger is not in the form itself, but just in the not listening to all the stories that are there.

Ortiz: Yeah. I mean, again, going back to what I said earlier about my son, our conversation this morning on the phone. Last time I saw him was about three weeks ago, and he wanted me to go out to Acoma with him and McCartys, but I didn't have time and so I said, I'm sorry and I apologized again and he said, that's okay. But I felt that it was important for me to have been there. That's why I apologized. So he could tell me what he was feeling, you know, his story. He wanted me to be there, maybe just for whatever, self-assurance, I guess, support, okay. But I couldn't be there. And how often is that the story? I think that if there's any problem with stories, such as stories told within families, it's because we don't listen to each other. You know, that's part of it. I know that it is hard to always be there, listening to each other's stories, but it is important, I think, that our stories be told to each other. And when society prevents stories from being told, or when one story is told to the exclusion of another, then only the story of America, only U.S. official history, is told, and then that other story is not being told. I think there's real danger in that because a certain judgment is made, and here in the United States it's oftentimes a political judgment. You know, based upon economic studies and scientific evidence and arguments.

Satterfield: I'm thinking about what you're saying and I can remember having a conversation with somebody about a story that I didn't like. I didn't like the way it concluded. But their answer to me was, it's their story. So in other words, because they're narrating it, they have the right to include or not include whatever they want and that—I don't know—I guess that's the other side of what you're saying. Can all stories be all-encompassing or all-inclusive, or are they by nature subjective, one person's experience, one group's experience?

Ortiz: Well, I think there are always value judgments that we make about each other. And because that is the case, well, we then have to take into account the fact that we still nevertheless respect each other. That sounds a little hokey, but it says, "Well, I'm sorry I don't have time to listen to you, but I still respect you."

Satterfield: Right, right.

Ortiz: Which is too famous in American civilization.

Satterfield: That has a bad ring to it, doesn't it?

Ortiz: Oh yeah, it sure does. And yet, that's what takes place over and over again. But I mean, there is I think a genuine sense of integrity that can be achieved when we have as a matter of principle respect among ourselves. I mean I respect and I love my kids, but sometimes I wish—and obviously I feel guilty about this—I wish I had been there at certain moments in their lives. You know, when they might have needed me. I suppose that is sort of the eternal pain of being a parent.

Satterfield: Right. A parent's lament.

Ortiz: To be there when the kid falls down or needs something, but sometimes we're not. Nevertheless, their stories are important. I think our parents are famous for telling their kids, "You can tell me anything." Some things you don't really want to hear.

Satterfield: Are you saying story in some ways is a basis for intimacy?

Ortiz: It is. Well, even though I may say that writing is important, I have always said the most common and immediate and intimate language is the oral tradition. Story, and especially spoken story, is where language is our most immediate contact. I mean, it doesn't have to just be by the voice, nor by writing, but how we behave toward each other. The story that we are living and that forms us and holds us, and how we respond within it—that's when it's most intimate. Telling about ourselves, you know. That's why I think one of the things I find about my own writing, one of the strongest features about my writing, is when I tell about my home and my parents, my family, my growing-up experiences. If there's anything immediate and most intimate, it's when I am speaking about those things. And I think I can say fairly, as observation, that this is what people, my readers and listeners, identify with.

Slovic: I'm interested in the way personal stories can evoke powerful feelings and ideas, for either an immediate audience or an audience of readers. Even if the readers have had very different experiences in their own lives, what is it about story in general, or particular kinds of stories, that has that evocative power? Why is it that we can listen to someone else's story and transfer the meaning of that story to the context of our own lives?

Ortiz: Well, you learn from other people, their experiences. Because you relate to those experiences and the way that they're told. But I think also that, that it's a way maybe of learning something new. I'm sure you've read things and said, "Hey, I've never thought of that before." Or, even if you have, you feel a certain kind of joyousness because somebody else has thought that same thing and put it in words.

Satterfield: Or put it elegantly, in a way you couldn't put it yourself.

Ortiz: Yeah. You kind of have camaraderie with that person, with that storyteller. I think good storytellers, you know, strike certain chords. Like the storyteller, the comic, the filmmaker Woody Allen. Woody Allen is talking about himself, and yet he does it in such a way it's as if he were inside of you talking about you, having the honesty and the courage and the clarity to . . .

Satterfield: . . . to voice all your neuroses?

Ortiz: . . . and the humor. You admire that, you respect that, and you maybe feel a certain kind of envy, and, yeah, I think you learn various things from it. It's a way of seeing. In fact, in one of my poems I say, "I said that I tell you about myself in order that you may see yourself." I was telling my friend David Levine about this man that I saw fall down on the street. He was coming from a pub, and I went across the street to pick him up, to help him up. I was working with the National Indian Youth Council at the time. He had been drinking, this man, so he had fallen down this winter day. I brought him inside and gave him some coffee, and he sat for a while and then he left. But I was telling David about him, and I wrote down other things that had to do with that—you know, about Indian people in America—and my conclusion was this: I let you know about myself, what I was feeling when I picked that man up and what it's like to be an Indian in America—I tell you about myself and what I am feeling in order that you may see yourself. So that was the story behind that. I think that if I am conscious of participating in a storytelling tradition, it is in order to teach. It's a device or a technique to teach, you know. Because when a story is told—and I grew up in this tradition—you learn from your elders. I mean, there're some guys that tell funny stories and some guys that tell pretty boring stories, but I always used to like to listen to them.

I remember this uncle, what's his name, Tom. Tom Chavez up at sheep camp, and he would tell me about when he was a kid. I guess he'd get on his horse and he would go visit this girl down by the village east of McCartys—it's not exactly a very big village, it's more of an area where there're hayfields and orchards around. So he would take his horse and he would go and ride the horse down there, and he would be out in the hayfield and he would call her. He'd call her, and she'd come out and then make an excuse to her parents and she would go to the outhouse and they would be together in the hayfield. And so, as a pre-teen—you know, I was about nine years old—I would listen very avidly to stories about Uncle Tom when he was a younger man and his exploits. And he would tell me about this. And then, you know, he would tell me about when he used to live in Chinatown in San Francisco. These are just the kinds of stories that you hear. But Uncle Tom didn't say, "I'm telling you this in order to teach you this."

Satterfield: These are not necessarily counseling stories?

Ortiz: Well, no. But you listen to them because you learn something about the person telling the stories. And you learn about the life back in earlier times. You're curious about an era that wasn't yours but that's made vivid by this person. My Uncle Philip, he was a good storyteller, too, but also kind of a bullshitter. But that's all part of the stories. So you learn something from them, not necessarily because they're teaching stories, but because you are open to them and they connect with you, they affirm you, make you feel important. I think that if poetry has any real value, it's because, as in the oral tradition, it gives you a sense of importance, a sense of value. And I suppose if we were to look at some stories that are denied telling, or denied hearing, that a judgment is being made, say, by the school system, by government policy, by even the National Science Foundation. If only the facts and figures are listened to, but not the stories of the people . . .

Satterfield: . . . then it's a denial of those values. That's what's happening in not listening to those stories.

Ortiz: Yeah.

Satterfield: We've been talking quite a bit over the last couple of days with various writers about stories and place. And I'm curious about a place like Acoma, which is home and a significant place to you, but also a place that other people visit looking for a sense of place, or looking to see what somebody else's sense of place might be like. Somehow in going up to Acoma, outsiders are pursuing a sense of place for themselves. Is that a difficult thing? Is it difficult to have somebody appropriate your own sense of place in that way, or is it a healthy thing, people living vicariously through you or through the Acoma community?

Ortiz: Well, it's uncomfortable when people see or expect only a certain image of Acoma, when they don't know or don't want to know the complete story. But I understand the complete story is very complex and detailed and it has to do with the religious and spiritual basis of the community—it really means everything. This story can be expressed obviously in other languages, English, Spanish—but some of the story is embedded in the Acoma language itself. If visitors, tourists, want to know only certain things that they already have in their minds, or perhaps they might be looking for certain exotic and esoteric information, then I think their visit can be of limited value.

Too often what can take place is that visitors perceive the new culture from the mindset of a consumer. Like the "Sky City" idea—Acoma's not Sky City. But I know that people get off on that. "The Sky City Casino, where the sky is the limit." I hate that—it sounds like a chamber of commerce line.

But too often that's what takes place. There's Desert Diamond here locally—Desert Diamond somewhere near Tucson, and then the Casino of the Sun. There's that aspect. That's what comes about. And then there are the stories that are very particular and distinctive to locales, that can be told, that should be told. I think these can become included into the whole story of haatse upeh-tahnih. Land knowledge. There are also certain things that are more particular to each person. When I was small we used to take our wagons—we would plant pumpkins and corn and some beans up in the valley at Acoma. I grew up at McCartys, which is the little village along the river behind the Interstate now. But we would take our horses, Charlie and Bill— we would drive on the old road by the river toward Acoma, which is thirty miles to the south, and I always loved going by there—I mean, going up this road. It was a dirt road then—it's paved now. But this old place, "kahmaataishruu" we called them, you know old places where the ancient people lived—it was a group of houses, it's all just a tumbledown of stones now. My mom would always say, make sure that you give salt to the Miihna Kquuyow and give cornmeal to the Miihna Kquuyow, which means offer cornmeal to the Miihna Kquuyow, Old Salt Woman, because she lived there. It was a custom, tradition, to show respect to that mythic figure. Because, my mom said, if you don't do that, the wind will blow, the wind will blow real hard. And I hated the wind around there. Anyway, in order to appease the Miihna Kquuyow, you gave her some cornmeal. We'd hang on to the back of the wagon pulled by Charlie and Bill, those were our horses. It's kind of a memory of that time. We would pass by a place called Ghoomih—we would sometimes have our lunch near there. "Tsuuscki-tsai-gaiyahmeshru" means Coyote. "Tsuuscki-tsai-gaiyahmeshru," where a coyote got trapped. There are some cliffs right there. And the story is that years and years ago, I guess a Coyote was going to get married or somebody was going to get married. So Tsuuschki, he was on his way there and got into some trouble—he was a gambler, so he met a party of expert gamblers and he gambled everything. He gambled his coat away, which used to be a real fine coat. Well, he lost that, so some mice gave him some scraps of fur and that was ehmee-eh eh chah-aitra. So he's had that coat ever since. That was a long time ago.

Satterfield: As I listen to you tell stories like this one, I wonder if the indirectness of story has something to do with your ability to make contact with your listener or reader. That you're not hitting them over the head with something, but you are sort of coming comfortably around the side? I expressed this to Terry Tempest Williams the other day as a kind of politeness. One of the reasons I'm comfortable with story is that I can say, here, look at this with me, rather than say, here, this is what I believe and you should believe it, too. There's a certain respectfulness about narrative that isn't true in other forms of expression that try to convey information.

Ortiz: I guess that happens. I know that some Americans—when I say "some Americans," I usually mean white people—want to hear Indian stories. And immediately there's a kind of stop light that goes on for me, because what they want is this esoteric, exotic Indian story. Certainly they just want confirmation of what they already think they know about Indian cultures, but this just isn't what real Indian stories do. I don't usually tell Indian stories as such, but I tell about the Indians—I tell about my own experiences or I tell stories I know or stories that have come about because I'm an Indian person. There's this one story about my father, because he was the Kuutsi naishtiya when he was older, meaning an elder in antelope clan, and he would go pray out in the early mornings. One time he was going out and it was winter and there was a little snow on the ground. Up at Acoma you couldn't quite see where the depressions were when they were snowed over. So he was singing "Chuuyuutitah," asking the Snow Spirits, "Where are you?" And as he was walking along, he fell into one of those water holes, frozen over, but covered with snow. He didn't know it was there. So he fell through the ice, and he says to himself that the Shiwana tudih yai-nahwah! He says, "The Snow Spirits must have said to me: 'Here I am, now you have found me.'" So that was his story. But later on he didn't tell me the story himself, it was my mother who told me the story. She says, one time your father came home and this is what he said. But anyway, that's an Indian story. To me, it's an Indian story because it's my personal reminiscence. But I think that it has importance, not because of its esoteric nature, but because it conveys a certain, very intimate knowledge, particular information about me and my parents and the love that they had in their lives and me for them and so forth. That's what the story really is—that is the story behind the story. It's story that is memory, it's story that is substance, because it tells about what my father did and it's a good memory of him. That kind of storytelling presents a very important quality about my parents' lives as Acoma people, as Acoma parents, and its importance to me because it's kind of like a memory stone. It's something that is theirs and that I hold as a quality that I can recall. I guess it evokes something, like the winter I know from my own experiences at Acoma.

Slovic: It's nice to sit in Tucson and remember the South Dakota winter.

Satterfield: When it's 120 degrees. But that is one of the reasons that we're so interested in narrative, because of that quality, because it evokes so easily, because you can store all kinds of memory and emotion and other things in what is really a very tiny story.

Ortiz: Well, that's the reason behind my book *After and Before the Lightning*. I used winter as an all-inclusive metaphor of my facing reality. But I think that within it I tell not only about the blizzard and the roads, but certainly about the people there dealing with the reality of winter and the reality of social, political, economic life that they know in South Dakota, or that is out there someplace else—South Africa or South Dakota, this is right now, this is what's taking place. Story is very central—the story that is behind these poems and within these poems. This is the storm. I conclude the book by asking, Why do we go into the storm? Because you appreciate and come to know beauty, I guess. Why do we live life?

Slovic: Part of what we're circling around, not by any particular design, is the way that narrative, or perhaps literature in general, often introduces readers to particularities of experience that may not match their own lives, so they engage in these experiences through the vicarious passageway of a literary text. What I wonder is whether this kind of indirect experience, or vicarious experience, can lead to profound and authentic and real emotional values or attitudes about the world. In other words, in brief, can a vicarious experience of life through literature lead to authentic attitudes toward the world?

Ortiz: Sure, I think so. In *Woven Stone* there's an instance where my father and my uncle David were driving along the road and they saw Yuusthiwa. I believe it's in the poem called "Yuusthiwa." It's a narrative poem. There was an old man. He was blind, or practically blind, but he would walk along the road at home in McCartys. I think his name, an American or Spanish name, was Juan Sanchez. He was also called "Shaarraowkah." I never could figure out if that was his nickname—"Shaarraowkah." It means tomato. Most people called him "Shaarraowkah," but Yuusthiwa was his Acoma name. And he was a lovely old man, but I remember when I was still small, you would see him walking along the side of the road. He was a real ancient man; last I heard, he was 112 years old. But one time he was walking alongside the road coming from Acoma, and so Uncle David, who was driving his truck, stopped. And the story was that every time a person would stop and invite the old man to get in, he would always refuse. The driver would say, "Guwaadze, how-duu-upah, come in, father," and he would refuse, saying, "Dzah dze how-duu-nieupuuskquunah, don't want in, thank you. I'm not getting in because I still have my feet and ways to walk." That's what my father would say, and then my mother would say, "No, he didn't say that. He said, 'No, I'm not going to get in because I'm still able to walk, not while I still have my feet.'" So that's the difference in their stories. But anyway, this time, the old man got in. He recognized my father, who was the passenger. And the old man got in, slowly, and then he said to my dad, "Oh, you're Dzai-rrai!" "Haah-ah," my father said. And then as they were driving along my dad said: "Naishtiyah, How did you come to be such an old age?" my father asked. And so the old man said, "Because I make use of the plants here and I live my life always being responsible and helping the people and the land and having a good spirit." And he said other things. He said, "That's how I have come to be such an old man." And so, I guess the reason why I tell this story of this old man is to be able to show the quality of the man himself and what he said about himself as story and then my father and my uncle David stopping for him and giving him a ride and then my father telling me this. So that all of it combined is really kind of an interwoven group of stories with layers and dimensions and various facets that creates, hopefully, on the written page, for the reader, a sense of particular values. A sense of this: that it's not just this old man whose American name was John Sanchez, who was sometimes called Shaarraowkah and who lived to be 112 years old—he's not just an interesting picture. The stories are actually a way of expressing a relationship that I, as poet and storyteller, have with that quality of life, a relationship that the reader can also vicariously, if that word should be used, find useful. The story enables the reader or listener to have a realization of that quality, that relationship. Does that make sense?

Satterfield: It's a wonderful answer and it goes back to where you began, showing story as a way for somebody to come in and learn something about themselves or acquire something.

Slovic: Is that poem in *Woven Stone*? I can't remember the exact poem.

Ortiz: It is. It's in the section called "Going for the Rain," and the specific poem is "Yuusthiwa."

Satterfield: Sometimes I worry about this project in certain ways. A couple of times when we've been describing this idea of narrative and narrative values and the importance of stories, people have said, "Oh, will you be talking to Native American storytellers?" And my reason for wanting to do that is to have different kinds of storytellers involved in the project, but I often feel when that question is being asked that it means, "Oh, the only real storytellers are Native American storytellers." It's a sort of reverse romantic notion, or sort of painting that portrait that everyone then has to live up to, as though every Native American person has to be a great storyteller, which is nothing we would expect of anyone else.

Ortiz: I don't think that because a person is Native American he tells good stories. I would speak personally and say that the stories I identify with are the stories that I like—the stories that I identify with. And that often has so much to do with the person that I'm speaking with, the kind of person to whom I'm relating. And I think, on the societal level, that our appreciation of story would depend on how we relate to each other. Not with prejudgments. Another idea that I've expressed in writing is that story brings us into being, because stories really do bring us into being, into existence. That is the nature of stories, actually. The story makes no sense until it brings us into being, into existence, into the reality of that existence. Otherwise, it's just information—otherwise, it's just facts.

Satterfield: Different people we've been speaking with have said that in different ways, and that's the cornerstone of the project: that apart from story, everything else is just information, and it doesn't live and breathe and have meaning until it can bring people, listener and teller, into being.

Ortiz: I'm trying to relate to what you asked earlier in the conversation about intimacy. When a story makes us intimate, then it's as if it reintroduces us to each other and confirms us, affirms us. That's really when the story is good. Because it gives both teller and listener validity, affirmation—it verifies us and values us. It makes us precious. We can't do without story in that sense. We can always get information and maybe objective knowledge, but without that sense of intimacy, we might as well not know each other. I think honesty has a lot to do with it. Honesty. But honesty can be hard to come by.

♦

Men on the Moon[2]

I.

Joselita brought her father, Faustin, the TV on Father's Day. She brought it over after Sunday mass, and she had her son hook up the antenna. She plugged the TV cord into the wall socket.

Faustin sat on a worn couch. He was covered with an old coat. He had worn that coat for twenty years.

It's ready. Turn it on and I'll adjust the antenna, Amarosho told his mother. The TV warmed up and then the screen flickered into dull light. It was snowing. Amarosho tuned it a bit. It snowed less and then a picture formed.

Look, Naishtiya, Joselita said. She touched her father's hand and pointed at the TV.

I'll turn the antenna a bit and you tell me when the picture is clear, Amarosho said. He climbed on the roof again.

After a while the picture turned clearer. It's better! his mother shouted. There was only the tiniest bit of snow falling.

That's about the best it can get, I guess, Amarosho said. Maybe it'll clear up on the other channels. He turned the selector. It was clearer on another channel.

There were two men struggling mightily with each other. Wrestling, Amarosho said.

Do you want to watch wrestling? Two men are fighting, Nana. One of them is Apache Red. Chisheh tsah, he told his grandfather.

The old man stirred. He had been staring intently into the TV. He wondered why there was so much snow at first. Now there were two men fighting. One of them was a Chisheh—an Apache—and the other was a Mericano. There were people shouting excitedly and clapping hands within the TV.

The two men backed away from each other for a moment and then they clenched again. They wheeled mightily and suddenly one threw the other. The old man smiled. He wondered why they were fighting.

Something else showed on the TV screen. A bottle of wine was being poured. The old man liked the pouring sound and he moved his mouth and lips. Someone was selling wine.

The two fighting men came back on the TV. They struggled with each other, and after a while one of them didn't get up. And then another man came and held up the hand of the Apache, who was dancing around in a feathered headdress.

It's over, Amarosho announced. Apache Red won the fight, Nana.

The Chisheh won. Faustin stared at the other fighter, a light-haired man who looked totally exhausted and angry with himself. The old man didn't like the Apache too much. He wanted them to fight again.

After a few minutes, something else appeared on the TV.

What is that? Faustin asked. In the TV picture was an object with smoke coming from it. It was standing upright.

Men are going to the moon, Nana, Amarosho said. That's Apollo. It's going to fly three men to the moon.

That thing is going to fly to the moon?

Yes, Nana, his grandson said.

What is it called again? Faustin asked.

Apollo, a spaceship rocket, Joselita told her father.

The Apollo spaceship stood on the ground, emitting clouds of something, something that looked like smoke.

A man was talking, telling about the plans for the flight, what would happen, that it was almost time. Faustin could not understand the man very well because he didn't know many words in the language of the Mericano.

He must be talking about that thing flying in the air? he said.

Yes. It's about ready to fly away to the moon.

Faustin remembered that the evening before he had looked at the sky and seen that the moon was almost in the middle phase. He wondered if it was important that the men get to the moon.

Are those men looking for something on the moon, Nana? He asked his grandson.

They're trying to find out what's on the moon, Nana. What kind of dirt and rocks there are and to see if there's any water. Scientist men don't believe there is any life on the moon. The men are looking for knowledge, Amarosho said to Faustin.

Faustin wondered if the men had run out of places to look for knowledge on the earth. Do they know if they'll find knowledge? he asked.

They have some already. They've gone before and come back. They're going again.

Did they bring any back?

They brought back some rocks, Amarosho said.

Rocks. Faustin laughed quietly. The American scientist men went to search for knowledge on the moon and they brought back rocks. He kind of thought that perhaps Amarosho was joking with him. His grandson had gone to Indian School for a number of years, and sometimes he would tell his grandfather some strange and funny things.

The old man was suspicious. Sometimes they joked around. Rocks. You sure that's all they brought back? he said. Rocks!

That's right, Nana, only rocks and some dirt and pictures they made of what it looks like on the moon.

The TV picture was filled with the rocket spaceship close-up now. Men were sitting and standing and moving around some machinery, and the TV voice had become more urgent. The old man watched the activity in the picture intently but with a slight smile on his face.

Suddenly it became very quiet, and the TV voice was firm and commanding and curiously pleading. Ten, nine, eight, seven, six, five, four, three, two, one, liftoff. The white smoke became furious, and a muted rumble shook through the TV. The rocket was trembling and the voice was trembling.

It was really happening, the old man marveled. Somewhere inside of that cylinder with a point at its top and long slender wings were three men who were flying to the moon.

The rocket rose from the ground. There were enormous clouds of smoke and the picture shook. Even the old man became tense, and he grasped the edge of the couch. The rocket spaceship rose and rose.

There's fire coming out of the rocket, Amarosho explained. That's what makes it fly.

Fire. Faustin had wondered what made it fly. He had seen pictures of other flying machines. They had long wings, and someone had explained to him that there was machinery inside which spun metal blades that made the machines fly. He had wondered what made this thing fly. He hoped his grandson wasn't joking him.

After a while there was nothing but the sky. The rocket Apollo had disappeared. It hadn't taken very long, and the voice on the TV wasn't excited anymore. In fact, the voice was very calm and almost bored.

I have to go now, Naishtiya, Joselita told her father. I have things to do.

Me too, Amarosho said.

Wait, the old man said, wait. What shall I do with this thing? What is it you call it?

TV, his daughter said. You watch it. You turn it on and you watch it.

I mean how do you stop it? Does it stop like the radio, like the mahkina? It stops?

This way, Nana, Amarosho said and showed his grandfather. He turned a round knob on the TV and the picture went away.

He turned the knob again, and the pictured flickered on again. Were you afraid this one-eye would be looking at you all the time? Amarosho laughed and gently patted the old man's shoulder.

Faustin was relieved. Joselita and her son left. Faustin watched the TV picture for a while. A lot of activity was going on, a lot of men were moving among machinery, and a couple of men were talking. And then the spaceship rocket was shown again.

The old man watched it rise and fly away again. It disappeared again. There was nothing but the sky. He turned the knob and the picture died away. He turned it on and the picture came on again. He turned it off. He went outside and to a fence a short distance from his home. When he finished peeing, he zipped up his pants and studied the sky for a while.

II.

That night, he dreamed.

Flintwing Boy was watching a Skquuyuh mahkina come down a hill. The mahkina made a humming noise. It was walking. It shone in the sunlight. Flintwing Boy moved to a better position to see. The mahkina kept on moving toward him.

The Skquuyuh mahkina drew closer. Its metal legs stepped upon trees and crushed growing flowers and grass. A deer bounded away frightened.

Tsushki came running to Flintwing Boy.

Anahweh, Tsushki cried, trying to catch his breath.

What is it, Anahweh? You've been running, Flintwing Boy said.

The coyote was staring at the thing, which was coming toward them. There was wild fear in his eyes.

What is that, Anahweh? What is that thing? Tsushki gasped.

It looks like a mahkina, but I've never seen one quite like it before. It must be some kind of Skquuyuh mahkina, Anahweh, Flintwing Boy said. When he saw that Tsushki was trembling with fear, he said, Sit down, Anahweh. Rest yourself. We'll find out soon enough.

The Skquuyuh mahkina was undeterred. It walked over and through everything. It splashed through a stream of clear water. The water boiled and streaks of oil flowed downstream. It split a juniper tree in half with a terrible crash. It crushed a boulder into dust with a sound of heavy metal. Nothing stopped the Skquuyuh mahkina. It hummed.

Anahweh, Tsushki cried, what can we do?

Flintwing Boy reached into the bag hanging at his side. He took out an object. It was a flint arrowhead. He took out some cornfood.

Come over here, Anahweh. Come over here. Be calm, he motioned to the frightened coyote. He touched the coyote in several places on his body with the arrowhead and put cornfood in the palm of his hand.

This way, Flintwing Boy said. He closed Tsushki's fingers over the cornfood. They stood facing east. Flintwing Boy said, We humble ourselves again. We look in your direction for guidance. We ask for your protection. We humble our poor bodies and spirits because only you are the power and the source and the knowledge. Help us, then. That is all we ask.

Flintwing Boy and Tsushki breathed on the cornfood, then took in the breath of all the directions and gave the cornfood unto the ground.

Now the ground trembled with the awesome power of the Skquuyuh mahkina. Its humming vibrated against everything.

Flintwing Boy reached over his shoulder and took several arrows from his quiver. He inspected them carefully and without any rush he fit one to his bowstring.

And now, Anahweh, Flintwing Boy said, you must go and tell everyone. Describe what you have seen. The people must talk among themselves and learn what this is about, and decide what they will do. You must hurry, but you must not alarm the people. Tell them I am here to meet the Skquuyuh mahkina. Later I will give them my report.

Tsushki turned and began to run. He stopped several yards away.

Hahtrudzaimeh! he called to Flintwing Boy. Like a man of courage, Anahweh, like our people.

The old man stirred in his sleep. A dog was barking. He awoke fully and got out of his bed and went outside. The moon was past the midpoint, and it would be daylight in a few hours.

III.

Later, the spaceship reached the moon.

Amarosho was with his grandfather Faustin. They watched a TV replay of two men walking on the moon.

So that's the men on the moon, Faustin said.

Yes, Nana, there they are, Amarosho said.

There were two men inside of heavy clothing, and they carried heavy-looking equipment on their backs.

The TV picture showed a closeup of one of them and indeed there was a man's face inside of glass. The face moved its mouth and smiled and spoke, but the voice seemed to be separate from the face.

It must be cold, Faustin said. They have on heavy clothing.

It's supposed to be very cold and very hot on the moon. They wear special clothes and other things for protection from the cold and heat, Amarosho said.

The men on the moon were moving slowly. One of them skipped like a boy, and he floated alongside the other.

The old man wondered if they were underwater. They seem to be able to float, he said.

The information I have heard is that a man weighs less on the moon than he does on earth, Amarosho said to his grandfather. Much less, and he floats. And there is no air on the moon for them to breathe, so those boxes on their backs carry air for them to breathe.

A man weighs less on the moon, the old man thought. And there is no air on the moon except for the boxes on their backs. He looked at Amarosho, but his grandson did not seem to be joking with him.

The land on the moon looked very dry. It looked like it had not rained for a long, long time. There were no trees, no plants, no grass. Nothing but dirt and rocks, a desert.

Amarosho had told him that men on earth—scientists—believed there was no life on the moon. Yet those men were trying to find knowledge on the moon. Faustin wondered if perhaps they had special tools with which they could find knowledge even if they believed there was no life on the moon.

The mahkina sat on the desert. It didn't make a sound. Its metal feet were planted flat on the ground. It looked somewhat awkward. Faustin searched around the mahkina, but there didn't seem to be anything except the dry land on the TV. He couldn't figure out the mahkina. He wasn't sure whether it moved and could cause harm. He didn't want to ask his grandson that question.

After a while, one of the bulky men was digging in the ground. He carried a long, thin tool with which he scooped up dirt and put it into a container. He did this for a while.

Is he going to bring the dirt back to earth too? Faustin asked.

I think he is, Nana, Amarosho said. Maybe he'll get some rocks too. Watch.

Indeed, several minutes later, the man lumbered over to a pile of rocks and gathered several handsized ones. He held them out proudly. They looked just like rocks from around anyplace. The voice on the TV seemed to be excited about the rocks.

They will study the rocks, too, for knowledge?

Yes, Nana.

What will they use the knowledge for, Nana?

They say they will use it to better mankind, Nana. I've heard that. And to learn more about the universe in which we live. Also, some of the scientists say the knowledge will be useful in finding out where everything began a long time ago and how everything was made in the beginning.

Faustin looked with a smile at his grandson. He said, You are telling me the true facts, aren't you?

Why, yes, Nana. That's what they say. I'm not just making it up, Amarosho said.

Well then, do they say why they need to know where and how everything began? Hasn't anyone ever told them?

I think other people have tried to tell them but they want to find out for themselves, and also they claim they don't know enough and need to know more and for certain, Amarosho said.

The man in the bulky suit had a small pickax in his hand. He was striking at a boulder. The breathing of the man could be heard clearly. He seemed to be working very hard and was very tired.

Faustin had once watched a work crew of Mericano drilling for water. They had brought a tall mahkina with a loud motor. The mahkina would raise a limb at its center to its very top and then drop it with a heavy and loud metal clang. The mahkina and its men sat at one spot for several days, and finally they found water.

The water had bubbled out weakly, gray-looking, and did not look drinkable at all. And then the Mericano workmen lowered the mahkina, put their equipment away, and drove away. The water stopped flowing. After a couple of days, Faustin went and checked out the place.

There was nothing there except a pile of gray dirt and an indentation in the ground. The ground was already dry, and there were dark spots of oil-soaked dirt.

Faustin decided to tell Amarosho about the dream he had had.

After the old man finished, Amarosho said, Old man, you're telling me the truth now, aren't you? You know that you've become somewhat of a liar. He was teasing his grandfather.

Yes, Nana. I have told you the truth as it occurred to me that night. Everything happened like that except I might not have recalled everything about it.

That's some story, Nana, but it's a dream.

It's a dream, but it's the truth, Faustin said.

I believe you, Nana, his grandson said.

IV.

Sometime after that the spacemen returned to earth. Amarosho told his grandfather they had splashed down in the ocean.

Are they alright? Faustin asked.

Yes, Amarosho said. They have devices to keep them safe.

Are they in their homes now?

No, I think they have to be someplace where they can't contaminate anything. If they brought back something from the moon that they weren't supposed to, they won't pass it on to someone else, Amarosho said to his grandfather.

What would that something be?

Something harmful, Nana.

In that dry desert land of the moon there might be something harmful, the old man said. I didn't see any strange insects or trees or even cactus. What would that harmful thing be, Nana?

Disease which might harm people on earth, Amarosho said.

You said there was the belief by the men that there is no life on the moon. Is there life after all? Faustin asked.

There might be the tiniest bit of life.

Yes, I see now, Nana. If the men find even the tiniest bit of life on the moon, then they will believe, the old man said.

Yes. Something like that.

Faustin figured it out now. The Mericano men had taken that trip in a spaceship rocket to the moon to find even the tiniest bit of life. And when they found even the tiniest bit of life, even if it was harmful, they would believe that they had found knowledge. Yes, that must be the way it was.

He remembered his dream clearly now. The old man was relieved.

When are those two men fighting again, Nana? he asked Amarosho.

What two men?

Those two men who were fighting with each other the day the Mericano spaceship men were flying to the moon.

Oh, those men. I don't know, Nana. Maybe next Sunday. You like them?

Yes. I think the next time I will be cheering for the Chisheh. He'll win again. He'll beat the Mericano again, Faustin said.

♦

Yuusthiwa[3]

"Whenever people are driving along and stop
to offer Yuusthiwa a ride, he refuses
and says, 'I still have my legs,'"
my father says, saying it like the old man,
a slow careful drawl. And my mother corrects him,
"'While I'm still able to walk.'"
Yuusthiwa has been sick lately;
either something fell on him
or else he got bit by something, she heard.
Apparently, he still gets around though
pretty much because like my father says
one fellow had said, "'That old man,
he's still tom-catting around, visiting.'
You see him in Acomita along the road
or in McCartys." I chuckle at the expression
picturing the old guy in mind; after all,
Yuusthiwa is only 114 years old at last count.

"One time, David and I were coming
from Acomita," my father says, "and we stopped
for him. Recognizing me, he got in and said
'Ahku Tsai-rrhlai kudha.' And as we drove
westwards up this way, he told us things.
I had asked him, 'Naishtiya, how do you come
to live as many years as you have, to be so fortunate
as to mature as healthy and firm as you are?'
And he said, 'If you live enjoying and appreciating
your life, taking care of yourself, caring for
and being friendly with others; if you use the plants
that grow around here, seeing and knowing
that they are of use, boiling them into medicine
to use in the right way in caring for yourself,
cleansing and helping your body with them;
that's the way I have lived.' That's the way
he said it," my father says.

3

WHERE THE POWER LIES: SEEKING THE INTUITIVE LANGUAGE OF STORY

Terry Tempest Williams, born in Salt Lake City in 1955, has lived her entire life in the state of Utah, apart from teaching stints at places like the University of Iowa Writers' Workshop and research trips to Spain and Italy. She earned degrees in English and environmental education at the University of Utah, and her first book, *Pieces of White Shell: A Journey to Navajoland* (1984), emerged from her master's thesis in education. Since then she has published such collections of essays and stories as *Coyote's Canyon* (1989), *An Unspoken Hunger: Stories from the Field* (1994), and, most recently, *Red: Passion and Patience in the Desert* (2001). Much of her work explores the poetics, politics, and erotics of place—the latter idea is demonstrated in the 1995 work of prose poetry, *Desert Quartet*, and is explored in her essay "The Erotic Landscape" (*Northern Lights*, Winter 1995). Critic Lorraine Anderson has stated that "Williams is committed to living an erotic life, in spiritual and physical dialogue with landscape" (Anderson, Slovic, and O'Grady 1999, 28).

Williams has also demonstrated in various publications, public presentations, and the following interview that she is deeply invested in the politics of the relationship between humans and the land. The political dimension of her work is vividly displayed in the 1991 volume *Refuge: An Unnatural History of Family and Place*, which explores the medical and ecological implications of nuclear-weapons testing at the Nevada Test Site. The epilogue to *Refuge*, titled "The Clan of One-Breasted Women," examines the transition from an attitude of passivity and acceptance to one of active, political resistance, an emotionally and socially risky choice within Mormon culture. Sometimes, though, as she says in *Refuge*, "The price of obedience has become too high" (286). Williams followed *Refuge* with a sequel of sorts in 2000, titled *Leap*. Williams's work has been honored with a Guggenheim Fellowship, a Lannan Literary Fellowship in Creative Nonfiction, and a "Spirit of the West" award from the Mountain-Plains Booksellers Association. She has also been honored by Physicians for Social Responsibility for "distinguished contributions in literature, ecology, and advocacy for an environmentally sustainable world."

In addition to the volumes of her own work, Williams has co-edited several important collections, including *Great and Peculiar Beauty: A Utah Reader* (1995) with Thomas J. Lyon and *The New Genesis: Mormons Writing on the Environment* (1998) with William B. Smart and Gibbs M. Smith. However, perhaps the collection most relevant to the focus of the following interview is *Testimony: Writers of the West Speak on Behalf of Utah Wilderness*, which Williams compiled with Stephen Trimble in 1995. *Testimony* includes statements by twenty American writers on the importance of protecting wildlands in southern Utah; it was hand-delivered to all members of the United States Senate and House of Representatives and was influential in inspiring President Bill Clinton to establish the new Grand Staircase–Escalante National Monument on September 18, 1996. At the ceremony dedicating the new national monument, the President held up a copy of *Testimony* and said, "This made a difference."

Williams's own contribution to *Testimony* (reprinted recently in *Red*) was the lyrical essay called "Bloodlines," which we have included in this book as a sample of her values-oriented narrative. Instead of asking, prosaically, for so many acres or square miles of red-rock country to be designated as "wilderness," she tells the story of a woman who has been raped by an unknown assailant and who, in response, has taken to leaving strips of red ribbon throughout her beloved canyonlands. The woman thinks of these ribbons as "bloodlines," reminiscent of Zuni fetishes, icons of nature's sacredness. Later, she finds an obsidian chip, cuts a "lifeline" on her palm, and impresses her own blood on a boulder. Despite its indirectness and, some would say, crypticness, this is a story that emanates the emotions of suffering and celebration. Pain of the human body codes for suffering and destruction of the external world. The red ribbons attached to the land mirror the ribbon of blood on the woman's hand. Just as we automatically value the health and wholeness of the human body, the story implies, we must learn to value the health and wholeness of the land that sustains us. This is the story that Williams told at the planning meeting in southern Utah, where Utah politician Jim Hansen responded, "I'm sorry, Ms. Williams, there's something about your voice I cannot hear." What Williams expresses in this story is vital, visceral attachment to land—wild land, land for its own sake, not land that can be mined or otherwise used for making money. Because her story does not use the language of law, economics, or resource management, just as the language of a typical layperson is likely not to use the terminology of these technical disciplines, a policy maker "cannot hear" it.

The same author, however, is quite capable of employing more traditional language of public testimony. Williams has occasionally testified before congressional subcommittees. In 1991, she spoke to the Subcommittee on Fisheries and Wildlife Conservation and the Environment concerning the Pacific Yew Act—this statement is available in *An Unspoken Hunger*. We have reprinted her more recent "Statement before the Senate Subcommittee on Forest & Public Lands Management Regarding the Utah Public Lands Management Act of 1995" in this volume, hoping to contrast it with "Bloodlines." Both are eloquent pieces of writing, and both have strong emotive and imaginative content. The "Statement" is more discursive, more analytical and argumentative—and thus would probably register more forcefully with legislators and resource managers. It includes quotations by scientists such as Edward O. Wilson and Mormon religious leaders, including Brigham Young—appeals to authority.

In the following interview, Williams contrasts the formal language of oped columns with the lyrical, mysterious, and even chaotic language of story. The former, she says, can help to open up discussion, but the latter operates in a more powerful and lasting way, inspiring new ways of thinking that emerge from the silence of uncertainty, even perplexity. The interview transcript, combined with the two contrasting writing samples, will give readers an opportunity to reflect upon the different kinds and degrees of effectiveness of different styles of narrative and testimonial discourse.

♦

A CONVERSATION WITH TERRY TEMPEST WILLIAMS

Prior to engaging the tape recorder, Scott Slovic and Terre Satterfield had been introducing the project and the predominance of cost-benefit analysis in designating the value of nature. Terry Tempest Williams was clearly very uncomfortable with the whole language of values research, and thus it took her some time to warm up to the discussion.

The interview took place at Williams's home at the time in the mountains east of Salt Lake City. We sat on her living-room floor, beneath a strikingly carved wooden snake on the fireplace mantel, and later at the dining room table. A few months after we met with her, Terry and her husband, Brooke, moved to their current home several hours south of Salt Lake City, in Castle Valley, Utah.

Satterfield: We acknowledge fully that "values" is one of those words that gets used differently by everyone who uses it, but we're interested in the way ideas—and, yes, values—are expressed in nature writing and how that differs from their expression in policy discussions and documents. Does narrative, for instance, provide a means of expression for attachments to landscapes or wild places that can't be articulated any other way? If we're truly interested in understanding citizen values about nature, is narrative the place to begin, the place to listen from?

Slovic: Charles Wilkinson has a few passages in his book *The Eagle Bird* where he says the very language in which policy issues are discussed determines the outcomes of the discussions. And he advocates, almost as an aside, bringing together the language of nature writing and the topics that are addressed in boardrooms. I think he means to say that using the concrete language of story and image would generate very different results.

Williams: And what's your hope?

Satterfield: Well, I guess one hope is that we'll begin to develop some evidence through these interviews with writers for the idea that cost-benefit analyses lack the kind of voice and meaning that are central to how everyday people talk about values. Perhaps, when introducing a discussion with concerned citizens, what the policy world refers to as stakeholders, the starting point for the discussion could be a narrative passage rather than a brainstormed list of costs and benefits. We could also let people create their own stories, give them the stimulus to create their own stories, to see what points of meaning or value appear there, points cleansed out of the other processes.

Williams: Do you mean settings where local people are gathered to comment on a plan for development or protection of an area?

Satterfield: Exactly. And I don't think the policy and academic community is closed to the idea. As unconventional as it sounds, I've often received a very enthusiastic response from those audiences when discussing this possibility.

Williams: This all sounds so objective, as though our hearts are not involved. Yet in truth this is not the case in science or policy. So I think when you enable the audience to breathe, to feel, to be human again, it restores their own creativity and imaginative capacities, so I can only imagine they were thrilled. It's like you brought them back to life.

Satterfield: Yes, living, breathing value is exactly the point, but I hope we haven't now contaminated our conversation by revealing our expectations for nature writers and the study of values.

Williams: No, it's just that in my world when I hear the word "values" it stops contemplation. I mean, I can just feel my heart rate going up. Because growing up in Mormon culture, being a woman, it's all about values and that really means orthodoxy, dogma, and conversation ceases. I pull back from that kind of discussion.

If you ask other questions, "What do you love? What do you care about? What questions shatter your sleep at night? What stories do you tell?" then the conversation opens again. But I reel at that word.

Slovic: So maybe this should be a study that explores the possibility of expunging the world of the "v" word.

Williams: Well, look at my body language. I mean, look at what's happened to me. When you start talking, all of a sudden my legs go up—it's like there's no way you're going to get inside of me. I mean, I am having an absolute physical reaction and it's because living in this community with the concerns that I have . . . people in this community would tell you I have no values.

Satterfield: Do you think I should have found a different place to start, a different word to start with?

Williams: I don't know. All I know is that I don't know how to talk about this.

Satterfield: So let's not. Let's take that other door and talk perhaps a bit more about narrative and why that works as a means to . . .

Williams: I'm not going to talk to you about that because I don't even know what "narrative" means.

Satterfield: The telling of stories—I think of it strictly as the telling of stories. The telling of an experience, the creating of story.

Williams: So when we're talking about story, are we talking about conversation? I mean, I know what narrative means when we talk about it in English class. That's a case where we talk about values and narrative but we can also talk about love and concern and stories—conversation, dialogue.

Slovic: Before we came here I worried that in talking to you about these issues we would make you feel dyslexic. Do you remember the conversation we had about landscape and gender in Reno a few years ago? I began it with a comment about gendered landscapes, and you said: "When I hear you talk, you make me feel dyslexic."

Williams: My brain goes haywire. It really does.

Slovic: But on the way over here I mentioned to Terre that you tend to think in stories, that you shape the world, and the world presents its meaning to you, by way of story and not by way of abstract interpretations of story. And so I had the feeling that rather than engaging in an abstract discussion with you, it would be more meaningful to see in what sense some of the prompts we provided might stimulate stories.

Williams: You see, here's one of the problems: I have been in and worked in policy circles and I can talk that world. I've been around the table when strategies have been discussed and created, and I'm very familiar with that language. The same is true of the academy. The difficult—let's see if I can articulate this for myself because I think it's how laypeople feel. Whether you're testifying before Congress or working at strategy sessions with a group like the Southern Utah Wilderness Alliance, there's a distance that gets set up. If you choose to speak in the language of story (a choice that's compounded by gender), there's a sense that these people can't really understand intellectually what we are talking about. They'll step back, provide an intellectual overlay, and "make sense of it." It's very demeaning. It negates in my mind what you are really trying to do.

It's similar to the problem with the word "value"; the word creates a separation and in my mind that's exactly what you're attempting not to do. There are separations between abstract terms and story, between the language of the intellect and the intuitive (the language of the poet, or the storyteller). I'm weary of the goal to interpret. Right there, the premise absolutely shatters.

Satterfield: Yes, this is a good point. Do those who work at eliciting values through story want only to break stories apart?

Williams: Yes, it brings me to tears; it's why the price is so huge for those who dare to speak the language of story to members of Congress, or around boardroom tables in Washington, D.C. There's always a judgment. Have you ever heard Ted Strong testify before Congress? He runs the Columbia River Intertribal Fisheries Commission. They say, "Well, he's an Indian. We are now going to be gifted by a story." There's always this mood: "Don't we all feel good?" Followed by the call to get back to work, back to the *real* nuts and bolts.

Satterfield: This suggests that narrative exists only in tribal populations and not in the rest of the world, including the political world.

Williams: Yet as human beings, what we really do is tell stories. How do we break down this hierarchy? Because of our friendship, Scott, I can say this, but this is part of what I think you're saying to me when you say Terry's not going to be able to be articulate in a linear way; we can let her move in the realm of stories and figure it out later.

Slovic: Maybe. I didn't mean it in a demeaning way, though. I meant it as a preference.

Williams: I know, but I'm pushing you because that's exactly what gets set up in these policy meetings. What we need to do, and again, I'm uncomfortable with the words "need," "ought," and "should" because we're saying we know what's right and they don't. But I think what we are desperate for, as human beings, is a world where there is no separation; it means the integration of the arts with the sciences, so that we're moving in all these worlds simultaneously. If we can't move in these directions, where we become shape shifters, then we are destined for loneliness, impoverishment. Lonely policies, impoverished policies, and sterile art.

It works both ways. As a writer, if I am concerned only about 5.7 million acres of wilderness, my work is at best rhetoric and at worst parody. I become a pawn for some organization. The important thing is that we learn to ask ourselves, "Are we really listening to each other?"

I want to know what questions are being asked around policy tables or dinner tables (which in many ways are the same thing). And, also, what are the spaces of silence? Are we comfortable in those moments of silence, in reflection? How do we allow for that kind of contemplation, that kind of reflective thinking, so that we are not just giving opinions? Washington is about opinions. A much better premise is: Can we care enough about each other to ask evocative questions? If you were to ask me what I value, and if I can get over my own physical reaction to that word given the culture that I'm encased in, then I value the evocative questions. I value the silences. I value someone who listens. I value the ambiguities, the discomfort. In that realm, because of the desperation that gets created, the stories arise. The blood rushes back into the language and the rhetoric dissolves.

Satterfield: One of the things that strikes me about the policy world, about the habit of bringing forth the storytellers, whether that be Ted Strong or yourself, is that, once delivered, the story just sort of sits there. It hangs in the air; no one knows what to do with it. There's no relationship between bringing in storytellers and what then happens at the level of policy. Is there some way to provide a better link between listening to storytellers and realizing the implication of story in some formal way? Or do we always run the risk of "killing" the stories by converting them into policy statements?

Williams: I don't think you can manufacture or manipulate this connection. Stories arise out of the moment and that's where the power lies. You can't know what story is appropriate for any given moment. I mean the stories are born out of an organic necessity, out of the heat, and that is the source of their potency.

I think it would be a stunning moment in Congress to have someone from each region read an example of the literature of place, whether it's a little hill or the Grand Canyon, whether it's the Sonoran Desert or the White Mountains of New England. People really love where they live; it's what sings to us. If we were to go back and listen to the great orations in Congress, we would see that many of them are place-based.

The big environmental groups are not that different. Not long ago I was talking to the director of the Wilderness Society. He was saying how busy he was and that he has no time for anything, and I said, through e-mail (which I love), "Do you read poetry?" He writes back, "I don't have time for poetry." And I thought, well, he reads e-mail. So I just snuck a basic haiku into a message. He writes back, "That's beautiful." Then, he says, "Send me another one." So I sent a little longer one. And he says, "Does this mean this?" And I say, "Yes." He then writes back sometime later and says: "You won't believe this, but we opened the governing council meeting with a poem!"

More took place in that strange exchange than when I was on the Wilderness Society board. It started with "I'm so busy" and went to "Do you have another poem?" and from there to falling in love with language. This is the breakdown of rhetoric.

Satterfield: What is different in the experience of hearing rhetoric versus hearing stories? Is there some harm that rhetoric does that story that doesn't do?

Williams: The way I've witnessed it at strategy meetings or in talking to people in Congress is that rhetoric is comfortable (once you have it down). You don't have to think; you've got the bases covered. Most people don't go farther than that.

Satterfield: So there's an arrogance involved?

Williams: It's just all on the surface. It's all perfect, you get what you want. The exchange is made, but there's no depth to it. What story does is take you out of the realm of what is secure and what is known. When you enter, you allow chaos to enter.

Satterfield: And why is that attractive or good for policy?

Williams: Because it's not predictable; it's where things get interesting. Maybe policy can't exist on that level of story or chaos, but then again there's the desire for arts and politics to blend. Look at the Wilderness Act of 1964; it has beautiful language because someone cared about that. If we as a culture fall in love again with language and stillness and slowness, that kind of attention becomes automatic.

Satterfield: Bill Kittredge said something along these lines, that story was not just a way for him to get something across, but also a mirror, a basis for reflection, a basis for reflection on the reader's part.

Slovic: The cracks in formal ideologies and mindless, inherited language start to appear.

Williams: Yes, everything quiets down. The body language changes. A silence enters in, and a trance sets in, one is brought into a trance. And I think that's the power of story. People forget where they are, and time and space dissolve. I did a really interesting experiment once with librarians. Librarians love words. I had three different pieces for three different purposes, three very different types of narrative. One was the op-ed piece that was printed in the *New York Times* in June of 1995 prior to a meeting of the Natural Resources Committee. It was the most straightforward, pedantic, factual exposition I could offer. You know, all the five w's: what, when, where, why, and who. I know for a fact that it changed the decisions at that meeting for the better. It made a difference. It opened the door for discussion.

The second piece of writing was an introduction for a book on Utah, and it appealed to the community whose roots are here. It was a very lyrical piece, a kind of ode to wildness. In as eloquent a language as I could come up with, it spoke to why community matters and why we can come together in the name of landscape. It was very non-threatening, more philosophical.

The last piece was the section called "Water" from *Desert Quartet*, which is about a woman who wears a dead frog around her neck, bathes in the river and dives into a pool, cuts her head, bleeds, surfaces. It uses the metaphor of hearing a chorus of frogs, and who knows what that means?

Which has had the least effect on public policy? I would say *Desert Quartet*. Which has had the strongest effect in terms of national policy? The *New York Times* article. But what was the life of that piece? Twenty-four hours at best, and then it was thrown away. Which of three pieces got read the most? No question, the *New York Times*. The next largest readership probably goes to the introduction. Was it understood? Yes. Did it make a difference? Probably not, but it was a nice thing to read. But what was the piece that held the silence? *Desert Quartet*. What was the piece that was probably least understood? *Desert Quartet.* What is the piece that has been read less than the others? *Desert Quartet.* Personally, which do I think will have the larger impact? I think it will be the *Desert Quartet* piece. Do you understand what I'm saying?

Satterfield: Yes, I think you're talking about creating silence, and time for thoughtfulness.

Williams: It's like this: when I was reading to the librarians, I never got through the *New York Times* piece because I was so bored by it. The second one was okay . . . it's my credo. But the other one: as I was reading it, I could hear different things, I went someplace else and it wasn't about me at all. It has a life of its own.

Satterfield: I often wonder about this, the issue of audience for nature writers. The publisher's accountant will tell you that nature writing is only a small portion of the market. And yet, when I'm talking to ordinary people about environmental values, I hear the voices of writers but I don't know the sources. Are writers putting to voice the words and ideas already out there, or are the voices of writers easily acquired by readers, through some kind of osmosis even? Your book is not necessarily on their reading list, but something is going on.

Williams: That's why I don't care about the numbers. I used to feel this missionary zeal. You know, there's only so much time left, the world is going to hell, and we have to get the word out. I don't feel that anymore. I think there's something else going on that we can't even begin to understand. And I think it is invisible and it is organic and it is happening across neighborhood fences, in the halls of Congress. In a way, Washington is the ultimate center of story. Politicians thrive on anecdote, but they would have you believe it is all policy, facts, and figures. That's the irony.

Satterfield: Let's change tracks here a bit and return to the characteristics of stories. If one of the things that values researchers want to do is set up value discussions or elicitation contexts, what are the pieces of stories—what a technician might call the "attributes of stories"—that help people think about their values?

Slovic: Yes, like the issue of the narrator. How do readers or listeners interact with the voice or storytelling style of the narrator?

Satterfield: Yes, the social-science community is not going to like the whole idea of narrators. They'll worry that if people read a story about an environmental problem about which they're supposed to offer opinion, the reader will just succumb to the narrator's opinion. Or does the influence of narrator work some other way?

Williams: Well, in becoming the narrator you measure yourself against humanity. You enter the process privately, with your own sets of judgments and assessments. It's how we find out who we are in the world. Stories dwell in ambiguity, and we go there to learn something of ourselves.

Satterfield: But I can just see how that would make the research and policy world nervous. Ambiguity isn't a very comfortable premise. Decision makers want to know clearly, and with some stability, what people think. They want to rely on that finding to help them guide decisions.

Slovic: Are we talking here about a very basic distinction between the sciences and the humanities?

Williams: I think it's just that we're an incredibly dualistic society. It's black or white, it's this or that, it's you or me. I have a niece who wants to be a scientist. Her brother is in literature and moving toward Harvard Divinity School. She just spent two weeks with him in London. I said, "How was it?" She goes, "I can't take it." I said, "What do you mean?" She said, "I'm so tired of sitting with my brother's friends where they just say there are no right answers." She said, "Every classroom I went to in his school was set up in circles. The minute I saw a circle, I thought, they don't know anything." She said she was so excited to get back to her science classes where they were all in rows!

And I said, "Abby, do you really believe that in biology things are more sure?" Again, the illusion. So I think storytelling begins to heal that split, so we see the world whole again, even holy. Even for a moment.

Slovic: Terry, this reminds me of the famous encounter, the infamous encounter, between you and Jim Hansen that Brooke has written about, using it as an example of fundamental differences between people, between Democrats and Republicans, between "peakers" and "non-peakers," to use Abraham Maslow's terms. This differs a bit from the idea that the split is surmountable, that there lives in everyone a fundamental impulse toward story. Do you think there is a basic division between people, some tending toward abstraction or quantitative information and others toward story? You seem not to agree with this, but . . .

Williams: The encounter with Jim Hansen at that hearing is so visual, and the people there were . . . you know, the glasses slipping, the flipping of papers, the yawning, the irritation, and then, finally, the infamous "I'm sorry, Ms. Williams, there's something about your voice I cannot hear." Well, you know, maybe he's talking about the microphone, maybe he isn't. On one level it's the microphone; on the other level, it's "I cannot hear what your voice is saying, and I will not hear what your voice is saying."

And in that context, it was so chilling. Every hair on my body stood up—it was horrifying.

What I loved is that I never said a word. The story of that event just started circulating, got out of control. His aide sent the record to see if that was what I remembered. And the words are there. That is the ritual of Congress, that's the ritual of a reading. It goes to what we were saying about how a classroom is set up. What is the atmosphere, how is the atmosphere created? And in that context, then, how is truth to be revealed? In Congress, it's set up so that truth can't be revealed because you are so intimidated that you are only speaking that which you dare to say in a highly controlled context of time and space.

I don't know if this is answering your question. There is another side to this. That is, when Jim Hansen and I were in his office. We were sitting down, and he showed me the pictures on his wall. We talked about his relationship to my uncle, about how much he loved the Bear River Bird Refuge. On some level, I think there is a deep regard that we have for one another. When the Friends of the Bear River Migratory Bird Refuge began a year ago, Jim Hansen and I were the speakers. You know, telling the same story. So, there are complexities, ambiguities, changes in context. There are rituals that the culture has set up so that you cannot hear one another and there really are major differences in opinion. But it may be that the differences are formed more strongly around or through the language we've used, not in the substance of the stories we tell.

Satterfield: So, it's not that the differences dissolve in stories, but that they're embraced in stories in some ways. Stories can contain difference in a way that other vehicles, or language styles, cannot.

Williams: There's a dignity in story, and I think there's a privacy allotted in story through the imagination that has a calming effect. You know, you're not put on the defensive.

Satterfield: The exchange you describe between yourself and Jim Hansen reminds me of some of my own discomfort. What I know the research world wants is evidence that stories can be used in some pragmatic way. So here I am studying this narrative vehicle, and yet when I go to play with it in some technical or social scientific sense, I feel almost sheepish. I feel something that is a bit like embarrassment. Maybe it's the feeling that people like to engage in stories in private, and I am asking them to make the process public.

Williams: You're bending the rules. You're rupturing protocol.

Satterfield: Yes, am I a fool in doing so?

Williams: And yet, it's the fool who carries the power. There's a great essay by Cecil Collins, a British artist, much in the tradition of Blake, who writes about the vision of the fool shattering both church and state with truth. The fool may not stick around long, because he or she can't, that's not how things are set up, but the fool's presence does open the windows. I mean, when you talk about embarrassment, I think, man, do I ever know about embarrassment. It's horrifying. On days when you're strong you can handle it, and on days when you're not strong . . . I can't count the times I've walked into this house full of self-doubt and embarrassment, humiliation. And yet, you don't know what the end of the story is. You don't know what the ramifications are. So, I—or you—play the fool because some part of us believes in it. A bigger part probably doesn't, but something else kicks in and there you are.

Slovic: The language of public officials, however, is often designed to say relatively little so as to avoid looking foolish, to cover up and conceal and keep things stable and in control. So it makes me wonder whether it's conceivable, or perhaps naive, to think about a revolution in language, a tolerance for the intuitive language of story in meeting rooms or congressional halls. Perhaps the language of the storyteller will always be that of the outsider and the destabilizer. And maybe that's the function of story, to regularly or irregularly intrude and disrupt, to force some kind of reconfiguration of formal policy through this process of disruption.

Satterfield: I like your point about story being the language of the outsider. That's the point in some ways. We're not trying to convert the language of policy, we're simply interested in allowing narrative to be the language of the public talking to the policy community or even the research community. As it stands, you don't get heard as an average person unless you can talk the official language, which may hide more than it reveals.

Williams: That is necessary and, really, it would be a catastrophe if artists ran government, or if the bureaucrats suddenly entered poetry.

Satterfield: I think of narrative as the language of inclusion, which really becomes important in the overall tendency in land management contexts toward dialogue, toward what is sometimes called "stakeholder participation." Narrative, or story, allows you tentatively to approach somebody that you couldn't be farther apart from if you tried. If you work in story rather than, say, technical language or even in openly politicized terms, there is a breaking down of barriers, a greater willingness to listen. This reminds me of Bill Kittredge's point: "It [storytelling] stamps on my desire to preach."

Williams: And storytelling has a life of its own. The ego dissolves. And when the ego dissolves, people can listen. Story allows us to enter through the back door. We don't even know what we're saying in a story. I really believe that. It just helps us think and begin to talk to others. Scott, I'd be interested in your opinion: aren't there endless interpretations for stories?

Slovic: Yes, there are many ways of reading, so a single interpretation doesn't deny the existence of other interpretations. The standard line of literature teachers, speaking to their students, is always: There's an effectively argued or explained interpretation and an ineffectively argued one, not a right or a wrong one. So, I think what aficionados of literature appreciate is not the way literature endorses a single view of the world, but the way it opens up the possibility of exploration. People interested in expedient statements of opinion—an attitude that may be fairly common among those who work in agency or government jobs—have many issues to think about, and they don't have time to devote hour after hour, day after day, to a particular issue. They want it boiled down. They understandably want expedience.

Williams: But they can also be calmed by story and healed by story. It's what keeps them sane.

Slovic: Terry, this brings to mind the book *Testimony*. One of the things that really interests me about that collection is the very different forms of writing used by the contributors. People like Barry Lopez and Rick Bass wrote relatively formal statements. You know, almost a kind of approximation of the language that they would expect their audience of politicians to be comfortable with. Yet your own contribution to the collection is a story I imagine your audience of Congressmen and Senators finding complex and mystifying. I wonder if you made a conscious choice not to write a *New York Times* type of piece. Perhaps you wanted to include a story that would challenge the readers.

Williams: Well, I remember Steve Trimble's discomfort with it.

Slovic: His piece is more down to earth, more linear.

Williams: But I didn't say to myself: "What's the most perplexing story I can give them?" I wanted just to tell a story that would be at the heart of what I felt. The story, "Bloodlines," was the only way I felt I could take on the emotional landscape I felt was at risk, that I could convey the abuse, the rape of the land, I saw as a resident there. I had a dream about that red thread, and I really pay attention to that. It's really a trust. I trust that that story, on some level, is understood, unconsciously. I truly believe Jim

Hansen would read that story and say, "What would you expect from her?" But on some level there may be a residual image that affects him. It's my absolute fierce belief in images—that it's the images that move us, it's the images that haunt us, even more than the words. Images are what the imagination plays with. And these are what prey on the rational mind.

Satterfield: Well, the image of place or places seems very important to the values literature in the social sciences. We know that people are drawn to places that they don't know of and will never see. Even so, such places remain very important to them. This comes up in a classic study about the *Exxon Valdez* oil spill in Prince William Sound, addressing what economists call "existence value." People who lived nowhere near the Sound, who couldn't find the place on the map, still expressed an attachment to this place. Their only experience with Prince William Sound is the one in their imagination, and they just wanted to know that it would continue to exist.

Williams: So it's in the mind, it's in the heart—it's in the knowing. I remember at age twenty, twenty-one, going to hearings in Denver—it was 1977—on the Alaska land spill. It changed my life. There was a blind piano tuner there; I remember he had blond hair. At the hearings, he said, "I will never be able to see Alaska, but just knowing it's there, I can continue to do the laborious work I do because while I'm tuning the piano, I hear the migrating swans."

Satterfield: What is it that we want to carry with us? What is the piano tuner wanting to hold on to? We pay a great deal of attention to the places where we live, but I think there's this whole other place in the mind that we carry around with us like a talisman. Or there's something we don't see, don't know, and couldn't really describe, that we desperately need to know exists.

Williams: I think it has something to do with inspiration. There's something inspirational about wild, open places. What does it mean to be inspired? When was the last time we were inspired, which means taken out of our daily lives and elevated to something new? It's what we want our politicians to do.

Satterfield: But what if, for a moment, it worked? What if stories inspired or elevated people, what if stories became more "acceptable" in policy circles? My fear is that the appreciation would be momentary, that for a brief moment policy people would live vicariously in or through this story, but then they would basically purge themselves of all the thoughts and feelings that a narrative can contain, leaving only the content behind. Story would become a sort of wastebasket, a place to set these things aside before getting on with the real world of business, politics, and so forth. It's not unlike environmental groups asking Native American speakers to their meetings. Often what happens is the Native speaker opens the meeting with a prayer or a story but is then not otherwise invited to the planning session or strategy meeting.

Williams: Well, I've allowed myself to be used repeatedly in that capacity.

The worst example I can think of was The Nature Conservancy's annual donors dinner, where the people in the room were all $500,000 donors, large oil companies. On one level, they couldn't have cared less. They were there because it made their companies look good. But I gave a reading, and I saw their eyes and I could tell a lot of them weren't moved at all. I know a lot of them were looking at their watches. But I also know that as years have gone by, I'll meet some of them again and they'll say, "I remember and it caused me to think about this," or it gives them some connection to their children.

They may invite you as a means of entertainment to salve their conscience. But what they don't anticipate is that you take it very seriously, that for you it isn't entertainment. Something gets translated, transferred, and they're touched. Again, it's the power of story and that's what we can have ultimate confidence in. It changes the energy. It's very difficult to talk about crunching numbers after a poem has been read. There has to be a pause. Sometimes the whole world gets turned upside down. The meeting's discussion takes a different turn.

Satterfield: What you're saying is that the impact doesn't have to be immediate.

Williams: No, and it usually isn't.

Satterfield: I recognize what you're saying. It's the long-distance echo that matters. It comes back to haunt that particular person sitting at that Nature Conservancy table.

Williams: That's right. Often I've given readings in law schools or in those kinds of settings; in some ways they have been the most difficult because you feel there's nothing coming back to you. You end and there's this kind of deadly silence, and you think, "I've failed miserably." But it's just that it takes a minute for the presentation to settle because it's a different atmosphere.

I keep thinking literature, art, paintings, dance, and music are offerings for the policy world. These media slow you down and make you think. We, the community of artists, are here—use us! The common point, the edge, actually, is a sense of democracy. There is a fierce sense of democracy in the arts, a freedom of expression. And I think there's a fierce sense of democracy in policy, too. I really do.

♦

Statement before the Senate Subcommittee on Forest & Public Lands Management Regarding the Utah Public Lands Management Act of 1995, Washington, D.C., 13 July 1995[1]

Mr. Chairman, members of this subcommittee, my name is Terry Tempest Williams. I am a native of Utah. My family roots run deep, holding me in place: five, six generations of Mormon stock run through my veins. Our family has made its living on the land for the last six decades laying pipe in the Utah substrate. We are a family of pipeline contractors and although I have never dug the ditches, I love and care for the men who do: my brothers, cousins, uncle, father, John Henry Tempest, my grandfather, John Henry Tempest, Jr., who is in his ninetieth year, even my great-grandfather, John Henry Tempest, Sr. We understand the power of continuity and our debt to these lands that have given us livelihood. As a Utah family, we would like to enter into the Congressional Record personal letters, four generations' worth, of why we care about wilderness, why we do not favor Senate Bill 884, and why we want more wilderness designation in Utah, not less. Some of the letters are forthcoming, some I have brought with me. These letters represent men and women, Republicans and Democrats alike, registered voters and voices too young to vote, but not too young to register their opinions. They are individual and original, some sealed, some open. It is a gesture of sincere concern for what we hold dear.

I appreciate this time to be able to share with you some of my own thoughts about the Utah Public Lands Management Act of 1995.

It is not a wilderness bill that the majority of Utahns recognize, want, or desire.

It is not a wilderness bill that honors or respects our history as a people.

It is not a wilderness bill that honors or respects the natural laws required for a healthy environment.

And it is not a wilderness bill that takes an empathetic stance toward our future.

It is a wilderness bill that lacks vision and undermines the bipartisan principles inherent in the Wilderness Act of 1964.

Quite simply, in the name of political expediency and with eyes capable of seeing only through the lens of economics, our public lands in Utah are being sacrificed. Our congressional delegation has told you that this issue must be resolved now, that this debate over the wildlands in Utah has torn our state in half. But I prefer to take the artist Frederick Sommer's approach when he says, "Quarreling is the cork of a good wish."

What is it we wish for?

In Utah, there was a man with a vision. He dreamed of a civilization bright with lights and strong of belief. He knew the industrious nature of work and picked the beehive as his symbol. He loved the land he saw before him, a landscape so vast, pristine, and virginal, that he recognized it as the kingdom of God, a place for saints with a desire for home. The desert country of the Great Basin and Colorado Plateau was an answer to prayers of spiritual sovereignty.

He sent families north into the mountains and south into the valleys where red rock walls rose upward like praying hands. He said, "We will create Zion among the wilderness." And with great stamina and imagination akin only to communities committed to faith, the building of culture among the pioneers began. Humble ranches, small businesses, and cottage industries of silk and wool sprung up and a United Order was dreamed.

Brigham Young, the colonizing prophet of the Mormons, brought with him not only a religion and a life but a land ethic.

> Here are the stupendous works of the God of Nature, though all do not appreciate His wisdom as manifested in his works. . . . I could sit here for a month and reflect on the mercies of God.

Time. Reflection. Mercy. These qualities were not revered as elsewhere in the Utah Public Lands Act of 1995. There is little gratitude extended on behalf of these sacred lands.

Only a few generations ago, Utah was settled on spiritual grounds. It is ironic that now Utah must be protected on spiritual grounds for the generations to come.

What do we wish for?

To be whole. To be complete. Wildness reminds us what it means to be human, what we are connected to rather than what we are separate from. "Our troubles," the Pulitzer Prize-winning scientist Edward O. Wilson writes,

> arise from the fact that we do not know what we are and cannot agree on what we want to be. . . . Humanity is part of nature, a species that evolved among

other species. The more closely we identify ourselves with the rest of life, the more quickly we will be able to discover the sources of human sensibility and acquire knowledge on which an enduring ethic, a sense of preferred direction, can be built.

Wilderness is both the bedrock lands of southern Utah and a metaphor of "unlimited possibility." The question must be asked, "How can we cut ourselves off from the very source of our creation?"

This is not about economics. This is not about the preservation of ranching culture in America. And it is especially not about settling a political feud once and for all. This is about putting ourselves in accordance with nature, of consecrating these lands by remembering our relationships to them. A strong wilderness bill as recommended by Congressman Maurice Hinchey, HR 1500, is an act of such consecration. At a recent family gathering, my uncle Richard Tempest, a former Republican state senator, said simply, "Wilderness is a feeling."

Mr. Chairman, if you know wilderness in the way you know love, you would be unwilling to let it go. We are talking about the body of the beloved, not real estate. We must ask ourselves as Americans, "Can we really survive the worship of our own destructiveness?" We do not exist in isolation. Our sense of community and compassionate intelligence must be extended to all life-forms, plants, animals, rocks, rivers, and human beings. This is the story of our past and it will be the story of our future.

Senate Bill 884 falls desperately short of these ideals.

Who can say how much nature can be destroyed without consequence? Who can say how much land can be used for extractive purposes until it is rendered barren forever? And who can say what the human spirit will be crying out for one hundred years from now? Two hundred years from now? A few weeks ago, Yosemite National Park had to close its gates and not allow any more visitors entry; the park was overcrowded. Last week, Yellowstone reported traffic gridlocks in the Lamar Valley, carloads of families with the wish of seeing a wolf. Did our country's lawmakers who held the vision of national parks in the nineteenth century dream of this kind of hunger? In the same vein, can you as our lawmakers today, toward the end of the twentieth century, imagine what the sanctity of wilderness in Utah might hold for us as a people at the turn of the twenty-first century?

We must act with this kind of vision and concern not just for ourselves, but for our children and our children's children. This is our natural heritage. And we are desperate for visionary leadership.

It's strange how deserts turn us into believers. I believe in walking in a landscape of mirages because you learn humility. I believe in living in a land of little water because life is drawn together. And I believe in the gathering of bones as a testament to spirits that have moved on.

If the desert is holy, it is because it is a forgotten place that allows us to remember the sacred. Perhaps that is why every pilgrimage to the desert is a pilgrimage to the self. There is no place to hide and so we are found.

Wilderness courts our souls. When I sat in church throughout my growing years, I listened to teachings about Christ walking in the wilderness for forty days and forty nights, reclaiming his strength, where he was able to say to Satan, "Get thee hence." And when I imagined Joseph Smith kneeling in a grove of trees as he received his vision to create a new religion, I believed their sojourns into nature were sacred. Are ours any less?

There is a Mormon scripture, from the Doctrine and Covenants section 88:44–47, that I carry with me:

> The earth rolls upon her wings, and the sun giveth his light by day, and the moon giveth her light by night, and the stars also give their light, as they roll upon their wings in their glory, in the midst and power of God.
>
> Unto what shall I liken the these kingdoms that ye may understand?
>
> Behold all these are kingdoms and any man who hath seen any or the least of these hath seen God moving in his majesty and power.

Without a philosophy of wildness and the recognition of its inherent spiritual values, we will, as E. O. Wilson reminds us, "descend farther from heaven's air if we forget how much the natural world means to us."

For those of us who so love these lands in Utah, who recognize America's Redrock Wilderness as a sanctuary for the preservation of our souls, Senate Bill 884, the Utah Public Lands Management Act of 1995, is the beginning of this forgetting, a forgetting we may never reclaim.

♦

Bloodlines[2]

There is a woman who is a tailor. She lives in Green River, Utah, and makes her livelihood performing alterations, taking in a few inches here, letting out a few inches there, basting in hems, then finishing them with a feather stitch.

While hiking in the San Rafael Swell, this woman was raped, thrown down face-first on the sand. She never saw the face of her assailant. What she knew was this: in that act of violence she lost her voice. She was unable to cry for help. He left her violated and raw.

The woman returned home and told no one of her experience. Instead, she grabbed a large spool of red thread, a pair of scissors, and returned to the Swell.

The woman cut pieces of thread and placed them delicately on the desert. Six inches. Three inches. Twelve inches. They appeared as a loose stitched seam upon the land. She saw them as bloodlines, remembering the fetishes of Zuni she had held that draw the heart down. She recalled rabbit, lizard, and rattlesnake. She continued to cut lines, from memory, of animals she had known, seen, and spent time with in these red rock canyons: deer, mountain lion, flicker, and raven. And on one occasion she recalled watching a black bear rambling down Crack Canyon. For this creature, she left a line of red thread three feet long. She cut one-inch threads for frogs and left them inside potholes to wriggle in the rain when the basins would inevitably fill.

Time and space shift.

It is fall.

The woman is now walking along the banks of the Colorado River. She takes her spool of red thread, ties one end to a juniper and then begins walking with the river, following each bend, each curve, her red thread trailing behind her for miles, stitching together what she has lost.

It is spring.

The woman is standing in the deep heat of the desert beside a large boulder known by locals as "the birthing rock." Tiny feet the size of her index finger are etched on stone. Ten toes of hope point to figures of women bearing down, legs spread, with the heads of children coming forth. She recognizes them as two beings seen as one, repeatedly.

The woman picks up an obsidian chip that has been worked by ancient hands; the flaked edge is razor sharp. She holds it between her fingers like a pencil, opens her left hand and traces her own lifeline from beginning to end. The crescent moon below her thumb turns red. She places her palm on the boulder and screams.

4

BEYOND HERE LIE ONLY DRAGONS: THOUGHTS ON WILD PLACES AND VIGOROUS LANGUAGE

Born in 1957 in Frankfurt, Germany, Gregory McNamee is the son of a military officer and had a peripatetic childhood, living in Germany, Texas, Oklahoma, and—what he considers to be his home state—Virginia. He studied classics at the University of Arizona, graduating Phi Beta Kappa in 1978, and completed a master's degree in English at Arizona in 1980. He taught English and journalism in Mexico before becoming editor of a weekly alternative paper in Tucson. In 1981, he joined the staff of the University of Arizona Press, serving as editor-in-chief from 1985 to 1990. During the past two decades McNamee has written, edited, or co-edited twenty-one books and authored approximately two thousand book reviews and articles for various books, magazines, and on-line publications, including *Outside*, *Orion*, *The Nation*, *New Times*, *Parabola*, *Newsday*, *Discovery Online*, *The Los Angeles Times*, and *The Washington Post*. He is a contributing editor to *The Bloomsbury Review* and to *Amazon.com*, for which he reviews books in a broad range of fields, and a nonfiction reviewer for *Kirkus Reviews*. He is also a consultant in world geography to the *Encyclopedia Britannica* and a regular contributor to it and its on-line adjunct, *Britannica.com*.

McNamee's publications include the short-story collection *Christ on the Mount of Olives* (1991), the volume of literary and political essays *The Return of Richard Nixon* (1990), the poetry collection *Inconstant History* (1990), a translation of Sophokles's *Philoktetes* (1987), and such books of nonfiction nature writing as *Gila: The Life and Death of an American River* (1994/1998), *In the Presence of Wolves* (1995), *Open Range and Parking Lots* (1999), *Blue Mountains Far Away: Journeys into the American Wilderness* (2000), and *American Byzantium: Photographs of Las Vegas* (2001). His numerous anthologies include *Resist Much, Obey Little: Some Notes on Edward Abbey* (1985), with James Hepworth; *Named in Stone and Sky: An Arizona Anthol-*

ogy (1993); *The Sierra Club Desert Reader* (1995); *A Desert Bestiary: Folklore, Literature, and Ecological Thought from the World's Dry Places* (1996); and *The Mountain World: A Literary Journey* (2000), among others.

As is evident from his list of publications, McNamee feels a particular affinity for arid landscapes—some of the most harsh and unapproachable and beautiful places in the world. Like such writers as Bruce Berger, Alison Hawthorne Deming, Gary Paul Nabhan, and Simon J. Ortiz, he has lived in the Sonoran Desert for many years, and much of his own narrative and political writing concerns his experiences in and thoughts about this landscape. Although a strikingly learned man, McNamee proved to be extraordinarily down-to-earth and concrete in our conversation about narrative and environmental values, steadfastly avoiding broad abstractions. Many of the authors whom we interviewed for this project—Simon J. Ortiz comes to mind first—emphasized the value of concrete, specific language as a means of communicating values and other important information. Concrete language may not always be a direct means of communicating, but it is a way to speak and write with powerful resonance. One of McNamee's interesting comments in the following interview addresses the distinction between "literary" language and "journalistic" language. He says, "Literature takes a long time to cook and journalism does not, generally speaking. . . . Journalism captures the immediacy of experience. When you're writing a book, you're cloistered. At least, I tend to be. When I'm writing magazine journalism or newspaper journalism, I'm on the phone with somebody or I'm out talking to somebody all the time." This sense of vital interactiveness, of being on the phone and gathering the latest information and points of view in preparing a journalistic article, gives journalism a special punch. During our conversation, McNamee also emphasized the genuine value of seemingly mundane forms of writing, such as book reviews. Unlike Terry Tempest Williams, who suggested when we interviewed her that some of her more oblique and artistic narratives would ultimately be the most lasting and influential of her works, McNamee argued that his numerous book reviews for on-line sites such as *Amazon.com* and *Tucson Weekly* were reaching enormous audiences and influencing the public's views of the world in ways that his more slowly "cooked," literary works were not.

For samples of McNamee's writings, we've selected the opening, narrative section of his essay "Yaak and the Unknowable World" from the anthology *The Roadless Yaak* (2002, edited by Rick Bass) and an on-line review of Roger Rosenblatt's 1999 book, *Consuming Desires*. When we interviewed McNamee, he had just returned from visiting the Yaak Valley in remote northwestern

Montana, and the essay he was writing about the value of that wild place was on his mind. He refers several times to the Yaak during our discussion of economic and non-economic measurement of values. The opening section of the Yaak essay is a poignant example of how McNamee tries to use story as a means of communicating his sense of the value of nature. In his review of Rosenblatt's edited volume, the first writing sample in this chapter, McNamee does not directly articulate his personal views of nature, of the world. He describes what Rosenblatt and his contributing authors say. Of course, the very selection of this book about consumption as a volume worth reviewing and the generally positive cast of McNamee's description is a form of values communication. Still, for the most part, this book-summarizing review is a way of simply and efficiently distilling central ideas from a significant new book and distributing them on-line to a potentially vast audience (potentially, anyone who does a web search on the subject of consumption). McNamee waits until the final, pithy sentence of the review to give his own explicit statement of values: "All this offers fuel for an environmentalist's fire and is likely to give marketing people fits—which is all to the greater good."

♦

A Conversation with Gregory McNamee

Terre Satterfield and Scott Slovic conducted this interview with Gregory McNamee in the guest cottage at the University of Arizona Poetry Center.

Satterfield: This project represents an effort to discuss with authors economic definitions of value. Many policy initiatives seek to include the public in management decisions by understanding what the public values. But the most common practice for doing this is cost-benefit analysis, although some have resisted this trend. Surveys of the value statements that the public supports are also common. What Scott and I are trying to do is to bring the nature-writing community into that discussion and to think of values in two ways: as distinctly moral trains of thought or expressions ("environmental ethics," if you will) and as something other than ideas distilled into a declarative statement, such as in "I believe x." Mostly, we're interested in values as expressed in narrative form.

We think narrative expression is important to lay people because most of us are more comfortable telling stories about nature and about experiences than declaring our values in a definitive, statement-like manner. We think of nature writers as our "theorists" on this point, and so we want to turn to writers to better understand why narrative forms work and also what their limits might be.

Slovic: I guess, backing up a little, there is the even more basic question: What comes to mind when you hear people using the word "values"? Does it seem to have any connection with the work that you do? Would you ever conceive of your writing in that way?

McNamee: Values certainly do have a connection with my work, though perhaps in a different way from the economic values you're suggesting. First, when I hear the word "values," I can't help but connect it with the phrase "family values," the two having been so wed. And I think of that phrase as having a rightist agenda attached to it. Only secondarily do I think of "values" as an economic term, as you say.

I haven't had much occasion to deal with the second meaning explicitly. A few years ago, though, I started off to write a piece for *Audubon* magazine, which had been running a series of "what is x, y, or z worth" pieces—what is a desert worth, and so on—that really annoyed me.

Satterfield: Were they partly trying to attach prices to things that aren't normally traded in markets?

McNamee: Yes, that's exactly right. But the thing that annoyed me, in a way, was that no one in any of the pieces that I read attempted even to take in the economic argument at all. And what I wanted to do was a piece on "what are mountains worth?" I wanted to go and talk to people whose job is to look at a piece of landscape and determine how much it's actually worth. Not just in aesthetic ways, but how you calculate the value of a mountain. I wanted to find an economic geologist whom I could take out and point to the Catalinas over there and to whom I could say, How much is that mountain worth? What would he guess, and why would he say that? On what basis do you—as certainly real estate speculators do—look at a picture of a slope and say: "Well, I can get x number of dollars in return each year if I spend a million dollars on a ski slope." I mean, there are people who do this.

Satterfield: Yes, they calculate what economists call "use value" or, more specifically, "recreational value."

McNamee: But environmentalists don't talk to them. As a journalist, it's necessary for me to go and talk to people whose values—there's that word again—I may not share. I want to find out who they are, to find out what I'm arguing against. So I really wanted to find somebody who would talk to me in that way.

Sadly, the piece was squelched in the course of a shakeup that's happened at the magazine. They have a new editor, so maybe some of these things are going to come back to life.

Slovic: So you never ended up writing it—you were proposing it?

McNamee: Right. But I've incorporated this approach in a long-term book I'm doing on gold right now. There again, I'm interested in how people arrive at an economic determination of the land. I'm trying to think in terms of the people who are the loggers and the people in extractive industries generally. How do they size up a piece of property?

Satterfield: Why did you chase down that particular angle? Why were you drawn to it?

McNamee: Because we talk about it all the time. In my own writing, I've called it the struggle between the politics of the long term and the short term. I think that the enemy, the real enemy in our lives, is the politics of the short term, of the immediate return. It's a world-destroying vision that lets us get in and get out as quickly as we can. It lets us extract and then say, "The hell with it!" So, I was curious. I wanted to find that demon. It's like the Eddy Harris book, *South of Haunted Dreams.* He rode a motorcycle from St. Louis, Missouri—I think he wound up in Atlanta. He wanted to find somebody who would call him "nigger." And he said so. He wanted to find somebody who would do that, and he couldn't. And I want to find a land racist. I'm looking for the land racist. That's what I'm doing.

Satterfield: And you think you'll find them among economic estimators?

McNamee: Well, I think somebody in there is going to say: "Look, we're on this earth, we have to make a living." But it's another thing to say: "We're on this earth, we have to make a substantial profit." I want to find those people. We have people like that in Tucson. One guy I can think of has been in the Tucson community for longer than I've been here. He's a land developer and philanthropist. He gives to the Jewish Community Center and various other kinds of organizations. But whenever land development is involved, he is somewhere in the picture. I've tried for a long time to get him to agree to an interview. I want to go and talk to him. I just want to say, "You're the land racist. And you know you are."

I'm being facetious. But, quite seriously, I want to find out what it is that motivates people, what it is that drives them. We talk all the time about the values of open space and open land and about riparian corridors that are unimpeded and wildlife corridors and migratory avian pathways and things like that. I want to find somebody who's against those. And I don't think you can find anybody who is really against them. I think the argument has to be constructed.

Satterfield: So part of what you're saying is that people won't necessarily be direct or honest about their values if they contradict popular ideas in the public mind. Nobody is going to come out and say: "I want to rape that land to make a profit."

McNamee: Yes. I was being very long-winded, but my point is this: when you talk about values, and the way that values discussions are commonly set up, I don't think you can find anybody who is going to say, "Yes, I believe that the land should be called 'nigger.'" Nobody is going to say, "I am anti-land, I am anti-water, I think we should mine and we should dam and we should destroy and no remediation or any such thing is necessary." So, to my mind, some of those values questions might have to be posed a little bit differently. If it meant the difference between your family making five thousand extra dollars a year to have that mountain sit over there or to have the top of it razed off, would you go for the five thousand dollars or would you go for that view? I think most people, when it's put in that kind of way, would say, "Well you can't eat landscape." It's a different kind of thing from asking: "Should the land be protected?"

Slovic: How does this show up in the genre of environmental writing? You've read about as much of it as anyone. Have you detected any particular patterns in the way writers treat issues of values? Have you seen any especially effective treatments of values in environmental writing? Are values latent or explicit in all of this literature? Who do you think is the most deft in addressing the value of nature?

McNamee: The most explicit discussion of values I've seen in a long time is in Jack Turner's book *The Abstract Wild*. It made a lot of people angry, and I have to figure that's where an interesting book lies. I hear that Rick Bass hates it with a passion. So, I figure, something's going on there.

Slovic: How did you respond to it?

McNamee: Well, I agree with Turner from a different point of view. I get very tired of abstractions generally.

Slovic: What kind of abstractions are we talking about here?

McNamee: Well, let's say the idea of a wilderness. What is the idea of wilderness? It's talked about quite a lot, and by people who don't have much experience with the real thing. There's a fellow, Karl Hess, for example. Karl writes a lot about public-lands issues. He's a libertarian, at least of a sort. His father, Karl Hess, was Barry Goldwater's chief speechwriter. Karl is the kind of guy who wears button-down shirts and very neatly polished cowboy boots, but I don't think he's ever stepped in a cowpie in his life. He lives in New Mexico and he's got a big cowboy hat and he writes these libertarian statements about land use and about why government ownership of land is bad and why government regulation of land is bad. And that's all well and good. I don't mind that, except I want Karl to go and step in a cowpie before he tells me that the market ought to decide about how land and resources are used. I really do. If he's going to write about public-lands issues, I want him to go and look at what a stream bottom that's been grazed dead by cows looks like. I want him to get the cowshit on his boots. I want him to see. That's an example of what I mean by abstractions.

Satterfield: So writing without a solid basis of experience is problematic?

McNamee: Yeah. I'm tired of Middlebury College instructors telling me what wilderness is all about when they've gone into the little park next to Middlebury College and walked around and seen a squirrel. That's what Jack Turner's book was about: an argument against abstraction. If you're going to be in wilderness, then something in it has to be able to kill you, and you have to be prepared for the possibility of that.

Slovic: That's Doug Peacock's definition of "wilderness" in his book *Grizzly Years*, isn't it?

McNamee: It sure is, and it gets right to the point. Now, part of an essay that I wrote not too long ago for Rick Bass's Yaak book [*The Roadless Yaak: Reflections and Observations About One of Our Last Great Wild Places*] is about a walk Rick and I were on. We came across the trail of a grizzly and it was very fresh. I wanted to go and find the grizzly and Rick wasn't averse to that, although he certainly lives closer to their turf than I do. We went off kind of stupidly, looking for the grizz 'cause I wanted to see one. We saw a little bit of one disappearing, I think, but nothing close. I was tempted, in the manner of so many outdoors writers, to dramatize that experience a little when it came to recounting it. "Oh, yeah, he stood up and waved at me!" But I stayed honest.

Slovic: You felt it breathing down the back of your neck! Don't you think you're kind of expressing a western perspective on what it means to really experience the nonhuman world in a concrete way? I think John Elder would dispute the notion that one needs to be in a dangerously wild place to have meaningful contact with nature.

McNamee: Oh, I don't particularly mean that. I don't mean "meaningful contact" in that kind of way. I think it is possible to go into Central Park and look at a squirrel and make some kind of connection with nature.

Any kind of connection with cycles other than market cycles is an improvement. But when I receive instructions on values and on how to live from other nature writers, I want to know what the writer's experiences of true wilderness are. I want to gauge from some depth of experience. In other words, I would rather listen to a rancher tell me about the value of public lands than I would some libertarian who works for the Cato Institute in a think tank. That's what I mean. Someone who has more experiential authority.

Satterfield: Increasingly, public agencies charged with developing management plans are attempting to develop value-elicitation instruments for receiving meaningful public input. So, we're kind of interested in pursuing this issue of how the general public acquires its sense of value. Where does literature fit in the scheme of things?

McNamee: Well, literature belongs, much as we would like to think otherwise, to a privileged minority. It always has and probably always will. So, if by literature, you mean literary writing of some kind, that's going to sway a small audience. And that audience is likely already to share the values that the writer is talking about. It's that preaching-to-the-choir phenomenon.

Slovic: Would you say that universally for literature?

McNamee: I think you see it in nature writing as a genre. Nobody is going to say: "Nature is bad and we should hate it." So when I see statements like "nature is good," I begin to get a little tired. I suppose I would like to see that communicated and subverted in some way, if nothing else, for humorous effect. I'm sounding like a libertarian myself. I don't really mean to. But if you mean to engage the public in a discussion of values of land, literature is not the vehicle to do it. Journalism may be.

Satterfield: Why? Let's look at this. What does literature not have that journalism has, and vice versa? Why does one engage and the other not?

McNamee: Well, partly it's the immediacy of response. Literature takes a long time to cook and journalism does not, generally speaking. Rick Bass's books grow out of magazine articles. My books grow out of magazine articles. Journalism captures the immediacy of experience. When you're writing a book, you're cloistered—at least, I tend to be. When I'm writing magazine journalism or newspaper journalism, though, I'm on the phone with somebody or I'm out talking to somebody all the time. I do a lot more advocacy when I'm asking people questions while I do a newspaper story than when I'm writing a book. Advocacy that's a lot more likely to change people's minds. This is very much on my mind because I'm doing this work on the wolf reintroduction, which is a question that was brought forward for public comment but was pretty well stampeded out as a possibility by the Wise Use Movement. I like the idea of wolves being reintroduced. And it wasn't until—I don't mean this to sound heroic—outside journalists came in and started talking about wolf reintroduction that some people could say: "Oh, yeah, I want that." They could open up to that kind of dialogue. I don't mean to say that journalists have come in with little white hats and saved the day. Journalists are as venal as anybody else in the long run. But this is how these questions and possibilities get opened up. I've seen the effect of magazine and newspaper articles in small towns. Nobody gets stirred up about books in small towns, but people will get stirred up about a newspaper.

Slovic: Yes, but part of what makes journalism good is good storytelling. You could also say that there are different types of journalism—direct-advocacy journalism and, say, story-intensive journalism. Which has a greater impact? Is it better to hit hard and fast and logically, or is it better to come in the back door with a good story?

McNamee: The answer is yes. [Laughter.]

Slovic: Let's shift direction a bit. As we came in the building a little while ago, you were commenting on your concept of the crucial elements in good nature writing. I'm interested in the various styles of language—philosophical, analytical, narrative, concrete action, description, or forms of imagery, and so on—that one might use in nature writing. Which of these elements or kinds of language do you think tend to contain useful thinking about values in environmental writing? Do you have any thoughts about this?

McNamee: Well, yes. Most of my own work in nature writing is done in the essay form. I have not done much, for instance, in the way of experimentation with dialogue in nature writing. In travel writing I use a lot of dialogue. In nature writing my own work tends to draw on anecdote to talk about larger issues. So, for example, in the piece that I mentioned earlier that I wrote for Rick Bass's book, I opened up that essay talking about the possibilities of a place where you can be within five hundred yards of a road and yet suddenly be in grizzly country. What does that mean? I use that as an entry into a larger discussion on my ideas of wilderness. What do I—or would I—like to think of real wilderness as being? What I mean by "real wilderness" is a place that human beings say is just flat-out off limits. Nobody goes there. No humans at all. Some chunk of territory that's off limits for the next hundred years. And maybe a hundred years from now we'll send a team in and see what happened. Just as a grand experiment, a grand vision.

Satterfield: Because you want to see how the land evolves, or because you think it's powerful to think of particular places as utterly nonhuman, or which?

McNamee: Because I want to see a restoration on the map of the old medieval notion: Beyond here lie only dragons.

Satterfield: What's the rest of your train of thought on this point? Why is an untouched place a good thing? What does it achieve?

McNamee: Oh, I don't know that it necessarily achieves anything. It's not a utilitarian experiment; it doesn't have a utilitarian end to it. It's really an ethical concern of mine about the restoration of limits. We've become unaccustomed to the idea that we should have limits of any kind. "If I want to go to the bottom of the ocean to see what's down there, dammit, I should be able to!"

Slovic: So you have the sense that we need, as a culture, to reflect on the idea of limits and how to restore our sense of limits. You've been using the example during this conversation of writing the essay for Rick Bass's collection on the Yaak Valley. In writing that piece, were you trying to convince the readership that limits are valuable? Reflecting on a place like the Yaak Valley, we can consider the importance of limits. Can you comment further on the form that you used in that essay? What aspects of that essay did you feel were likely to be most potent with your general audience? How is it structured?

McNamee: Well, it's structured very much as a speculation. After the initial anecdote and movement into larger ideas of wilderness, I then say something about my idea of a wilderness that goes beyond all hitherto existing definitions because I want there to be places where nobody does go. Let me give another anecdotal example, an experience I had out in the western desert near here. I was doing a magazine story and was camping out in ruins of an old mining town. I was sitting and cooking over an open fire, and some kit foxes came up and sat outside of the fire circle and watched me for a while. Eventually one of the foxes just sort of came over to me and sniffed me and sat down. This feeling overcame me—I decided subsequently that the feeling that overcame me was a sense of shame. I actually recall the feeling of that sense of shame and thinking, "You poor dumb kit fox. You don't know enough not to trust me. You don't know that I'm the enemy." I wrestled with this because I was writing a travel piece about this wilderness area and I thought, hmmm, if I tell people how comparatively easy it is to get to this place, people are going to want to come here, and this kit fox is in trouble. So I exaggerated the piece some. I said it's really very fearfully despoiled and there is no water. You will die if you come.

You can't take on very large policy issues—or at least I can't—outside of the essay form, the argumentative essay or argumentative journalism.

Slovic: In a sense you're conceiving of your writing and the various techniques that you use as a way of conveying some sort of value that you've intuited and that you're trying to communicate in a persuasive way?

McNamee: Yes, when I'm trying to influence people, trying to make them change their minds about why we should or should not build on a place, I tend to write anecdotally—to say, "I was in this place, this is why this place is important to me, and here's why it should be important to you."

Satterfield: By "anecdotally," you mean you sort of paint yourself in as a character who knows this place and has some particular experience that the audience might align with?

McNamee: Yes. It's a device, a means of giving readers a connection with something, so they might say, "Hey, if I were there, I might be doing that, too." I wrote a piece about the Endangered Species Act for *The Arizona Republic* on why the Act should be reauthorized. The best thing that anybody ever said about it was from a plumber I know, a guy from Boston who is not particularly well read. He read it somewhere and walked up to me and said: "Greg, I got the feeling you was talking to me when I was reading that piece." And I thought, that's the highest praise I could think of, particularly since I was writing about this fairly complex and fairly abstract issue.

Satterfield: I'm getting the feeling as you talk about journalism that it isn't really how I think about journalism. I mean, you really are talking about journalism as conversation, in part as story, expressed by anecdote, rather than, say, the disclosure of previously unknown information, unearthed by investigation. Facts that might surprise or alarm somebody into action.

McNamee: Well, that has its place. And I do quite a lot of that kind of writing, too. But if I really want to change somebody's mind about something on a deep level, then I want to have a conversation. I don't want to make a purely logical argument.

Satterfield: When you begin a compelling piece like this—say, one that represents a particular idea or value position—does your own position evolve in the process of writing? Do you have the same position in the beginning that you have at the end? Or is there something in the act of writing that results in a new or altered position?

McNamee: Again, the answer is yes, or it's a bit of both, I think. In the course of advocacy, if you want to convince your readers of the wisdom of your position, then presumably it's something you've thought through well beforehand. You are not using the writing as a process of discovery. I can't think of a specific instance of my own advocacy journalism where I didn't more or less know what I wanted to say.

Slovic: When you're doing a project that has mixed goals—you're trying to tell a good story, and you also have a message—how do you achieve both goals without muddling the message and undermining the aesthetic or literary force of such a project?

McNamee: Well, that's a good example of the importance of beginning with imagination, with a kind of speculation, as I tried to do in the Yaak Valley piece. Another piece in which I put that to use was my book on the Gila River [*Gila: The Life and Death of an American River*]. My speculation in this case was that a river that had flowed for 100 million years—or perhaps 60 million years, no one's quite sure—was destroyed by human behavior. There was a river that existed in some recognizable form for many millions of years, and in the space of three generations, we killed it. Imagine that: we killed a river. How did we do that? How did we come to value water so little in this desert that we allowed ourselves to do that? How can we imagine the river back into existence? How do we imagine changing an economic course so that we can bring a river back from death? Speculations all. The narrative followed pretty naturally from that; it helps when you're writing about a river, you can use riverine narrative flow, you know, beginning to end.

Slovic: Do you ever worry about a story carrying the weight of a message and badgering the reader with your art?

McNamee: Sure. There's a difference between having a message and being a propagandist. And that's the dividing line for me. I don't believe that art and politics can be separated, but I believe that art and propaganda can. If you are sloganeering, you're saying, "Listen to me, I'm going to make you agree with me." I'm not interested in doing that kind of writing, and I'm not really interested in living that way, either.

Slovic: What about Barry Lopez's piece "Apologia" and his encounters with roadkill? To me it's about environmental values in a way. If we're going to talk about a piece of writing that is literary and that explores issues of environmental values in a way that might inspire an audience to reflect on these issues, it's hard to think of a much better example of evocative, probing language that sidesteps straightforward "sloganeering."

McNamee: Well, it has a beautiful simplicity. One of the things I talk about with my nature writing students is the value of declarations. I talk about Ed Abbey, at the opening of *Desert Solitaire*, who says: "This is the most beautiful place on earth." That's not a factual statement, it's a value statement. The point is, he's willing to put it on the line and say, "This is the most beautiful place on earth," when of course there are so many beautiful places on earth to claim one's heart—I have about a hundred of them on my personal map of the planet. Whenever I read Barry's piece, I think of a comment that Aldo Leopold made: "To be an ecologist is to be aware that you live in a world of wounds." That, in itself, is a declaration. When you find a declaration that you admire in a piece of nature writing, underline it and think about it. I've wondered if Barry was not responding to that quotation from Leopold when he wrote that piece about encountering dead animals on the road, or thinking about it. It's certainly what that piece is about, to my mind: the interconnection between life and death.

Satterfield: Let's change tracks here a bit. Can I ask you how and if you think about the social implications of your work?

McNamee: Yes, I do think about the social implications of the work all the time. One of the truest things that Ed Abbey ever wrote, I think, is that "we are the voices of the voiceless." We speak for the powerless, and particularly—and I say this to my writing students in nature writing all the time—we are writing for those without language.

Slovic: What is it that gives you faith in the importance of what you're doing?

McNamee: Hmmm. I wonder if I have that. There was a quote that I read from Reinhold Niebuhr not too long ago, that was talking about just that: about having to have faith in the future in the knowledge that it takes more than a generation to get anything done. So I often think that maybe it doesn't matter what I say right now about something, but maybe in five or fifty years it will matter, maybe I've planted in somebody's ear the notion that there could be a living river in the Southwest and that somebody will do something about it.

Satterfield: Writing for those without language seems really crucial to me, as part of the issue with studies of value is that people may have tremendous difficulty articulating some value positions. What are your thoughts on that, both in terms of people as readers using nature writing as a vehicle to clarify their thoughts, and why articulation might be difficult in the first place?

McNamee: Well, let's see, there are a number of different issues bound up in that question. I've already mentioned the distinction between art and propaganda, saying that part of my work is stating my values and saying these are the things that I believe in. I also find that I have a set number of values. A very fixed and very small number of values. My interest is in telling lots of different stories that illustrate those values. That's where the interesting stories come from—the stories by which I can express my values. And my values, as I say, are really very few: I believe you shouldn't beat your wife, drink or drug or otherwise sin to excess, or rape the land. [Laughter.] Seriously, when it comes to articulating values, you find very few people listing the Ten Commandments.

Satterfield: Is that because, stripped naked, they're dull, or just not compelling? They don't have life, they don't breathe, they don't have meaning unless in some ways they have story attached to them?

McNamee: Quite often, yes. It's the little wrinkles in the stories that are the interesting things, and not necessarily the values that are attached. I once did a translation of Aesop's fables from the Greek as a means of keeping my Greek alive—way back when, I earned a college degree in classics. When you strip away those morals and look at the stories themselves, they say the same thing. But they say a different sort of thing, too. The fox and the grapes story is not all about Christian values of hard work and the vanity of human wishes; it's a different kind of story, with deeper implications than might appear on the surface. I'm more interested in looking at the stories not because the values are not interesting—it's that, stripped naked, the values are unobjectionable, and how we get to them is the more compelling part of the process.

Satterfield: Interesting. I look at a value statement in, say, a survey and I might agree with it entirely, and yet it just makes me shudder as well because it's had the life blood drawn out of it. There is nothing to attach it to—or elaborate it—that draws me in. Regardless, yours is a good point. It's fundamental to the project in that I take your point to be it isn't that a value statement *couldn't* be stripped to the bare bones. It's just much less useful in that form.

McNamee: Yeah, again, it's those little wrinkles. They personalize things, and they give us a way to participate in the story through interpretation.

Slovic: Greg, in both your own story writing and your responses—as a reviewer or scholar—to other writers' work, you're emphasizing natural-history writing. I'm wondering if you think this kind of writing, in some ways, is stigmatized for the general readership as implicitly bearing a particular ideological perspective. Is this a limiting factor? I remember a student's response to Rick Bass's *Winter*. He said, "This writer is trying to make all of us hug trees like he does." That hadn't occurred to me, actually. I see the book as being about moving to a place, finding it interesting, feeling out a place. I don't remember seeing a message anywhere in there, where the author says all of you should go out and hug trees.

McNamee: No. Nor do I, and in fact quite the reverse. It seems to me that what Bass is saying in *Winter* at various points, is that, man, this is hard work! I mean, this is not ideal, this hauling wood and clearing underbrush and making sure the water pipes don't freeze. Driving yourself crazy by experiencing cabin fever and making sure you make contact with your neighbors so that you can take care of each other and just the hard work of living in less than convenient circumstances. So I'm intrigued by this student's response.

Slovic: He wrote this full paper about how he's being pushed and bullied by this writer to become a "tree hugger" and insisted on using that phrase. So, I'm wondering whether this entire type of writing carries with it a baggage of preconception. When you're writing your book reviews for *Amazon.com*, analyses of texts in the genre, do you feel yourself trying to break through this preconception?

McNamee: Well, again, that's a multi-level question, it seems to me. Yes, the genre of natural-history writing is going to appeal to a certain kind of reader, generally speaking. Probably somebody of liberal sensibilities in some way or another, although I can think of many exceptions. Nonetheless, this is why I object to preaching to the choir so much, because it's so clear to me that the audience is already converted. The audience is already interested in preserving nature. So you don't need a lot of special pleading. That's why I like Richard Nelson's *Heart and Blood*, to cite one particularly well written book about nature. He doesn't go out of his way to say, "Man, you really gotta like deer." I was very grateful to him for not doing that, not making special pleading about what cute little bambies deer are. But there are many examples of books that do do that, that sermonize and valorize and propagandize. So the genre is probably suspect among certain readers.

Slovic: What is it that we can do—either in our teaching, in our writing about the genre, or in producing new nature writing—to work toward reaching a broader audience?

McNamee: I don't know if there's an answer to that question insofar as attracting the readers is concerned, except to write as well as we possibly can. Natural-history writing, as I have told my students, is as American a form as jazz, and it will always find readers—perhaps not many, but always.

Satterfield: If part of our goal is to get narrative expressions of value taken seriously as a place to reflect on or to look for public thinking on the subject, we do have to address the sentiment that nature writing is just overly romantic bull of some kind. Why would we want to indulge it at all? How would you respond to that? Because certainly we'll have to respond to that.

McNamee: Well, because it's about lessons that are learned from the land, that are learned over periods of years of living with the land, from years of observation. Those lessons can be told only through narrative, and only personally—which is to say, not sentimentally.

Satterfield: It seems to me you're saying that from the point of view of learning, natural history writing is the only place, or the best place, where you can both learn that information and express that information.

McNamee: Yeah, that's right. It's the best vehicle we have.

Satterfield: I have one last question. Earlier you said that you had a few fundamental values that permeated much of your life: don't rape the land, don't beat your wife, I can't remember what the third one was. One of the things of interest to those who study values is that some think that values are very malleable; they shift and change all the time. Have you got any thoughts on that question?

McNamee: No, I don't think values are malleable, unless you advocate situational ethics in all things. That would be a question to ask Edward O. Wilson. Are values biologically based? Because they do seem to be at root, they do seem to be a constant and universal of a certain kind. "It's not good to kill mom." So what is the biological basis for having those values? What is the biological basis for preserving land? It's probably the same as not befouling the nest.

♦

A Review of *Consuming Desires: Consumption, Culture, and the Pursuit of Happiness*[1]

Travel wherever you will around the world, and it seems that everywhere you go people are addicted to the same things. The triumph of consumerism—the doctrine exemplified by the obnoxious bumper sticker, "He who dies with the most toys wins"—is inescapable. Roger Rosenblatt (reputed for his work on PBS and in *Time* magazine) assembles a stellar cast of contributors to argue against consumerism in this collection of essays. Some of those contributors offer paeans to disappearing virtues such as thrift and modesty; others tender modest and immodest proposals to reduce our desire for material goods, which Rosenblatt gently calls "a strange basis for a civilization, but an effective one."

In his introduction, Rosenblatt recognizes that he and his colleagues are swimming against the tide. After all, he notes, something like 90 percent of the American workforce is now engaged in making and selling consumer goods and services, from cheeseburgers to computers; and nearly everyone is behaving as if we had all suddenly come into Jay Gatsby's wealth, a point that Harvard-based social critic Juliet Schor underscores when she remarks, "The new consumerism is less socially benign than the old regime of keeping up with the Joneses," less benign because both more conspicuous and more closely bound with our notion of who we are, our things have come to serve as markers of social class and self-esteem alike.

The essays included in this volume are of universally high quality, but there are some real standouts: William Greider examines our unwillingness to reduce waste and the forces at work against offering high-quality, durable and affordable goods to all segments of society; Edward Luttwak ponders the new face of American indebtedness, which now, he says, has "reached the unprecedented level of 89 percent of total household income"; Stephanie Mills considers the moral dimensions of excessive consumption in a time of extinction and biological crisis.

All this offers fuel for an environmentalist's fire and is likely to give marketing people fits—which is all to the greater good.

♦

Yaak and the Unknowable World[2]

Kamchatka. For hours I have been traveling with the arc of the sun, crossing time zones and continents, flying the great circle from Los Angeles to Shanghai. Between those two huge megalopolises, far below, has passed territory that a Puritan elder, one of those dour thinkers who first shaped—and who continue to shape—American ideas about wilderness, would call a hellish wasteland: the glacial inlets of British Columbia, the old-growth forests of the Alaskan coast, the tundra of Beringia. And now Kamchatka, a place of childhood dreams nursed by an often visited globe and by peripatetic parents, Kamchatka, wilderness pure and primeval, uncut by roads, seemingly unvisited, a russet forested world stretching unbroken from horizon to horizon.

Just weeks before I had been in another wilderness, the Yaak Valley of northwestern Montana, tucked away near the Idaho and British Columbia lines. It is but an atom of wildland compared to the huge landmass of the Kamchatka Peninsula, but it is surpassingly wild nonetheless, a place where wildlife corridors do not run at right angles, a place through which a Yellowstone-bound wolf might find safe passage on the underground railroad from Canada. Small it may be, but it is largely unmediated by human presence.

I had traveled to nearby Troy, Montana, to provide desperately needed moral guidance to a cutthroat gang of musicians who were then touring taverns and trailer parks in the northwestern corner of the state, but Yaak was the real reason I had traveled so far from home—Yaak, about which I had been reading for so many years in the journalism and essays of my friend Rick Bass. Rick is not shy about sharing Yaak, unlike me, who selfishly salts away my favorite places, the little wild corners of Arizona, New Mexico, Sonora. And so on a sweltering July day we set out from the banks of the Yaak River up a spiny knoll in the all-too-evident footsteps of an adolescent male grizzly bear—I say that he was male and adolescent on account of the hormone-charged trail of savaged tree trunks and half-chewed shrubs he had left in his wake, but I have no stronger evidence for his identity—through a tangled association of coralroot, tallgrass, mistletoe, blackberry, lodgepole pine, spruce, alder, cedar, ponderosa pine, an Amazonian density of vegetation bewildering to me, used to the comparative austerity of the Sonoran Desert.

We never did catch up with that bear, although I like to believe with more hope than proof that we saw the barest glimpse of his tail rounding a draw a quarter of a mile or so ahead of us. The grizzly surely knew we were in pursuit. It is probably to the good that we did not meet him. It is certainly to the good that he had a place in this world big enough that he could afford to tolerate our attentions.

"Among the most sinister phenomena in intellectual history is the avoidance of the concrete," says one of my great heroes, the Bulgarian philosopher Elias Canetti. Traveling into Yaak—and, for that matter, flying over the reddish eternity of Kamchatka and Siberia—gave mere abstractions about which I had read in books and on maps an unforgettable face. Portions have been ravaged over time, to be sure, but Yaak is one of the few wild places, few *real* places, left in the contiguous United States. It is a place where the processes of nature—growth and decline, decay and regeneration, birth and death—are laid bare before us. Having now gazed into its face, I am even more firmly convinced of its value, and of its being precisely the sort of place that demands our protection—against logging, mining, ranching, and other activities—in those last roadless areas, certainly—that favor short-term gain over long-term good.

We have too few such places. It is time, now and finally, to declare that what we have we will not allow to be taken.

5

STORY AS COMMON GROUND

Born in Hartford, Connecticut, in 1946, Alison Hawthorne Deming has made a literary subject out of her own itinerant lifestyle, her encounters with and attachments to a variety of places within the United States and in Mexico and Canada. Several of her essays consider her connections with New England culture and landscape, as a descendant of American novelist Nathaniel Hawthorne. She also writes of her annual, summer stay—since childhood—on Grand Manan Island, off the coast of New Brunswick, Canada. In 1990, having worked from 1988 to 1990 as Writing Program Coordinator at the Provincetown Fine Arts Work Center in Massachusetts, she moved to Tucson, Arizona, where she became director of the University of Arizona Poetry Center and eventually a professor of English. Many of her poems and essays address the experience of moving from the Northeast to the Southwest. She has also been a visiting professor at the University of Hawaii and has spent time writing and doing research in Alaska, Oregon, and Mexico, and these experiences as a brief visitor to new places have also become an important part of her writing, particularly in her books of essays, *Temporary Homelands* (1994), *The Edges of the Civilized World* (1998), and *Writing the Sacred into the Real* (2001), and in her second book of poems, *The Monarchs: A Poem Sequence* (1997).

In addition to her longtime fascination with the experience of place, Deming has long been interested in the natural sciences—both the discoveries of science and the scientific way of looking at the world. This fascination comes through in her first poetry collection, *Science and Other Poems*, which received the Walt Whitman Award for poetry in 1994. The contrasts and confluences between the scientific and artistic world views emerge as well in many of her essays, such as "Science and Poetry: A View from the Divide," which appeared in 1998 and was reprinted in Lee Gutkind's *A View from the Divide: Creative Nonfiction on Health and Science*. She articulates the supposed distinction between science and poetry as follows:

> Scientists are seekers of fact; poets revelers in sensation. Scientists seek a clear, verifiable, and elegant theory; contemporary poets, as critic Helen Vendler recently put it, create objects that are less and less like well-wrought urns, and more and more like the misty collisions and diffusions that take place in a cloud chamber. The popular view demonizes us both, perhaps because we serve neither the god of profit making nor the god of usefulness. Scientists are the cold-hearted dissectors of all that is beautiful; poets the lunatic heirs to pagan forces. We are made to embody the mythic split in Western civilization between the head and the heart. But none of this divided thinking rings true to my experience as a poet. (Deming 1999, 13)

Many of her comments in the following interview echo this statement, arguing that "everyone is intrinsically a storyteller," including scientists and policy experts. She emphasizes the importance of the language of story in addressing issues of environmental values and policy, because story is a "reflective" medium, not a "persuasive" one. Story, for Deming, is a means of teasing out and probing meaning, not hammering an ideological opponent with one's personal point of view. Much of Deming's work, as poet and essayist and editor and arts administrator, is aimed at seeking common ground, bringing people with disparate points of view and styles of communication in contact with each other. Her recent anthology, *The Colors of Nature: Culture, Identity, and the Natural World* (2002), co-edited with Lauret E. Savoy, seeks to identify important differences and fundamental commonalities in the views of nature among writers from various cultural backgrounds. Along similar lines, Deming's statements about narrative in the interview emphasize how narrative discourse functions to overcome argument and adversarialism and helps disagreeing parties to find common ground.

The essay included as one of Deming's writing samples in this book first appeared in *The Georgia Review* and was then used as the "Tucson" chapter in her 2001 book, *Writing the Sacred into the Real.* Much of this essay, especially the opening section, describes (tells the story of) Deming's living situation in Tucson in the late 1990s, embedding her concerns about the rapid growth and environmental degradation of the city in details of her experience. The purpose of this story is not to ram her conservationist views down readers' throats, but to explain the source of her concerns and to show her ambivalence about urban growth and environmental protection and about mixing art (poetry and literary nonfiction) with activism. This essay is about language as an agent of cultural analysis and cultural change as much as it's about Tucson, Arizona. But by using her life in contemporary Tucson as the narrative core, Deming is able to give readers a way of reflecting upon their own communities and their political involvement or disengagement. Her essay, properly read, is less a diatribe than a meditation.

The second sample consists of the first three (out of sixty) brief poems from her 1997 "poem sequence," *The Monarchs*. These poems show how Deming moves between reflections on butterfly intelligence and examinations of human efforts to balance intellect and emotion in navigating geography and relationships. Although these are poems—taut, image-filled sentences, presented in short lines so that even the line breaks contribute to the emphasis on words at the beginning and end of lines—they are also peppered with scenes and with vignettes (brief stories). The poems, especially in their treatment of butterfly migration habits, clearly value the insights of the natural sciences. At the same time, the playful, colorful language suggests implicitly the value of image, story, and the indirectness of metaphor. Is butterfly intelligence a metaphor (a way of representing) for human intelligence? Or is human intelligence simply another way of getting at the meaning and processes of butterfly intelligence? Perhaps it doesn't matter. Perhaps what Deming is hinting at is the complexity and wonder of all forms of intelligence—insight, clarity, sympathy, appreciation. At times, as in the representation of the street fight in the second poem and the memory of whaling in the third, she comes at the idea of intelligence indirectly, by offering bits of present-day experience and bits of history that seem problematic, less than laudable. But these poems, like the essay "Getting Beyond Elegy," are not diatribes or manifestoes—they are nuanced explorations of topics that may be of far-reaching relevance to contemporary society and to individual readers. They are quests for "common ground."

♦

A Conversation with Alison Hawthorne Deming

Scott Slovic and Terre Satterfield conducted this interview in the guest cottage at the University of Arizona Poetry Center.

Satterfield: Let's begin with a discussion of the language of "environmental values," as the term is conventionally used. A moment ago we were discussing narrative as a vehicle for representing environmental values and the sticky point of whether such representation permits appropriate reflection or, instead, works toward persuasive ends. I've spoken to you already about the world of research, which largely thinks of value as an economic expression. That doesn't, however, preclude an interest in other definitions of the term or other modes of expression. Mainly, all of us want to know how better decisions can be made—the kinds of decisions that are sensitive to how people value the land or timber or species that might be at stake.

Deming: Well, it makes complete sense. Everybody's really tired of the way we make decisions—you know, our public decisions. They're all polarized, they're all argumentative. Experts are brought in to back up foregone conclusions. They're not brought in as part of the conversation or a sharing of stories. Even public hearings are so polarized—it's just a joke! So I can see story as one of the ways that you might possibly break down polarized decision-making processes.

Satterfield: Why do you think it might work in that way? What is it about stories that can take that problem on?

Deming: Well, there's the question. My first response is to say that it's because stories are a reflective enterprise, not a persuasive enterprise. Basically, you tell a story because you want someone to understand what you have experienced and why you believe what you believe. It's really very different from starting with: *This is what I believe and this is why you should believe it too.* Story is also our way of finding common ground. You know, "Oh, how was your trip? Oh, have you been having a good time?" "What have you been doing?" You start at a place that is the meeting point—that point is the telling of a story, which is very different from arguing for your position. It doesn't have that climate of being on the defensive, of looking for the places where you can insert your argument. I think story diffuses power.

Satterfield: How is that different from somebody saying, "Here are my calculations. This is how I arrived at my opinion or conclusion"?

Deming: One relies on collective data and the other values individual experience. I mean that, to me, is the problem with numerical measurements. We seem to believe, as a culture, that collective data is always more significant than individual data. And it's not.

Satterfield: Or that individual data is only meaningful if it can be verified en masse?

Deming: Yes.

Slovic: So if we take story seriously, we want to understand the crucial elements. What are the elements—the parts—in stories that might inspire other people to tell stories?

Satterfield: Yes, because if we really want to listen to other people's values, one way to do that is to encourage their telling of stories, stories that capture what are sometimes value positions or insights.

Deming: What are the elements of a story that might trigger someone else's stories?

Slovic: Yes, or trigger their responses.

Deming: Well, story usually has an emotional hue to it. There's a tone to story and so when you're engaged emotionally you're more likely to want to reciprocate with a story. In the end, it's pretty hard to tell a story without it having an emotional hue.

Satterfield: That's really interesting. This is one of the themes that's been coming through in our interviews with other writers. Terry Tempest Williams spoke in terms of breath, suggesting that story breathes, has a life.

Slovic: She was speaking, like you, about emotion.

Deming: Emotion is what data avoids; it strips out emotion. Because if you have emotion, it can't be real, can't be verifiable. It's not to be trusted. On the other hand, it's emotion that makes us care about one another. And it's the emotions we feel for the natural world that make us want to preserve it. It's not that we know the numbers in terms of the loss of biodiversity. It's that it breaks our hearts, that those numbers break our hearts. In story, emotion is usually conveyed through images, I think, and we know that certain images evoke or trigger certain emotions in us.

Satterfield: Why is that? Is it because these are culturally shared images?

Deming: That's a good question, a question that looks at the nature of consciousness. I mean, image works because it's a kind of embodied presence. Image feels sensory. It's as if you're experiencing it with your senses, not your intellect. It unifies the mind and the body in a way that numbers don't. We know it to be a primal way of processing our experience. We know it through dreaming and through fantasy; you know, through daydreaming. I mean, we all dream in images, nobody dreams in data. Nobody really dreams in argument. You dream in images. But I don't know how to bring that into public policy or research on values.

Slovic: Do you think everyone is intrinsically a storyteller, or are there storytellers and non-storytellers?

Deming: I think everyone is intrinsically a storyteller.

Slovic: Yet it seems at the same time that people don't trust story. Why is that?

Deming: We live in a culture built, supposedly, on the great rugged individualist, but the truth is that we believe that experts know the truth, while a story is just a story, something that happened to *me*. It's a function of living in the age of experts—tribal people didn't have all this text around to encode the knowledge of experts. Story in that context held a much higher place because it was the basis for conveying all information.

But another thing about story, why it's important and universal to some extent, or storytelling at least, is that it has to do with its relationship to time. Story takes place in time, it gives shape to a piece of time and it helps people cope with the sense of time dissolving, even as we're experiencing it. Our feelings are out of control with the passage of time whereas story stops it, contains it. Story says that time has a beginning, a middle, and an end, and this is how it fits. It creates a kind of order in the stream of time which is, I think, deeply satisfying to people.

Slovic: It seems to me, speaking of time, that efficiency is of great importance in the public world. Public testimony is a kind of ceremony where the quest is not for the narrative but for the conclusion.

Deming: The challenge of trying to get this into public policy is that only the person who comes with data is respected. If you imagine a public hearing, the person who stands up and says, "I want to tell you a story about how I feel about this community," is met with rolling eyeballs.

Satterfield: On the other hand, this practice continues. Story persists in all kinds of places, whether in congressional testimony or public hearings. It's kept alive and we have to wonder why.

Deming: Yes, but if I think about reporting, I'm left with the image of "one person told a story, another person told a story." You have, perhaps, fifty stories and an unmanageable pile of material, but how do you turn that into something that's useful?

Satterfield: Unfortunately, I don't have an easy answer for that. One possibility is to analyze that mass of material for content—to find the pattern in the grains of sand.

Deming: Anthropologists do that very well sometimes. They produce a broader narrative through wonderful little ways of grouping.

Satterfield: Yes, something like a clustering exercise might work, but what I fear doing is reducing the quality or genius of individual narratives into statements or claims, especially if it destroys the imagistic content in the story.

This morning, Scott and I were talking about whether some stories or images are nationally shared. Oddly, we could think only of disasters as examples. We both thought of the Valdez oil spill at Prince William Sound, which has now become a kind of national moral narrative.

Deming: I think of the reintroduction of the wolves. For a lot of people it's a positive, shared story. Or the recovery of the bald eagle following the banning of DDT. A lot of people know and share this story.

Satterfield: So, it's the reclamation stories that capture the imagination.

Slovic: It's odd that reclamation stories might be potent, especially because reclamation takes place over an expanded period of time and doesn't necessarily have a fixed conclusion. Disaster stories usually have conclusions or moments of crisis that trigger our imagination in a very different way.

Satterfield: Yes, but stories of sustained environmental disasters can be very compelling too. Long-term contamination is a good example. It's something that Kai Erikson writes beautifully about. Image may be less potent there, but chronic contamination still terrifies us because it never ends. We don't know whether exposure will result in cancer in our lifetime or whether genetic damage will be passed on to the next generation. It's a different kind of shock value.

Slovic: Still, if I'm thinking about potency of image, I gravitate toward the Alaska example because it is more circumscribed. I can pinpoint the event.

Satterfield: Maybe what we're talking about is the difference between television-generated images and images in a written text—say, a piece of poetry. Can people reflect on an image, a visual image, in the way that they can a textual one?

Deming: I don't think it's the same. With television the viewer's experience is controlled. But with a book you can take your time. If you get to a place where you feel moved, you know, you put the book down, you close your eyes, you think about it, or you go back, you read that section again. From there you might even try to imagine the place. There's something about having to turn the words into your own visual image that's more engaged. Television not only gives you the image, it gives it to you quickly and then it announces that it's moving on to another image, say, Bosnia. It doesn't allow for reflection or resonance. Very few people tape things and then pause on an image. There is clearly something about mental reflection or mental engagement. It's a contemplative state, a meditative state, but not a passive thing. Whenever you can help to induce more reflection, more thinking, less utility and speed in the way we operate as people, it is to our good.

Slovic: In principle this makes a lot of sense, to think differently about utility and efficiency, about speed, especially when we're talking about public consultation. And yet on a pragmatic level, this is the kind of thing that would never sell to the research or policy community.

Satterfield: If we think of those responsible for monitoring or eliciting public opinion, the general rule is to seek efficient methods of inquiry. We may want to think expansively about topics like narrative and value and to resist the dominance of economics. Clearly we can't offer everyone involved two hours a day for contemplative storytelling, so how might we maintain some pragmatism without being absurdly idealistic?

Deming: We can talk about the values that make a culture one in which you feel proud and satisfied to exist. Do we really have to argue that historic values and spiritual values are not frills but very important?

The whole argument strikes me as futile. We can't, of course, expect corporations to hold different values. They hold the values they do because it's in their nature to do so. Generally speaking, what drives our culture is economic interest, which also has the power to denigrate those who give testimony to what other values are important. I keep going back to this question: How do you dignify testimony for the importance of beauty?

Satterfield: Some of the authors we've been talking to have a different take on this topic. They wonder not about how to dignify these values but about how to make these values clandestine. They believe that many policy agents are already influenced by natural historians. They've been reading Aldo Leopold or Terry Tempest Williams. The argument then becomes: You're already recognizing the importance of these writers, these narratives; let's just bring that influence out into the open and proceed from there, develop it.

Deming: If they are influenced by writers, I can only hope that in the midst of the meeting about cost-benefit analysis, some writer is triggering an emotional response in people. If they remember their emotional response to the land, people will remember their passion for the issue. If nothing else, literature can replenish the energy that is depleted by the coldness of the cost-benefit arguments.

Satterfield: I'm not sure it's a loss of energy, but maybe a loss of engagement. Earlier you were talking about narrative's capacity to engage. You seemed to be hinting at a comparison to rhetoric. Any thoughts on that, on why rhetoric does or does not work?

Deming: Well, often rhetoric is taking place in a combative, or polarized, situation. Invariably people have already formed their opinions and are hammering on one another to change their views.

I also think we're a very debunking culture. We have a great distrust of experts because we see them being used for rhetorical purposes and think that we ourselves are being manipulated by them. Yes, most people are pretty scientifically illiterate and so don't know which expert is making a rhetorical argument or which to listen to. We become cynical and tend to say, "Oh, Exxon's paying him to say that" or " The Sierra Club's paying him to say that." We feel like spokespeople are there to manipulate us. It confuses our desire to make our own decisions.

Satterfield: Your mention of scientific literacy reminds me of a related topic: the relationship between science and values. To what extent do you draw your sense of value from knowledge of science or literature on science?

Deming: Oh, to a tremendous degree.

Satterfield: And why is that?

Deming: Well, I have a tremendous respect for the enterprise of science. I think the ability to look at something with intense focus, to attend to it with great scrutiny, is the tremendous gift of science and a poetic gift at that.

Satterfield: Are you thinking of science in this sense when you use the term "experts"?

Deming: No, there I'm really talking about experts paid to make an argument for one side versus the other. Their goal is not to tell us about the current state of knowledge, or to tell us how cautious, or not, we should be, given the limitations of what we know.

But if I want to renew my sense of the natural world, I can do a number of things. I can go out into it, and I can also read the work of scientists who are doing research in a manner that concerns me—say, people studying the monarchs.

Slovic: With regard to the preparation for your book on monarch butterflies, what is the relationship between reading about monarchs and your direct experience of monarchs? How do those different types of information work together?

Satterfield: And when you're reading about monarchs, too, are you reading monarch literature from peer-reviewed scientific journals or are you reading other sources?

Deming: The point with the monarch book is that I wanted to go out to their wintering sites in Mexico and California. I also wanted to know something of the data on monarchs and about the people who had devoted their lives scientifically to this creature. So I looked at the work of the leading researchers, generally scientific books. Lincoln Brower and Fred Urquhart are two major monarch researchers. I also looked at a compendium of papers published in the 1990s including some of the newer theories and research projects under way. I can't overestimate how much it meant to consider the people who followed this creature and who devoted a good portion of their professional lives to understanding it. My knowledge was slight, was poetic, personal. My real love for the monarch was fed not only by the specific knowledge that these people had acquired and the questions they were asking, but also by the fact that their attraction to this creature was such that they would devote an entire professional career to understanding it. That's absolutely beautiful. There's no way on earth that I can say that those scientists are robbing the world of a sense of wonder with their cold, analytic data gathering. They're simply not.

They also challenged me to think about certain behavior that might have once been called instinctual. Behavior we don't think of as intelligent behavior. I then wanted to read other people who were writing about the nature of intelligence, particularly books about animal intelligence.

Satterfield: Are you suggesting in some sense an alternate means for researching monarchs, a means for working with the tension between "cold, hard data" and strong feeling?

Deming: I see the question as, "What is data good for? What is it good for, what is it not good for?" It's great for making economic arguments, because the terms of economics are numerical. But it's not good for spiritual or aesthetic concerns because their terms are non-numeric. Data can strike me as cold and harsh because it's used where it shouldn't be used.

Satterfield: How did your collaboration or interaction with monarch scientists work? Did you discuss your work with them while proceeding?

Deming: Well, I often talked to Bob Pyle; he's a good friend, he's read all the monarch material, and we've been to the Mexico site together. Another entomologist from Arizona, Steve Buchmann, and ethnobotanist Gary Nabhan and I went down together. Bob would always check my science to make sure I hadn't screwed something up or gotten it wrong. I wanted to be accurate, even though I was taking the science and putting it into a story.

Slovic: I've been listening to you talk both about reading science and visiting monarch wintering sites. So you've acquired a knowledge vicariously, that is, through the work of others, and also directly, through site visits. How does direct sensory experience affect your sense of meaning in a way that the vicarious experience does not? What if you hadn't visited the sites, but had read the story as worded by others?

Deming: Well, it's a matter of distrust of story. You know that every account of a place that you hear is another person's version, and not your own. As a natural historian, you want to know how it will affect you, how it will change you to be in the presence of something. So, it's about authenticity, and it's about it being my story and not just repeating somebody else's story. If you're a fiction writer, you do that all the time. Some fiction writers write about places they've never been, astonishingly. So, it is possible for the imagination to transcend the need for that initial work. But I find I need to feel that I've embodied the place in order to write.

Satterfield: How does this need fit with your earlier comments about story as the only communicative means for taking somebody by the hand and going to the place in question with them?

Slovic: Or, is story a viable medium if and when ordinary citizens are being asked to provide their values for a place they may not have visited? Can people estimate meaning if it's not part of their direct experience?

Deming: Well, this is a central question for those of us in this field. Do we, for instance, really want to encourage any more people to go to the Galapagos? It's the Edward Abbey syndrome: you write about a place and it's soon destroyed by visitors seeking a parallel experience.

Slovic: But Abbey also writes about Alaska and the desire to *know* Alaska even if one never goes there. So one can promote the desire to write effectively enough so that people are left with a sense of satisfaction.

Deming: Yes, and part of that writing effort is driven by honesty: the need to avoid romanticizing the beauty of the place or the need to address the economic and cultural impact of outsiders on, say, wintering areas in Mexico. But part of what we're also doing is preserving these experiences for those who aren't likely to have them.

Satterfield: And are they transferable experiences?

Deming: Well, in one sense a small number of people may plant a patch of milkweed in their backyard so the monarchs will stop there on their way north or south. And this may happen because the vicarious experience was satisfying. But I also think it's the nature of human desire to want more. So, there will always be those who say: "God, I really would love to go there!" A purely romantic writing style tends to speak only of beauty, whereas a natural historian may put a little moral consciousness into the matter as well. The writer may impose the question: Is it a place you want to go or is it a place you want to leave alone? We might ask that the vicarious experience be sufficient.

Satterfield: Do you ever worry about the criticism that this implies a division between an elite who are allowed that experience or can access that experience in some ways and those who cannot?

Deming: The field of nature writing and the conservation community generally remain pretty white; it is still connected to its roots as an upper-class white movement. There are more Native American writers now in the field. But cultural exclusivity and the absence of a multiplicity of cultural views about experiences in nature remain a problem. We don't see Mexicans writing stories about what it's like to hike through the desert to cross the border and work illegally. Those are experiences of nature, but we don't hear about those. We would be much richer if we heard these other stories, but generally we haven't.

Satterfield: We've got just a few minutes, so I would like to close with some final thoughts on narrative. Do you think of your writing as helping people generate or find within themselves their own values? Are you articulating what's already there? Do you thinking you're influencing them?

Deming: This is something that we wrestle with all the time. I often feel as though I should be out picketing or whatever [laughs]. But everybody's born with a gift; writing is the gift I've got. I'm not good at that other work. I cry if I go to public hearings, I rage, I lose my temper. Then I listen to the arguments of a very sober urban planner who knows how to use the tools of the game, and I know that's the person who should be at the public hearing and that I should be at home at my desk.

But to the other point: does my work reinforce existing values? Well, I love it when I'm asked to give a talk to an environmental group or when activists come to a reading. I think that this kind of writing really does help them to recharge. They're playing a very hard game out there against these incredibly aggressive forces.

But you also asked about narrative. I don't tend to separate narrative and poetry. A lot of people are very intimidated by poetry and so they don't read it. Yet, if I read poetry to them, it has a tremendous impact on audiences. Some forms of poetry are very confusing on the page, but when they get the bodily experience of the poetry because the music of the reading enters them, that can be very powerful.

♦

Getting Beyond Elegy: Nature, Culture, and Art[1]

> You are right to require a conscious attitude from the artist toward his work, but you mix up two ideas: *the solution of the problem, and the correct presentation of a problem.* Only the latter is obligatory for the artist. In

"Anna Karenina" and "Onegin" not a single problem is solved, but they satisfy you completely just because all the problems are correctly presented.
—Anton Chekhov, Letter to Alexei Suvorin

I'm living on a dirt road northeast of the Tucson city limits, just south of the Coronado National Forest and at the ankles of the Santa Catalina Mountains. It is the spring of 1999. Out my big picture windows I look up to the craggy bare ridge, slope speckled with saguaros and desert scrub. In the yard, bare dirt, one giant forked mesquite busy with Gila woodpeckers, and more saguaros—giant, many-branched elders that have presided over the scrub for more than one hundred years.

My place is a funky little studio, once a tack room, once a painter's workplace, once a daughter's hippie hangout, the landlady tells me. She's sorry she doesn't live in the attached house anymore. That's rented out too. I can tell from her readiness with the stories that she misses the life she had here. The main house was built in 1937. The tack room added in the 1960s. Once she owned sixty acres. There's an aerial photograph in the main house labeled "High Saguaro Ranch." Now she's down to four acres, and next door a new paved street bears the sign "High Saguaro Road," following the time-honored custom of developers to name new neighborhoods after what they destroy in building them. For a while the owner's then-husband ran helicopter tours over the Grand Canyon. I think that was when things were coming apart for her here. Now she's married to someone else and works in real estate in—Tennessee, is it, or Kentucky? It's hard to remember when all of our business has been on the phone, the fax, or by electronic deposit.

She sounds happiest telling the older stories—how they bought the place in 1970 from the president of Kraft Foods, how his wife used the tack room for a studio, how his pal Perry Como liked to visit because they kept those small horses here, how she used to have big parties and play the piano and everyone sang. I can't imagine the place as an executive getaway. It has a rough, handbuilt look, painted saguaro rib pillars on the porch, mortar slopped into place adequate for the job but with no sign of the refined craftsmanship going into the stone walls in the new gated community climbing the hillside to the north. Maybe that's the point. This really was a getaway, a place to loosen the formalities of the working life, not a place to show off.

The exterior walls of the house and studio are desert stone flecked with mica and grained with quartz. One of my indoor walls is made of the same kind of stone, and one wall provides two picture windows that connect me with the desert's daily life. Each morning two rabbits hop across the yard, usually meeting the flock of Gambel's quail that skitter along like windup toys. Often there's a solitary roadrunner that stands still staring, and several tiny verdins working the bark of the paloverde. In two months I've learned the difference, at last, between the Phainopepla and the pyrrhuloxia.

And I've learned a great deal about the temperament of the latter, a wedge-headed cardinal-like bird, more gray than red and with a yellow bill. One determined male pyrrhuloxia has discovered that a rival lives inside the sideview mirror of my car. Every morning at dawn he launches his attack, slamming his parrotlike bill into the glass again and again, wings in overdrive to keep up the assault until he retreats in exhaustion. The mirror is etched with his bill marks. It gives me pleasure, when stuck in the traffic jam I must endure twice a day in order to live here, seeing those battle scars on the glass and recognizing in them the futility of my anger.

My first night here I heard a scuffling in the gravel outside my door and opened it to find javelinas (collared peccaries) on the doorstep, a chorus of soft grunts that never quit, as if they could not move without vocalizing. Five of them in all, two of them young that hung back in the darker night. The boar came close enough to sniff my hand, then recoiled. Again it approached, dared to take a whiff of me, then pulled away. Again—and this time I touched the coarse black bristles on his forehead, the snout bubblegum pink, hairless, gleaming with moisture and vented with big round flexing nostrils. Grunt, sniffle, shovel along the ground, circle, approach, and jerk away. And then they were gone.

Some nights the coyotes wail and yip. The sound is not what I expect, more chaotic and shrill, pack noise, never individuals. I wonder if they cry out excited over fresh kill, or just to hear their freedom heckle the night. When the noise quiets, a lone dog chained in a neighboring yard replies, its bark an unconvincing posture of ferocity set against that wilder song.

Some nights I hear the great horned owl—*hu-hu-hu-hoo!-hoo!*—and I pray for the rabbits in my yard. One night I heard paired owls in conversation outside my window. I was talking on the telephone with my lover, and ours was a conversation I did not want to have. And all through it, the tenderness and the crying and the pleas, I heard the owls say with no confusion *hu-hu-hu-hoo!-hoo!* and then came the long silence.

Desert night. When the moon is full everything is so white I wake startled in the dark, thinking it must have snowed. And when the moon is empty, the stars are so white and numerous I think, Who needs the moon anyway?

I'm living in the desert to see and hear these things before they are gone. There's no pretty way to say it. The desert is filling up with condos, mansions, and golf courses. An acre of Sonoran Desert, according to a January 1999 *High Country News* article, "much of it teeming with saguaro and prickly pear cacti and ironwood trees, disappears to development every two hours."[2] Tucson has a strong community of artists, writers, scientists, and activists working for preservation and conservation, but so far every major zoning dispute over the past twenty-five years has been lost to developers. In the early 1970s the population of Tucson was 400,000; now it is 823,000 and growing. Another 400,000 people are expected to move to the metro area over the next twenty years. The city occupies a broad bowl surrounded by five mountain ranges, the sprawl climbing up the sides of the bowl. The total annual vehicle miles traveled in Tucson in 1970 was two million; in 1997, sixteen million; expected in 2020, twenty-eight million. Citizens have managed to prevent freeways from cutting through their urban neighborhoods. But this is a qualified victory, since the traffic is driving everyone, including at least one fervent pyrrhuloxia, crazy.

> Number of rabbits, mice, rats, birds and reptiles eaten by a typical Tucson housecat each year: 80.
>
> Number of toads, rabbits, snakes, lizards, small birds, javelinas, coyotes and bobcats killed each year by automobiles in and around Saguaro National Park: 7,100.[3]

Tucson's best hope for controlling sprawl is the proposed Sonoran Desert Conservation Plan. While it will take several more years to complete and implement, the plan is visionary in its scope, aimed at protecting not only sensitive habitat and ecological corridors, but also the cultural and historic characteristics that make the region unique, including ranches as well as historic and prehistoric sites. Development, of course, will not wait for the plan. Indeed, my fear is that developers will hasten to reap their profits before new restrictions come into play, blading away the desert and slapping together more and more colonies (picture them as bacteria on a culture plate) of the bland and placeless sameness that has come to mean economic progress in the New West. In the foothills northwest of the city, developers have spent two years bulldozing land for proposed development of 9,000 homes, four golf courses, and three resort hotels. If the Conservation Plan becomes a reality, growth in the desert will look quite different from this wholesale transformation of wilderness into a microburst of human habitation. Instead, we might see pockets of intense development interspersed with sprawling ironwood and saguaro forest; riverbeds long dry restored to flow through the city and floodplain nourishing stands of mesquite, cottonwood, willow, and the wildlife they harbor; and archaeological sites illuminating the 12,000 or so years that human beings have lived in this valley made prominent enough to eclipse a few golf courses—all in all a more gracious balance between people and the land, between our moment in history and those that precede and succeed us.

Through the scrub beyond my yard I see the flicker of earthmovers, blades, and pavers carving into the foothills above me. Already five monster homes lumber into my line of vision—houses bigger than anyone needs, houses that boast, "I've got mine and I'm closing the gate behind me." Paved driveways wind up the incline, transforming wild land into building lots. In another year or two, the hillside will be clustered with mansions lording it over the valley, an enclave of secessionists at peace with their safe little world behind walls, while in the city that twinkles below like starlight, the toxic waste piles up, homeless people sleep on the sidewalks, and young men "wearing colors" play at war, bleeding real blood on the streets. Do I just hate the monster homes and developments because their owners are rich and I am not? Aren't they entitled to their comfort, pleasure, and safety? I don't care if people build houses in the desert. I just want some desert left after the houses are built. I want one person's comfort not to ride like a cement mixer on the back of another's. I want to have some place to go where I can celebrate creation without having to lament. I want to get beyond elegy. I want my love for natural beauty to be a force for protection, and I want art to be the form for my love.

My life in Tucson is filled with contingencies, and living on the outskirts is one of them. I did not come here to return to the austere reclusiveness of my earlier years. For all my love of nature, I spend most of my days indoors, as I have done for the past decade, working for a cultural institution. It's meaningful work, teaching writing and directing the University of Arizona Poetry Center, and it's what brought me to Tucson in 1990. When I first came to the desert I wanted to live outside of the city and get to know the place through its wildness. I pictured a diminutive ranch with wagon wheels in the yard—something out of a Hopalong Cassidy movie. But I was forewarned by tales of sprawl and bought a city house five minutes from work. This winter, when my daughter and her family were casting about for a place to spend a few months refocusing—she on painting and he on letting go of his job as pastor of a liberal Protestant church in Illinois—I offered them my house, thinking at last I'd seize my chance to get to know the rural neighbors—pocket gopher, scorpion, Gila woodpecker, and noble saguaro.

And I have gotten to know them within the context of my job, enjoying their company in my off hours. I worry that I should be more of a conservation activist—piloting slow-growth initiatives, lobbying city hall, laying down my body (or at least my language) in the path of the pavers. But, as much as protection is my passion, it is not my profession, and I suffer as most people do trying to find the appropriate form for expressing what I believe so deeply. Instead of doing political action, I organize literary readings, send poets to teach in prisons and inner-city high schools, run a poetry library, and teach students how to write. I think of these tasks as cultural activism—nurturing lives devoted to creating meaning rather than to amassing things—because the crisis between our culture and its natural foundations is a crisis of beliefs and values at least as much as it is a crisis of policy and governance. Nevertheless, I feel inadequate as an opponent to the destruction I deplore when asked, as increasingly I am, to address grassroots environmentalists—professionals with their hands in the dirt of ecological restoration, nature education, conservation planning, and wildlands preservation. What good is a poem or an essay when nature is dying and we are to blame?

This frustration that the work of writing and cultural advocacy is not enough to protect the things we love was what led me to collaborate with Richard Nelson and Scott Russell Sanders in an open letter to readers of *Orion* magazine in 1995. The letter was a call to transform the terms of the public discussion about our way of life, our home places, and the fate of the earth. It was a complaint that the dialogue about how we inhabit the earth has been taken over by the voices of money and self-interest, the loudest among them talking "mostly about property rights, economic growth, and the rights of individuals and corporations to pursue profit without restraint."

My frustration also called me to rethink my own role as an activist. I came of age during the era of three significant activist efforts: the civil rights movement, the antiwar movement (both Vietnam and nuclear), and the women's liberation movement. These all erupted out of sleepy post–World War II complacency—the antiwar effort working to take apart social systems that were unjustifiably brutal, the civil rights and women's liberation movements to take apart systems of oppression that deny equal opportunity for all people. The nature of oppression is that it depletes the oppressed of hope and energy, awareness becoming dulled in order that one can endure: *It's just human nature to be brutal. We can't change things, so why try?*

I confess I never had much stomach for the combative mode of activism—though I did march in the Spring 1968 Mobilization for Peace in New York City, and I had peacenik friends studying how to build bombs so that they could be more effective insurgents. Rather than trying to dismantle the existing social order, I tried to invent a new one, moving to a farm as far away from ground zero as I dared go, working in alternative schools and women's health clinics, learning how to be a self-respecting single mother, and writing poems on a homemade desk slapped together from an old barn door. Those actions felt more radical to me than pouring blood on Pentagon walls because they gave me a sense of agency in my life—I was an actor (the star!) in the play of my life. That sounds woefully individualistic to me now that I know human culture is the most powerful evolutionary force on the planet and that it is folly to think any individual can be separate from it, but my intentions then were broader. "Radical" meant working "at the root," making myself a better person, working from scratch to create cultural institutions that were more humane than the dominant ones. I'm thankful that others continued the public acts of demonstration. But I don't disavow my choices—they were in keeping with the goal of an artistic life: to wrest from the personal some form that speaks universally.

My work today follows that pattern, though what's changed is that I've found a satisfying role not only in art but also in the cultural life of art—that is to say, I feel that my time is equally well spent in making art and in working to create a culture in which art can thrive. This kind of culture work can exact a toll, of course, on one's art practice. But it is important work to do, and particularly so if one can cultivate the perspective that neither of these two kinds of work is in opposition to the other. Rather, they are part of the whole in living out a commitment to art, an expression of one's citizenship. And I am convinced that it is a radically good thing to cultivate in others a commitment to artistic, intellectual, and spiritual pursuits. To give our inner lives the status of things, as Edward Sapir claims, is a step in the right direction for an overly acquisitive culture. Better to acquire a few more poems and prayers than a speedboat and plot in a subdivision on the bare flanks of Mt. Lemmon.

By now it will be apparent that geography has been a touchstone for my imagination, this essay having become so similar to other peregrinating works of mine—*Temporary Homelands* and *The Edges of the Civilized World*—for which travel has been a spur to keener attention and intimacy with place. *Touchstone* is a word used almost exclusively these days for its metaphoric meaning: a thing which serves to test the genuineness or value of anything. The origin of this definition is mineral—a smooth dark stone used for testing the quality of gold and silver alloys by rubbing them against it and noting the color of the mark made on the stone. I know one of the pieties of nature writing says that one can only have intimacy with nature and form community by staying in one place, answering to it and for it against the culture's assaults. But when I have tested my own experience for its genuineness and value, I find that I have consistently deepened my understanding of the intricate weave between nature and culture by learning about them in different places.

I consider it implausible that human culture will settle back into an agrarian way of life in which geographic mobility is shunned in the interest of staying put. Human beings are thrilled by the technological prowess that keeps them moving all over the planet and beyond. We are not going to stop these movements, unless, of course, disaster demands it of us. For those who wish to celebrate the agrarian way of life, I hold no antagonism. Indeed, there is much to admire in long study of one place. But what interests me, and what feels useful to me at this time in history, is to transpose what can be learned from more settled lifeways to the change and velocity of contemporary life. How, in a culture that is in love with its freedom and mobility, can individuals learn to conserve and preserve not only their own backyards but what is likely to become someone else's backyard in a year or two or twenty? The essay, poem, or story can become a paradigm for reestablishing the spiritual intimacy with nature that we have lost from lack of physical intimacy.

I know that mobility can instill an ethic of impermanence, of leaving one's mistakes and failures behind, rather than fixing them and fostering healing. But America is no longer an unsettled land, and as it grows more crowded, its membranes more permeable to the rest of the world, one finds that pulling up stakes and moving on leads one to face the same mistakes and failures played out in a new setting. We live in the same old story of fallibility and overreaching goals that has been the bane and boon of human existence from the start. It does us good to face up to that—our stunning potential for messing things up—for without such awareness we don't feel the need for restraint. And we do need mechanisms—morality and law, plans and paradigms—to restrain us, because it is in our nature to dominate, control, and succeed against the competition. For all of our goodness, we are not benign animals. In the first era of global exploration and colonization, human mobility was at its most heedless peak: Go wherever you want and claim it at whatever expense to local nature and culture. Today, human mobility is more democratic. Granted, galloping capitalism can turn a place into the economic colony of a few monster corporations. Nevertheless, our mobility has become less a way to run away from ourselves and more a way to see ourselves more clearly.

When I moved to Tucson in 1990, I had just begun to work in prose after writing poetry for twenty years. I had written an essay about Grand Manan, the island in the Bay of Fundy where I spend my summers, and had realized in the writing how interested I was in the way the place and its people are one thing, as form and content are in a poem. I had also realized there was a good deal of content I wanted to explore that would require me to stretch out further into prose. And the questions I was asking at the time were all nourished by the move: How had my relationship with nature been shaped by family and culture? How does the human order fit into the larger natural order? How does nature act upon me as opposed to the dominant paradigm of people acting upon nature?

Of course, I fell in love with the West's magnificence, a scale and intensity of beauty that humbled me before its power. None of the sheltering blue hillsides, tidy seacoast villages, or fresh mown velvet green pastures I was accustomed to swooning over in the Northeast. Here the mountains scraped up past the treeline to make their jagged statements to the sky. And the desert spanned into the shimmering edge of nowhere, its creatures adapting to harsh aridity with such inventive survival strategies that life seemed indomitable. Yes, there was sprawl, but in the spaces between the explosions of Sunbelt boom, there was the serene and open space of wild land. That expansiveness invites a freedom of mind, I think, and makes one challenge old assumptions about the meaning of nature. The geologic nakedness of arid land gives a vivid sense that human power is small beneath that of the larger planetary forces. Whatever damage we inflict, one can easily think while gazing into the Grand Canyon's gullet that, in the long version of Earth's story, nature will endure.

I find it ironic that the stereotype of the Westerner is that of the rugged individualist, because my move to the West did more to make me understand myself as a cultural animal than to enhance my sense of independence. As a member of the dominant cultural group I do not often see my whiteness, which is particularly invisible to me when I move in the monochromatic social circles of my Eastern roots. But Tucson, like much of the West, is culturally permeable, and here I have had the chance to learn from a place where Mexican and Native American people give definition to the community. And that has made me more apparent, often humblingly so, to myself. Not only is our mass culture one that denies the fact of ecological disaster. It is also a culture that denies the fact of cultural inequity and the ferocious wounds that the European conquest inflicted upon America's indigenous people.

My ancestors, as civic leaders in Puritan New England, had a hand in inflicting those wounds. One incident in particular haunts me. I learned of it only recently while researching family history for an article on the Salem witch trials. William Hathorne, a distinguished soldier in King Phillip's War (1675–76), made his fortune in one day when he captured four hundred peaceful Indians who had gathered in Dover, New Hampshire, for trade and festivities. He arranged a ruse, telling them about a game his people used to play in England. The Indians should pretend to attack the soldiers and then the fun would start. When the game began in earnest, the Indians were captured and sorted out by strength and size like so much timber, with two hundred of the strongest chained body to body and loaded into slave ships that carried them to Bermuda to be sold. The crime earned the young soldier and his business partner close to a million dollars, and he was celebrated in a sermon by Cotton Mather for his bravery in inflicting such a stunning wound upon the savages.

I am deeply ashamed and sorry that my ancestors had a hand in these injustices, even more so because they were respected and pious civic leaders. This is a terrible grief we all must carry, a terrible remorse at human cruelty and blindness, now that we know more about the crimes committed by our own ancestors—and everyone else's—than did any other people in history. It is easy to feel compassion for the victims. But how do I feel compassion for my own ancestors? How do I honor and respect my elders when I am ashamed of them? The only way is to face up to them, to name the evil they did as evil, and to acknowledge that the capacity for evil lies in everyone. They were victims of the time in which they lived, blind to the injustices they caused. We too must be blind, and when I try to imagine the deeds for which our descendants will find it most difficult to forgive us, I am quite convinced that it will be our cavalier destruction of the natural world.

In 1997, I was asked by the Orion Society to lead a conversation at a colloquium convened in honor of Gary Snyder when he received the John Hay Award for his writing and activism. My assignment was to address the question, Does activism compromise one's art? The question was very American, as Snyder pointed out. In Europe and Asia an artist is a public person—seeing the responsibility to use some of his or her skills on behalf of society. I answered the question by saying, Yes, of course compromise occurs. The work of activism exhausts us and makes us grieve; it takes us from our studios; it makes us scholars, negotiators, combatants, administrators, and business heads when we would prefer to be makers, dreamers, healers, and dancers. And if art is made to serve our activism, it can lose its elemental engagement with the unknown; its freedom to be outrageous, obscure, absurd, and wild; its need to speak the truth as it cannot be spoken in political discourse.

Asking this question is like asking, Does culture compromise nature? Does love compromise solitude? Does eating compromise prayer? Does the mountain compromise the sky? All of these are relationships of complementarity, correspondence, call-and-response, the mutualistic whole of existence. Gathering in Snyder's home place, listening to stories of the Yuba Watershed Institute and the building of the Ring-of-Bone Zendo, and celebrating the poet's work provided a lesson in how radical an act it is in this culture to live a life devoted to something other than capitalism. Yes, we all participate in the currently dominant system. Yes, we are all complicit in environmental degradation and overconsumption simply because of our position in the global food chain. But we can make life choices that nurture more meaningful and sustainable relationships. To live a life devoted to art, to spiritual practice, to service to one's community and ecosystem, restores faith in our collective human enterprise. Work on the culture is work on the self.

Art can serve activism by teaching an attentiveness to existence and by enriching the culture in which our roots are set down. Culture is both the crop we grow and the soil in which we grow it. And human culture is the most powerful evolutionary force on Earth these days. The grief we feel at abuses of human power is the first positive step toward transforming that power for the good. Legislation, information, and instruction cannot effect change at this emotional level—though they play a significant role. Art is necessary because it gives us a new way of thinking and speaking, shows us what we are and what we have been blind to, and gives us new language and forms in which to see ourselves. To effect profound cultural change requires that we educate ourselves about our own interior wildness that has led us into such a hostile relationship with the forces that sustain us. Work on the self is work on the Culture.

The reciprocating relationship between self and culture was brought home to me recently when Chinese dissident poet Bei Dao came to Tucson to give a poetry reading. Considered by many to be China's foremost poet of the pro-democracy period, Bei Dao is currently living in exile in the United States, his work accused of inciting the Tiananmen Square uprising in 1989.

He spoke informally with students and local poets about Chinese writing during the past thirty years. He was in high school, seventeen years old, when the Cultural Revolution began. His formal education ended and he became a Red Guard. In 1969 he was sent several hundred miles south of Beijing to work. He was a construction worker there for eleven years. In the countryside he discovered poverty and backward conditions, seeing how different life was from the propaganda he'd been given, and he lost his enthusiasm for the revolution. Then he began to study literature and to write.

Books were banned, except those speaking the official discourse of the state, such as books on Marxism and Mao's thought. Bei Dao and his friends read whatever they could get their hands on—books stolen from closed libraries or banned books confiscated from houses: classical Chinese poetry, Lorca, Kafka, *Catcher in the Rye.*

Bei Dao founded the magazine *Jintian* (*Today*), published from 1978 to 1980 during the Democracy Wall movement, when many people who had suffered during the Cultural Revolution began to come to the capital to express their dissatisfaction. *Jintian* was the first unofficial literary magazine published in China since the Communist takeover in 1949. The first issue's sixty pages were posted on the Wall, with blank sheets of paper beneath each printed page so that readers could let the editors know what they thought. The magazine was also distributed to various cultural organizations in Beijing—publishing houses, universities, and literary institutes. There was tremendous excitement about this new writing, and poetry groups sprouted up all over the place.

"Writing was a forbidden game," Bei Dao explained, "that could cost one one's life." The poetry they published amounted to a new language, since "for thirty years in the Chinese language there had been no personal voice at all."

The official line on Bei Dao's poetry was that it was politically subversive because it expressed intimate thoughts, asserting the rights of the individual to his or her own private experience. And the more obscure Bei Dao's poems became, the more subversive the authorities considered him. What struck me most profoundly was how different this notion of the political was from the sensibility of most poets in the United States. For us, aesthetic subjectivity is considered an escape from politics. In Bei Dao's experience of Communist China, subjectivity meant entering the political arena.

Once an interviewer asked Bei Dao to comment on his statement that "poets must not exaggerate their own function, but even less should they underrate themselves." He replied, "On the one hand poetry is useless. It can't change the world materially. On the other hand it is a basic part of human existence. It came into the world when humans did. It's what makes human beings human."[4]

That language is a key tool for cultural change is evident in the long story of human evolution and in the short one of Mao's Cultural Revolution, as well as in the manipulations of advertisement and the affirmations of prayer: language makes us the speed learners among species, and this power can be used for good or ill. All good literature helps to renew language—to restore its capacity to link the inner life with outer experience, and to sing the song of the soul on the stage of history. And environmental literature, at least since Rachel Carson's *Silent Spring,* has had a remarkably tangible impact on both the ethics and the politics of conservation. This literature has created a common language with which to bear witness, to praise and lament our wounded relationship with nature. It has made more sensuous, and therefore more real, our increasingly abstracted relationship with flora and fauna. It has made invaluable discoveries of science accessible to readers untrained in scientific disciplines, discoveries central both to understanding our predicament and to finding remedies for it. It has served as a collective act of preservation for places lost, lifeways lost, species and cultures lost, forests and mountainsides and rivers lost, and faith in our own kind lost.

I don't mean to say that when a forest is gone you can replace it with a poem. When a forest is gone, you cannot replace it. But with written words you can bear witness, you can hold a memory of the forest for others to experience and celebrate, you can grieve over the loss and rage against the forces that have leveled the forest—and through grief you can fall in love with forests again, and through that falling you can believe again in the human capacity for love, and in the faith that we might learn to protect what we love.

Excerpt from *The Monarchs*[5]

1

They hang in Santa Cruz by the hundreds of thousands,
shingled over each other like dead leaves
high in the eucalyptus grove,
Unable to move below fifty degrees,
but getting here from everywhere west of the Rockies
in time to winter out the cold.

Their navigation takes science—an animated
scrap of paper flying two thousand miles
for the first time each year (a nine-month
life) and making it. And art to know
to move when the idea strikes. Idea?
A butterfly idea? What could be smaller
or more frantic—yet correct. The beauties survive.

I like to think the same intelligence,
whatever makes the monarchs fly,
is at work in my friends who shed
jobs and marriages the way a eucalyptus
ruptures out of its bark as it grows.

Sometimes when I'm driving I forget the car—
riding thoughts instead into
what I should have said when he said,
"I guess you just don't want
to be married to anyone." Then I look up,
there's the sluice of the highway,
and I don't know how I got through the last city.

It's called *unaware memory*, what activates
when the body just does what it should.
No one remembers to accelerate,
which muscles to flex. The body
just does it because
the event is sufficiently rehearsed in the nerves.

2
What does intelligence have to do with
the mean end of Market Street
where the dying pitch tents,
unloved and contagious,
where the street screamers rail
against against against,
ones whose inside
has become the outside and the sidewalk
melts away before their pelting diatribes?

I walked by, invisible there, except
to the sorry man who approached—
"I'm not feeling too good today. Can
you help me out?" I didn't know
if he wanted my money or my mouth,
until he teased, "Oh, c'mon . . . no way?"

Safe back in my car, my blue upholstered
living room, my little local heaven . . .
stopped at the light, I saw the corner bloom
with argument—two kids on the way
home from high school, the bandannaed longhair
pinning his girlfriend to the ground,
from where she screamed, "I don't want you near me!"
at first flinging the words in his face,
then, "I don't want you NEAR me!" the pitch
intensified, reaching for the businessmen
who began to slow down along the sidewalk.

One ran up, "Let her go." Nothing. Then,
"Get OFF her!" hesitating, a thought of safety,
then lifting him like a dog by the back, the kid raging—
"Who the fuck are you! Who the FUCK are you!"
Thrashing, unable to wake up
to what had happened, still dreaming he had the right
on a street full of strangers to have his way.

3
Bypassing Santa Cruz
I descended toward Monterey Bay, a bedazzled traveler,
Connecticut Yankee ogling
the strange expanse of wealth and winterless weather.

They call it winter when the rains turn foothill grasses
velvet green, when lemons fall to the street,
when the monarchs sleep nestled in the eucalyptus leaves,
When the garlic fields quit and the lactating whales
return from the Sea of Cortez.

But I grew up in the cold—

a town where children, in summer, swam in the effluent
of an explosives plant and, in winter, skated across
the surface of a dormant gray brown world.
Call it Anywhere, U.S.A., its brick factory
now glitzed into upscale
shopping mall and all of us, the golden postwar cohort
for whom new school buildings went up
and the flag came down, half-mast, all of us
scattered like so many dandelion puffs into the urban fields.

Here on the last coast,
the tin-walled factories where herring boats used to unload
now dish out Anywhere junk by the busload. In the famous aquarium
the travelers, myself eagerly among them, marvel at how relentless
the life forms have become—pressing noses to glass
to observe one that bores through shale
to establish its niche, another with a body all
undulation and engorgement, venous, and hungry to move.
Outdoors,
historic grainy photos slipping through my mind,
I see the rubbled carcasses, remaindered bones
that once lined this beach, black smoke of whale oil,
and I long to know their stench
because it would be
something true—those massive, black,
underwater angels harvested to light our ancestors'
dinner lamps, the hunter and the hunted now diffused and risen,
spirits in the luminous air.

—after Czeslaw Milosz

6

MAKING STORIES OUT OF EVERYTHING: VALUING THE ORDINARY

Ofelia Zepeda, a member of the Tohono O'odham (formerly Papago) tribe, was born in 1954 in Stanfield, Arizona, a rural cotton-farming community. She earned her master's degree and doctorate in linguistics at the University of Arizona, where she is currently professor of linguistics. The former director of the American Indian Studies Program at Arizona, she is co-director of the American Indian Language Development Institute (AILDI), an annual summer institute for American Indian Teachers.

Zepeda is also editor of Sun Tracks: An American Indian Literary Series for the University of Arizona Press, in which her own collection, *Ocean Power: Poems from the Desert*, appeared in 1995. More recently, she published the poetry chapbook *Jewed 'I-hoi / Earth Movements* (1997), together with a CD of her reading poems in O'odham and English. In addition to her literary work, she has published important studies in linguistics, such as the first grammar of the Tohono O'odham language, *A Papago Grammar* (1983). She received a grant from the Endangered Language Fund for the Tohono O'odham Dictionary Project and has been centrally involved in developing language curricula for the Tohono O'odham nation and for other Southwestern tribes. She was guest editor, with Teresa McCarty, of the *International Journal of the Sociology of Language* for a special issue on *Indigenous Language Use and Change in the Americas* in 1998 and for a special issue of *Bilingual Research* on *Native American Languages* in 1995. In 1999, Zepeda received a MacArthur Fellowship for her work as a linguist, poet, editor, and community leader working to preserve Native American languages and revitalize tribal communities.

Our conversation with Zepeda emphasized various aspects of storytelling and cross-cultural communication. In American society, it's common for us to refer to "story" in a general, universal way, as if all stories are basically the same. It quickly became apparent in Zepeda's statements during the interview that she had in mind several different kinds of stories when she used the term "story"—especially, the distinction between everyday stories and traditional or ceremonial stories. Soon it became clear, too, that the relationship between teller and listener was extremely important. Often this relationship determined whether a speaker would tell a full, long version of a story or a more abbreviated version, leaving out special details. This kind of abbreviation could even happen when speaker and listener are of the same tribal group, perhaps because of a difference in age. Sometimes there is an awkwardness even when an O'odham student seeks to collect traditional stories from tribal elders. Zepeda works frequently with Native American students at the University of Arizona, teaching them to tell their own stories and to gather stories from their families and other members of their communities, as a means of cultural preservation.

Although it was clear from our discussion that there is sometimes an awkwardness, even a prescribed "silence," when tribal members communicate with outsiders, Zepeda nonetheless indicated a few specific occasions when Pueblo or O'odham people made special efforts to participate in public hearings in order to assert land claims. She emphasized the difficulty of making indirect, story-based language fit the requirements of a public hearing. Elderly tribe members, even those whose English is poor, are often called upon to speak at hearings, as their words and presence have particular validity, particular authority, in the O'odham community. Often native speakers will try to emphasize universal ideas, such as the value of "home," when giving public testimony. Perhaps the most difficult aspect of participating in a public, cross-cultural process of communicating wishes and values is the problem with presenting indirect stories to listeners expecting efficient, direct presentation of information. It's interesting to see how even the language of the following interview juxtaposes the direct, question-style of academic interviews with subtle, humorous anecdotes. The interview was not limited to a precise period of time, and we have also had the luxury of reading, editing, and rereading the transcript of the conversation. Zepeda describes stories as a way of easing into a topic and offering a "roundabout" way of teaching an audience. She says stories "leave you hanging and really somewhere along the line the light clicks on." People living in story-based communities hear the same stories repeatedly, so that key ideas get planted in their imaginations, become part of their world view.

We have included three samples of Ofelia Zepeda's poetry, starting with the little piece called, in English, "It Is Going to Rain." We've included the O'odham version that was published on the facing page in the 1997 collection *Jewed 'I-hoi / Earth Movements*. This poem responds to the seemingly innocuous statement by "someone" that "it is going to rain." The speaker of the poem disagrees, saying simply, "I think it is not so," and offering four specific reasons for thinking that it will not rain, all of them based on precise physical sensations. For agricultural people living in the Sonoran Desert of Arizona and northern Mexico, rain is an extremely important natural phenomenon, not something to be taken lightly. So the anticipation of rain is crucial to survival. "It Is Going to Rain" asserts the value of rain, the value of sensory experience, and the value of subtle knowledge of one's home environment. And the language of the poem, in a way, is quite narrative—it is a precise, abbreviated vignette about a dispute over the expectation of rain. The full setting of the dispute is not presented—only the essential details that reveal the values suggested above.

The second poem included in this book, from Zepeda's 1995 collection *Ocean Power*, is "Kitchen Sink." This selection represents the idea in the title of this chapter, the notion that stories can be made out of everything, even—and perhaps especially—out of ordinary things, such as kitchen sinks. Actually, the poem is not specifically about the speaker's kitchen sink, but it uses the perception of light through the kitchen-door window near the sink as a way of measuring the changing of the seasons. The "story" here is not one of a specific incident, but of the speaker's annual process of perceiving seasonal change. As in the previous poem, the value of sensory experience in helping people to know the natural patterns of their places is highlighted. Zepeda's gentle, self-deprecating humor appears when she comments that afternoon, when the sink is "full with sunlight," is not necessarily the best time to be washing dishes, so bright is the light reflecting off the water.

"Lard for Moisturizer," also from *Ocean Power*, is a humorous and insightful poem about the most ordinary of climatic phenomena in a desert landscape—dry air. In particular, this poem tells the story of how the speaker's family treats that most mundane of desert maladies—dry skin. So playful and endearing are the narrative details of the poem—the family's use of assorted lotions and moisturizers ranging from Jergens to petroleum jelly, and sometimes even to lard—that it's easy to miss the fact that this is a poem about adapting to the realities of environment. In much of American culture, we have become accustomed to using technology—from air conditioners to humidifiers, from heaters to dehumidifiers—to overcome the unpleasantness of climate. Zepeda's poem suggests that even "native" people suffer physical hardships as a result of climate, but instead of trying to avoid reality and distance themselves from it, they can make a game out of adaptation. This poem, too, is a summary of years of experience rather than a detailed immersion in a specific scene, until the concluding passage about the aunt who "goes straight for *lard*."

Although Zepeda is clearly writing from a specific cultural background, her poems are easily accessible to outsiders. Her topics—rain, light coming through kitchen windows, chapped skin—are universal. And although her work may sometimes admonish readers/listeners to pay more attention to the world about them, her tone is non-confrontational and often gently joking. Readers of all backgrounds can learn much about the natural world and about the language of story from Ofelia Zepeda's writings and from her comments during the following interview.

♦

A CONVERSATION WITH OFELIA ZEPEDA

Terre Satterfield and Scott Slovic conducted this interview with Ofelia Zepeda in the guest cottage at the University of Arizona Poetry Center.

Slovic: A big part of this project is to talk with people whose work addresses the meaning and importance of the natural world using frameworks other than dollar amounts.

Satterfield: We refer to this as our "narrative-values project" but basically we're exploring the possibility that storytelling is as good as (and perhaps better than) other common means for thinking and talking about values. One outcome of the project would be to get the language of story and narrative into the world of policy and try to de-emphasize the notion that "value" is strictly a dollars-and-cents phenomenon. This is all quite exploratory. We've been getting people, laypeople from all kinds of places, to provide their own stories as well as asking writers to talk about story and values from a professional point of view. Several writers have mentioned that telling a story that has a certain quality or magic to it allows the storyteller to convey something that is virtually impossible to convey in any other way. So that's probably as good a place to begin as any.

Zepeda: When I think of the word "story," I remember that there are different kinds of stories. You have stories that everyday people tell. And then there's the type of story that some of us experience sometimes because of who we are, because of the background or cultural community that we come from. And so to me there are different levels, different kinds of stories. I don't know which one you want me to talk about. I always get my students to tell me about their lives, and to me that has a certain magic about it also. To me, the difference there is their age and their background, and my age and my background and being a professional person. What they choose to tell me and what I actually get from what they tell me are very different things.

Satterfield: I want to hear about both those things actually. [Laughter.]

Zepeda: Well, to me the term "story" has a lot of these compartments. I always tend to get a number of independent-study projects with students. That means that I get to spend an hour to two hours a week with particular students at a time, every week for the whole semester, sometimes for years. And I get both graduate and undergraduate students, but our undergraduate population is still fairly young. This semester I have 180 students, including four native people—three are O'odham, one is Pima. I get to know them. Some I've known before—in fact, I went to high school with one woman. We each have had different experiences, but the way she tells me about things already has background. The others are people I've just met. Even though some of them are from my tribe, I've known them for only maybe a year or two. But it always turns out that because they're O'odham, I think I know of their family in one way or another. Perhaps I've met their mother or their father somewhere along the way. So, when they tell me stories, I'm already working with a little bit of a background because of that common tribal affiliation. In other cases, it kind of stops because of the large gap in age and life experience. That's why some stories are unique—because they build on common experience.

Slovic: What kinds of questions do you ask to lead them to tell stories?

Zepeda: Well, there's a young guy who's doing a biography of his mother. And his mother was one of the few O'odham women who went to a boarding school and then got hired out to go work for an Anglo lady in California as a housekeeper or something like that. That was part of the chronology. He was telling me about his mother, but then we had a discussion about other places that O'odham people work. Because she was fairly young when she went off to boarding school and then to California on her own to work for this Anglo lady, I asked him what other kinds of work his mother did besides housekeeping. And he said, "Oh, she worked in the fields, in the cotton fields." And I said, "Where?" He answered, "Over there, where everybody else worked." There are these two major areas near the reservation, two towns, and one of them was where I was born and raised. Our family did the same thing; we worked in the fields picking cotton and chopping wood and stuff. And he said that was the kind of work his mother did too when she was younger.

One of the stories that he tells of his mother is about homesickness. She was hired one summer, as I said, by a California lady and went to California. The lady bought her a one-way train ticket. His mother took the train ride and went to California and got terribly homesick. And so the lady said, "Okay, if you want to go home, I'll get you another ticket. You can go home." This guy actually has his mother's original ticket, and it says she was supposed to go to Tucson. But as the mother tells the story, she never came back to Tucson. She says she got off in Casa Grande. There's a train stop there, too, and Casa Grande is one of those cotton-farming towns as well. She got off in Casa Grande, but my student said that his mother then walked—which is quite a walk—to Stanfield, which is the place where I'm from, where all the O'odham have temporary settlements for picking cotton. It's about fifteen miles or so to drive, so I don't know how she walked that. She must have gotten off the train in Casa Grande because she knew parts of her family would be out there in the fields. She got off in Casa Grande and just walked and found the rest of her family and worked with them for the rest of the summer.

Anyway, I have these kinds of connections with the students who are telling me their stories, because, as I said, that's what my parents did. The same work. In the case of this young guy, it was his mother's experience, not his. But it's a long story—it has events in it.

Slovic: So the students who are working with you are often telling family stories?

Zepeda: Yeah, pretty much.

Slovic: Do they run into any obstacles, things that they don't know how to talk about, and do you help them through some of that? Give them some guidance in how to tell a story like that?

Zepeda: This young guy has already talked to his mother and in fact he's sort of been interviewing her on and off for a while now. There's another guy who's collecting stories. Now the person he's collecting from isn't related to him and he's fairly elderly—he's seventy-seven, I believe. It's difficult to collect from somebody you are not related to, whose life you really don't know. And also the type of material this guy is collecting involves a very traditional story—one that is really found only with O'odham who are in Mexico, not the ones who are in Arizona. But my student's family is originally from Mexico and so is my family, and so I know his mother and some of his relatives as well. I know the population that he's trying to tap into—they're fairly elderly people from Mexico and there are not that many of them. But collecting this very special kind of story is difficult no matter who you are because of the nature of the story itself. I've never heard the story in its entirety—even he, my student, has a version of it that's fairly short. It's not real detailed yet. The main challenge for him, the problem that he has, is not so much to recollect the story, but to ask the guy to fill it in. He can see that. He can see when his storyteller has not elaborated or told the whole story. There might be a reason for this. And still, we don't know what's not yet there in the story. If he goes back and asks him again, "Why didn't you say any more about this particular event?" the man might choose not to say anything. Or he could tell the story again and fill a lot more in the next time around. So things like that come up. This particular student just has to ask somebody of the same age the right kind of questions and he'll get the right kind of story. My student has spent a lot of time with this old man, but there's sort of an awkwardness sometimes in trying to collect stories. He's also collected from other people who are younger, and people that he knows. There he gets a lot more information, just because he feels more comfortable with those people.

Satterfield: Is this just about awkwardness or are there intentional places of silence—points where the pieces of the story don't get filled in? Perhaps there's a lesson there—either for us when we're collecting stories or for you when you're talking to your students—that might be helpful. You know, why is that piece not being filled in? Not so much pushing for that missing piece—"Please tell me that, please"—but to say, what is it about this section that shouldn't even be part of the story or shouldn't be told? I mean, here we are collecting stories and maybe some of what we want to know is why there are silences about certain things.

Zepeda: Yes, I know there are some tellers who will preface their stories by saying that. There's a collection—I translated it, and I'm transcribing it now—that an Anglo woman was collecting. She wants me to transcribe the whole tape. And the lady who's telling the story does say at the beginning that she's not supposed to talk about this thing the Anglo lady's asking for, this story about whatever. And then she says, "It's also kind of the wrong time of the year to tell the story and I feel funny talking about it." So then she says, "I'll just tell the short one." [Laughter.]

She says, "That should be okay." So I transcribed that whole thing, because that was her preface to this story. She tells the story, but it is a shorter version of a long, more detailed, traditional story. And so this lady got the short version and, as I said, there's a lot of detail missing from it. People often know why they leave things out. But sometimes they won't say it unless you go and ask them, "Was there a reason you didn't go into that?" And they'll tell you. And then sometimes they say, "Oh, I don't remember it!" [Laughter.] "I thought I told you. I guess I forgot."

Satterfield: Can you talk a bit about the difference between a traditional story and a personal story that somebody might tell? Not so much in reference to form. It's more that we're interested in story as a way in which people convey something that is meaningful to them, particularly when they don't want to convey it directly, as in a blanket statement. And maybe there's some insight for us there, not so much in the details of the story, but in just what makes a story a "traditional" story. Is it because it has a particularly potent message? Is it because it's been around for a long time?

Zepeda: Yeah, here's the way I use the distinction, in the case of the two things that my students are doing. The one who's collecting from this old guy—he's interested in one of the stories that they pass down and it's part of a more elaborate ceremony and ritual. It has a very specific context and not too many people tell that story. It's a very specialized piece. That's the way I look at it. It's quite different from my student telling me about his mother's work or something like that. To me, that's not a traditional story—that's just the telling of a life experience.

Satterfield: So, with the traditional story, is that a way of saying that only a few people are being told the story, partly because there are few people who can really understand the story or should receive the story?

Zepeda: Yes, and typically because of the nature of the ritual. You are supposed to apprentice into the practicing of the ritual. And the apprentice part doesn't happen until men are fairly mature, in, say, their late forties or early fifties. They've heard the story all along the way and could possibly tell it. But it is a small group of people who know it well enough to tell it. So the number involved in it, or having access to it or the status to tell it, is very small.

Satterfield: We haven't run into that too much. We've been using "story" very broadly and haven't paid perhaps sufficient attention to the way in which there's not only such a thing as, say, a professional storyteller, someone like yourself, but also the way in which there might be a "professional audience," too. Sometimes there are stories that are meant for only certain ears.

Slovic: Do you think of your poetry as a kind of story? Or do you have a different sense of the language in your poetry?

Zepeda: I think some of my poems certainly are stories. When I tell them, they have a background to them. And when I do a reading, I'll set a background so it becomes part of the whole thing. It gets longer that way and it also gets that story format.

Slovic: When you give a reading, do you usually make a point of reading some of the poems in O'odham and some in English?

Zepeda: Well, there are about four or five of us O'odham who've been writing for the last fifteen years or so but weren't published for a long time. We used to get invited to do readings around Tucson and Phoenix. We'd do the readings and all of us wrote in O'odham as well. And one colleague of mine is also a singer. So we'd have poetry in O'odham and in English and sort of combine that with traditional song. It was an interesting performance. We sort of had a circuit [laughter] that we'd do. So now, even though our audience typically is predominantly non-O'odham, if we're reading in Phoenix or Tucson, they still enjoy it, and they request that we read in the O'odham language. "Will you read at least a couple of pieces?" We were planning to anyway, just for the audience's experience. We get interesting responses when we do that. Even now, when I read in different parts of the country, I'll read in O'odham. To me, it's just part of what I write. I'll read in both English and O'odham instead of saying I'm going to read only in English because I'm at Dartmouth College, you know. [Laughter.]

Satterfield: One of the nice things about that, over and above the story or the poem itself, is that there's a certain sound of the language that listeners then take away with them. They really don't know what the phrases mean, but they'll be glad to have the sound in their heads in some way that changes the English version.

Zepeda: Yes, we always get comments afterwards—we get all kinds of comments about what they think O'odham sounds most similar to. You get everything from Chinese to whatever. [Laughter.]

Slovic: Let me change the direction of our conversation. We feel that there are certain ways that people think about the world that are very difficult to make abstract, difficult to turn into numbers or dollar expressions. So we're relying on writers to give us advice about why story is important and why it needs to be included in the language of public policy, rather than only abstracted or boiled-down statements or numeric summaries.

Satterfield: Statements from a survey or dollars from a cost-benefit analysis.

Slovic: Yeah. Do you have any thoughts about that?

Zepeda: Well, it's really hard for me to grasp what that is. The thing that you mentioned: policy. I can't really understand the question. What comes to mind is one of the pueblos where they had a case for reclaiming some lands, traditional lands. One of the arguments that they brought into the contemporary court case rested on their traditional stories—stories that they've always known and always told within their community. These stories made references to very specific things and very specific places. I don't know if it was solely based on their using those references—maybe there were other things, but the stories were very important parts of the evidence.

Satterfield: That's a good example. A similar thing has happened in British Columbia. Part of what the court decision was saying was, "This is a legitimate way of transmitting historical information; story is permissible evidence in court." I suppose we haven't been thinking about story in its historical context in this project, but rather just as a way of talking about certain things.

Zepeda: Yes, but cases of this type are very rare. There are a lot of instances where tribes, especially small tribes, are trying to get federal recognition. Many of these don't have enough documentation to prove their existence. They have tried to use things like story to document their own native existence or whatever, but with less success.

Satterfield: This may be a tough question, so dismiss it if you want to. If you had to finish the sentence that began, "The main purpose of a story, the main reason I use story, or the main purpose of story in my mind is . . .," how would you answer that? What is the main goal of telling a story? Or telling an ordinary versus a traditional story if you want to distinguish between them in that way?

Zepeda: Well, for instance, if I tell a story about my father, I use it to set a kind of background or something like that. Or I might do it for somebody else, someone who needs that background. Earlier I was saying this about poetry. Normally I do that—I tell a short story of some sort beforehand.

Satterfield: To provide a kind of context for . . .

Zepeda: I don't know. I guess I assume that the audience will understand the poetry better with a bit of background. They will get more out of it, maybe it will be more enjoyable, more interesting.

Satterfield: And are there other purposes different from that? That's one example.

Zepeda: Well, I teach a class on the story of native languages which can sometimes be pretty dry. So I use stories there a lot of times to give background to some linguistic point, you know, some sociolinguistic point. It helps make the point, and hopefully students learn something more easily because of that. So in a classroom I use story as a teaching tool.

Slovic: Why do you think students can learn something more easily if you tell them a story?

Satterfield: Yes, this is a key point for us: Why is it that you can remember something if it's told in a story form that you can't remember otherwise?

Zepeda: When professors do that and set that little context, the story is non-intimidating, as long as you can relate the story to the lesson's major point. A lot of times it just makes it comfortable for students. And it's just a way of getting into the topic—you *ease* into it rather than head into the facts. [Laughter.] You don't necessarily have to use hard-core traditional stories—medium-range ones, I don't know what they call them, stories in the language, work just as well. These are stories that are supposed to teach you how to behave and so it's the same process. They tell you this roundabout story and it's entertaining and so forth, or it can be sad or melodramatic, but in the end, it leads up to some specific thing that you're supposed to learn. They'll never tell you directly, "Well, this is what you're supposed to get out of this story." They just leave you hanging, and somewhere along the line the light clicks on.

Satterfield: Is the point of not telling the story directly the wish to not hit somebody over the head with it? This morning we were talking about not coming out directly with your central message. Aside from comfort, it's sometimes the case that listeners or readers will learn better by figuring it out for themselves. There's an open-ended quality rather than, you know, saying, "I'm handing you this piece of wisdom." If you leave them something with a little space in it for them to walk around in, in their mind, it's more powerful because there is a place that they've arrived at by themselves. It's the opposite of being instructed directly as to what to do.

Zepeda: I think that's certainly what happens. You know a friend of mine over in anthropology always comments on how storied language is very indirect. The storytellers expect you to infer a lot of information from what they say. And, you know, a lot of this comes from old people talking to you or your parents talking to you, in the old days, and some people still do it now. They talk to kids when the kids are half asleep. Unconscious kinds of things. Something gets planted. Little kids or teenagers and so forth get this very, very indirect lesson. Sometimes you just totally miss it. And it's not a good thing if you totally miss it. But parents repeat it a lot throughout your growing-up years. Eventually it gets in there. But it's not direct at all. It's extremely indirect and you can certainly misinterpret it and get yourself in trouble.

Satterfield: It's possible that there are a lot of contexts where that indirectness is the only way to say certain things. In fact this is one of the motivations for this project. We know that people who manage public lands, watersheds, estuaries, forests, and so on, are legally obligated to ask the public what they think or want. Yet, it might be the case that many people ("the public") can speak directly only about less important things. The more important things get, the more they need to talk about them indirectly. Through story.

What about stories that might be told when someone is trying to convince a land manager that it's important not to mess up this place, not to put that copper mine there, and so on? There are intangible reasons why it matters deeply to all kinds of people, and those are the things that are the hardest to articulate. Do you have any thoughts on the way story could be helpful there?

Zepeda: Well, some of us have sat through those kinds of discussions. Like here in Arizona, when they were having hearings on making English the official language of the state, many of us went to testify before the state legislature. We were all talking about language, and the importance of keeping our own language, not legally forcing people to use English. Part of the richness of this region is because of the language. For all the tribes in the state, it's not just the language, it's also the land including all these regions and all their names. It's not so much *because* of the language, but because of the people *and* the language *and* the place. It's all tied up, and no matter what tribe you're from, whatever part of Arizona, the argument is always the same. A lot of what happens in a story about, say, Mount Taylor or about San Francisco Peak, is just that—it's about specific places. I even think some of the legislators can identify with ideas of "home" and all that good stuff. We didn't discuss it before these meetings, but when we got there and did our testimony, this was the theme over and over again.

Satterfield: Did that repetition, the over and over again, make the point about story, land, and place more powerful or less powerful? I mean, I can see certain situations where a story that's repeated several times loses its clout and I can see the opposite being true.

Zepeda: That has a lot to do with who's presenting it. In some cases, we brought some old guy over—everybody did the same thing too. [Laughter.] One of those old O'odham people. Their English wasn't very good, so they sort of rushed back and forth, but they had translators. The thing is, that gives us validity, the bringing along of the old people. A lot of this oral stuff exists in their memory and so because there were different tribes with different languages and from different places, each time it worked well. It was a nice representation of the different groups even though we basically have the same thing in mind. Every perspective was slightly different, just as [are] the geography and language and the culture and the people.

Slovic: On that occasion, how much time did you have to give your testimony?

Zepeda: Well, it didn't matter if you sort of rambled on and on. But you didn't have that much time. Each testimony was fifteen to twenty minutes.

Slovic: How did it feel trying to say these things about language and place in merely fifteen minutes?

Zepeda: Well, we were given an agenda. We had an agenda to go by and it was fairly strict. We had advice from people who were familiar with doing this type of testimony in front of that audience. We were told to pay attention to the schedule because if everybody keeps running over, they'll stop the whole thing. They're very strict. We knew this was the case and that this was the population we were going to be dealing with. So we tried to pack as much as we could into the time that was given.

Satterfield: Do you have a sense of what the people listening to these testimonies would then do with the stories? Were they just something pretty that they would take home with them? What do you think happens there? Our worry is that we get story or narrative in the door, but then it just becomes the afternoon's entertainment or something like that.

Zepeda: In the case of an audience like that, I think each one of them takes away something different. It's not what their take is on the Indian population in general for our state. Some people are extremely sympathetic to the native population and so it's already like preaching to the congregation, but we know that, and we'll ask them to sort of lobby to help us. They're the ones that we are fairly sure take stories seriously. We ask them to let others know that this isn't just for show. In a lot of cases it's how our people make a point, make an argument, convince somebody.

Slovic: I think there's an interesting connection between the time span of public testimony and the way you write poetry—both tend to be brief. You write in the lyrical mode, which has the effect on the readers of very quickly introducing an idea and bringing the reader into a scene or situation. I think part of the effectiveness of this style is not to drag it out too much, but to quickly evoke a feeling in the reader and then to leave it hanging in the air. The reason I started asking about the time that you had to testify at the public hearings is that part of our concern, as we try to think toward the long-term goal of expanding the way people talk about environmental management, is that at the managerial level, people are very concerned about efficiency, about doing things quickly.

Satterfield: Getting to the bottom line.

Slovic: Getting to the bottom line, whether it's numerical or economic or some other kind of bottom line. Of course, the thing about story, and art in general, is that it often takes much more time to create a proper atmosphere and communicate a message indirectly. Is it possible in any forum, spoken or written, to take, say, a poem, and make a profound point about how one feels about or "values" a place? It's encouraging to hear what you say about this particular occasion where you were able to work within the time limits.

Satterfield: Here's another angle on this. A hearing might use oral storytelling, but how does that differ from the written page? What happens in one form that does not happen in the other?

Zepeda: Well, I guess it sort of depends. For me it's often depended on who or what has control over the written page. If there's no control over the written page, it seems to me that whatever existed orally when you've written it down verbatim can go on and on and on and on. Whether anybody wants to read it or publish it is the second part. Then there's a different kind of control: audience control, which places certain conditions on what needs to change to make it readable or publishable. The press wants a written form. They're not interested in the oral form at all. And there are certain conditions that you have to meet if it's going to be a written piece of text, a publishable written piece of text.

Satterfield: Is it unnerving to have an oral narrative fixed on the page?

Zepeda: It can be if you are really hung up on the oral and you want to have the print be a representation of what was said, at least the best representation that you can have, going from oral to print. So certainly if somebody chops it all up, then you say, "Well, it's not the same story—it's not my story anymore." But it's also true that a story will have a different effect when you read it as opposed to when you listen to it.

Satterfield: Any thoughts on why that is or what makes a good storyteller? I might refer to someone as a really good storyteller, but I'm not sure I could articulate why. Have you got any thoughts on that yourself?

Zepeda: I don't know. I know people I like to listen to because I think they tell something. It doesn't even have to be stories or anything. I just like listening to them talk. I don't know what it is about them. There's a guy that we know—he loves to talk and he talks very well in O'odham and in English. I like listening to him a lot and he always makes a story out of everything. Little things. He just makes stories up on the spur of the moment, you know. So that's kind of fun—he's fun to listen to and it's nice for him to do that. I see him only at meetings and he always starts out with some little story. But other people don't like it. They think it wastes a lot of time and they say, "Oh gosh, now he's going to tell one of his stories!"

Satterfield: How about stories that emphasize particular senses? How important is describing taste and smell and sound and touch and other things in the telling of story? To you, is that high on the list of what's important, or do other things come more into play, such as descriptions of emotion?

Zepeda: I know that description has a high position, description of just about any of those, whether it's emotion or landscape or behavior of an animal or something like that. For somebody to be able to say it in a certain way, a way that you never thought of yourself, gives you this nice little picture. Even a single word can do that for me. This weekend we had a meeting—a little O'odham group that's working on a dictionary project. There was the woman who wrote some dictionary entries in O'odham, and she gave a little sentence with the O'odham word that in English someone else had defined to mean "to flutter." Flutter.

Satterfield: Like a butterfly?

Zepeda: No, well, butterfly didn't really come up, but . . . bird wings. But as they thought about it more, and they talked about it for a long time, just this one word—it came to light that it's actually the act that a bird does to straighten out his feathers or get water off. We didn't think flutter was the [right] word in English. We don't know what the word is in English, but we do know what it is in O'odham now. So we had to sort of clean up the O'odham part for that one particular word. The feathers have to be on the bird and not just a feather hanging out the window or blowing in the wind. It has to be attached to a bird. [Laughter.] So, yeah, just little words and things like that kind of bring a clear picture.

Slovic: Is O'odham a language that's especially good for describing certain kinds of experiences? Are there certain things, certain subjects, for which it's a stronger, more precise language than English?

Zepeda: Well, in certain ways it is precise. But I don't think I can make the generalization that it is more precise than English. We always say—I don't know how true it is—the speakers place very high value on how a person uses language, in everyday talk or as a singer or orator. We do see that as a special gift, a talent. I assume, then, that the language is such that certain people can manipulate it in a certain way to describe conditions or whatever. But, to me, the striking thing that the language does is much more subtle. It takes a while to figure out what this language does very well compared to English or Spanish. A lot of it comes in the different levels of poetic language. Anybody can do that kind of language and they can do it talking about anything, whether it's horses or pigs or farming or whatever. People place quite high value on it, that a person can do this. Certainly, the O'odham language is set up so that certain speakers can manipulate it in that way. People also refer to the way speakers use the O'odham language with humor. There's always something funny. Not necessarily a joke, but just a subtle play on words.

Slovic: Is that part of what you are trying to do in your poems, too?

Zepeda: Sometimes, yes.

Slovic: Do you know many non-native speakers who seem to understand the subtleties of it?

Zepeda: Yes, because some of it can carry over into English, so they can participate as well.

♦

B 'o e-a:g Maṣ 'ab Him g Ju:kĭ[1]

B 'o 'e-a:g maṣ 'ab him g ju:kĭ.
Ṣag wepo mo pi woho.
Nañpi koi ta:tk g jeweḍ mat am o i si ka:ckad c pi o i-hoiñad c o ñenḍad.
Ṣag wepo mo pi woho.
Nañpi koi ta:tk g da:m ka:cim mat o ge s-wa'usim s-we:ckad.
Ṣag wepo mo pi woho.
Nañpi koi ta:tk g hewel mat s-hewogim o 'i-me:
Ṣag wepo mo pi woho.
Nañpi koi hewegid g s-wa'us jeweḍ
mat g hewel 'ab o 'u'ad.
Ñia, heg hekaj o pi ṣa'i woho matṣ o ju:.

It Is Going to Rain

Someone said it is going to rain.
I think it is not so.

Because I have not yet felt the earth and the way it holds still
in anticipation.
I think it is not so.
Because I have not yet felt the sky become heavy with moisture of
preparation.
I think it is not so.
Because I have not yet felt the winds move with their coolness.
I think it is not so.
Because I have not yet inhaled the sweet, wet dirt the winds bring.
So, there is no truth that it will rain.

Kitchen Sink[2]

The light from the kitchen-door window comes through in a special way.
I can see the seasons change in my kitchen sink.
The movement of the sun is shadowed in that sink.
During the afternoon the sink is full with sunlight.
Not necessarily a good time to be washing dishes.
Later in the summer there is a sense of urgency as the shadow gets longer
and begins to slant
as the sunlight starts to edge out of the sink.
I pretend the sunlight is going down the drain.
The light cannot be stopped by the plug in the drain.
It seeps down around the inner seal where water cannot go,
becoming a part of the darkness that is always a part of drains and pipes.
Winter is coming.
The air is probably cooler already.
I know this because of my sink.

Lard for Moisturizer[3]

I turn the vertical blinds,
attempting to capture the southern light.
The sun is now at the south corner.
The December wind is cold,

magnifying the weakness of the sun's light.
This light is difficult to contrast
to the searing, still heat of three months ago.
I think of that heat now, but I can't really remember it.
I welcome the gentle warmth of the winter sun.
With this sunlight I think of home and the activity that moves to the east side of the house,
to catch the weak winter morning sun.
My father sits on that side for hours doing small repairs.
My mother and her laundry tubs move to that side also.
Bent over her washtubs of clothes, her back to the sun.
Arms moving back and forth washing, pulling on the rays of the sun.
My sisters and I hang out clothes,
being grateful only that it isn't raining.
Sun and winter wind dry the clothes quickly.
The only casualty of this work is our hands.
Hot water, cold water rinse, cold wind, and mild dry sun.
As outdoor people our parents
found small relief in lotions and moisturizers for the skin.
Our family kept the Jergens lotion people in business, we used to say.
Early in December moisturizing lotions were fine, but by January and February we were ready
for the hard stuff, petroleum jelly.
Our parents went to bed each night with a slight sheen of grease on their hands and face.
We did the same.
A minor epidermal comfort.
My sisters and I laugh about one aunt who doesn't even bother with moisturizing lotion
or even petroleum jelly, she goes straight for *lard*.
We've all seen her do this.
When she makes her tortilla dough
with the last step she greases each ball of dough.
As she finishes, any lard left over she simply rubs into her hands as she would lotion.
My sister mimics and exaggerates the description,
showing us how she rubs the lard on her face, arms,
and then lifts her skirt and rubs a healthy handful on her brown, chapped knees.

7

THE BUILDING BLOCKS OF STORIED EXPRESSION: ADVICE FROM A TEACHER OF WRITING

As he explains in the questionnaire responses below, Richard Shelton has spent most of his life living in arid regions of the American West, places where far fewer people would be today were it not for feats of engineering that have brought water for irrigation and air conditioning in the summer. He was born in Boise, Idaho, in 1933. After spending his first two years of college at Harding College in Searcy, Arkansas, he left to join the U.S. Army, serving at Fort Huachuca, Arizona. In 1956, he married Lois Bruce. He received his B.A. in English at Abilene Christian College in 1958 and then began teaching English to seventh- and eighth-graders at Lowell Middle School in Bisbee, Arizona, while working at the University of Arizona on his M.A., which he completed in 1960. Following graduate school, Shelton began teaching as an instructor at the University of Arizona, eventually becoming Regents Professor of English in 1991. He also served as director of the Creative Writing Program from 1979 to 1981 and was instrumental in hiring Edward Abbey to teach writing at Arizona. He continues to teach popular introductory literature classes today, nearly half a century after beginning his career.

With a series of books of poetry from the University of Pittsburgh Press in the 1970s, and with poems and prose pieces in more than two hundred magazines and journals, Shelton established himself as one of the leading celebrants of the harsh and exquisite landscapes of the desert Southwest. These books include *The Tattooed Desert* (1971), *Of All the Dirty Words* (1972), *You Can't Have Everything* (1975), and *The Bus to Veracruz* (1978). His *Selected Poems: 1969–1981* appeared from Pittsburgh in 1982. *The Tattooed Desert* won the International Poetry Forum's United States Award in 1970. More recently, his first book of nonfiction, *Going Back to Bisbee*, received the Western States Book Award for creative nonfiction in 1992. He published a collection of fictional vignettes, *The Other Side of the Story*, in 1987. Another volume of desert poems, *Hohokam*, was published in 1993. His public-education efforts on behalf of the desert include work on three projects for the University of Arizona Film Bureau: "Sonora: The Hidden Desert" (1980), "Another Day" (1981), and "The Sound of Water" (1982).

"Requiem for Sonora," collected here as a sample of Shelton's poetic articulation of environmental values, may be the single best-known poem about the Sonoran Desert. The poem personifies the desert, representing the wind as a small, lonely child wandering through canyons under moonlight, sleeves tattered by thorns. In the second stanza, the poet speaks directly to the desert, now addressing it as one might address one's lover: "Oh my desert / the coolness of your face." For those who think of the desert as a landscape of unremitting heat and dryness, references to water and coolness will seem surprising and misplaced—but for a person long familiar with desert reality, the cool of night and winter and the moisture of monsoon season are as significant as noon on a midsummer day, and perhaps more so. The poem continues, in section 2, to fret that the desert is becoming a "last resort / for tourists," resulting in the transformation and loss of all that belonged originally in this landscape, from coyote to ocotillo, to saguaro. The third and final part of the poem returns to the trope of speaking directly to the beloved desert, using language that might be appropriate for addressing a human lover. In addition to being a love poem, though, this is also a "requiem," a memorial to something either dead or in the process of dying. "Oh my desert," the piece concludes, "yours is the only death I cannot bear." In addition to several specific references to desert animals and plants and landscape features that show the poet's familiarity with details of place, the requiem-for-lover strategy produces a poignant combination of mourning and attachment, inspiring a sense of painful loss even for readers who may not be familiar with the Sonoran Desert. In his responses to John Daniel's questionnaire, Shelton emphasizes the importance of evoking sensory and emotional experience for readers of his work—"Requiem for Sonora" clearly does both.

Toward the end of his questionnaire responses, Shelton is particularly critical of our tendency in American society to over-emphasize the importance of economic concerns in our treatment of the natural world, our typical failure to value the spiritual and aesthetic qualities of nature. This is why we allow mining and ranching interests so much free rein in the West, he suggests. His own work, by contrast, disallows ownership. "Requiem" ends by stating that the speaker does not belong to the desert, nor the desert to him.

The second poem offered following the questionnaire responses, "Sonora for Sale," uses religious allusions to indicate that a kind of sacrilege occurs when we think of the Sonora (and presumably other places and phenomena in nature) as things that can be bought and sold, used for our own benefit. The phrase "dragging our feet like innocents" in the second stanza hints that we may think of ourselves as being innocent of any wrongdoing ("*like* innocents"), while in fact we are as culpable as "the guilty . . . [who are] in possession of everything." In "dragging our feet," we are moving too slowly to correct the mistakes of our society, to realize a new way of being in relation to the world. It is significant that Shelton uses the first-person plural pronoun, "we," in this poem, as it implicates himself and his reader in the economic mentality that is on the verge of destroying the desert. The third stanza yearns for a potent warning—unfortunately, the stars shine forth from the distant past, not from the future. It is the responsibility of the poet, using the rhetorical gentleness of the self-implicating "we," to notify his audience that "the desert / . . . is all we have left to destroy."

♦

QUESTIONNAIRE RESPONSES FROM RICHARD SHELTON

Richard Shelton mailed us his responses to the narrative-values question set; they are recorded verbatim here.

Q1: Why do you think you became a nature writer?
Shelton: I don't think I am a "nature writer." That is a very ambiguous term and what it means seems to depend on who is using it. Much bad writing falls into this category, as well as some superb writing. I consider myself a literary writer whose work often reflects the natural world in which I live. But I don't like to be pigeon-holed even in that way. My work reflects my passions—my loves and hates and needs. Many of those passions are rooted in the natural world. I feel passionately about the Sonoran Desert and hate passionately the forces that are destroying it. These passions naturally show up in my writing, both poetry and nonfiction. But I also feel passionately about people and often write about them as well.

Q2: Do you see your work as an attempt to articulate the value(s) of nature?
Shelton: I hate to be such a pedant, but again the term is a problem for me. I question "value of nature." How would a pantheist respond to this ques-

tion? I guess I'm some kind of modified or failed pantheist in the way I feel about the natural world. My feelings always concern specific places or flora or fauna. I believe in the numen of a place or plant or animal. That is, an indwelling spirit, a god. Consequently, my attitude toward many individual attributes of the natural world is a kind of worship. I can't talk about the value of a river or trees, even its aesthetic value, any more than the worshipper can talk about the value of the god worshipped. My response is, I fear, almost totally emotional. That's probably why my response to the natural world most often seems to channel itself into poetry, another slippery term.

Q3: Which statement is closer to the truth in your case, or are both true?
A. You write in order to express your sense of nature's value.
B. You derive a sense of nature's value from the process of writing.

Shelton: The first idea is by far more true for me, although again I quibble with the term "value." Perhaps I might modify it to say that I often write in order to express my worship of some place or part of the natural world. Or sometimes my fear of it. Or even, a couple of times, my hatred of it—the wind that batters us in the spring, or the heat of late June in the Sonoran Desert. But there is some sense of truth in the other statement as well. Often after I have decided to write about something or have been led to write about some element of the natural world, my appreciation of it will increase. Research, for me, is the most enjoyable part of much writing because it directly increases my ability to understand and draw closer to the thing itself. I guess the two statements, if modified a little, are complementary in my case.

Q4: What mode(s) of expression work(s) best for you in articulating the values of nature: Exposition? Argument? Description? Narrative? A combination? Please explain.

Shelton: Probably a combination, but it would depend on the particular piece of writing and its genre. In poetry, I depend on description and the image, exposition, and sometimes a small narrative. In nonfiction I depend largely on narrative and description, with sometimes some limited argument. I don't think argument in literature is usually very moving, however accurate it might be. This is perhaps one of the reasons that so much of what appears under the rubric of "environmental writing" is so hard to read and often so ineffective. I want, as a reader, to be shown rather than told. Narrative and the image (description), it seems to me, can be most effective. Some exposition is often necessary. Argument, I guess I will generally leave for the politicians and preachers.

Q5: Why is this mode the most successful? How does it appeal to/elicit understanding in the reader or listener?

Shelton: I'm interested in approaching the reader through his or her senses, rather than simply through his or her intellect. Sensory impact, like falling in love, can have a strong effect on one's attitudes and even behavior. Concrete imagery enters the mind through the senses. The more of the senses the image affects, the more effective it will be in general, although of course context often determines the image. A narrative, which is probably the basic element of all literature, is often little more than a series of images, which explains the power and appeal of film.

Q6: Do you feel that a responsive reader learns environmental values from your work, or that your work alerts the reader to values already held?

Shelton: Both, I hope. Readers have told me that a certain poem or prose piece made them see, really see, something they had passed a thousand times before but had never noticed or experienced. I consider this the ultimate tribute. To bring light, to open eyes, to show, perhaps not a theory or argument, but a thing. I feel that one of the major reasons we do not value the natural world enough to protect it is that we do not see it or experience it in enough depth and with enough impact. It seems to me that these concerns for the writer are both aesthetic and moral. Some are so much concerned with the moral that they lose track of the aesthetic. Consequently, the writing, however accurate and strongly felt it might be, has little impact.

Elsewhere, especially in the nonfiction book *Going Back To Bisbee,* I very deliberately use narrative to take the reader to a little-known river that is threatened and try, through description and narration, to make the reader fall in love with the river. I feel that this river can be saved only if enough people fall in love with it, as I am in love with it.

Q7: What do you see as the strengths and limitations of narrative as a carrier/elicitor of natural values?

Shelton: The term "narrative," in its broadest sense, is probably the basic element of literature, but that sense includes the fact that a single line of poetry often presents a little story, or even a word often contains an entire story. There are tiny seeds of narrative everywhere, and often they are not consciously noticed by the reader, but they are effective nonetheless. I think, as contemporary writers, we should produce contemporary narratives involving the natural world, but they should be informed by an awareness of earlier narratives, partly because these will give our own attitudes more depth and texture. If our narratives are informed in this way and include liberal doses of descriptive imagery and emotion, passion, humor, etc., they will have the best chance of presenting the natural world.

Q8: Has your sense of the importance of narrative changed over the course of your writing life to date? If so, how? If you didn't begin as a writer of narrative, how did it happen that you became one?

Shelton: I think I always had a strong feeling for narrative but have become more conscious of it since I began writing nonfiction seriously. When I started writing *Going Back to Bisbee*, I thought it would be mostly description and exposition. As I got into it, I realized (with the help of my astute wife) that the stories were the best part. Readers have agreed. Although the book contains a great deal of information about the natural and unnatural world and takes on both the ranching and mining industries, it is the stories that have caused it to be in its eighth printing and going strong.

Q9: Are there values that can *only* be told in and learned from narrative?

Shelton: It sounds to me like this question was loaded by a fiction writer. I don't think the elements of good writing can be divided that completely. I can't imagine good narrative without some description, imagery, and exposition. If the question means "good" narrative, that is, narrative including these elements, I would probably say yes, it is certainly an effective way to approach the natural world.

Q10: Can natural values be fully and accurately expressed in purely rational terms, or is there inevitably an emotive content?

Shelton: Probably, but not effectively. Scientists attempt this in certain contexts, but it will not interest most readers.

Q11: Is there inevitably an ethical or moral content to these values?

Shelton: Again I am troubled by "values." Many people, of course, have no ethical or moral attitudes in relation to the natural world. Others seem to have such attitudes instinctively. I am wondering if these attitudes (stewardship, etc.) are not the result of an aesthetic element—one's sensitivity to natural beauty or organic form or function. I don't think many children have such attitudes naturally, although I could be wrong about this. I know such attitudes can be taught, enhanced, encouraged, etc. I'm not sure I understand the question. Both ethics and morality vary from culture to culture.

Q12: Why are these values difficult for many people to express?
Shelton: Largely because many people don't have any such values to express. Otherwise, there are cultural reasons. It isn't fashionable. This last is changing, I believe. As with wolves, we learn to express our concern and value for things just as they are going out of existence. It is difficult for many people to express anything beyond what is necessary to survive and obtain sensory satisfaction. And many people who might otherwise try are put off, I believe, by much of the writing about nature today. It is simply so bad, and there are so few good models.

Q13: In your opinion or experience, what would be the best ways to elicit these values and identify them in people who may harbor them but find them difficult to articulate?
Shelton: At the bottom of this is the problem of sensitivity and feeling, passion. The question implies that these are already there, but somehow latent or undeveloped. I think what such people need is mostly exposure and some encouragement through good writing and good films. They are afraid to express their feelings because they feel ignorant, feel that they don't know enough about the subject. They have encountered a certain kind of writing about the natural world that stressed facts and figures, and they don't have any. I think exposure to some of the really good literature concerned with the natural world could lessen their insecurity and give them permission to express their feelings in largely subjective terms. I know that the work of Terry Tempest Williams has done this for many people. And I have received many letters saying, in effect, "Your poem about the desert gave me the courage to write my first poem, also about the desert, and here it is."

Q14: In your opinion, are these values "held," so to speak, or are they more closely integrated with one's being? Are they learned or innate?
Shelton: I think I answered this in my response to Question 11.

Q15: Do you believe that environmentally responsible behavior flows from having a conscious sense of the values of nature? From an unconscious sense? Or it there no reliable causal relationship between values and behavior?

Shelton: This is an incredibly big and difficult question, and it's like the chicken and the egg. Most environmentally responsible behavior probably flows from a conscious sense of the values of nature, but this conscious sense might be disguised by or included in other systems of belief, especially religious belief. Also, such behavior can probably flow from aesthetic sensitivity alone, which might be considered one of the unconscious senses. This question doesn't seem to take into consideration the idea of sensitivity at all, which I believe is innate in some people (although possibly learned at a very early age) and totally lacking in others. Without the basic sensitivity, the rest is, I believe, useless. If a person can't feel something for elements of the natural world, I think teaching is probably a waste of time. However, teaching and experience can certainly awaken and increase a dormant sensitivity to the natural world.

The highly touted positive environmental practices of many Native American tribes was, I feel, largely the product of their religious beliefs and world view. In matters that were not included in their religious beliefs, they were sometimes extremely insensitive to the environment.

Q16: Has your own sense of the values of nature changed over time? If so, how? Can you identify particular experiences that contributed to the change(s)?

Shelton: My awareness of that sense of value has changed and become more conscious and more clearly delineated, but I'm not sure my evaluation of nature has changed very much. I guess what I mean is my sensitivity. I've always had, I think, an aesthetic sense, and I have never been able to separate my feeling for beauty from my feeling for nature.

Perhaps because I was largely a solitary and lonely child, I turned to the natural world for whatever it was I needed. I was often threatened physically as a child, and I learned to hide by climbing a tree or burrowing into the tall weeds. My first encounter with the deep woods was incredibly powerful and my first experience with an ocean, which didn't happen until I was almost twenty, was cataclysmic. One of the worst things about growing old is that this raw-edged sensitivity has a tendency to wear down and become less shattering. So maybe in recent years, while my conscious, intellectual evaluation of the natural world has continued to increase and become more refined, my real feeling for the natural world is decreasing. It's much easier to embrace environmental causes than it is to be truly sensitive to a landscape or a tree or a toad.

Q17: Do you consider beauty a value of nature? If so, please hazard a definition of natural beauty.

Shelton: I've already answered this. My definition of natural beauty would be, probably, a very conventional one, and would apply just as well to art in general. It would vary with the beholder. It would have something to do with harmony, appropriateness, the apt integration of parts. Sometimes it would involve function as expressed by form, and sometimes it would include the element of surprise. It would please and excite. If I sound like I'm paraphrasing Aristotle, I probably am, only he said it much better.

Q18: Do you find more value (non-utilitarian) in some things and creatures of nature than you do in others? If so, what do you think accounts for the difference?

Shelton: Of course, and everything accounts for the difference. Probably part of it is cultural and part of it was determined by early experiences. If I was taught as a child that spiders were ugly, then they were and are ugly for me unless I have deliberately attempted to overcome this prejudice (and probably fear) and have taught myself to see their incredible beauty. But some things (like sunsets and mountains, etc.) appeal immediately to our conditioned idea of beauty, so they require less effort to appreciate. We instinctively prefer big, dramatic scenes with pleasing color contrasts, etc.

Most of this is learned, but some is learned later. When I first came to the Sonoran Desert I was very unhappy, having been drafted and sent, kicking and screaming, to this God-forsaken place on the Mexican border. The landscape frightened and repelled me. After I had been in that landscape a few months and had solaced my loneliness with its sunsets and vistas, I knew I needed it in a way I had never needed any other landscape. And that relationship has persisted now for forty years.

I have tried, again and again, to figure out why. Why this place. Why the desert. Perhaps it is as simple as acculturation, which isn't simple, of course. I was raised on the edge of the Great Basin Desert, in Boise, an artificial landscape made possible by great engineering feats of irrigation.

Then I went to college in West Texas, the northern Chihuahua Desert. All I had ever really known was desert or desert oasis. Without realizing it I had acquired a basic need for great space and vistas, for a certain quality of light, for sparseness of vegetation, for mountains at a distance, for certain colors, etc., and when I came to the Sonoran Desert, there it all was. It didn't take me very long to respond, even though my immediate situation, a draftee in the Army, was not the greatest. As soon as I was in a position to choose where I would live, I chose to stay.

Q19: Do rocks have rights? Trees? Whales? Planets? Is there a concept other than "rights" by which you prefer to identify the worthiness of natural things and creatures?

Shelton: The concept of "rights" exists only in the world of humans. In the natural world, the complex interrelationships are much too tight to admit such an idea. Each thing or creature exists because it relates in a certain place in certain ways with other things or creatures. Man is the only creature that doesn't seem to understand this and has, by means of technology, tried to remove himself from the system. The idea that we can confer "rights" on things of the natural world is frightening. The concept of "rights" is basically political. It has nothing to do with the natural world. Only humans have need of such concepts, since we insist on trying to function somehow outside of and beyond the natural world, pretending it and its principles do not exist. If we insist on discussing these issues in terms of "rights," it will not be the rights of the stones we are talking about, but our own.

Q20: Does wilderness have value in and of itself? To what extent is wilderness an objectively identifiable thing, and to what extent is it a category of mind projected onto natural surroundings?

Shelton: Perhaps this is a semantic issue. The definition of "wilderness" seems to be changing rapidly, as in Alison Deming's book, *The Edges of the Civilized World.* Or Ken Lamberton's *Wilderness and Razorwire* discusses the natural world as he finds it inside a prison, and calls it "wilderness." The government agencies entrusted with protecting "wilderness" in this nation have proven unworthy of our trust and we must fall back on other, less pristine definitions.

This is not to say that we should not fight on for those few areas remaining that are even semi-wilderness. But it is and will be a rear-guard action. Perhaps if we can understand the essence of wilderness as it is described by Deming, Lamberton, and others, we can apply it retroactively and come to cherish the small and limited as well as the large and pristine.

The strict and traditional notion of "wilderness" is becoming increasingly unreal, a dream, and that very dream is perhaps hampering its preservation.

Q21: How important is direct sensory experience of nature to having a sense of natural values and being conscious of those values?

Shelton: I don't think that without the direct sensory experience of nature one can be human. One cannot value or understand what one has not experienced.

Q22: Aldo Leopold wrote: "A thing is right when it tends to preserve the integrity, stability, and beauty of the biotic community. It is wrong when it tends otherwise." Do you agree? How would you modify his definition to better reflect your own view?

Shelton: It's a good if somewhat abstract and intellectual quotation. I agree with it intellectually, but it wouldn't influence my behavior.

Q23: Leopold wrote of the land community, by which he meant the entire biota in a place. Is community in some sense a natural value of your own? How so?

Shelton: Of course such ideas are legitimate and visible, if sometimes expressed in ways that seem to bore nearly everybody, even those who believe in them adamantly. The community must also include the human community (because it has the power) when it is involved. And when is it not involved? Perhaps a better union between aesthetics and activism would help bring the human community to a passionate feeling for the land community and the community of living things.

Q24: What is the most important value of nature, if you believe there is one?

Shelton: I suppose it is that without nature, nothing on this planet as we know it would exist, including us.

Q25: What is the least understood or appreciated value of nature? Why is it poorly understood or appreciated?

Shelton: I'm not sure I could pick out one. The way everything is dependent on everything also has not, until very recently, been well understood.

My most immediate problem is the concept of a desert as empty space. People don't want to look at empty space, but they are willing to throw their trash into it.

Q26: Do you believe that we have made progress toward a generally held land ethic—an ethical sense that values the things and creatures and systems of nature—since Leopold called for one in the 1940s? What do you see as the chief obstacles to such an ethic? How optimistic or pessimistic are you about our chances of realizing a land ethic?

Shelton: Yes, we have made some progress, but very little. The ranching and mining industries are still in control of the West. While they have lost a few local battles, they have not been curtailed on a national scale. Ranchers are still subsidized by the taxpayers. Mining laws still place everything at the mercy of the mine owners. The period of dam building seems to be over, but there is no agreed-upon plan to save the rivers.

Yet, there is much more interest in issues of the environment, especially in regard to forests, than there once was, although it seldom gets translated into political action. It takes a very long time to educate people so that their land ethic can be expressed with sufficient force to those in politics.

Q27: Is it a land ethic in Leopold's sense that we most need, or is it something else?

Shelton: Leopold's land ethic model might be a good place to start. A complete overhaul of our educational system would also help.

Q28: What piece of your work best expresses your sense of the value of nature?

Shelton: The poem "Requiem for Sonora."

♦

Requiem for Sonora[1]

1

a small child of a wind
stumbles toward me down the arroyo
lost and carrying no light
tearing its sleeves
on thorns of the palo verde
talking to itself
and to the dark shapes it touches
searching for what it has not lost
and will never find
searching
and lonelier
than even I can imagine

the moon sleeps
with her head on the buttocks of a young hill
and you lie before me
under moonlight as if under water
oh my desert
the coolness of your face

2

men are coming inland to you
soon they will make you the last resort
for tourists who have
nowhere else to go

what will become of the coyote
with eyes of topaz
moving silently to his undoing
the ocotillo
flagellant of the wind
the deer climbing with dignity
further into the mountains
the huge and delicate saguaro
what will become of those who cannot learn
the terrible knowledge of cities

3
years ago I came to you as a stranger
and have never been worthy
to be called your lover or to speak your name
loveliest
most silent sanctuary
more fragile than forests
more beautiful than water

I am older and uglier
and full of the knowledge
that I do not belong to beauty
and beauty does not belong to me
I have learned to accept
whatever men choose to give me
or whatever they choose to withhold
but oh my desert
yours is the only death I cannot bear

♦

Sonora for Sale[2]

this is the land of gods in exile
they are fragile and without pride
they require no worshipers

we come down a white road in the moonlight
dragging our feet like innocents
to find the guilty already arrived
and in possession of everything

we see the stars as they were years ago
but for us it is the future
they warn us too late

we are here we cannot turn back
soon we hold out our hands
full of money
this is the desert
it is all we have left to destroy

8

FROM IMAGE TO EVENT: CONSIDERING THE RELATIONS BETWEEN POETRY AND PROSE AS CONVEYORS OF ENVIRONMENTAL VALUES

Like Alison Deming and Gary Nabhan, John Daniel views the landscapes of the American West with transplanted eyes. Born in Spartanburg, South Carolina, in 1948, he moved west to attend Reed College in Portland, Oregon, in 1966. Caught up in the emotional and political hubbub of the late sixties, Daniel left Reed without his degree and spent more than a decade as a climbing bum in the Sierra Nevada, occasionally working on logging crews in southern Washington, and working for the railroad in Klamath Falls, Oregon. During these years, he was teaching himself to write poetry, in part by reading on his own and sometimes by corresponding with established writers, such as the poet William Stafford. During the late 1970s, Daniel became a "poet in the schools," supported by the State of Oregon to teach poetry to children in elementary schools in rural eastern and southern Oregon. A major turning point in Daniel's life occurred in 1982, when he was awarded a Wallace Stegner Fellowship in Creative Writing at Stanford University. He stayed at Stanford until 1988, teaching as a Jones Fellow in poetry and as a lecturer in Freshman English after the one-year Stegner Fellowship ended. Daniel left Stanford in 1988 and has lived in Oregon for the past decade and a half, first in Portland for several years and, since 1994, in the small town of Elmira, half an hour's drive west of Eugene.

At Stanford, Daniel came under the influence of such distinguished authors and teachers as W. S. Di Piero, Kenneth Fields, and Denise Levertov. But perhaps the deepest influence on Daniel's understanding of himself as a writer and as a person living in the West was distinguished novelist and essayist Wallace Stegner. Daniel and his wife Marilyn actually lived in a cottage on Stegner's property in Los Altos Hills during most of their years at Stanford. Under the guidance of his mentors at Stanford, Daniel developed the manuscripts of his first books, the poetry collection *Common Ground* (1988) and the book of essays titled *The Trail Home* (1992). In 1988, he also became the poetry editor of *Wilderness* magazine (the publication of the Wilderness Society); a decade later, he edited the volume *Wild Song: Poems of the Natural World*, pulling together selected pieces from *Wilderness*. A second collection of Daniel's poetry came out in 1994: *All Things Touched by Wind*. This was followed by *Looking After: A Son's Memoir* (1996), the story of Daniel's efforts to make a home for himself in the West and the story of his mother, particularly her decline into Alzheimer's after she came to live with John and Marilyn in Portland in 1994. Both *The Trail Home* and *Looking After* received the Oregon Book Award for literary nonfiction. Daniel contributed to Milkweed Editions' Credo Series in 2002 with the volume *Winter Creek: One Writer's Natural History*. He also collaborated with photographer Larry N. Olson on the book *Oregon Rivers* (1997).

In the following interview, Daniel discusses the linkages between values and narrative language from the perspective of a poet who often depicts specific moments of insight and an essayist who makes prominent use of anecdotes and specific scenes. Two of the important ideas expressed in the interview include his intuitive suggestion that values must be associated with emotions, and his argument that the human imagination is triggered by material experience, by the senses and the verbal approximation of sensory experience. He states, "If it's a value, it's worth something. And if it's worth something, you're going to have an emotional sense of that." In other words, we learn to recognize what's important to ourselves and to others by gauging the intensity of our emotional experience. At another point in the interview, echoing his essay "Some Mortal Speculations," from *The Trail Home*, he makes a practical claim about why story and imagery have such emotional salience for readers and listeners: "The imagination thrives on locality and material things and small things that you can grasp in your hands and turn and look at again."

The two samples of Daniel's writing offered here suggest the limitation of merely abstract, intellectual understanding of the environment in guiding human society to a sustainable, healthy relationship with the rest of the planet. "Remembering the Sacred Family," a piece from *The Trail Home*, argues that we must take to heart the admonitions that run through Native American stories, the philosophical statements of Emerson and Thoreau, and familiar contemporary writers such as Gary Snyder and Annie Dillard—the exhortation to *feel* our connectedness to the world, not merely to *know* it. He writes, "As long as the greenhouse effect is a story on television or in the *New York Times*, and not an absence of bread on our tables or the presence of salt in our drinking water, it is unlikely to prompt us to use fossil fuels twice as efficiently as we now do—the order of change necessary, some scientists are saying, to mitigate global warming." This sentence implies the importance of understanding something as physical, tangible reality, not merely as a dry concept. The Zuni story of Payatamu, the man whose daily ritual is responsible for the sun's rising, is a vivid example of connection between the human and the natural.

On the other hand, much of Daniel's writing is built from his own, primary experience—mundane, typical experiences that the writer casts as significant by way of his careful, vivid, emotion-laden language. It's not that the experiences he has are altogether different from those of another, ordinary person—it's just that he attends to them and to language itself with enough care to make the *value* of experience clear. Take the opening lines of his poem "Ourselves," from *Common Ground*: "When the throaty calls of sandhill cranes / echo across the valley, when the rimrock flares / incandescent red, and the junipers / are flames of green on the shortgrass hills. . . ." Words like "throaty," "flares," "incandescent," and "flames" imply not only physical phenomena, but emotional intensity and concern. The odd, yet fitting, description of juniper trees as "flames of green" indicates that the poet is not referring just to *literal* fire with his imagery, but also to fire of the mind, to emotion. The adjective "throaty," attributed to the voices of sandhill cranes, also seems to apply to a husky, heartfelt emotionality in the voice of the human speaker.

Because of Daniel's expertise in using imagery and story to convey his sense of environmental values and because of his proximity to the offices of Decision Research in Eugene, where Terre Satterfield was working when we began this project, we asked him to help us prepare a questionnaire for "nature writers" about the connections between narrative language and environmental values. As noted in the Introduction, three of the authors included in this book—Bruce Berger, William Kittredge, and Richard Shelton—responded in writing to Daniel's questionnaire. The questionnaire served as a loose foundation for the face-to-face conversations Satterfield and Slovic had with the other nine writers.

♦

A CONVERSATION WITH JOHN DANIEL

Scott Slovic and Terre Satterfield conducted this interview with John Daniel at the offices of Decision Research in Eugene, Oregon.

Slovic: Terre and I have sometimes characterized nature writers as lay ethicists, particularly environmental ethicists. One of the questions fundamental to this project is how does writing in the manner that you do permit you to express what you couldn't express using some other mode of delivery?

Daniel: Well, I've never used any other mode of delivery, except talking, I suppose. I was telling Scott that I don't want to exhort any more. I feel that I've done that in some of my essays—not all of them. I've written in a polemical mode. Somehow that seems archaic now, and it also emphasizes a polarization.

Satterfield: Is that because it reifies existing conflicts?

Daniel: Yes. Lately I seem to be drawn to more of a big-boat approach. There is plenty to blame on all of us—plenty of blame to go around, and plenty of changes that need to occur in the ways we live. I've also come to suspect that people turn off. If they want to be preached to, they go to church. Preaching can appeal, but at the same time, it activates an automatic resistance, I think, in a way that telling a story, without an overt didactic burden, does not. Story seems to entice an almost primal receptivity. I mean, we like to be told stories, we like to hear stories. We've always liked it, you know, long before writing. Story is a way to appeal to the generosity of a reader's imagination rather than the tracks of his or her conceptual thinking. And it puts us all together in a way. The story stands for all of us, the story is all of us. There's that implicit sense anyway.

Satterfield: Have you become uncomfortable with a polemic mode, what you referred to as an "archaic" mode, because of something you've come to feel for yourself, or has your audience changed?

Daniel: I guess I feel that the rhetoric is archaic—the rhetoric sounds archaic to me now.

Satterfield: It's just tired itself out in some ways?

Daniel: Maybe it's tired *us* out. We're trapped in our polarized discourse. But I also feel uncomfortable in that I'm fully implicated in the whole [ecological] catastrophe. I drive my car and truck, I turn on my lights when I want, I listen to my stereo, I live in a house made of fallen trees, I'm not using my life as a laboratory for environmentally responsible living. I do some things: I recycle, I take small conservation measures here and there. I write about this stuff, which I think is worth something. But nobody is in a position to preach, and also people are just numbed with word of disaster. Nobody wants to hear about the rain forest. I mean, I just heard on the radio coming in that there are two hundred more fires a day starting in Mexico. Two hundred a day. But what do you do? What you do is, you just shut down. I think polemic doesn't work because people don't hear it. You can talk about or imply the end of the world only so much.

Slovic: Is it a kind of sky's falling phenomenon? Because the sky hasn't fallen, so warnings cease to be meaningful. The world hasn't come to an end in the projected twenty-year period.

Daniel: The sky probably is falling. Global warming is happening. But somehow it's not going to work to call people to arms about that and pretend to know what will work. People don't want to feel invalidated in their lives and they don't want to feel that they bear the responsibility of the world on their shoulders. This is why you shouldn't teach kids about the dire straits of the rain forest. You should take kids to the stream out back and show them water striders. Just start where you are. Start with the tangible, the sensual. The imagination thrives on locality and material things and small things that you can grasp in your hands.

I mean, think of what we went through, are still going through, with the nuclear age. Who can even comprehend the danger? We need to be alarmed, and, yes, worry. But it doesn't begin with polemic. Polemic is almost a call to revolution. I guess I'm an evolutionist and not a revolutionist.

Satterfield: Can you elaborate a little further on your thoughts about presenting information in a polemical way, a form you described as restrictive, imaginatively speaking?

Daniel: Well, polemic tells you how you should think or feel and cracks the whip. It's constrictive. Stories suggest possibilities beyond themselves—they're not essentially about information. A story has a narrative life with people and possibilities working themselves out in some way and yet suggesting other ways the situation might have gone. It's expansive.

Slovic: What are the qualities that allow that to happen? What mechanisms are at play there that make it work in those ways?

Daniel: Fair question, and I'm not sure I can answer it. I'm not sure I know how it works. I'm just reasonably convinced that it does. When you listen to a story, if it's a decent story being told by a decent storyteller, you're inside it. I think the listener is invited inside the story. But when you're presented with information, you're not invited into anything. You've got facts out here. But the reader is not invited to participate in a drama.

Slovic: John, when you talk about multiple possibilities, are you thinking about providing story to audiences either electronically or with books that have multiple endings? The reader chooses the direction he or she wants. So on a more subtle level, there's room for the reader to imagine dimensions of the story that the writer may not have intended. That's where the reader becomes involved.

Daniel: No. I mean that Edward Abbey's stories in *Desert Solitaire* don't reduce to a single meaning or point. Electronic hypertext doesn't interest me. They talk about the tyranny of the author, but I *want* to be led by an author. I mean, if it's a story I'm responding to, I'm happy to be led. That doesn't mean it's a totally passive and helpless process—it can be very active. To be led doesn't mean you're bound, gagged, and blinded.

Satterfield: That's interesting. You seem to be suggesting a kind of tension, walking the fine line between leading somebody along and allowing the reader or listener to be active at the same time.

Daniel: It is that line, yes. Nobody likes to be bossed around. That's part of what's wrong with polemic, maybe—nobody likes the authoritarian aspect of that.

Satterfield: Where does journalism fit in here as a mode of presenting information? Stepping aside from more negatively charged terms like "polemic," much journalistic reporting is more narrative in style. Other writing tends toward a "just the facts" style.

Daniel: Journalism is always more interesting to me if the author is in it—infused into it as a distinctive voice, and in it as the personal pronoun "I." I mean, even if I dislike the author [laughs], that's more interesting to me. I want that sense of a human being observing things, working the material through his mind and feelings. When I've done journalism myself, that's what I've tried to do.

Slovic: I want to go back a little bit to our discussion of the language of critique and the language of confession. What may at first glance seem to be a finger wagging, a kind of supercilious relationship with an audience, might actually be a statement of complicity. Yet, it's also true that one of our archetypal narratives as a culture is the story of George Washington cutting down the cherry tree and then apologizing. It's a statement of confession: I admit I did this terrible thing. What I'm interested in is the phenomenon of confessing one's own culpability.

Daniel: Yes, it's as though the confession strengthens the faith of all concerned—like an AA meeting. Everybody tells their story, and that's a kind of strengthening of the faith.

Satterfield: How much of that is just an equalizer—you know, just saying that when it comes right down to it, you and I are the same and can therefore talk to each other? And how much of it is a way of saying, I'm not here to preach? I have these faults, and therefore I have no right to preach—so will you listen to me?

Slovic: I think one of the particular requirements for an author, though, in doing so is at once to demonstrate humanity and, at the same time, not to relinquish authority. You're still the person on stage, you're the person who has the right to speak on the occasion of producing this text, and so you need to be authoritatively confessional.

Daniel: You're the one that's speaking, whether or not you've got the right. You have to earn your authority, and I think confessing can strengthen authority. I think paradoxically you strengthen your authority by acknowledging your fallibility. I look for that in memoirs. I want to be in the presence of a narrator who says: I'm not sure I'm remembering this right, I'm not sure what I did was right. You trust that voice. That's the one you want to follow.

Satterfield: Is part of that creating intimacy or creating relationship with your imagined audience? Why does this make for a more effective exchange? Is it creating a relationship with you as author? You, the author, told me something about yourself, and I immediately can then imagine you as a real human being whom I like and therefore will listen to what you have to say.

Slovic: Does this apply to writing on any topic? Is it your goal somehow to convince your audience to agree with you? Generally as you enter a piece of writing, either fiction or literary nonfiction, would you feel better if your audience said, "Yes, you've explained it to me, that's what I already thought"? Or, would you prefer, "I used to think differently but you've changed my mind"?

Daniel: I don't really think mind-changing occurs in those terms. I think the kind of writing that I do, that nature writers do, can only help form the minds of people who already have an affinity and already have leanings in that way. I don't know if writing ever changes a person's mind. And so my goal isn't to make the reader agree with me; it's more a matter of showing. As with Joseph Conrad—"My task above all is to make you see." And he's talking about seeing in a very sensory sense, as well as in the sense of understanding. The goal is to body it forth in images, as wholly as possible.

Slovic: In the piece on Wallace Stegner in the paperback edition of your book *The Trail Home*, you write about encountering Stegner's "Wilderness Letter" early on in your life. You write, Stegner did not change my mind about wilderness, he *formed* it. What did you mean by the phrase "he formed it"?

Daniel: I meant that he gave words to it. Because when I read him I was new to the West. I was doing some mountaineering, some backpacking. I was kind of reveling in the wild West—an eastern kid kind of thing—and I loved it. But my love was unspoken. Wallace Stegner gave me one of the first embodiments of language that felt like it represented my love and enlarged my whole sense of wilderness as a historical force. Adrienne Rich says of poetry, "It is a way in which people can hear their own unspoken thoughts spoken." That's what it feels like—something really rings. If I hadn't found his language, I don't know—I suppose my love would have found other formulations. It's not like it wouldn't have found expression, but . . .

Slovic: Since then you've taken those formulations and spun off your own versions. But you needed an initial forming or framing in order to launch your own.

Daniel: Oh absolutely, absolutely. I mean, nature writing comes from experience, but it also comes from other writing. Sometimes it comes from reading more than from experience of nature.

Slovic: Well, do you think we, as a culture—people in general, non-writers—have a language appropriate for expressing how we feel about our experiences in the natural world? Do you have a sense that people have what they need, the raw materials of language, to express what's important about their experience?

Daniel: They probably have the raw materials, but they don't have the will or the real internal need to have it come from within. People at readings sometimes tell me they're grateful to have it expressed for them. That doesn't mean they don't have the raw materials. I guess it means they're not engaged with language in the way that a writer is. So, raw materials maybe, but most people are a long way from being able to make something freestanding out of that raw material.

Satterfield: This is a problem central to the study of environmental values. People may have the raw materials or perhaps strong feelings on the subject, but cannot articulate them and so fall prey to—or accept by default—purely scientific or economic arguments. Other categories or values become invisible. But maybe this is true more broadly. Perhaps there are even places where even you can't go with your writing. I'm thinking particularly in terms of expressions of values.

Daniel: You bet. Language is a blunt instrument. All it can do is lead one to the top of a small hill and point. And I think the most profound truths can be expressed only in paradox, and imperfectly at that. I usually think of music taking up where language leaves off; somehow it can reach places that perhaps words can't. I think everything is essentially inexpressible. That's kind of a funny thing for a writer to be saying, I guess.

Satterfield: Public discussions about a policy—say, a public meeting with representatives from a regulatory agency about how to manage a local estuary—are sometimes called, in academia, "value deliberation exercises." I often wonder whether people are able to say what matters most to them in these settings. So I'm wondering what you think about writing for a reader versus, say, a public reading or presentation, with an audience. How do these differ? How does writing a story down on a piece of paper compare to a reading where you've got a room full of people? Does something change in the way that story and meaning are conveyed—is one better than the other for deep thought about values?

Daniel: Reading aloud can bring a piece of writing to life, but by and large I think we're not good listeners. I'm certainly not. I go to readings, but I don't like them very much. The invention of writing probably ruined most of us as listeners. I think of literature more and more as a private relationship in which a reader engages with a writer in silence and solitude.

Satterfield: Maybe there's a similarity between story telling and thinking about values—the format or conditions under which a discussion is set up between value-elicitor and respondent is essential. Some conditions work better, create some kind of contemplative space that makes certain types of thinking permissible. I can't quite put my finger on it.

Daniel: I know, it's elusive, but it's genuine.

Slovic: It may be that when we hear a story that is presented to us that inevitably evokes some kind of powerful emotional response or probes our values or attitudes in some deep way, we want to be able to reflect on this in isolation and we don't know what to do when we're part of a large audience.

Satterfield: Let's talk a little bit about the emotion-values connection—it's come up a few times in our other interviews. For me, it seems important to ask whether it's possible to have a value without having emotional investment in it.

Daniel: I think it isn't. I have nothing to base that on, no philosophical argument about it, but I just don't see how it's possible. If it's a value, it's worth something. And if it's worth something, you're going to have an emotional sense of that. I'm not even sure that understanding is possible without an emotional content, an emotional excitation of some kind.

Satterfield: How does that work for you as a storyteller? How do you elicit—or do you consciously elicit?—that in the reader, an emotional investment in your subject matter, nature? Do you think of yourself as using certain vehicles to make that work?

Daniel: Not certain vehicles or forms. You elicit it in the reader by discovering it in yourself. I'm kind of new to storytelling. I mean, narrative's been this growing thing for me. But as any kind of writer you hope for the flash of discovery, something new, when you're going from tired phrasing to something unexpected that interests you. Something that elicits your own attention, you know, that you're somehow clarifying some circumstance, in a way that you didn't see it/feel it before. And the feeling just seems to come right with the seeing—the emotion seems to come right with the seeing. It only realizes itself as you go along. It's kind of like a groping, a nearsighted groping, without your contact lenses.

Slovic: Can you say a little more about being a newcomer to narrative?

Daniel: Yeah, I'm new to it as a sustained mode. My poems have been little narratives, a good many of them, and elements of essays have been narrative. There's only one thoroughgoing narrative in *The Trail Home*. It's a story about a packrat, the second essay in the book. My storytelling expanded from little bits of poems to streaks of poetic narrative and personal narrative in essays, then to a book-length narrative in the memoir about me and my mom, *Looking After*. Yeah, I feel like I'm just discovering story. I've just kind of given myself to it in the last few years.

I think I began to use narrative because I needed to tell stories by which to understand my life. I hit the biggest need in my forties, when I suddenly became interested in the past because I didn't fully understand the present. I hadn't cared much about the past before that time. Story, narrative myth, may be the only way that I'm capable of understanding my life. The point is not to document it or record it but to imagine it, by which I don't mean to make it less real, but to make it more real. To put it into images. I don't think a story really lives, for me, unless I have imagined it, unless I have put it into the language of the senses. In doing so, it inevitably becomes inaccurate in a documentary sense, but real in a mythic sense. So a story is myth in both senses—it's a story so true that you'd want to live your life by it, but it also contains myth in the other sense of factual falsehood.

Satterfield: Can you define a little more precisely what you mean by "narrative"? It's a word that we're using in a very fast and loose way during our conversations with writers.

Daniel: I think it means telling a story. But I guess the kind of narrative I'm talking about is personal narrative. It's the art of turning one's own experience into a story—a story that I'm telling for myself and for any interested reader. It involves, of course, a sequence of events, one thing leading to another. Like evolution.

Satterfield: You've also used the word "experience." How is that a key piece?

Daniel: Well, experience isn't a story—experience is simply a flux that has to be formed to make a story. Memory forms it—selects, sorts, adds, transforms—all of which we're perfectly unconscious of. Then the writer further forms memory's version of experience, shaping it into scenes and summary, into narrative. The key tool here is imagery, the language of the senses. The "itch of haydust in the sweaty shirt and shoes"—that's an image from a Gary Snyder poem. It's sensory imagery, more than anything else, that activates the reader's imagination. Images supply the verisimilitude that gives a very artificial written construction—though we call it nonfiction—the spirit of life.

Satterfield: How do you manage trying to include information in a story you're telling? You must commonly encounter that problem.

Daniel: Yeah, I manage it, or hope I manage it, gracefully! I'm just writing a very little essay about an intermittent stream where I live. We have a little creek bottom through part of our acre, and I'm getting to know that stream a little. I write about its sounds and how it starts up in early November when the rains come and about going out on the deck to hear its kind of silvery lilt from down there. The sound of water flowing again.

Then I tell how in February 1996 the little stream turned into a thirty-foot-wide torrent—it was really flooding. The house wasn't threatened—we sit high and were thrilled by it, just like I'm thrilled by thunderstorm and surf. But that little flood was eroding the creek bottom where I'd broken the sod for gardening. And then I say, at that time soil was moving all over the state of Oregon, sometimes massively, sometimes catastrophically, a lot of it set loose by clearcuts and logging roads. Within these passages are bits of information about soil movement during other flood events, how in the flood of 1964, more soil moved in two hours than in the next thirty years combined. It's episodic and catastrophic. I don't say it like this in the essay, but I go into that and it seems kind of a natural movement. Then I take it back to my place where I start thinking, hmm, what can I fairly ask of this creek bottom? What do I owe it? You sort of move back and forth between the personal and the broader information.

Satterfield: I'm a little confused here. In talking about information infused in narratives, we've talked about myth as well as the importance of bringing information to life but not necessarily working with un-truths.

Daniel: Well, a myth is story truth. A myth is not the news from the newspaper, but the real news. It's a lens, you know—it's experience seen through the lens of who you are now. A lens clarifies some things and distorts others. It puts a frame around what the reader sees. Ed Abbey is not telling the documentary truth of his experience in *Desert Solitaire*. He's not a journalist. He's a literary artist.

This is a very contentious topic, of course. There are a lot of honorable people who disagree on what kind of myths or falsehoods a writer can introduce.

Slovic: It's contentious in an acute way in the environmental context where you have people who have various types of quantitative or hard information—hard facts from various perspectives, economists, political scientists, ecologists. And then you have what Garrett Hardin calls "the merely eloquent." In the book *Filters Against Folly*, he cautions against placing too much stock in the merely eloquent who might lead us astray with beautiful words and ideas that are not rooted in some kind of material knowledge.

Daniel: Well, as a reader you're always at the mercy of a writer. But I think we sense when we're being led astray, when we can't trust the authority of the writer. We're all capable of being fooled, of course. When you read a story, you enter a kind of wilderness. There's no nature trail with signs. [Laughs.] I mean, if it's going to elicit your full human being, you're liable to see some things that aren't there, be shown some things you're not sure of. But many nature writers are coming at it from more of a science-writing angle. They have, and of course should have, an allegiance to things as they saw them. Myself, I draw on science and try to get it right, but I'm not a scientist or a naturalist. I'm talking more about narrative essay or memoir, where personal narrative is the main vehicle.

Slovic: In your recent work, you've pivoted from a more journalistic and philosophical kind of nature writing toward the genre of memoir. But nature remains a prominent part of what you're writing about, in addition to the personal stories. How is it that you came to be a so-called "nature writer"?

Daniel: That's a good question, but I don't know how to answer it. I would say it would be worth hazarding a story to find out. That's how I would approach it. I would start with memory, that's all I have—perhaps one early memory of being a kid in Charlotte, North Carolina, eating dirt in the backyard. My mother came out and put a stop to that. I was eating nature. It would be really interesting to write a personal essay, a narrative essay about that. That could be very valuable to me. I might understand all sorts of things, even if I was remembering them inaccurately.

I also think it had something to do with being a solitary kid. I kind of liked to just kick around in the woods by myself. I was in the woods looking for secret caves, buried treasure, and stuff like that, but nature was working on me. There was an affinity. When I came west, I fell in love with mountains, open spaces, rocky coast. I dropped out of college and hiked and climbed. It's as though adventuring in wilderness awakened my own wildness. Then in the seventies I moved to south-central Oregon and stayed ten years. That sagebrush steppe country was the first landscape I slowed down enough to really see, and it's where I began to write. I was born as a writer there.

Since then, I've written to express my sense of nature's value, but I've also derived my sense of nature's value from the process of writing. It's always both. If I had a fully realized sense of nature's value, I probably wouldn't write at all. I'd probably just sit on my back deck and enjoy that realization.

Slovic: That's interesting because typically, in social science, a pool of study respondents might be asked to express or articulate what they value, rather than explore it or wrestle with it through writing. The oddity is that there is so much artificiality in this task. The research community treats ordinary groups of respondents, non-writers, as if they have a more fully realized sense of value than people who devote their lives to exploring this.

Satterfield: Yes, such tasks do assume that ordinary people have at their fingertips fully formed ideas on the subject, while it might be wiser to develop a process that allows people to build or construct their ideas about nature as they go. There is a growing literature on this, generally known as "constructed preferences." But how to "construct" or "build" a more ethically focused deliberation on value is a very difficult problem.

I'm wondering what you think, as a teacher of writing, is easier for people to do. Is it more manageable for the average, non-literary person to construct his or her own stories or simply to respond to questions or other sorts of prompts in order to think through value positions?

Daniel: It's easier to respond to the questions and prompts, but it might be more worthwhile to have them construct their own. It's always easier to work off of something that's there. But you might not be getting all the way to the seat of their values.

Satterfield: When I elicit narratives from study participants, I tend to get romantic or stereotypic stories—protagonists who are overly heroic, prose that is clichéd.

Daniel: That's a good point. What you're getting is what I see from students, first drafts of essays and poems that are full of clichés. They're still on the surface, using that prefabricated language—chunks of meaning and actual phrases. They haven't yet found their own way. They might need a quarter or a semester to work on a piece.

Satterfield: But this kind of time investment is not an option for most policy studies and researchers, so I'm eager to find the means—through writing or whatever structure or medium—for people to explore the value basis of their positions more fully.

Slovic: What about specific environmental values? One of your questionnaire items is: Do you consider beauty a value of nature?

Daniel: Beauty may be the chief value of nature. I like Robinson Jeffers, who says, "The greatest beauty is organic wholeness, the wholeness of life and things, the divine beauty of the universe." I think in terms of beauty as wholeness, and of art recapitulating nature. I think all artists are interested in making whole things—wholeness is what we're about.

Slovic: What about the idea of the rights of nature? Do rocks have rights?

Daniel: I don't like the idea of rocks having rights, or trees or whales, for that matter. "Rights" is just so human a term. It's a legal term. It's something that's defined by, dispensed by, others. It seems very imposed. Nature's not a body politic.

Slovic: Do nonhuman things have ethical standing, then, and are human beings compelled to act within an ethical framework when their behavior will have an effect on nonhuman things?

Daniel: Sure. But I guess I see it as more religious than legal. It's not because natural phenomena have rights, but because of their innate value. You can call it "rights," "natural rights." But somehow that just isn't what it's really about. Things in nature have value and they have necessary standing in our valuations, but rights can be taken away, too. Most people are afraid of losing their rights.

Satterfield: What about wilderness and the value of wilderness, a very contested idea of late? To what extent is wilderness an objectively identifiable thing and to what extent is it a value category that we have projected onto certain landscapes?

Daniel: It's both. There seems to be a lot of debate about wilderness theory right now, but for me, it's important not to lose sight of the objective thing, which is the original gift—of which we are a part, of course. I'm thinking of the world as given to us, as distinct from the world as we've transformed it. Wilderness, I guess, can be a lot of things, but it seems to me it always has to come down to land and life as unfettered as possible, places we leave alone. We're getting kind of idea-heavy when we talk about wilderness. That's fine. But it's also land, it's also creatures, it's stuff, matter, matter, contact! [Pounds desk.] There it is.

Slovic: How does Aldo Leopold's notion of a biotic community that encompasses more than human beings fit into this context? He used the phrase "Land Ethic." Does it help at all to use a term like "community" if we're trying to understand how to extend the ethical context beyond humans?

Daniel: For me, "community" is a little like "rights." It's an apt metaphor, useful, but also limited. I like "commonwealth" a little better. The land and life in any one place is the common wealth. "Community" is probably a little too orderly for the stuff of nature, which is full of—is based upon—killing and extinctions. "Community" sounds too much like a human environment. I don't think we'll ever improve our relationship with nature by imagining it in political terms.

Satterfield: So, whether you're talking about community or rights, or some of the other current phrases, it seems that the language still isn't quite apt or that language about nature and values is changing. I mean, many of these terms are not very old, but already there is a sense of discomfort about them. It's interesting to me how quickly we start to evolve a resistance to certain kinds of characterizations.

Daniel: It may just be the inexactness of language—any metaphor is insufficient. I mean, it's all metaphorical, each term has an aptness. But evolution is the thing. We won't stop, we won't reach one way of expressing things and quit. "Community" goes way back. I mean Leopold was using that idea in the thirties and forties, and writers before him probably were as well.

Back to the question about Leopold and his idea of the "Land Ethic." There are localities where people are consciously trying to live according to a land ethic, and I admire them. But for the greater society, no, this concept wouldn't mean much. I used to be more disturbed by this, but I'm now convinced that nothing humans do is going to totally scuttle the experiment of life on Earth. It's going to proceed regardless of us. And as Stephen Jay Gould said, it has always been the Age of Bacteria. We'll just start all over again. David Brower told a joke about one slime mold saying to another (in the cracks in a rock, with the nuclear clouds rising in the distance): "Next time, no brains!" [Laughs.] I actually draw some pleasure from that thought.

Satterfield: Let me ask you a different question: Is it better to proceed with notions of a land ethic or wilderness ethic, or is it better to aspire to good versions of occupied territory or of occupied land? I think one of the authors we've spoken with made a point about managed landscapes—Tuscany or Provence—examples of places that are beautiful and natural in some ways, but profoundly managed and unnatural as well.

Daniel: Absolutely. We'll never be able to protect and defend anything we want to call "wilderness" if we don't find sustainable ways of living in the land we do inhabit. Look across the landscapes of America and you see, in various ways, land chewed up by this organism—made of us—that we call "the economy." We've got wilderness protected by law for now, but not much, and that can be changed in the blink of an eye. If we decide that the commodity value in wilderness is greater than our sense of value in the landscape as is, then designated wilderness will be undesignated. What's more, global warming and acid rain do not respect wilderness boundaries. If we don't come to terms with the ways we live, anything worthy of being called wilderness just won't be there. But I don't want to abandon the idea of wilderness, big wilderness, either. We don't have to live everywhere or even go everywhere. There are creatures that require wilderness. We should have the good manners to leave them alone.

♦

Remembering the Sacred Family[1]

The milky light returns. It comes imperceptibly into the openness of the field. Imperceptibly, in stillness, the trunks and limbs of the oaks begin to define themselves, to emerge from the vagueness of shadow into their curving distinction. Certain birds know the change before I do—their restrained, almost solemn chirping is what wakens me, and looking out the bedroom window, I see the light is on its way.

It comes every morning, this miracle, and I rarely see it. Usually I sleep well past dawn; when I go outside the light has already arrived, complete and unremarkable. I go about my business, noticing from time to time the warmth or the cold, the brightness or lack of it, but by and large as unconscious of the solar radiance I move through as of the ground I walk on. The sun is something I assume. It happens outside my being, with my awareness or without.

Recently, though, I read about a man with a very different view of the sun. In a Zuni story translated by Dennis Tedlock, a medicine man named Payatamu goes out every morning to a shrine on a rock where he brings up his Sun Father. One morning as he walks to perform his ritual, a witch girl tries to entice him into her field. "He's going to come up anyway," she says, "just the way he's been coming up. " Payatamu replies, "No, it's because of me that he comes up."

Out of context, his remark may be taken as anthropocentric arrogance—the sun is subservient to human will. But that is not Payatamu's meaning. He goes to bring up his Father not with a sense of self-importance but in a spirit of duty and humility. He goes every morning. This particular day he wavers, however, and he and the girl agree to play a high-stakes game of hide-and-seek, the loser to die at the winner's hands. Payatamu sprinkles a cornmeal road and follows it up to his Sun Father, but the girl finds him and cuts off his head. The Sun says, "I must go in at once, for I've been coming up because of you." The ritual practice is broken, and disaster falls. The world lies dark.

Our own culture tends to dismiss such ritual as based on a primitive understanding of life. But in fact it is primitive only in the sense of *primary*—of or connected to first things. Payatamu, in his ritual of dawn, takes part in a primary reciprocal relationship with the sun. He and his people are dependent on its light and warmth. The corn they grow, the deer they hunt, they themselves cannot exist without it. Mysteriously, it fills their human needs, and so Payatamu does his part to keep it rising. He believes that its beneficence occurs because human beings, through proper thoughts and words and practices, approach it with humility and reverence. In short, he does not take the sun for granted. Until the morning of his fatal wavering, he takes responsibility for the sunrise.

We, in our reasonable way, take no such responsibility. Like the girl in the story, we think the sun is going to come up anyway. We understand the recurrence of light and dark to be a mechanical regularity of the planet's rotation. Nature goes on, we assume, regardless of our attention or inattention. And we go a step further. Consciously or unconsciously, we assume that nature will go on even if we actively abuse it, forcibly extracting its "raw materials" and pouring into it the poisonous waste products of our industrial civilization. We have inflicted this assumption on North America for four centuries now, justifying it in the name of such values as comfort and progress. We have created and sustained what we like to call a high standard of living. But the environmental dysfunctions we have caused and contributed to provide ample evidence, if evidence did not exist before, that it is our own understanding of life that is primitive, in the sense of crude or naive.

There is nothing naive about the message of the story of Payatamu: a human falters in his responsibility to the nature that sustains him, and as a result he dies and the world is threatened. That story is a culture's way of reminding itself—through its oral tradition, one generation to the next—of a truth it can't afford to forget. Our own European cultures must once have carried similar stories with similar themes, but we have for the most part left those stories behind, along with our sense of responsibility. The truths they once told have dissipated to bland generalities without force to guide our lives—"You can't fool Mother Nature," for instance—and have been bastardized to such purposes as selling margarine on television. We Americans, like other industrialized peoples, appreciate the natural world, but what we appreciate is not our interconnection with it. We tend to value it with a sentimental aestheticism, as something beautiful or peaceful or magnificent, or with the residual pride of our frontier experience, as the formidable foe against which we struggled and prevailed.

As we subdued the continent with our technological genius and burgeoning numbers, cautionary voices were raised by observers who saw in nature not just beauty or fearsomeness but also our kinship with it. The writings of Henry David Thoreau, George Perkins Marsh, and John Muir aroused an ecological conscience that helped bring to birth the modern conservation movement. From the beginning, however, the character of that movement has been minority and reactive. It has necessarily fought rear-guard campaigns against the excesses of our exploitive civilization, trying to save this stretch of wild river and that threatened forest, and more recently, trying to hold air and water pollution within certain limits. Conservation has not set our society's agenda; it has had all it could do to defend against it.

In the twentieth century, one conservation writer above all others tried to give the movement a broad philosophical view and a positive vision of what it needed to achieve beyond its reactive skirmishing. Aldo Leopold, writing fifty years ago, argued that humanity's expanding ethical concern needed one further expansion. We have advanced from the day when humans could own other humans as property, he noted, but land—which in Leopold's usage includes the entire biota—is still considered mere chattel, affording its owner privileges but entailing no obligations. The next step in the evolution of ethics, Leopold said, must be an ethical relationship between humans and the land. We must come to see the land as a community to which we belong, not a possession at our disposal. Calling such a land ethic "an evolutionary possibility and an ecological necessity," he believed it existed in his own time in embryo and saw mixed signs of its chances for development.

Had he lived into the sixties and seventies, Leopold would have been heartened by that period's bloom of environmental awareness and the landmark legislation that resulted. Had he lived into the eighties, he would have lost heart as he saw many of the earlier gains stalled or reversed under the Reagan administration's malign stewardship. If he were alive today, he would see America still squandering its resources—strip mines still ravaging the Appalachians, the Mississippi still carrying far too much topsoil out to sea, the western mountains being sheared of their trees at a rate he would have found unbelievable. And aside from what we are taking from the land, Leopold would have been stunned by what we are returning—toxic fumes to the sky, corrosive rain killing trees and lakes, rivers and groundwater laced with carcinogens, sludge dumps along our coasts, marshlands poisoned by agricultural runoff, and the atmosphere slowly warming around us as the overheated engine of industrial society roars on.

The chief incentive for change, Leopold hoped, would be humanity's growing awareness of its connectedness to and dependence on the natural world, as revealed by the science of ecology. And, in fact, the ideas of ecology have gained a certain currency since Leopold's time. The two Earth Days have done much to plant them in the public's mind. They are taught in schools and appear in media stories. "Our Fragile Planet" has made the cover of *Time* magazine. But for most of us, ecology remains *only* ideas, topics we read about and absorb from television and occasionally discuss at dinner. Like the sunrise, they remain effectively outside our lives, which continue, by and large, to follow the course of least resistance. We may believe in a land ethic, but we aren't living a land ethic.

It's possible that the threat of environmental calamity will scare us into changing our ways. The specters of dead forests and rising oceans and skin cancer may cause us to veer from the way of life that produces such consequences. But our tendency is to see environmental problems as either remote from where we live or remote in future time. If the trees in our neighborhood seem healthy enough, acid rain is an abstraction. As long as the greenhouse effect is a story on television or in the *New York Times,* and not an absence of bread on our tables or the presence of salt in our drinking water, it is unlikely to prompt us to use fossil fuels twice as efficiently as we now do—the order of change necessary, some scientists are saying, to mitigate global warming. We economized for a short time in the seventies, but only because gasoline wasn't in the pumps. When it returned, so did our profligate energy habits.

Industrial civilization is sustained by a powerful inertia. Businesspeople tend not to abandon practices that bring profit. Consumers tend not to repudiate the comforts, conveniences, and spendthrift ways of a society used to abundance. And politicians, with few exceptions, tend not to arouse prosperous businesspeople and comfortable consumers. To those who prod them they say, "I care about the environment," or "I am an environmentalist," as if all questions were answered by saying the word, and the public tends to let it go at that.

Much of the inertia that thwarts environmental concerns is a function of what we call "the economy." In our ordinary speech we liken it to an organism with a life of its own. We speak of it as strengthening, weakening, heating up, cooling off, being slowed or stimulated, being healthy or depressed. We pay obsessive attention to this organism, and we zealously encourage its growth. Higher gross national product, higher profits, higher Dow Jones averages, more jobs, more housing starts, upturns in the "leading economic indicators"—these we equate with progress, health, and a better future, and nothing seems to make us realize that the growth we worship is fueled by finite resources and spews its dangerous wastes into a biosphere with finite powers of absorption. Few are teaching us that in the human economy, as in the economy of nature, growth within limits is health while growth without limits is disease. The symptoms of our irresponsibility are multiplying, but the growth economy remains virtually sacrosanct.

Even among environmentalists, the growth economy is a blind spot. Conditioned into the movement's reactive mode, we tend to find fault with outside entities—oil and timber corporations, polluting utilities or chemical plants, the Forest Service and other public agencies, agribusiness. Those entities have plenty to be faulted for. They need to be confronted and their irresponsible actions curtailed. But everyone who uses wood and paper products and consumes electrical energy and drives cars and eats the produce of corporate farms and blindly invests money for the highest return is accomplice to the excesses of the growth economy. As environmentalists we attempt to restrain it. To the extent that we consume in the habitual American way, we feed it. The organism is made of all of us.

It's true that environmentalism has successfully halted or curbed some depredations of the growth economy. But it's also true, and maybe in the long run more significant, that the fortunes of environmental organizations are substantially linked to the fortunes of the economy. When times are prosperous—at least for the middle and upper classes that traditionally form the environmental constituency—membership and contributions are high. When the economy enters a recession, as in 1990, membership and contributions fall off. Even among many of those sympathetic with its goals, environmentalism is seen not as a necessity but as a luxury, one of the first to be dispensed with when times are hard. Whether the environmental cause can succeed in this country with that basis of support—and with the movement's vitality, as measured in numbers of members and dollars, dependent on the vitality of the very growth economy that makes environmentalism necessary—is questionable at best.

The problem is that we as a people do not fundamentally believe that our excesses will do us harm. Native American cultures, by contrast, were constantly reminding themselves of that truth. A story from the Wasco people, collected by Jarold Ramsey in *Coyote Was Going There,* tells of a young man who is visited by a spirit Elk. The Elk empowers the boy as a great hunter, promising to provide for him in every necessity. In return, the boy must kill only what he needs, not more. But the boy is prodded by his human father into killing all the elk in the countryside, five entire herds. He even tries, without knowing it, to kill his own spirit Elk. The Elk draws the boy deep into a lake, where he sees the spirits—in the story they are called persons—of all the animals he has slaughtered. The Elk rebukes him for breaking their pact and abandons him. The boy is cast out of the lake, goes home to explain his guilt to his gathered friends, and dies.

I have omitted much of the plot's complexity—in particular, the boy's divided allegiance between the spirit Elk and his human father, which gives his fall a tragic dimension—in order to distill what I understand to be the cautionary point: if you kill more animals than you need to live, you will die. Like Payatamu in the Zuni story, the boy breaks a reciprocal bond with nonhuman nature, and disaster results. And like the Zuni tale, the Wasco story was told through generations because it carried wisdom the tribe couldn't afford to forget.

Such wisdom doesn't arise from a vacuum. Indians were, and are, no more innately gifted with ecological awareness than we are. The people who walked into a New World twelve to thirty thousand years ago doubtless brought with them a heritage of customs and traditions, but they also may have come with something of the irresponsibility that European settlers later brought with them. The existence of stories like that of the boy and the Elk suggests that early Indians may have committed excesses amid the seemingly infinite abundance of North America and won their wisdom through hard experience. But the Indians had a great expanse of time in which to learn responsibility, and were sufficiently limited in population and technology that they and their environment could recover from their mistakes. Our own situation is more precarious. If we can't find a way to teach ourselves and remember through time our own reciprocal bond with nature, we are capable of doing enormous damage to our world and ourselves.

But how can we learn the wisdom we need? If environmentalism remains a minority reactive force, if Leopold's land ethic has evolved as idea but not substantially as practice, if our economy stifles environmental values, if our own cultural heritage is inadequate to guide us, where will wisdom come from? I don't know. It may be that we will learn only through the experience of catastrophe. But possibly we may learn in a less bitter, dangerous, and stupid way. It will not happen by means of reactive environmentalism alone, important as that is. It will require something more than popular awareness of the ideas of ecology. I believe that to realize the ethical relationship to land that Leopold envisioned and Indians have lived, we need to rediscover—and perhaps are rediscovering—a religious relationship to the natural world.

Black Elk Speaks, the story of an Oglala Sioux warrior and seer, begins like this:

> It is the story of all life that is holy and is good to tell, and of us two-leggeds sharing in it with the four-leggeds and the wings of the air and all green things; for these are children of one mother and their father is one Spirit.

Like Leopold, Black Elk sees land as a community to which humans belong. But he sees a particular kind of community—one of relationship by birth, a family. And it is a sacred family, whose mother is Earth and whose father is Spirit.

In Black Elk's words, as in the stories of Payatamu and the boy and the Elk, ecologically responsible behavior is implicit. You cherish all natural beings as you cherish your human family, for all are sisters and brothers, and all are manifestations of divinity. You are no more likely to injure the Earth than you are to injure your mother. If the Sun is the Father who sustains you, you will take pains to keep him rising. Every act required to maintain human life is of religious significance, undertaken with humility and reverence; every act embodies a complex understanding of humanity and nature evolved through thousands of years in the land of this continent where the rest of us are green newcomers. Taught in story, song, and ritual through generations, reciprocal responsibility with nature is assumed and thoroughly practiced.

To say this is not to idealize traditional Indian cultures. Those societies had severe limitations. Their people were acquainted with hardship and evil. But they had—and, insofar as traditional cultures survive, still have—an ecological awareness far superior to our own. In this regard, their traditions have much to teach us, and our situation is sufficiently grave that we should care very much about learning it. We are not likely to solve our ecological problems until responsible behavior becomes as immediate and deeply rooted in our culture as it was among the Indians. And that will only happen, I believe, when we regain a religious sense of nature akin to theirs.

The point is not that we should learn the Sioux language and perform the Sun Dance, or that we should plant corn in dry places and sing it up with Zuni songs and rituals. We can't simply borrow another culture's religious sensibility, evolved through ages, as we borrow a coat. Nor is it crucial to believe that certain words and actions cause the sun to come up. But it is very crucial to understand the sensibility from which such words and actions flow, to understand that the continuance of life depends on the thoughts, words, and acts of each of us, just as the rising of the Sun depended on Payatamu's daily pilgrimage, just as the boy's power depended on his honoring the pact he made with the spirit Elk.

An understanding of land as sacred and familial is obviously foreign to our secular worldview, and it may seem foreign to the Judeo-Christian tradition that forms the mainstream of what religious life we have. But as Wendell Berry has argued eloquently for years, Christians who hold the creation in contempt are not following Scripture but defying it. One can't serve God by misusing or destroying His work. What's more, the Christian mystical tradition, ranging back through Julian of Norwich, Hildegard of Bingen, and Saint Francis of Assisi, affirms the oneness and sacredness of nature in a way that Black Elk would have understood. Our European ancestors for many centuries felt themselves to be part of a cosmic chain encompassing all

Being. And far deeper in the past, before the Christian era, our forebears were tribespeople who saw a holiness around them to which they felt themselves somehow akin. The sense of the sacred family is not something new and unattained, like Leopold's land ethic. It is both a cultural relict and a latent possibility in us all.

More than a possibility. In a diverse variety of forms, the sense of the sacred family is very much alive today in this country and the rest of the industrialized world. It is present in the life and work of Wendell Berry, and in others who find in Christian tradition both the justification and the necessity of responsible ecological behavior. It is present in the concept of Gaia, the living organism of Earth, developed as a scientific hypothesis by James Lovelock and embraced as a religious as well as scientific idea by thousands of his readers. It is present in the revival of interest in ancient pagan rituals and healing practices associated with the Goddess. It is present in the work of Gary Snyder, and in others who express in the terms of Eastern religions their sense of divine immanence and the kinship of all being. It is present in the American nature religion of Emerson, Thoreau, Whitman, and Muir, mutated and re-expressed in the twentieth century by such poets and writers as Robinson Jeffers, A. R. Ammons, and Annie Dillard. It is present in the broad biocentric view through time of the deep ecologists. It is present in the spiritual dimension of the Green and ecofeminist movements. And it is present in thousands, perhaps millions, of individuals such as myself whose experiences of the natural world have a religious character that calls for expression but seems to fit no established form.

I don't suggest that these various religious manifestations can be reduced to the same belief, but they have much in common with each other and with American Indian religions: a sense of the sacredness of nature, a view of humanity as one life form related to all others, and a recognition of our need to assume responsibility toward the nonhuman world. Taken together, these modern versions of the sacred family may constitute an emerging spiritual rediscovery of ourselves and nature. And such a rekindling of our religious imagination, it seems to me, is as important to our future as any amount of letter writing, lobbying, demonstrating, or direct action, because it represents a potential change of the magnitude I believe we need. It represents a force, very likely the only force, that stands a chance of overcoming our prevailing secular religion—our orthodox and primitive belief in the growth economy and the unlimited development of technology.

When those givens are called into question, the cry immediately goes up—even from many who are sympathetic toward environmental causes—

that we can't go back to the life of an earlier time, that anyone who suggests such a thing is a simplistic Luddite. It is true that we cannot wholly abandon our present way of life, and we do not need to. But in this century we have reached the point where the dangers of continued economic growth and technological development have begun to outweigh the benefits. To acknowledge this is only realistic. And isn't it simplistic to assume that the cure for the troubles caused by growth and development will be found in more growth and more development? Sometimes, as anyone who has lost a trail in the forest knows, going back to find your way again is the most practical thing to do. Sometimes it is the only thing to do.

And paradoxically, to limit voluntarily our economic growth and technological power, to relinquish some of our control over nature in order to join it again, would not weaken us. It would empower us. In withdrawing from the sacred family, we have not only shed its responsibilities, we have also lost its privileges. The cost is the loneliness of our disconnected state, the great bereavement of no longer knowing ourselves at home in the natural matrix that gave us birth. True power comes from relatedness. Where is the power among us, in all our expertise and technological might, to equal that of Payatamu, who participates in the mysteriously benevolent power of the sunrise? What we can only watch from the bare room of our rationality and greet with a diffuse aesthetic response, Payatamu is part of.

In the Zuni story, the world lies dark after Payatamu is beheaded by the witch. Until his body can be found and restored and his ritual practice renewed, the Sun Father won't rise. Payatamu's brothers know they won't be able to find him by themselves, and so, in humility, they ask the help of their grandfathers who live in all the directions—mountain lion, bear, badger, eagle, vulture, true coyote, juniper coyote, and crow. Each searches and fails, and then the brothers ask their "father who lives at the nadir, the mole"—the slightest of animals, and, of course, the one best suited to tracking in darkness. The mole finds Payatamu's severed head in the witch's jar and teams with the hawk and the owl to steal it. Payatamu is restored, and the story goes: "aaaaaaAAAAAA THE SUN CAME UP."

In such a world, humans are not alone. Their relations are all around them, each with special powers and each empowering the others. It takes the entire family together, the great and the small, the human and the animal, to keep the world unfolding as it should. The mole says, "If he's alone it won't work," and his comment is true for every being alive.

Our own world, the signs are clear, is working less and less well. It will take many wills laboring together to turn it back toward health. Remembering the sacred family, I believe, has an important part to play in that change. It cannot be made to happen, by proselytizing or persuasion, and it will not happen overnight—religious transformation, like ecological disaster, creeps slowly. We are not used to seeing nature as holy and akin to ourselves. But we are capable of seeing it so, and that way lies the best hope we have of avoiding the calamities now looming and those we don't yet discern. The path of the sacred family leads back, then forward, toward a world in which the very term "environment" may become unnecessary, a world in which we do not act upon the land but in and of the land, so at home in our surroundings that it makes no sense to speak of an external environment. We *are* what we act upon and what acts upon us. When we separate ourselves, we come to no good. If we're alone, says the mole, it won't work.

♦

Ourselves[2]

When the throaty calls of sandhill cranes
echo across the valley, when the rimrock flares
incandescent red, and the junipers
are flames of green on the shortgrass hills,

in that moment of last clear light
when the world seems ready to speak its name,
meet me in the field alongside the pond.
Without careers for once, without things to do,

without dreams or anger or the rattle of fears,
we'll ask how it can be that we walk this ground
and know that we walk, alive in a world
that didn't have to be beautiful, alive

in a world that doesn't have to be.
With no answers, just ourselves and silence,
we'll listen for the song that waits to be learned,
the song that moves through the passing light.

9

PHOTO AND WORD: THE POWER OF SUGGESTION IN VISUAL AND VERBAL "LANGUAGE"

Stephen Trimble attributes his lifelong fascination with landscape to his father, a geologist, who taught him to "listen to the landscape." After many years of talking with and writing about Native Americans in the West, he has also tried to adopt a "native" way of looking at the land—a perspective based upon an indelible, long-term sense of attachment.

Trimble himself has always lived in the American West. Born in Denver in 1950, he was educated at Colorado College and later earned an M.S. in biology at the University of Arizona. He began his career as a writer and photographer in 1969, while still an undergraduate. From 1972 to 1975, he worked as a seasonal ranger and naturalist for the National Park Service, and then from 1979 to 1981 as an editor and publisher at the Museum of Northern Arizona Press. Since then, apart from various roles as visiting lecturer and consultant at universities, arts organizations, and government agencies, he has worked as a freelance artist. His writings have appeared in periodicals ranging from *American Indian Art* and *High Country News* to the *Los Angeles Book Review* and *Sierra*, and in fourteen books to date. His first book was *Great Sand Dunes: The Shape of the Wind*, published in 1975 by the Southwest Parks and Monuments Association. More recently, he published *The People: Indians of the American Southwest* (1993) and, with Gary Paul Nabhan, *The Geography of Childhood: Why Children Need Wild Places* (1994). One of his best-known publications is *The Sagebrush Ocean: A Natural History of the Great Basin*, which appeared in 1989, with a foreword by Barry Lopez; this book received the Sierra Club's Ansel Adams Award and the High Desert Museum's Earle A. Chiles Award. He has also edited the anthology *Words from the Land: Encounters with Natural History Writing* (1988; expanded edition 1995). With Terry Tempest Williams, he compiled and distributed the influential volume *Testimony: Writers of the West Speak on Be-*

half of Utah Wilderness in 1995, a book that directly contributed to the establishment of Grand Staircase–Escalante National Monument in 1996. Trimble is equally well known for his work as a photographer, having contributed to such periodicals as *Audubon*, *Life*, and *Newsweek* and to several books, ranging from *Navajo Pottery: Traditions and Innovations* (1987) to Ann Ronald's *Earthtones: A Nevada Album* (1995).

On March 27, 1996, Wisconsin Senator Russell Feingold and New Jersey Senator Bill Bradley argued before the U.S. Senate on behalf of wilderness preservation in southern Utah, explicitly referring to and quoting from *Testimony*. In addition to offering their own arguments on behalf of wilderness designation for some of Utah's federal lands, Senator Bradley read excerpts from New Jersey author John McPhee's contribution to *Testimony*, while Senator Feingold read the entirety of Trimble's essay. Feingold commented on the piece as follows: "That short piece of writing is so powerful, Mr. President, because it is a timeless statement about how people feel about natural places. For myself, I personally know the value of wild areas. For the last nine years, I have spent my summer vacations on Madeline Island, immediately adjacent to the Apostle Islands National Lakeshore in northern Wisconsin. I have always found the quiet beauty of the Apostle Islands refreshing and invigorating." And later, "In places like the Apostle Islands and southern Utah, Wisconsinites have found opportunities to develop a consciously sympathetic relationship to the rest of the world" (*Congressional Record*, 27 March 1996, S2914). It is difficult to think of a more direct and powerful connection between the work of writers and the politics of environmental policy.

But not all of Trimble's work has been applied so directly to specific environmental initiatives. In fact, much of his writing in a much more general and fundamental way supports education about and appreciation of underappreciated and exploited landscapes. The two samples of his work presented here include an essay about wrestling with the ethical dilemmas of a wilderness photographer, an artist trying to make a living from his work and yet realizing that the companies that buy the work may not support the protection of wild places or human health and well-being. This piece is, essentially, a story about the writer's personal struggle with environmental and professional values—a struggle to decide how to be practical and, at the same time, how to do the right thing. In the following interview, Trimble proposes that one of the key facets of the language of story is that it functions as *suggestion* rather than as *assertion*. In his story about the dilemmas of a landscape photographer supported by the business of advertising, he offers a narrative that may well be suggestive and compelling to any reader who has had to make compromises in his or her own work, trying to balance values and pragmatism.

The second sample of Trimble's work comes from the concluding pages of *The Sagebrush Ocean* and demonstrates how the author's contemporary experience of the Great Basin Desert, especially the view of it from its westernmost edge, near Reno and Lake Tahoe, converges with the stories of earlier visitors such as Clarence King and Israel Russell and with Walter Van Tilburg Clark's fictional narrative about Reno and Mount Rose. This is how the suggestiveness of story works—by the association of remembered texts (other people's stories) with one's own immediate perceptions. What Trimble is presenting in the concluding pages of this important book (one of the most popular books ever published by the University of Nevada Press) is that the meaning—or value—of place can be demonstrated through intertextual resonance. When one story reminds us of another story, which in turn reminds us of our own experience and inspires us to tell our own stories, this is evidence that something important is happening, that our imagination and our feelings have been kindled. This is what was happening when Senator Russell Feingold read Trimble's essay about southern Utah to the U.S. Senate and then told the story of his summer visits to northern Wisconsin. This is what happens whenever we read something and are inspired to tell our own stories—this is often how values come to be articulated through narrative.

♦

A Conversation with Stephen Trimble

Scott Slovic conducted this interview with Stephen Trimble at his home in Salt Lake City, Utah.

Slovic: One of the important things about your work that differs from that of the other writers we've been talking to is that you're not only a writer but also a photographer, and many of your projects involve a combination of narratives and visual images. What do you think about the differences in the ways we perceive static, or stationary, images and how we listen to a story or perceive it over time?

Trimble: When you listen to a story, you soon drift into all kinds of other places in your world and in your life. Something in the story will make you think of one of your own stories. And something in a character's personality will make you think of your daughter or your wife or your mother. Stories are so suggestive, and as they carry you to a time, they carry you to all kinds of places.

For instance, I listened to Stegner's *Crossing to Safety* on tape while I was photographing around Nevada. And so, particular sections of *Crossing to Safety* match up with particular landscapes in southern Nevada because that's where I absorbed the story. I happened to reach the climax of the book when I visited the beautiful little desert pools in Ash Meadows National Wildlife Refuge, and so that moment of the story is tied very specifically to being on the south side of Mount Charleston. The book and the refuge landscape are totally contrasting landscapes, but for me they will always be bound together. That's the way story works—it engages you with whatever happens to be going on in your life in that particular moment.

A photograph to me is much more like a piece of art on a wall. You respond to the color and the graphic imagery and the content with whatever you are bringing to it as a person—but it's a much more momentary kind of spark.

Slovic: When you are telling a story, when you're reporting on an encounter or producing a more literary story, are you focusing on the drama of the encounter or are you conscious to some degree of trying to communicate an idea, a sense of importance or value?

Trimble: It would depend on the story.

Slovic: Can you think of any concrete examples of stories that have led you in one direction or another?

Trimble: Yes, very much so. In "Sing Me Down the Mountain," from *The Geography of Childhood*, I just wanted to tell the story—tell this emotional story in words that capture the sense of that chapter in my journey. It's very straightforward. There's a straight line from my life and what happened to me, through my need as a writer to distill that experience into words, to the endpoint, where I pass it on to you.

The essay that I wrote for *Testimony* has a much more specific purpose. I wanted to move the readers and change the way they think about wild country in Utah. And in that case I knew my readers precisely—specifically, the members of Congress. Yet I wanted to reach them in a way that wasn't didactic and obnoxious.

Much of my writing is an effort to make people aware of things that I have discovered. I want my readers to understand. I have a very definite sense of all those different needs when I'm writing.

Slovic: I wonder if we can talk even more concretely, without making you overly self-conscious, about strategies for achieving these various goals. For instance, an essay like "Sing Me Down the Mountain" could easily have been shifted into a more didactic mode. To me that essay, to a great extent, is about relationships, various kinds of relationships, from being a friend to a dog to being the father of a human child, and about partners. And you could have developed a moral concerning relationships with people that lead us to care about places, and yet that is kept in the background. Are you conscious when you're telling such a story of the potential implications of that story and of your efforts to avoid making those implications too prominent and overt?

Trimble: Well, I think initially I'm not conscious. And as I rework and rewrite, I become more conscious of the potential moral. I'll often write the more didactic sequence of paragraphs toward the end of the piece and then cut them because they end up sounding sappy and moralistic. Sometimes they creep into the finished piece when they should have been cut. I believe it's so much better to let the reader make that jump, because it's going to be more meaningful. Readers hate to be lectured to. It's only the wisest of human beings who can do that without alienating their readers.

I think all of us who write this kind of work—all of us who write about the natural world and how much we care about it—cross that line. Barry Lopez writes like a dream, but he also is deeply concerned about the ethical and moral aspects of our lives, and sometimes he goes over the line. And there are people who can't read Edward Abbey because of his fierceness. It's that fine judgment that you make about yourself. As for me, I'm afraid that I've been the master of summary rather than the master of story.

Slovic: Can we talk about the difference between summary and story in your mind?

Trimble: I've been discovering that much of my writing is summary. And I don't mean that in an entirely positive sense. I've been incorporating a massive amount of information in my head and distilling it—ideally—into a great story, but nonetheless summarizing it for lay readers. This is what I've done when I've written about the desert and Indian people. I think I'm very good at it, and I think that it serves an important purpose. But I also think that it doesn't reach as many readers as I would like to reach.

Slovic: What does a story have that summary doesn't?

Trimble: More emotional content, more soul. "Sing Me Down the Mountain" is a story that makes most people think, yet I had no intention of conveying the kinds of information that these other pieces do. *The People* is filled with stories and I think comes far closer to taking information and turning it into story. But I think writing a novel is really the highest form of storytelling.

Slovic: In writing?

Trimble: In writing. Yes, just to create a piece, to write a novel, to generate a piece of writing that long that holds the reader, doesn't let the reader down, is just a magnificent achievement.

Slovic: On this issue of what a story is and how it carries information, how does it carry values that might have an important effect on audiences?

Trimble: That's one thing we haven't talked about. I feel that story is absolutely critical for people learning about landscapes. The reason that I came to natural-history writing and landscape writing was the land itself. When I went to southern Utah, I reacted to the land with a great deal of emotion. Then, as I finished college in the early seventies, I discovered *Desert Solitaire* and it was like being given an enormous gift. I discovered this writer who had pondered exactly the same experiences and had done his very best to translate them into stories. And they're great stories—it's a powerful book.

When I started canoeing the Green River, I discovered Ann Zwinger's book about the Green River, *Run, River, Run*. Again, it was a gift. I want to understand a new place on as many levels as I can, as this place that I love. And to do that runs the gamut from being there and photographing it myself so that I see the place graphically and in color with full attention, to listening to other people's stories about the place, all the way from the first explorer to the contemporary poet.

Slovic: You are talking about a very particular relationship between a reader and the text. In a sense, you, as a reader visiting the particular landscape, become uniquely primed to appreciate the text. However, if this literature is ever to have a meaningful effect on a vast audience, then I think it's important to consider the audience that is unfamiliar with the landscape being represented in a text. We need to consider the encounter with a piece of writing on its own terms and in isolation from the landscape that produced that text. What do you think is the potential for natural-history writing to move and motivate readers who have no direct contact with the places?

Trimble: Well, I think a work like *Walden* is the ultimate answer to that question. Great literature changes the world and in some cases that literature involves the natural landscape. But it's self-defeating to worry about having that kind of effect as a writer. All you can do is to do your best to put the story out there and hope that it's universal enough to reach people.

When I have written specifically to change votes—as in *Testimony*—I've tried to do so by being as universal in feelings as I could. On the whole, I'm a pretty esoteric and provincial person. I'm enthusiastic and engaged with things and places that I love, and I simply write as an act of faith. If I can capture my love and passion with words, if the work is powerful enough and meaningful enough, it will change people's minds. But I don't spend a lot of time thinking about that, because you can't. You can't.

Slovic: Charles Wilkinson's point, in *The Eagle Bird*, is that some of the frustrations people feel with modern environmental policy come from a language problem, from the fact that language, the formal, impersonal, quantitative language of environmental law and environmental policy, pushes ideas in a certain direction. Some people might argue that it would be beneficial to reform the very language of law and policy, to introduce narrative writing, nature writing, into the professional language of law and policy. Is there any possibility of doing that in your mind? And do you think even a book like *Testimony* is a first step in that direction?

Trimble: I think it helps and I think it's a worthy, worthy task. I think it also goes in the other direction—from the environmentalist-nature-writing perspective toward the people who are out on the land, the rural westerners who hate environmentalists. There, again, the anger is there partly because of language.

Slovic: What is it that they don't like about this language?

Trimble: Well, the word "wilderness" is a flare, and yet environmentalists (or whatever you want to call these people who are out there working trying to identify the wild places that they want to protect) are actually trying to preserve the same thing that most rural ranchers are trying to preserve. They're trying to save open space and the chance to live your life with long horizons that are untrammeled.

Open space is really the ultimate goal for both, and there is a lot of common ground between the environmental community and rural people who are so filled with hatred toward the environmental community. Language gets in the way and could help solve the problem. Being out together on the land is one way to start to make the language become more parallel.

Slovic: If "wilderness" is a key word for ranchers or rural people, are there any other words from the environmental community that anger or worry rural people? Red-flag words?

Trimble: Yes. "Environmentalist" is one. It's the whole elite flavor of those words that gets in the way of people who are dealing with water, soil, cattle, horses, and weather. Particularly when the environment *is* water, weather, and soil. When a hiker and camper and climber go to these places, those are the words they too use. But when you go home you talk about "wilderness" and you call yourself an "environmentalist" and you join "environmental organizations"—the two parties never come together because of the way the culture works.

Language has a lot to do with it. The language of the rancher, the person living on the land, is incredibly concrete. The language that environmentalists use to describe the look of the place becomes more and more abstract the farther they get from it.

Slovic: Are there any words that *ranchers* use that frighten environmentalists or annoy environmentalists?

Trimble: Yes. Production kinds of words. Head of cattle, units of production. But the ranchers I've talked to speak with great sadness about how the urban environmental community simply doesn't understand what they're about. Some ranchers are angry and verbal and eloquent. Others don't, in fact, use many words. They fit the Gary Cooper–Virginian stereotype to some extent.

The thing I've been impressed with is how observant they are. I learn about the land when I go out with ranchers because they're looking at new growth in each clump of grass and matching that up with the patterns of storms over the last two months and predicting ahead of time what that's going to mean for their animals. They know full well the animals will die if they don't have the right combination of weather and grass. It's very, very elemental.

Hikers are out there on a much more temporary basis, and in some ways their journeys are more spiritual than elemental. They don't necessarily see much about the place because they are also very much engaged in their own head on their journey into wild places. I certainly don't denigrate that. I go there for those reasons, too. But my personal catch phrase is "pay attention." The whole goal in life for me is to pay more attention than I'm paying to whatever it is in front of my nose. Whether it's land or people or relationships or stories. Ranchers are very good at paying attention to particular sweeps of things because their lives and their business depend upon it.

Slovic: Some people refer to landscape literature or the literature of hope, but I tend to think of writing about nature as the literature of attention.

Trimble: Yes, but the attention is squarely on the natural world in a way that a brilliant writer like Alice Munro, perhaps, focuses attention on relationships, on the nuances of human relationships. It's a similar skill directed at a different subject.

Slovic: If you wanted to know how people felt about something or "attended" to something, say perhaps a revered place such as the Grand Staircase–Escalante region in southern Utah, would it be wise to ask them to state directly their feelings? Would you ask them how important something is to them? How would you approach them?

Trimble: I would ask: "What is the most significant thing that ever happened to you in the world of nature and why was it important and can you relate that in any way to the preservation of this other place?" I would try to entice them to tell stories. Because if you ask them those other questions, those big abstract questions—how important to the nation something is—they will likely spit back at you what they read in the mailing they got from the Wilderness Society.

Slovic: How do you spark stories? You have a lot of experience wandering around getting people to talk to you. Do you find that there are certain kinds of questions, like the one you just mentioned, that tend to relax people and make them willing to tell story?

Trimble: I think you can often get people going by asking them about their childhoods. What place do you remember from your childhood? What place do you remember with enormous affection, that has had a lasting effect upon you? It's a technique to use with someone who is inclined to think of you as an adversary.

If someone perceives me as an environmentalist, and they don't think of themselves as one, then it's very difficult. When I was working on *The Geography of Childhood*, I went down to Wayne County, Utah, to interview middle-school kids about their attitudes toward landscape. It's an extremely rural county. I talked with the teacher who was sponsoring me about how to broach the subject, because they all live in families that, for the most part, hate environmentalists—or, they think that they hate the values that people who call themselves "environmentalists" stand for.

We couldn't use even the word "nature" without it being a red flag. Eventually, we asked the kids how they felt when they were outside. What did they do there? They talked about watching their uncle's sheep up in the hills and riding horses. I've always thought it works far better for me to go to their world when I'm doing field work. People love to reminisce and in doing so tell you a lot about how they feel.

Slovic: And from these conversations, are you able to get a sense of what's important to people? Does it take a lot of fretful interpretation, wrestling with ambiguity? Or are there cues as to what's important, meaningful?

Trimble: Well, the cues are often simply a change in tone of voice. To start with, people will tell you what they think you want to hear. You usually have to listen to that before you get to the good stuff. And I think it works better to work with a notebook than it does with a tape recorder. There's an engagement with the conversation that just works far better.

Slovic: Part of this project's goal is to contribute to the way that information about what's important to stakeholders is gathered so as to encourage the incorporation of narrative explanations into the value-elicitation process. To do so would require not only seeking out certain types of informants who may be especially comfortable with story, but finding a way for people from various political and geographical perspectives to speak more fully to non-utilitarian or philosophical points of view.

All of us who use spoken words or literature to communicate certain ideas about people in the natural world understand this necessity. But it is difficult to introduce both this material and this language to economists, politicians, resource managers, or policy analysts. We're stymied by the question, "How do we find a way to bring to your attention—as you sit in your offices at the Department of the Interior formulating policy statements—the way that people actually think and process information and articulate their feelings about things?"

Trimble: An incredibly daunting question.

Slovic: For me, it is perhaps the ultimate question. Otherwise we're involved in entertainment. Or I am at least—I'm entertaining people when I introduce them to this literature, as a teacher and a literary scholar.

Trimble: Well, you're not. What most of us are doing is not entertainment. It's working at that same change in values through all kinds of circles and paths. If we can reach readers with sufficiently powerful language, they're moved to change, their behavior will change, however subtly. But to actually get to that interface between power and government action is very hard—there's such a cultural difference. The politicians and lifetime bureaucrats may not speak the same language, they may not look at the world from the same basic values.

The same is true in the small-town communities. The material that I gathered from these kids in middle school in southern Utah showed that their families still believe they are there on a mission from God. They were sent to the desert to make the desert blossom like the rose and to tame the wilderness. There is this absolute religious component to how they view the world that I don't share and that the preservationist community does not share. From my point of view, it's hard to bridge the gap—it's hard to get the right words to describe the environmental aspects of the problem and the importance of setting aside as much acreage as possible as designated wilderness.

Slovic: Before we leave altogether the different languages and cultures across the policy and public worlds, I am wondering if I can ask you a bit about *Testimony*, in particular, and your sense of how it was received by its intended audience, which was a policy audience, and by other readers.

Trimble: I think it worked far better than we could have imagined. The introduction is called "An Act of Faith." That came from a phrase that just popped out of my mouth after a press conference on the Capitol lawn. A cynical reporter came up and said, "What if nobody pays any attention?" And I said, "Well, this is an act of faith on our part." We have no idea whether anyone will pay any attention, we've done our job and now the words are in their hands. Perhaps a Congressional staff person will pick the book up, take it home, read it, and be moved by one of the essays only to go back to the member of Congress and say, "You know, let's rethink this." That's what we really hoped for.

Slovic: Do you have any concrete evidence of the response?

Trimble: We do. What we have is the *Congressional Record*. Bill Bradley and Russ Feingold were up there in front of Congress waving *Testimony* around and reading essays into the *Congressional Record*. Bradley read a section of McPhee's piece and Russ Feingold read mine into the *Congressional Record* and said, "This connects with my childhood!" He connected what I was saying about special places on the Colorado Plateau with his memories of lakes in the upper Midwest.

Terry [Tempest Williams] and I were in Washington and went to great lengths to disassociate ourselves from all the official environmental organizations. We wanted to represent ourselves as writers and to speak for the larger community of writers, though we relied heavily on SUWA [Southern Utah Wilderness Alliance] for contacts. We worked out of their offices, used their contacts with the press, and they told us which Congresspeople to visit. But we spoke as individual writers, not as lobbyists for an organization.

The book itself reached a much larger audience than it would have otherwise because of contacts I had with Universal Press Syndicate. I do one travel story for them every year and they ran what was essentially a feature article on the project in their outdoor adventure travel column. It was syndicated to four hundred newspapers. The feature ran with a headline along the lines of "The Pen is Mightier than the Bulldozer." And I was enormously gratified to have that exposure.

Slovic: I'd heard that you also handed the book out to less supportive members of Congress. What is the point of handing a book to someone like that? Is it a symbolic gesture?

Trimble: It's a symbolic gesture. It's an act of politeness, handing the book to them. We were going to give a copy to every member of Congress, and it was simply a gesture of a certain amount of respect for our own community to give a copy in person to those members of the delegation from here—representing Utah, so to speak. With the conservative Utah members, however, it was probably a complete waste of time.

Slovic: In recent years, I've been talking with some friends, writers and literary scholars, about how there is something fundamentally ineffective about the way environmentalists, including nature writers, tend to operate. They communicate in a fairly sincere mode, lacking the jauntiness and the wit and the rambunctiousness of a Rush Limbaugh or his cohorts. People are saying what's needed is a kind of green Rush Limbaugh. But I wonder if that's even possible. Can the ideas and feelings in the environmental community really be presented in such a raucous, seemingly carefree manner? Except perhaps by someone like Edward Abbey.

Trimble: There's Dave Foreman. He's wonderful. He's very much the person you're describing. But our wise elders are much more like Old Testament prophets—Dave Brower, before he died, and Barry Lopez. In public, they tend to be much more stern and moralistic and hard to like, hard to warm up to—even though in private they can be warm and funny. But Dave Foreman might be outrageous enough on the order of Rush Limbaugh to attract a good audience.

Slovic: I find myself thinking about this in the context of my university classes. My students haven't necessarily gravitated to my classes because they want to study environmental literature. They're just there checking off some requirement or another. If I'm participating in a trickle-down filtration process by which these ideas and turns of phrase work their way out into their world, then how can I best achieve this distribution to my students who sometimes actually say, "This is all starting to sound so similar"? I often feel as though I need some of that jauntiness that disrupts people's expectations. Often readers don't notice, or don't want to notice, the complexity of a certain voice. Even that of Edward Abbey. One of the directions for the evolution of this genre, environmental writing, could be to disrupt people's expectations of the dry and serious tone of this work.

Trimble: Perhaps then we can at least just get the books onto their nightstands, into their homes. Perhaps [laughing] the words will fly into their brains. That might be the way it works, the way ideas journey through the culture. You never know.

Slovic: I really like one of the words that you used at the beginning of our conversation when you were talking about the "suggestiveness" of the story. I think that's rather fundamental to this whole process. Ideas and feelings are often *suggested*, not directly asserted. The thing about this literature, and more particularly about the use of story, is that it operates on the level of indirectness and ambiguity.

Trimble: That's absolutely true. Well, it's very much like Keith Basso's stories of the Apaches, collected in *Wisdom Sits in Places*. The elders tell you a story that may have no apparent relevance to what it is they want to teach you. But you get it somehow. They're suggesting a moral and a tale—a moral in the tale. It's a technique that goes back thousands of years.

Slovic: In some of the passages in that book, Basso breaks down the different kinds of story—you know ultimately that there will be some kind of moral, a lesson, in many of the stories.

Trimble: That's right. When we were talking about how to elicit stories from people, I was thinking that one advantage I have in spending most of my time interviewing people, particularly Indian people, is that there is a rich tradition of storytelling. Even with the most urban Indians, there's sympathy toward telling stories to strangers that not all Forest Service rangers or local community bureaucrats have.

Slovic: Yes, this is crucial. It may be that the people who are interested in environmental values in this technical sense and want everything boiled down into numbers come from communities of people who are disenfranchised from story. These are often the people with the power to frame policy or to make important legal decisions, and yet they come from an unstoried, or a destoried, part of our culture. If they're not inclined to be interested in literature or the arts or personal stories, there is a great impasse. How do we guide people who have lost their understanding of story to care about story again?

Trimble: As a parent, my thoughts return to reading to children at bedtime.

There's an unwritten message in that: that story is incredibly important. It's the one time of the day when the child gets one parent, one-on-one, absolutely every day. "Hurry and get your teeth brushed so that we can read a story together before you go to sleep." There's an enormously powerful message in that.

♦

A Wilderness Photographer in Marlboro Country[1]

I

On a serene afternoon in August, 1985, I left Santa Fe for the half-hour drive to my little adobe house in New Mexico's Pojoaque Valley. The highway bears north between the trench of the Rio Grande and the high spine of the Sangre de Cristo Range. Summer clouds were building over the mountains, piling into the most spectacular thunderheads I had ever seen. I gunned my truck, racing for home and cameras.

On a small hill behind my house, I shot two rolls, photographing as the clouds rolled over the peaks. I photographed until the last flicker died within the storm clouds—ominous mushrooms fired by golden and red light. I was thrilled to have seen this event, and exhilarated to have the chance to photograph it.

The storm itself was not unusual. In July and August, warm air, high altitude, and Gulf moisture create what Southwesterners call the monsoons—afternoon thunderstorms that build, roil, rain, and disappear over several hours. By sunset, the sky clears, washed clean, and ready for a glitter of stars.

But these clouds were especially remarkable in their form. They towered over the Pecos Wilderness, while the sky above me was a radiant blue. The sun at my back lit the tableau; color and form changed with each interval closer to sunset. The drama climaxed right over Truchas Peak, a cardinal sacred mountain for Tewa Pueblo people.

II

October, 1989: my daughter was a few months past her first birthday. She had had a restless night in a cabin outside of Torrey, Utah. My friend, Chuck Smith, woke up early and wandered out into the piñon-juniper woodland for a morning pee. His wife and my family stayed snug inside. I was too groggy to be up at dawn for photographs.

Chuck returned and called me awake. "Steve, you *have* to go outside and see the cliffs. Terrific light . . ."

I roused myself, grabbed my tripod and cameras, and hurried outside. The sun had risen into a narrow opening eastward beyond the Henry Mountains. Silver storm clouds filled much of the rest of the sky arching over the Waterpocket Fold. Orange light shot across under the cloud cover, firing the Moenkopi sandstone cliffs under the dark ceiling of the storm. I knew the intensity of color would last only a few minutes. I gritted my teeth against my own full bladder and photographed as fast as I could, changing lenses, trying a polarizing filter to intensify the contrast between cliff and sky, quickly shooting a series of pictures.

And then the light was gone. I went back inside and curled into the warm hollow of my wife's back and drifted once more into sleep.

III

What do you say when the phone rings, and Exxon wants to use your photographs of pristine nature in an ad promoting their corporate sensitivity to the environment? I would say no. What do you say when Philip Morris offers you big bucks to use your photos to sell Marlboro cigarettes? I said yes.

The Chicago advertising agency representing Philip Morris called me after they saw a book of photographs of the Colorado Plateau that I had edited called *Blessed By Light.* They wanted, first, a big red cliff, and, later, a thunderhead. They wanted my photographs for Marlboro ads—but needed computers to add cowboys and horses to the foregrounds of each. "Now there's a special place in Marlboro Country." "Come to Marlboro Country."

I have told you the stories of these images. I saw no cowboys or horses in Marlboro Country; no one smoked cigarettes there. Although there was a woodstove and a cold beer not far away, wilderness began at the doorstep. Philip Morris, of course, used these pictures and what they communicate about wilderness for corporate purposes, for mythmaking, profit, and the despicable enticement of people to cigarettes.

I am a professional photographer, and so I was delighted to see my photos used so conspicuously, to be paid so well for their use. I was unsettled, too. I do not smoke, and do not like anything about smoking. I hope my children never start. But I also know that the Marlboro image is powerful and unchanging and that my particular images will not target any new audience, will not convince any one person to begin smoking.

And then there is the issue of *using* the wilderness. Politically correct critics suggest that even conservation-oriented photo books of pristine wilderness are at best boring or nostalgic, at worst destructive. Conservationists worry that more books of "perfect" and beautiful landscape photography will make the public complacent. Some call such photographs pornographic, a perverse misrepresentation of the wilderness as a *Playboy* centerfold, an unreal beauty without flaws or complications.

I can only imagine what such commentators think of using wilderness images for advertising cigarettes.

I thought through the conflict in values. My solution has been to allow the use of the photos but to send some of my profits back to where they originated, back to the wilderness.

And so I tithe. A portion of each Moenkopi cliff check goes to the Southern Utah Wilderness Alliance, to fight the dam proposed below the base of the very cliff in the photograph. A percentage of the payment for the thunderhead over sacred Truchas Peak goes to the Native American Rights Fund, to lobby for passage of the Native American Religious Freedom Act, to fight for the protection of sacred places.

The wilderness gives itself to photographers. We have an obligation to think about what we take. And what we give in return. Our exchange resembles that of a native hunter who thanks the spirit of a deer he has slain for its gift of life and who then leaves behind a piece of meat for Mother Earth. With these kinds of agreements with the wilderness, with this kind of attention paid, the lessons of the experience can be understood. In this way, the wilderness may continue to survive, as our refuge and teacher, and, yes, as our place of work, as well.

♦

Excerpt from *The Sagebrush Ocean*[2]

Perhaps more than anywhere, the Great Basin reveals its nature where it meets a landscape most dissimilar, as at the Sierra Nevada. Writer after writer waxes emotional looking east from the high peaks to the desert. The Carson Range, the first Basin range, straddles the transition in both topography and history.

The view from these mountains includes many worlds and suggestions of many times. The centuries of the Washoe, the People, who named Tahoe and lived closest to this land. The little lake off to the west called Donner, scene of tragic deeds that make one of the West's most harrowing stories.

At the south end of the Carson Range lies Jobs Peak, on whose summit a lightning bolt struck Clarence King in 1867; his "brain nerves were severely shocked," but he recovered to publish his version of the view from the peak, finish his survey of the fortieth parallel, and become first director of the U.S. Geological Survey. Across the valley southeastward lies the Virginia Range, mother of the Comstock Lode and generator of enough human energy to help forge a Mark Twain. On the summit of Mount Rose stand the ruins of an old stone weather station built by James E. Church in 1905 and prototype for the modern science of snow surveying.

Mount Rose hangs as talisman over every event in the life of Tim Hazard, central character in Walter Van Tilburg Clark's 1945 novel *The City of Trembling Leaves.* In Tim's day (and in Clark's Reno boyhood), to reach Lake Tahoe from Reno one walked over Mount Rose. The Mount Rose Highway did not exist. Tim went up to the mountain at crucial times in his life, yearning for its "purity."

Tim took his great love, Rachel Wells, to Mount Rose. He shared his meadows, his mountain, and his gods with her. "Until you are greatly moved by the beauty of mountain sadness and loneliness, and for a moment perceive time according to stars and wholly without mathematics . . . there is almost no use in coming."

From the summit:

> Far down in the basin in the west, lay Lake Tahoe, shrunken, and fitted neatly into all its bays and inlets in the wooded mountains. . . . But it was when they turned east that the world spread out under them, pale, painted, turbulent mountains, range after range toward the sky which curved beyond the shoulder of the world, all of them subdued by sun except the very last, a thin and broken edge of snow. In the north-east, through a distant pass, glittered an illusory sliver of Pyramid Lake. . . . It was the pale, burning and shadowed east that led the mind out.

The last time I stood on the summit of Mount Rose, smog lay over the Truckee Meadows too thickly to see Pyramid Lake. Tahoe was barely visible and no longer had the quiet and unblemished purity that moved Clark to call it an "unconscious saint." When the National Park Service sent out an investigator to evaluate Lake Tahoe's suitability as a national park in the twenties, he deemed it too developed to be suitable; today we lament a lake thoroughly casinoed and condominiumized.

Clark was right. The real Basin ranges—"pale, painted, turbulent mountains"—draw your eye eastward.

On Mount Rose, Tim Hazard said: "This . . . is what I've been after. . . . It was the suspension, without desire, without regret, with only the lucid, independent present, which was the gift of the mountain."

We share in this mountain's gift. We live in the present, with the desert.

In this desert lies an ocean of shrubs, several hundred mountain ranges, a few dozen ranches and towns, and considerably more dune grasshoppers, kangaroo rats, and Pinyon Jays. More than anything else, however, in this Great Basin lies a message about time.

I look out from Mount Rose to the eastern ranges, to the sharp raw blocks studding the smooth Basin, the lilting sequence of basin and range leading away toward Utah. I look into a haze, the present distilled from the past, the future discernible in the rawboned tans to some sufficiently visionary seer.

Dynamic plants and animals dominate the Great Basin's past. It has been a desert for only a few thousand years. Before that a lake covered much of this view, forest the rest. Still earlier this land was grassland, jungle, ocean.

A century ago, Israel Russell ended his classic work on Mono Lake with a prediction: "If the imperfect data now at hand may be trusted, it seems as if the last geologic change of climate had not yet culminated, and that increased humidity in the Great Basin might be expected in the future."

The future of this sagebrush ocean is bound to bring change. Time, climate, life, and history have "not yet culminated" here. They never will.

10

PACKING INFORMATION IN THE FORM OF STORY: VIEWING NARRATIVE FROM THE PERSPECTIVE OF SCIENCE

It's difficult to imagine a more suitable person to consider the topic of "narrative" from the perspective of science than Robert Michael Pyle. Like one of his favorite authors—lepidopterist and novelist Vladimir Nabokov—Pyle is a renowned butterfly scholar and enthusiast and a lover of playful, colorful words. Born in Denver, Colorado, in 1947, Pyle spent his youth exploring the High Line Canal in suburban Aurora—these experiences, and the implications of urban sprawl and the loss of open space in and near cities, became the topic of his 1993 book, *The Thunder Tree: Lessons from an Urban Wildland.* At the age of eleven, he began collecting butterflies in Colorado, actually meeting the prominent ecologists Charles Remington (who would serve as his advisor in graduate school at Yale two decades later) and Paul Ehrlich at the Rocky Mountain Biological Laboratory when he was still a junior-high student. In high school, he received a National Science Foundation pre-college grant to spend the summer of 1963 at Jackson Memorial Laboratory in Bar Harbor, Maine, an experience described in the writing sample "Spark-Infested Waters" following this interview. Pyle left Denver to attend the University of Washington, completing a B.S. with an independent major in "nature perception and protection" in 1970 and an M.S. in the College of Forest Resources with an emphasis on nature interpretation. He spent 1971–72 on a Fulbright-Hays Scholarship at the Monks Wood Experimental Station outside of Cambridge, England, studying butterfly conservation. Pyle started the Xerces Society for invertebrate conservation in 1971 and two years later began the Ph.D. program in the School of Forestry and Environmental Studies at Yale University. By the time he started his Ph.D. program, he had already published nearly forty articles.

Pyle published his first book, *Watching Washington Butterflies,* in 1974 and that same year began writing the butterfly-oriented novel *Magdalena Moun-*

tain, which he continues to toy with today. After completing his Ph.D. in 1976, he took a series of temporary positions as a college instructor and conservation consultant. He bought his home in Gray's River, Washington, in 1978. Throughout the 1980s and 1990s, Pyle published numerous butterfly field guides and works (books and articles) of literary natural history. *The Audubon Society Field Guide to North American Butterflies* appeared in 1981. His breakthrough literary work, *Wintergreen*, appeared in 1986 and received the John Burroughs Medal for outstanding natural-history writing, the Governor's Writers Award, and the Pacific Northwest Booksellers Association Award the following year. He published his Colorado book, *The Thunder Tree*, in 1993, followed by the "cryptozoological" study of the natural and cultural history of Sasquatch, *Where Bigfoot Walks: Crossing the Dark Divide*, two years later. In 1999, a literary butterfly book, *Chasing Monarchs: Migrating with the Butterflies of Passage*, came out, chronicling his eight-week journey in the fall of 1996, as he followed monarch butterflies on their annual migration through the western states into Mexico. Pyle published *Walking the High Ridge: Life as Field Trip*, a Credo Book from Milkweed Editions, in 2000. The title—"walking the high ridge"—comes from an epigraph by Nabokov: "Does there not exist a high ridge where the mountainside of 'scientific' knowledge joins the opposite slope of 'artistic' imagination?" Pyle clearly believes that there is no intrinsic gap between the scientific, economic, and managerial views of the world and the artistic view with its attachment to beauty and emotion.

The first writing sample included in this chapter is Pyle's well-known essay "The Extinction of Experience." He begins the essay by describing the neighborhood in which he grew up, showing how it changed with the process of urban development, and then exploring the ecological implications of these changes. Although the opening of the essay is largely "narrative" (it's the story of the author's youth in suburban Denver), the language also demonstrates a familiarity with scientific discourse and ideas. The story part of the essay builds to the explicit statement of the "moral" of the essay: "Many people take deep satisfaction in wilderness and wildlife they will never see. But direct, personal contact with other living things affects us in vital ways that vicarious experience can never replace." The implication of this statement is that there is no substitute for direct exposure to natural phenomena if we are to learn to value these phenomena—this gives a sense of poignant urgency to the earlier discussion of the loss of urban wildlands and the consequential "extinction of experience." In the following interview, Pyle makes it clear that he believes science and narrative must be combined carefully, precisely—not casually thrown together. But he argues, too, that scientific information can be effectively used in a narrative context. Perhaps this form of expression is the unique territory of the technically trained individual, such as Pyle himself. In any case, the implication is that scientists might learn to communicate their knowledge and concerns in accessible and piquant ways, engaging to general audiences.

When asked directly to comment on the concept of "environmental values," Pyle responded immediately, "I guess the phrase 'environmental values' means everything to me. I mean it's my whole life." And he proceeded to discuss his career-long engagement in both natural science and environmental activism, carefully explaining that his love of nature and his tendency to criticize human beings in no way diminished his love for his own species. Often Pyle's values are articulated through statements of sheer celebration, through stories of delight. The second sample of his writing in this volume, the short essay "Spark-Infested Waters," does exactly this. Responding to a recent experience swimming amid bioluminescent plankton off the Florida coast, he recalls his high-school NSF experience in Maine, when he first experienced this natural phenomenon: "And when I clapped hands overhead, showers of shooting stars fell all around, transporting me back to 1963, another bay, and a night alight with fascination, infatuation, and a summer storm of living sparks." Fascination and infatuation—with both nature and people—are the dominant emotions of this narrative. This small essay is a charming demonstration of the environmental values that Edward O. Wilson described with the term "biophilia"—love of life (all life). There is no abstract sermon about this in "Spark-Infested Waters"—the two, intertwined stories are enough.

♦

A Conversation with Robert Michael Pyle

Terre Satterfield and Scott Slovic conducted this interview on the front porch of Pyle's century-old farmhouse, known as "Swede Park," in Gray's River, Washington, not far from the mouth of the Columbia River.

Slovic: We wanted to start by having you describe the various categories of writing in which you work. You are rather versatile and your writing covers a wide range of modes of expression. I wonder if you could in a fairly leisurely way give us a kind of anatomy of the different kinds of writing you do.

Pyle: I primarily work in the exploring, discursive, lyrical essay. I blend a certain amount of scientific fact and journalism into that form. I use a lot of factual information but I also try to be conscious of the importance of the exploring line over and above the facts; I'm wary of the facts taking over.

However, I am a conservative when it comes to essays and the nonfiction–fiction distinction. I don't agree with some of the current (it's not just current, it has been done many times) ideas that some of my friends propound: that the essay form and fiction run together. Memory is a relative thing and all that, but I really do think that one has a certain responsibility to the reader. If you are going to call it an "essay," it better pretty much have happened that way. I don't believe in the subtle bending toward fiction. I think it becomes guile; if it's just your selective memory at work and you go ahead and write it that way because it's *your* memory and so it's true to you, fine. But if you are less lazy than that, or you decide to check it, and you find that the facts were otherwise, then I think you need to go with them. So I work in an essay that I characterize as conservative in that sense, but free-ranging in most other senses. I do mostly what I call "refractive" rather than "reflective" writing; I mean reflection as in a mirror where the writer is the instrument of the material. I am spoiled by being able to voice opinion and personal shades of experience that I don't think work very well in journalism.

Increasingly I write poems, often . . . [pause] when something strikes me. Like yesterday I had a wonderful experience. There were two bats in the house when I came home, stuck in the house. They were moribund, but not dead. So, I gave them some water and they both responded to that; one of them flew off. I put the other bat on a big shelf fungus on the red oak over there. When I came back to it later, it had crawled down, and was hanging beautifully under the bracket fungus but still very weak. So I went out with my butterfly net and started feeding it insects. The bat was very weak and tentative at first and scared of my tweezers, but soon it began really going for the insects I presented. I gave it thirty or forty small moths and flies—this tiny little bat! Eventually it perked up and flew from my hand; it was wonderful. I know I will write about it, but I don't know if it will be a poem or an essay. So increasingly poems do capture or suggest themselves to me for the same sort of experiential reasons that essays do.

I do write short fiction that is very different from the other forms—the stories that I write are wildly different. A lot of them tend to be organized around freeways, experiences that I would never write an essay about. It's almost a therapeutic kind of writing, an exercise in delight. And I do write what you could call left-brain, analytical, reportorial kinds of pieces in which I try to become a transparent reporter rather than a bent lens, an individual lens. But that tends to occur when writing in the realm of science.

I guess what I'm trying to say is that I'm willing to completely remove myself as a poetic presence where necessary, for instance with some science writing, because I believe it is a completely different and equally important thing to do. It irritates me, really, when people ineptly combine the two. I think that the two can be combined to great advantage, but it takes great care, and again great attention to context. One needs to write fact such that the reader takes the fact as a given. If the next paragraph is a poetic response to that fact, it's a tough trick to pull and an even tougher trick to find an editor or publisher who will even let you do both. And most of the time, it's rather badly done.

Satterfield: What are the circumstances under which you might choose to stick with the scientific as opposed to a narrative nonfiction or essay form. How do you make that choice?

Pyle: Good question. My training is largely scientific, although I put together a self-directed plan, cutting many corners to serve my purposes. My Ph.D. dissertation did not have a highly mathematical and analytical component to it. I am not a deeply statistically or mathematically minded person, although I appreciate the quantitative approach because it's important to be able to characterize the world as it works in physical terms. There is extraordinary beauty and strength and fascination to be found in asking how physical phenomena operate. The wealth of the world to me is represented in the elegance of evolutionary adaptation and the fit of form to function and vice versa.

Satterfield: You seem to be tacitly suggesting a tension between scientific and literary explanations. You've expressed your appreciation for both and you've suggested that the two forms should not be combined, but when you speak of science, a poet's aesthetic fascination emerges that complicates this opinion.

Pyle: See, I try to have it both ways; I think I've earned that. I don't mean to sound arrogant, but I have written a certain amount of science in which I try to remove myself as a refracting lens. I deeply appreciate the work of scientists who explicate the world without their own artistic or ego involvements and I appreciate the scientific method. I get fed up with some of my friends and colleagues who are terribly dismissive of science because of its reductionism. We don't understand the elegance of what scientists are about. I appreciate that on one level I can step back and say,

"Right, that parnassian butterfly is responding to particular climatic conditions or the presence of that plant." But that is not what it made me *feel;* I want to be able to write about what I feel.

I would like to be the kind of writer who can have it both ways, who has the kind of versatility to go back and forth, to write one moment about how I see the world as an experienced naturalist, always trying to become a more experienced naturalist, and in the next moment, if I feel like it, to write a poetic response to it. I think the essay allows you to do that. I don't think science writing does because science writing is intended to be the interpretive medium between the scientist and the reader. We are supposed to be able to rely on the science and to assume that we would see the same thing were we to go out and conduct the same experiments, make the same observations. This is the opposite of what you want from the poet.

Satterfield: Is your preference for the essay form primarily based on the purposes you've described or is it a viable form from the reader's point of view as well?

Pyle: Well, I think it's both a preference and an appreciation of the different service that it performs for the reader, or the different reward it provides the reader. There are readers, by the way, who are keyed to one or the other, readers who live more in their left brain or their right brain, to use that model. There are those who have very little patience with fact, but are overborne with emotion and feeling, and there are readers of exactly the opposite inclination.

That, I think, is the third element. It's not only my personal preference. It's not only trying to achieve different effects for the reader, but it also, frankly, is doing what we are enabled and partly enculturated to be good at. There are writers who never will be good at expressing themselves lyrically, and others who will never do the opposite. I aspire toward having more arrows in my quiver, to being able to respond to the world on lots of different levels.

For example, the monarch book—I had a wonderful letter recently from a friend, Jerry Powell, one of the greatest lepidopterists in modern history. He has spawned a whole generation of graduate students who have gone on to do wonderful things in parnassian butterfly and moth studies. Now Powell is very much a rationalist, and a cut-through-it kind of guy. In his letter, he told me that *Chasing Monarchs* was the first book of its sort he'd read in years. He reads a lot, but usually more technical material. He wrote two pages of criticisms and gently corrected me on some biology I got wrong. He said he found the book frustrating at first, because he kept wondering where the data was. Once he realized there wasn't going to be any data as such, he sat back and enjoyed the journey and the story—and the rest of the letter was laudatory. It was a wonderful letter to get and it made me think about my purpose in writing the book.

Slovic: Once he finally was able to set aside his expectation for a kind of factual fidelity and focus on *chasing monarchs,* what do you think he was appreciating about the book?

Pyle: Well, he is a naturalist, and the book contains a great deal of natural history and not all of it was in need of correction. But I think he liked the progression of the journey—I mean it's a pretty straightforward road book (what one reviewer called "*On the Road* with monarchs"). If you tell a road trip well, it's hard to resist.

But I should also tell you that Jerry Powell was the first editor I ever had in my life, for articles I submitted to *The Journal of the Lepidopterists' Society.* The *Journal* had been founded by Charles Remington when he was a graduate student at Harvard in the same laboratory where Vladimir Nabokov worked. That was in 1947, the year I was born. I met Remington when I was twelve, in Colorado, and he encouraged my interest in butterflies. A few years later, when I was entering college, Jerry Powell was editor of the *Journal* at Berkeley. When my mother died in 1967, I wrote an obituary of her for the journal. It was an appreciation, really, because a lot of the lepidopterists knew her. I also wrote a couple of pieces about butterfly phenomena I'd observed. These were part of my early struggling attempts to try to sort out these very same kinds of questions. At the time, I was much enamored of the Victorian writing style typical of the early naturalists. They weren't particularly precise, but their language was lovely in its time and context.

So, I wrote these early pieces aping the nineteenth-century naturalists, and Jerry would not let a young man off the hook about that. Even in this [recent] letter, he says, "You use more adjectives per page than any writer that I know." He even quoted "shades of the azure clouds," which refers back to the writing I had submitted to him about an extraordinary swarm of butterflies in Colorado in 1967, thirty-three years ago. He rejected it at first given all my azure clouds of butterflies, but he eventually published it after he worked me through it, making it more precise. So you can imagine getting this letter after all these years; it really had quite an impact on me.

Satterfield: Do you think he is a special case of a very empirically oriented and hard-headed scientific thinker who also has an openness to this more narrative or lyrical mode of writing, or do you anticipate that most scientists as well as people working in the fields of environmental law and policy would be interested in these other forms of expression?

Pyle: I don't think Jerry is a special case. I think that most scientists are susceptible to being moved by lyricism and narrative. It is just that their training leaves behind a pretty hard and thick and tall wall.

Satterfield: Remember, one of our purposes in conducting these interviews is to understand the role of narrative better in the context of expressing both technical or scientific information and what is often called "environmental values." Is there something in narrative that renders these two kinds of content visible, or does the form obscure or clutter these materials?

Pyle: Well, it should make things more accessible. One of the reasons that I have a foot in both areas is that I *feel* I have an obligation to bring both these components together. Many of the very best writers have done that. Thoreau did exactly that. Nabokov did it in spades, and Rachel Carson did so as well.

I'm not making comparisons, but these are people that I do aspire toward precisely because they accomplished both of these ends. If you read Gary Nabhan's *The Desert Smells Like Rain*, you will get wonderful natural history, scientifically reliable information, but in a way that is palatable and delightful. The science writer often fails in this; an awful lot of science writers employ journalistic tropes that verge on the cutesy and the cliché because they feel obliged to make it "pop" in the popular-culture sense of the word. It might be good for a giggle, but what is it going to sound like in five years? It's not literature for the ages, that's for sure.

Slovic: You used the terms "palatable" and "delightful." I'm curious to know what it is about narrative expression, I mean on a philosophical level, or a psychological level, that we as human beings tend to find palatable, pleasing, delightful. And how does this compare to other forms of language? Are we talking about a kind of language that is and should remain completely separate from the realm of environmental policy? Is it ridiculous to bring such ideas as palatability and delightfulness into the realm of official discussion?

Pyle: Well, what comes through in most of the public discussions and meetings are not only the facts and the law but also questions of beauty and all of these intangibles. The county commissioners are resistant to considering such things because they're not points of law. They are afraid of being sued if they turn down a development application that is not based on law. But I have seen enough instances where language of the heart in smart balance with language of the head has brought about the desired conclusion. Not necessarily even a political end, but a desirable conclusion where people consider things from a broader spectrum.

I'm not able to separate a political response to the world from an artistic response to the world because everything that inspires our artistic response is under threat. I mean it just is. I suppose that some people are able to completely dissociate themselves from that, from the prevailing peril, but somehow I have to believe that alternate expression, literary—or "narrative"—expression, will make a difference.

Satterfield: But does this not then run squarely into the enlightenment premise that emotional dimensions of experience are regarded as extraneous, unnecessary, maybe even intrusive?

Pyle: Yes, that's why scientists, including those capable of being moved by narrative expression, are reluctant to admit it. They believe that things progress by means visible to the scientific method; so do I, but I believe that literature can also illuminate reality, so getting a letter like Jerry's utterly reinforces that for me. The differentiation of the factual and emotional, or just the nonfactual (I'm not wedded to the term "emotional"), can be completely subverted in essays or narrative nonfiction. I believe that if you are able to approach both sides of experience, the emotional and the observational-factual, in the same piece of writing, which is then read seriously, you have a chance to convince with both artfulness and fact.

Satterfield: What about these questions in the context of public hearings? Typically there are people who are using emotional appeals and narrative to put forth what matters to them and others who are using a more technical language.

Pyle: My experience is actually rather disheartening in that respect. I have seen many instances of the facilitator announcing that "we are not here to consider emotional things." The usual thing is to simply exclude that content up front. So, frankly, I think the evolution of the facilitator, and the facilitated meeting, has been one of the most insidious developments in public discourse that I have ever seen. Previously it would just be a hearing, and anybody could get up there and talk. Oh, man, talk about an emotionally stultifying impact. It's a great way to organize a lot of information, but it's also an extremely cynical and adept way to defuse the emotions of the public. Even when it's organized by the facilitator toward a good political end, it's still deeply cynical.

Slovic: We have all seen public hearings that probably produce enormous tomes of testimony, and yet what are the managers to do with this, with these tomes? I discussed this with an environmental lawyer I know, and she said, "The most honest thing that public officials could probably do would be to take these volumes of testimony and just shred them on the spot, and say this is essentially what is going to happen." Instead, they put them on display, and say these are available to people, but they are seldom used by people making decisions. So how do we make linkages between the events at which these testimonials are gathered and the meetings of the officials who are tasked with the formulation of policy statements or making of practical management decisions?

Pyle: By insisting that they consult their own hearts as well as their heads, and giving them the kinds of stories that show how to integrate thought and feeling. I have great sympathy for these agencies; they are taxed with the enormous burden of public response that comes with this era of increased public involvement. But what they have taken to doing is excerpting statements from the hearings that best fit the agency's goals. I don't mean to say that there aren't well-intentioned individuals conducting hearings, but I still think the public consultation processes as they stand have the power to deeply distance officials from participants' emotions—from the public's feelings—about the issues under discussion.

Slovic: How does that distancing happen? Is it because the meetings are too structured? Is it because to call something a "hearing" suggests a formality that renders certain kinds of value expressions taboo or embarrassing?

Pyle: Well, sometimes the structure is almost jury-like. Participants are frequently given verbal cues that keep them focused on a limited set of facts. The facilitator will often re-state the questions for the questioner in an editorializing manner, and there is often a certain amount of persuasion to stick to the point—that is, the facilitator's point. There is no secret about it. There is an onus that rides with expressing your heart in these situations.

Satterfield: But this is why the language of values is so ambiguous. Technically, the term "values" encompasses a definition that speaks both to dollar worth and also to belief, commitment, meaning, moral content, etc. In the kinds of consultation processes we're discussing, facilitators will often say "we want to know what your values are," but one is often expected to respond not with a narrative about what matters and why but with something more like an abstract statement of philosophy or belief.

Slovic: On the other hand, I have sometimes attended meetings where

Native American activists are permitted, even respectfully encouraged, to offer narratives of place as a way of communicating how their values or world views are linked to specific places.

Pyle: Exactly—it is so patronizing. By making permission group-specific, racially specific, it marginalizes the impulse of *all* people toward narrative-style expression. Earlier today I was reading about the battle between the Quinaults and the Cowlitz. The Quinaults don't want the Cowlitz to be recognized as having a say over archaeological remains, and so on. In that dialogue, they can talk about spiritual values, about values of the heart. They can even talk about ghosts, for that matter. But Euros are assumed to be devoid of this orientation. Or maybe it's just that to express such values, in such a manner, is to betray one's culture. Different rules for different cultures.

But then writers sometimes play a similar role. We're allowed, as I was at a recent technical conference on the Cherry Creek watershed in Denver, to speak in heartful terms. I did this by evoking each participant's own special place, the place responsible for making them care about management. You should have seen the faces in the audience; it was like exercising mass hypnosis. They were enraptured. I purposely used language that went beyond all the formal talks because I was in a privileged position, speaking "as writer."

Satterfield: So writers get away with something that your audience members wish they could?

Pyle: I'm not sure. I just know that when I'm keynoting, speaking at a luncheon, whatever, I am there in order to take listeners out of their frame. Hard-headed people: you can draw them into this state of mind that is rapturous. You look out over the audience, and you see this sea of faces. Of course, the rapture doesn't last very long, because then we get down to talking about facts and ideas and challenges.

Satterfield: But when talking about enchanting people as you were just now, are you trying to open the door to a wider breadth of possible value expressions or are you wanting to persuade audiences to accept your point of view, and is that a good thing?

Slovic: Yes, are you undermining rationality? Are people wedded to the expository language of science and politics afraid of a narrative language for its perceived lack of rationality, even though they might recognize that this is the only language through which we can talk about certain things?

Pyle: Well, there are a lot of people who have a clear agenda. But I don't think we should fear the artistic imagination, the opposite slope if you will. Still, I do grow tired of a certain amount of soft-headedness; one can become too personal, flaccid, and end up with oatmeal for ideas. That doesn't help at all.

Slovic: We have talked on other occasions about precision; is this what you mean?

Pyle: Yes, it really is. I think of precision in several different respects. One of them is simply as a literary technique, just being careful, using the right words. But precision means looking harder, looking more deeply, looking with more tools, expanding your repertoire of perceptive skills. I often work with students on paying attention to sensory detail, which is not something we can do all the time, as we'd all become mad with the sheer level of stimulus. But if you can work with people so that they become aware that the Swainson's thrushes are singing a little bit more now than they were an hour ago when it was a little bit warmer . . .

In other words, try to be aware at different levels of different sensations. Go forth and actually touch more than they do, smell a great deal more. Part of precision is experiencing more deeply, and then trying to match that to the language. That's the very hard part. Try writing about smell. It's terribly difficult to express properly, but it must be done and done well. I did my Master's in nature interpretation with a real master, Grant Sharpe. I didn't stick with that field, but he gave me some insights that have affected all my writing. For example, interpretation seeks not just to deliver information, but to evoke the curiosity of a visitor to a natural place. Also, if it doesn't relate to the visitor's experience, then clearly it can't make much of a score. I think these principles apply equally well to writers and readers. If our discourse can relate to the experience of citizens and policy makers, to arouse their curiosity, then it might break through to wider possibilities of resolution.

This is what I think narrative does very successfully. Once you can start telling a story, and get people drawn in, you open them to a broader way of looking at things. I like the phrase given me by a Navajo wrangler, "Take your imagination out of your hip pocket"—doing that causes vulnerability, expansiveness. Frankly, you are trying to find a chink in the armor of objectivity. Because it is a kind of armor, I am convinced, even though I am a proponent of the scientific method. I am convinced that commerce and industry gird themselves with an armor of the invulnerability of reason. Yet I think reason embraces emotion. How could it not? We're emotional beasts.

I've seen a number of decisions made where people have been affected, finally, by something beyond sheer dollars and cents. I wrote about an example in an essay on Hendrickson Canyon, only 160 acres, but also the very last old-growth forest in this entire county. We have been worrying the issue of its protection like a dog with an old toy for twenty years. We finally got the canyon set aside because doing so made sense, but also because we got an awful lot of people to express their feelings about it. Or the South Nemah Cedars, which is a significant old-growth cedar reserve in the next county over. That came about largely because the commissioner of public lands was out there nosing around without his staff, when a member of our group told him a story about an old hollow cedar tree. He wanted to see it. Our friends led him to the ancient cedar, and he got down inside of it. Then he went back to his office in Olympia [the state capital] and raised Nemah from Number Twenty to Number One on the list of lands to be considered for protection. Here is a policy maker, an elected official responsible for six million acres that are supposed to produce income for the schools of the state and their trusts, and yet he was influenced by a narrative, by the feelings the place evoked in him.

Satterfield: Let's move our attention, for a moment, to the central subject of this book, which is environmental values. Can you tell us first what that phrase means to you, what comes to mind?

Pyle: I guess the phrase "environmental values" means everything to me. I mean it's my whole life. I don't mean to sound sanctimonious but I'm a naturalist, which has been true for my entire life, and I was an activist from the beginning. Thea and I helped found the Conservation Council at the University of Washington in our earliest days there. But to say I'm a naturalist is not to say I'm misanthropic. I look at my own species with a jaundiced eye, and yet I am also a lover of my species. My particular philosophy is one that allows me to easily incorporate humans and their foibles into natural history. So, I cannot imagine living a life in which environmental values or conservation are not the number-one subject. That's why it's so distressing when I hear an entire presidential campaign in which the only reference to conservation involves *growing the economy while protecting the environment.*

I live in a place where people still, to some extent, draw their livelihoods from the land. There's going to be a meeting tomorrow night that I don't think I will be attending in which people are going to be discussing agency plans to buy out this valley for the flood plain. Let the river run its course, not try to stop it any more. Of course, the local people who still have a sense of community and history here are extremely offended by this idea.

As a naturalist, I find it an absolutely glorious idea, but I am also a member of this community who wishes to live and thrive here in a modest manner. So my deeper values say, yes, let us live on the fringes as makes sense—let us not try to dominate the valley as they've tried for a hundred years, a pattern that has finally failed. But I also try not to rub my beliefs in my neighbors' faces, nor would I say that they don't have environmental values.

Satterfield: How does the term come into play in your writing? Are you attempting to inculcate something like your version of environmental values? Are you hoping that readers will spot something that is already there but latent, or . . . ?

Pyle: To some extent the question has everything to do with why I began writing. One reason was my fascination with butterflies and the rest of the natural world, and my desire to make a contribution to our knowledge about both those things. But the second reason was a hope for influence. A lot of my early writing was just out-and-out propaganda, rhetoric.

Satterfield: But you abandoned propaganda—why?

Pyle: Well, I don't think I did. I think I just became more subtle.

Satterfield: Because you catch more bees with honey?

Pyle: To some extent, that's true, but it's also a matter of having a little more respect for the reader's ability to sort it out, to suck it out of what I am saying. I also just think it's better writing. Laying it right out there in one's face is neither elegant nor graceful. I think one can grow tired of a steady diet of conservation journalism. It can be distressing to the point of rendering the reader moribund.

Slovic: We are entering, again, into the question of what constitutes permissible and impermissible writing. If the engineers become too fanciful, the space shuttle will crash, or the bridge will fall under its own weight. But how does the idea transfer to environmental policy, which is supposed to reflect, to some extent, public opinion? If the formulator of a policy statement moves into rhapsody, will the policy be coherent? Will it operate as a blueprint that will enable legislators and citizens to understand how a place or a particular resource should be managed?

Pyle: That's a very good question, but I don't think it's really equivalent. These people are not writing literature. They are not writing reportage. They are not writing scientific papers. They're making cultural determinations, and this is a different thing. A cultural determination frankly, in my opinion, absolutely ought to incorporate every possible kind of tool. An urban plan is not like a space shuttle—it neither flies nor crashes. The field of new urbanism attempts, for instance, to make city plans that no longer separate the nonhuman externalities from human behavior, which had been the hallmark of urban design since the World Wars. It's a return to the organic growth that preceded the wars. That was often a bit of a hodge-podge, but it led to diversity and interesting places.

Slovic: This hodge-podge model sounds rather like the preference you mentioned earlier for essay forms in which one could combine both human passion and defensible technical or scientific information. But we never really got around to discussing how one accomplishes a synthesis of this kind. Do you mark the text when shifting from one mode to another? And if so, how is that done in your own writing?

Pyle: Sometimes it's done with a direct transition, but that can be over-slick. In *Wintergreen* I move back and forth—from slithering across a greasy glass of wild, metaphorical celebration and whimsy to a fair amount of fact. Here's an example:

> Eruptions occur daily. Out of the twigs of trees, catkins pounce on unsuspecting scenes. Hazel's long canary danglers, alder's rufous tassels, and pussy willow's pearly tail-tips all break the silence of the branches. Below, unexpected pushers break out of the banks of shale and orange siltstone slides. Among the limp, rotted rags of last year's horsetails, the new crop appears. The green, vegetative plants that first resemble the myriad evergreen seedlings that sprinkle the roadside before drying out and dying. . . .

You can read that paragraph and find information that you could equally get from a botanical text, but it's stated in a way that's often metaphorical. I just trust the reader much of the time to be able to say, "Okay, hazel, and alder, and pussy willow catkins all come out at the same time. Okay, good, I'm glad to know they all come out then, and the pussy willow is gray, and the hazel is yellow, and the alder is rufous." The facts are all there, but they are stated in language that gives my personal take on those colors. In some ways it's more precise this way than if I had used terms like staminate, acuminate, and fuscous.

Then in the next paragraph, "Meanwhile, up in the forest fringe, a revolution takes place in the salmonberry brakes. Unrest at swollen nodes hints of leaves to come, while riots break out at the flower buds as cerise packets of petals unfold." No reader is going to be dumb enough to think there's actually a riot going on—it's strictly metaphorical, but at the same time the information that's given is rock solid, and cerise is a precise description of those colors. To some extent it's a matter of trust, but I guess when I speak of context I mean a sense of utter honesty, that you're not stating anything that any sensible reader could read and think it was fact when it's actually lyric perception. I mean, in that particular passage I think I combined the two all the way through. I think any sensible reader is going to come away from that both with a sense of my take on the place and also with a sense of the actual progression of the season.

Satterfield: So, again, it's a form of precision through which the reader can come to know, see, and hear exactly what you're trying to convey both technically and experientially.

Pyle: Well, that's right. But now you see if the alders came a month later than hazels, but I tucked them in there for poetic reasons, that then would be a dishonesty. In the essay form, you cannot manufacture something in order to make it *seem* real when in fact it is not.

Satterfield: But this is very tricky to police. A lot of people would not see that distinction which might, in turn, be what a lot of scientists would say about the hazard of this synthetic language.

Pyle: That's true. There's a great deal of ignorance about natural history out there, so it's easy to mislead.

Satterfield: Or if your goal as natural historian is to teach, then you have to establish some indication that you're doing an accurate job, that you are deserving of trust.

Pyle: That's right. That goes back to the old nature-faker debate with Roosevelt and Burroughs versus Seton Thompson. The way some would make things up in pursuit of narrative punch—Seton Thompson would actually manufacture material. It's like Disney's photographers first herding the lemmings over the cliff, therefore leading to an image that generations of people have believed is actually true, that lemmings really do go looking for cliffs to jump off of.

Slovic: This has been a heated debate in recent years, following, for instance, Annie Dillard's revelations about her cat, or the nonexistence of her cat. And John C. Van Dyke has been accused of not really observing the southwestern deserts that he writes about up close, as he professed to have done.

Satterfield: So the concern with new forms then is how to establish an ethos, a set of rules or precedent, that will not be transgressed? Does such a thing exist for natural historians but not for those who write *like* natural historians?

Pyle: Yes, I think it does. The great gift of the scientific method is that people who are schooled in it realize that there are certain standards even when one is not conducting a controlled experiment. Joseph Grinnell, the great zoologist from Berkeley, came up with a method of note taking, a Grinnell journal, that enabled you to lay out what was observed in a very objective manner. Another teacher of natural history that I know draws lyricism out of his students, but he also has them keep a Grinnell journal. Some teachers will try to mush the two together, and I've experimented with both in my own journals, and frankly people are better equipped, if they have a bit of scientific training or solid natural history training, to distinguish the purposes of the two. When people just try to mimic that, and they have neither the knowledge nor the rigor, it fails. There is such a thing as artistic rigor. Again, it comes down to precision, careful observation, and honesty. But scientific rigor, in the absence of experimentation, is simply viewing and trying to relate what you perceive in the sharpest possible terms. I don't think science and metaphor must be mutually exclusive. But I do think that there is a strong burden of honesty to be adhered to there.

Satterfield: We were talking about issues of trust, credibility, and authority, and the extent to which these rhetorical stances or relationships between a speaker and an audience are embedded in the kind of language that's being used. We have sort of been trained through multiple generations in western society to think of science or science-like language as possessing a truth-carrying quality that is implied by invoking certain terms.

Pyle: That's so, and sometimes it does; but so-called science-like language has no monopoly on truth. I recently heard a lecture on the writing of Thoreau versus the work of Susan Fenimore Cooper. The lecturer's point was to distinguish in their writing the representation of anthropocentric versus biocentric values. But it really seemed to me to be a question of style: Thoreau wrote people into his work more than Cooper did. But that doesn't necessarily mean that the one author holds a different or truer value perspective than the other.

Slovic: Yes, it may just be a different style of self-representation. Norman Mailer versus John McPhee. There is an interesting discussion about Annie Dillard's persona in *Pilgrim at Tinker Creek* that the author presented in an article written years after the book came out. Originally, she began writing that book from the perspective of a male persona. She then decided that wouldn't work and ultimately moved toward a relatively gender-neutral persona. It would be very hard to get a fix on the identity of the narrator if you didn't know who wrote the book.

Pyle: Well, many women will tell you, especially those of Dillard's generation and older, that they were taught to retreat from the expression of self in literature. The two pieces of writing I referred to may reflect this. Thoreau was a great scientific writer, but he was also a personal essayist, full of opinion and refraction and allusion; while Cooper was not as comfortable expressing herself personally.

Slovic: To close, let's address a practical point. If you, Bob, were addressing a policy audience and you wanted to make the point that the language of narrative is a significant medium through which to express ideas about environmental values, how would you make that point? How would you address that audience?

Pyle: I tend to look for people's personal fascination, perhaps with insects or monarchs or their own special place, which is often very distinct from their public involvement. I attempt to find something vivid in their imagination and then invite them to tell their own heartfelt stories. This helps to establish a realm of good faith and trust. I think a lot of natural-history writing begins with the premise that there's such a bond between the author and his or her audience because there is an implied relationship between speaker (writer) and listener (reader) that is unique to natural history. And I try to let those who are skeptical know that I honor the line between fiction and nonfiction, that narrative does not necessarily mean manipulation, error, or lack of scientific rigor.

To give you an example of how narrative can affect policy, I have long been working with many others to try to get the Dark Divide roadless area in the Washington Cascades protected as wilderness. The science of the situation should be enough to clinch the case. But I find that some of the Forest Service bureaucrats and politicians are really more interested in the Bigfoot stories that come out of the Dark Divide, which I wrote about in *Where Bigfoot Walks*. The power of a good myth, whether it corresponds to the facts on the ground or not, is that it gives people something to go on, to grab hold of. When the Dark Divide is formally protected, I bet it will owe at least as much to the persuasive power of wildness as embodied in the Sasquatch stories as to the biology of the place.

♦

The Extinction Of Experience[1]

> We need not marvel at extinction; if we must marvel, let it be at our own presumption in imagining for a moment that we understand the many complex contingencies on which the existence of each species depends.
> —Charles Darwin, *The Origin of Species*

I became a nonbeliever and a conservationist in one fell swoop. All it took was the Lutherans paving their parking lot.

One central, unavoidable fact of my childhood was the public school system of Aurora, Colorado. My path to school for ten out of twelve years followed the same route: down Revere Street, left at the fire hall, along Hoffman Park to Del Mar Circle, then around the Circle to Peoria Street, and on to whichever school was currently claiming my time. Detours occurred frequently.

The intersection of Hoffman Boulevard and Peoria Street was two corners sacred, two profane. On the southeast squatted the white brick Baptist church. Across Del Mar lay a vacant lot full of pigweed, where Tom and I cached brown bananas and other castoffs foraged from behind Busley's Supermarket in case we needed provisions on some future expedition. Then came the Phillips 66 gas station and the Kwik Shake, a nineteen-cent hamburger stand whose jukebox played "Peggy Sue" if you so much as tossed a nickel in its direction. On the northeast corner lay Saint Mark's, the red brick lair of the Lutherans, marginally modern, with a stained glass cross in the wall. I spent quite a lot of time dawdling in the vacant lot among the pigweed and haunting the Kwik Shake after school, but I seldom loitered in the precincts of the churchgoers.

Lukewarm Methodists at best, my parents flipped a coin and took us to Saint Mark's for the Easter service. The next Christmas I was roped into being a wise man, and I felt both silly and cold in my terry cloth robe. Later, when my great-grandmother came to live with us, she hauled me off Sundays to the Southern Baptists. Gimma desperately wanted me to go down the aisle and be saved. A shy boy, I wasn't about to prostrate myself in public before a bunch of people with big smiles and bad grammar. Besides, I couldn't see the sense in confessing to sins I didn't feel I had properly enjoyed as yet. Had I been compelled to choose among them, I'd have taken the cool, impersonal approach of the Lutherans over the Baptists' warm-hearted but embarrassing bear hug of a welcome. But Gimma passed on, and my parents pushed in neither direction, so I opted for the corporeal pleasures of "Peggy Sue" and pigweed and put the soul on hold.

Behind the Lutheran church lay another, smaller vacant lot, where the congregation parked in the mud. The new community of Hoffman Heights had been built partly on a filled-in lake. The water poked up here and there, making marshy spots full of plants that grew nowhere else around, like cattails and curly dock. The far corner of the Lutherans' lot held one of the last of these.

One September day, coming home from school, I cut across the boggy corner, almost dried out with late summer and tall with weeds. Pink knotweed daubed the broken mud and scented the afternoon air. Then I noticed, fully spread on the knotweed bloom, a butterfly. It was more than an inch across, richly brown like last year's pennies, with a purple sheen when the sun caught it just right. I knelt and watched it for a long time. There were others flitting around, some of them orange, some brown, but this one stayed put, basking. Then a car drove by, disturbing it. The last thing I noticed before it flew was a broad, bright zigzag of fiery orange across its hind wings.

A couple of years later, when I became an ardent collector, I remembered the butterfly in the Del Mar marshlet clearly. My Peterson field guide showed me that it was, without question, a bronze copper. The orangey ones had been females. Professor Alexander Klots wrote in his *Peterson Field Guide* that it is "the largest of our coppery Coppers" and "not uncommon, but quite local. Seek a colony," he wrote, "in open, wet meadows." Dr. F. Martin Brown, in my bible, *Colorado Butterflies,* explained that the species extended no farther west than the plains of eastern Colorado, and called it *very* local (which I translated as "rare"). He went on to say that "the best places to seek *[Lycaena] thoe* in Colorado are the weedy borders of well-established reservoirs on the plains," which the Hoffman Heights lake had certainly been. I eagerly prepared to return to the spot at the right time and obtain *Lycaena thoe* for my collection.

Then, in early summer, the Lutherans paved their parking lot. They dumped loads of broken concrete and earthfill into the little marsh, then covered it with thick black asphalt. Gone were the curly docks, the knotweeds, the coppers. Searching all around Aurora over the next few years I failed to find another colony, or even a single bronze copper. Concluding that a good and loving god would never permit his faithful servants to do such a thing, I gave up on the Lutherans and their like for the long run.

Biologists agree that the rate of species extinction has risen sharply since the introduction of agriculture and industry to the human landscape. Soon the decline might mirror ancient mass extinction episodes that were caused by atmospheric or astronomic events. In response, we compile lists and red books of endangered species and seek to manage conditions in their favor. This is good, if only occasionally successful.

Our concern for the absolute extinction of species is highly appropriate. As our partners in earth's enterprise drop out, we find ourselves lonelier, less sure of our ability to hold together the tattered business of life. Every effort to prevent further losses is worthwhile, no matter how disruptive, for diversity is its own reward. But outright extinction is not the only problem. By concentrating on the truly rare and endangered plants and animals, conservationists often neglect another form of loss that can have striking consequences: the local extinction.

Protection almost always focuses on rarity as the criterion for attention. Conservation ecologists employ a whole lexicon of categories to define scarceness. In ascending order of jeopardy, the hierarchy usually includes the terms "of concern" (= "monitor"), "sensitive," "threatened" (= "vulnerable"), and "endangered." All types so listed might fairly be called "rare." But people tend to employ that term when some other word might be more precise.

Most species listed as endangered are genuinely rare in the absolute sense: their range is highly restricted and their total number is never high. Biologists recognize a fuzzy threshold below which the populations of these organisms should not drop, lest their extinction likely follow. That level is a kind of critical mass, the minimum number necessary to maintain mating and other essential functions. A creature is profoundly rare when its members are so few as to approach this perilous line.

Perceived rarity is often a matter of the distribution of a species over time and space. The monarch butterfly, for example, is virtually absent from the Maritime Northwest owing to the lack of milkweed, while across most of North America it is considered a commonplace creature. Patchy and fluctuating from year to year when dispersed in the summertime, monarchs become incredibly abundant in their Mexican and Californian winter roosts. Yet the migration of the North American monarch is listed as a threatened phenomenon because of the extreme vulnerability of the winter clusters.

Another orange and black butterfly, the painted lady, appears in northern latitudes by the millions from time to time. In certain springs, such as those of 1991 and 1992, these butterflies block entire highways with their very numbers. In drier years, when their southern winter habitat produces little nectar, nary a lady might be seen in the temperate regions come summertime. Nevertheless, this thistle-loving immigrant is so widespread globally that its alternate name is the cosmopolite. Are these insects common or rare? Evidently they can be either. Painted ladies and monarchs stretch our sense of rarity.

The concept becomes a little less slippery when we speak of sedentary or specialized animals and plants such as the bronze copper. But are such creatures actually rare, or merely "local," as Professor Klots described the copper in 1951? The fact is that as the countryside condenses under human influence, that which was only local has a way of becoming genuinely scarce. Somewhere along the continuum from abundance to extinction, a passenger pigeon becomes a pileated woodpecker, then a northern spotted owl, then nothing at all.

In light of the relativity of rarity, it is not surprising that scarce wildlife preservation resources go almost entirely to the more truly rare species. But, as with Ronald Reagan's decision to restrict federal aid to those he considered "truly needy," this practice leaves many vulnerable populations subject to extinction at the local level.

Local extinctions matter for at least three major reasons. First, evolutionary biologists believe that natural selection operates intensely on "edge" populations. This means that the cutting edge of evolution can be the extremities of a species' range rather than the center, where it is more numerous. The protection of marginal populations therefore becomes important. Local extinctions commonly occur on the edges, depriving species of this important opportunity for adaptive change.

Second, little losses add up to big losses. A colony goes extinct here, a population drops out there, and before you know it, you have an endangered species. Attrition, once under way, is progressive. "Between German chickens and Irish hogs," wrote San Francisco entomologist H. H. Behr to his Chicago friend Herman Strecker in 1875, "no insect can exist besides louse and flea." Behr was lamenting the diminution of native insects on the San Francisco Peninsula. Already at that early date, butterflies such as the Xerces blue were becoming difficult to find as colony after colony disappeared before the expanding city. In the early 1940s the Xerces blue became absolutely extinct. Thus local losses accumulate, undermining the overall flora and fauna.

The third consequence amounts to a different kind of depletion. I call it the *extinction of experience.* Simply stated, the loss of neighborhood species endangers our experience of nature. If a species becomes extinct within our own radius of reach (smaller for the very old, very young, disabled, and poor), it might as well be gone altogether, in one important sense. To those whose access suffers by it, local extinction has much the same result as global eradication.

Of course, we are all diminished by the extirpation of animals and plants wherever they occur. Many people take deep satisfaction in wilderness and wildlife they will never see. But direct, personal contact with other living things affects us in vital ways that vicarious experience can never replace.

I believe that one of the greatest causes of the ecological crisis is the state of personal alienation from nature in which many people live. We lack a widespread sense of intimacy with the living world. Natural history has never been more popular in some ways, yet few people organize their lives around nature, or even allow it to affect them profoundly. Our depth of contact is too often wanting. Two distinctive birds, by the ways in which they fish, furnish a model for what I mean.

Brown pelicans fish by slamming directly into the sea, great bills agape, making sure of solid contact with the resource they seek. Black skimmers, graceful ternlike birds with longer lower mandibles than upper, fly over the surface with just the lower halves of their bills in the water. They catch fish too, but avoid bodily immersion by merely skimming the surface.

In my view, most people who consider themselves nature lovers behave more like skimmers than pelicans. They buy the right outfits at L. L. Bean and Eddie Bauer, carry field guides, and take walks on nature trails, reading all the interpretive signs. They watch the nature programs on television, shop at the Nature Company, and pay their dues to the National Wildlife Federation or the National Audubon Society. These activities are admirable, but they do not ensure truly intimate contact with nature. Many such "naturalists" merely skim, reaping a shallow reward. Yet the great majority of the people associate with nature even less.

When the natural world becomes chiefly an entertainment or an obligation, it loses its ability to arouse our deeper instincts. Professor E. O. Wilson of Harvard University , who has won two Pulitzer prizes for his penetrating looks at both humans and insects, believes we all possess what he calls "biophilia." To Wilson, this means that humans have an innate desire to connect with other life forms, and that to do so is highly salutary. Nature is therapeutic. As short-story writer Valerie Martin tells us in "The Consolation of Nature," only nature can restore a sense of safety in the end. But clearly, too few people ever realize their potential love of nature. So where does the courtship fail? How can we engage our biophilia?

Everyone has at least a chance of realizing a pleasurable and collegial wholeness with nature. But to get there, intimate association is necessary. A face-to-face encounter with a banana slug means much more than a Komodo dragon seen on television. With rhinos mating in the living room, who will care about the creatures next door? At least the skimmers are aware of nature. As for the others, whose lives hold little place for nature, how can they even care?

The extinction of experience is not just about losing the personal benefits of the natural high. It also implies a cycle of disaffection that can have disastrous consequences. As cities and metastasizing suburbs forsake their natural diversity, and their citizens grow more removed from personal contact with nature, awareness and appreciation retreat. This breeds apathy toward environmental concerns and, inevitably, further degradation of the common habitat.

So it goes, on and on, the extinction of experience sucking the life from the land, the intimacy from our connections. This is how the passing of otherwise common species from our immediate vicinities can be as significant as the total loss of rarities. People who care conserve; people who don't know don't care. What is the extinction of the condor to a child who has never known a wren?

In teaching about butterflies, I frequently place a living butterfly on a child's nose. Noses seem to make perfectly good perches or basking spots, and the insect often remains for some time. Almost everyone is delighted by this, the light tickle, the close-up colors, the thread of a tongue probing for droplets of perspiration. But somewhere beyond delight lies enlightenment. I have been astonished at the small epiphanies I see in the eyes of a child in truly close contact with nature, perhaps for the first time. This can happen to grown-ups too, reminding them of something they never knew they had forgotten.

We are finally discovering the link between our biophilia and our future. With new eyes, planners are leaving nature in the suburbs and inviting it back into the cities as never before. For many species the effort comes too late, since once gone, they can be desperately difficult to reestablish. But at least the adaptable types can be fostered with care and forethought.

The initiatives of urban ecologists are making themselves felt in many cities. In Portland, Oregon, Urban Naturalist Mike Houck worked to have the great blue heron designated the official city bird, to have a local microbrewery fashion an ale to commemorate it, and to fill in the green leaks in a forty-mile-loop greenway envisioned decades ago. Now known as the

140-Mile Loop, it ties in with a massive urban greenspaces program on both sides of the Columbia River. An international conference entitled "Country in the City" takes place annually in Portland, pushing urban diversity. These kinds of efforts arise from a recognition of the extinction of experience and a fervid desire to avoid its consequences.

Houck has launched an effort to involve the arts community in refreshing the cities and devoted himself to urban stream restoration. When streams are rescued from the storm drains, they are said (delightfully) to be "daylighted." And when each city has someone like Mike Houck working to daylight its streams, save its woods, and educate its planners, the sources of our experience will be safer.

But nature reserves and formal greenways are not enough to ensure connection. Such places, important as they are, invite a measured, restricted kind of contact. When children come along with an embryonic interest in natural history, they need free places for pottering, netting, catching, and watching. Insects, crawdads, and tadpoles can stand to be nabbed a good deal. Bug collecting has always been the standard route to a serious interest in biology. To expect a strictly appreciative first response from a child is quixotic. Young naturalists need the "trophy," hands-on stage before leapfrogging to mere looking. There need to be places that are not kid-proofed, where children can do damage and come back the following year to see the results.

Likewise, we all need spots near home where we can wander off a trail, lift a stone, poke about, and merely wonder: places where no interpretive signs intrude their message to rob our spontaneous response. Along with the nature centers, parks, and preserves, we would do well to maintain a modicum of open space with no rule but common courtesy, no sign besides animal tracks.

For these purposes, nothing serves better than the hand-me-down habitats that lie somewhere between formal protection and development. Throwaway landscapes like this used to occur on the edges of settlement everywhere. Richard Mabey, a British writer and naturalist, describes them as the "unofficial countryside." He uses the term for those ignominious, degraded, forgotten places that we have discarded, which serve nonetheless as habitats for a broad array of adaptable plants and animals: derelict railway land, ditchbanks, abandoned farms or bankrupt building sites, old gravel pits and factory yards, embankments, margins of landfills. These are the secondhand lands as opposed to the parks, forests, preserves, and dedicated rural farmland that constitute the "official countryside."

Organisms inhabiting such Cinderella sites are surprisingly varied, interesting, and numerous. They are the survivors, the colonizers, the generalists—the so-called weedy species. Or, in secreted corners and remnants of older habitat types—like the Lutherans' parking lot—specialists and rarities might survive as holdouts, waiting to be discovered by the watchful. Developers, realtors, and the common parlance refer to such weedy enclaves as "vacant lots" and "waste ground." But these are two of my favorite oxymorons: What, to a curious kid, is less vacant than a vacant lot? Less wasted than waste ground?

I grew up in a landscape lavishly scattered with unofficial countryside—vacant lots aplenty, a neglected so-called park where weeds had their way, yesterday's farms, and the endless open ground of the High Line Canal looping off east and west. These were the leftovers of the early suburban leap. They were rich with possibility. I could catch a bug, grab a crawdad, run screaming from a giant garden spider; intimacy abounded.

But Aurora slathered itself across the High Plains, its so-called city limits becoming broader than those of Denver itself. In reality it knew no limits, neither the limit of available water nor that of livability. Of course the lots filled in, losing the legacy of their vacancy. The park actually became one, and almost all of its fascination fled before the spade and the blade of the landscaper's art. By the time the canal became an official pathway, part of the National Trail System, most of the little nodes of habitat embraced within its curves and loops were long gone. As butterflies fled before bulldozers, the experience I'd known was buried in the 'burbs.

In a decade I recorded about seventy kinds of butterflies—a tenth of all the North American species—along the canal. In doing so, I learned perhaps the most important thing the High Line had to teach, which was also the saddest. It had to do with the very basis of ecology, that organisms ask their own specific needs of the landscape, and when these cease to be met, they vanish unless adaptation happens fast enough to accommodate change and allow species to survive.

The admiral butterflies flitting along the High Line Canal were survivors. Butterflies related to both red and white admirals lived in central Colorado approximately 35 million years ago, as shown by Oligocene fossils from the shale beds of Ancient Lake Florissant. Sharing many characteristics with today's relatives, they kept up with changing landscapes and climates and prospered. They will change further, just as wood nymphs change their spots over time, refining their protection. But because few butterflies can adapt fast enough to outpace a Caterpillar tractor, they must depart or die out when development comes. Altered habitats along the High Line have provided all too many examples.

At first, faunal changes on the canal were largely additive. Itself a product of human intrusion, the old irrigation ditch came to provide habitats for many opportunistic animals and plants. When I began studying its butterflies in the late fifties, the High Line was probably at the peak of its diversity. Habitats had matured and gained complexity for the better part of a century. New species were still coming in, riding the long pipeline of life downstream from the Rockies or up from the prairie.

One season, my mother and I found a large colony of painted crescentspots in a field beside Toll Gate Creek. This southern butterfly had never been recorded in Colorado outside the Arkansas River drainage. Here it was, deep within the basin of the Platte. How it crossed the Divide, the piney plateau that serves as a biogeographical barrier between the watersheds, we hadn't a clue. But once beyond, it began spreading rapidly. The Platte River flood of 1965 took out most of the original colony, but it came back from remnants. Then the painted crescent, more adaptable to disturbance of canalside habitats, began to replace the formerly common pearl and field crescentspots. The painted and gorgone crescentspots, feeding on bindweed and sunflower, respectively, became the common species on much of the eastern High Line, while the pearl and field crescents, dependent on asters, retreated to a few less disturbed sites. With change, something was lost and something else gained.

As change intensified with the growing population of Aurora, losses began to outnumber additions. Many of the habitats I'd known were erased by rampant development of housing tracts and malls. Places where black swallowtails, purplish coppers, and silvery blues once flew became other kinds of places, where they didn't. The only colony of Olympia marblewings was sacrificed, along with their crucifer hosts, mourned by no one but my butterflying buddy, Jack Jeffers, and me. A bluegrass playing field for a new school appeared in their place—the very field where I would throw the discus all through ninth grade. Even as the platter flew high above the new green turf, I thought of the mustards and marbles that would not be back.

None of these butterflies became extinct in the strict sense, for they survived elsewhere, in places still wild and rural. Still, through these local losses, I learned about extinction. Like spelling or multiplication tables, it was a lesson learned by rote, for it was repeated again and again. My work with the butterflies of the High Line Canal has gone on for thirty years. For half that long, a group of friends has gathered each July to hold a butterfly count centered at the site of the Thunder Tree. These ongoing censuses have revealed that since 1960, some 40 percent of the butterfly species on my High Line Canal study sites have become extinct or endangered. This is a greater rate of loss than Los Angeles, San Francisco, or Staten Island has experienced. The decline corresponded with the growth of Aurora's population from about forty thousand to more than a quarter of a million human beings.

On a recent visit, I saw many more kids walking along the canal than in my day, and in many more colors, but none of them were catching bugs, trapping crawdads, or running from spiders. Merely putting people and nature together does not ensure intimacy; to these kids, the canal path might have meant little more than a loopy sidewalk, a shortcut home from school. But I wondered how much was left to find, if anyone wanted to look.

The next day I followed the High Line Canal out onto the plains. A few dozen tall cottonwoods marked off an unspoiled mile strung between a freeway and a new town. Where the ditch dove into a culvert beneath a road, an old marshy margin survived. Monarchs sailed from milkweed to goldenrod.

Then I spotted a smaller brilliancy among the fall flowers. Netting it, I found it was a bronze copper—the first I'd seen in more than thirty years, since the Lutherans paved the parking lot. It was a male, and a female flew nearby. Maybe, I thought, releasing the copper near her, some kid with a Peterson field guide will happen across this little colony before the end of it.

Had it not been for the High Line Canal, the vacant lots I knew, the scruffy park, I'm not at all certain I would have been a biologist. I might have become a lawyer, or even a Lutheran. The total immersion in nature that I found in my special spots baptized me in a faith that never wavered, but it was a matter of happenstance too. It was the place that made me.

How many people grow up with such windows on the world? Fewer and fewer, I fear, as metropolitan habitats disappear and rural ones blend into the urban fringe. The number of people living with little hint of nature in their lives is very large and growing. This isn't good for us. If the penalty of an ecological education is to live in a world of wounds, as Aldo Leopold said, then green spaces like these are the bandages and the balm. And if the penalty of ecological ignorance is still more wounds, then the unschooled need them even more. To gain the solace of nature, we all must connect deeply. Few ever do.

In the long run, this mass estrangement from things natural bodes ill for the care of the earth. If we are to forge new links to the land, we must resist the extinction of experience. We must save not only the wilderness but the vacant lots, the ditches as well as the canyonlands, and the woodlots along with the old growth. We must become believers in the world.

♦

Spark-Infested Waters[2]

A few weeks before my sixteenth birthday I flew from Denver to New York in an old Constellation airliner with four props and three fins on the tail. I was part of a passel of would-be scientists, spending the summer at a genetics laboratory on the coast of Maine courtesy of the National Science Foundation. Our parents arranged for me and the only other kid from the West to meet in the city, then take a bus together up north. She was a pretty and brainy girl from southern California, and by the time we got to Bar Harbor in a cold rain, I was a goner.

On a thoroughly magical night during that summer of 1963, our group gathered beside a seashore campfire in Acadia National Park to roast weenies, sing "Michael Row Your Boat Ashore," and watch the Perseid meteor showers. Most of us had long since paired off, and my bus partner and I were in the full throes of young love with the Perseids bursting all around us and the fine calcium-carbonate sand of Shell Beach sticking to our skin.

Then someone yelled "Look!" and pointed out into the bay, and we all gawked. As if the meteors had hit the water and exploded, the Atlantic was alive with green fire. We had no idea what we were seeing until one of our leaders told us the sea really was alive. "It's plankton," he said. "Makes its own light. Shines just like fireflies." Fireflies! They did shine with much the same cool green glimmer. There are no fireflies in the West, and my girlfriend and I were rapt with them—just as we were with the smell of the tidal wrack on the seaside rocks, one another, the shooting stars, and now another thrill, the shimmering plankton. One is easily rapt at 16. We wanted to run out into the neon sea in the worst way, to be among the green galaxy in the ocean while the meteors arced down overhead. But the Atlantic at Bar Harbor turns your toes blue—especially at night. It would have taken more than a campfire and a beach blanket to warm us up.

Such saltwater fireworks are the bioluminescence of certain dinoflagellates, unicellular marine protists that make up nine-tenths of the rich soup of pelagic life known as plankton. They possess scintillons—packets of luciferin and luciferase, the same substrate-and-enzyme matchbox that oxidizes to produce bioluminescence in fireflies, glowworms, and certain fungi.

The best known genus, *Noctiluca* (night light), spirals through the water powered by twin flagellae, and may be as big as two millimeters across. They can make the sea reddish or yellowish by day (hence, "red tide") but by night, their cold power illuminates the waters blue-green, wherever they bloom in the world's seas.

Over the decades, I have seen the green blaze on the waves here and there around the world, from the North Atlantic to the South Pacific, the China Sea to the Bay of Biscay. And I have met the phenomenon in literature from *Moby Dick* and *Kon-Tiki* to *The Voyage of the Beagle.* But it wasn't until last fall, when Orion's Forgotten Language Tour visited southwest Florida, that I finally had a chance to swim with the sparks.

After giving evening readings, we writers made for the beach behind our hotel. Walking over the famously shelly sand of Sanibel Island and into the bathwater Gulf, we all exclaimed "Wow" in various writerly inflections to see the chartreuse brilliants rise from our steps and circle our legs as if we were human sparklers. I stood still, transfixed, my legs illuminated by key-lime footlights. And when I swam, the amniotic ocean parted in curtains of watery gauze bejeweled with electric emeralds. Diving, there was plenty of light for plucking slippers, whelks, and calico scallops from the seafloor. We ended up splashing one another wildly, giggling as skeins of greeny sequins glittered in our hair and dripped down our limbs, lighting up and flicking out almost faster than we could register their half-lives.

I swam with the night lights every night on Sanibel, barely able to tear myself away for bed. Usually a sinker in water, I drifted easily in the buoyant brine of the Gulf, suspended by water and light—or as one Caribbean captain put it, "floating in stardust." And when I clapped hands overhead, showers of shooting stars fell all around, transporting me back to 1963, another bay, and a night alight with fascination, infatuation, and a summer storm of living sparks.

11

TELLING IT SLANT: THE VALUE OF NARRATIVE INDIRECTION

Born in 1938 in Evanston, Illinois, Bruce Berger was raised in Phoenix, Arizona, before leaving the West to attend Yale University, where he graduated with a degree in English in 1961. In addition to his work as a writer (and specifically as a writer devoted to environmental topics), Berger has worked as a professional pianist in Spain from 1965 to 1967 and in Aspen, Colorado, from 1968 to 1974. Today, he spends his summers in Aspen and works as a pianist in Baja California each winter.

Berger's early publications include *Hangin' On* (1980) and *Notes of a Half-Aspenite* (1987). He next published *A Dazzle of Hummingbirds* (1989) and *The Telling Distance: Conversations with the American Desert* (1990); the latter volume, a collection of essays, received the Western States Book Award for Creative Nonfiction in 1990 and the Colorado Book Author Award in 1991. *There Was a River*, a nonfiction book originally published in 1979, was reissued in an expanded edition in 1994. Berger published a poetry collection, *Facing the Music*, in 1995. And more recently he has published *Almost an Island* (1998), essays about the natural history of Baja California and the stresses placed on nature by contemporary human culture.

In much of his work, Berger expresses his sense of nature's powerful impact (and especially the *desert's* impact) on human psychology. His work suggests that the sensory and emotional experience of nature is an essential, basic aspect of our lives as human beings. Just as John Daniel emphasizes the importance of a visceral, emotional understanding of our connectedness to the more-than-human world, Berger's essay "The Mysterious Brotherhood," from *The Telling Distance*, is an essay about kinship, about the fundamental connection between humans and nature (nature being represented, specifically, by various species of cacti). In particular, for Berger, it is the sense of the mortality of cactus, revealed by the exposed skeletons of these plants, that links us with them. He was driving through Arizona one evening when he stopped for a walk among the cactus, and this vision of how cactus dies occurred to him and inspired the essay. He spent the next twelve years writing the essays for that book—fifty of them, including the introduction—that "combined desert observation and experience with speculation and literary experiment."

It is fascinating to see Berger's resistance to some of the concepts described by John Daniel's questionnaire. Although the two authors, in their essays and poetry, seem inclined to articulate and explore similar issues, Berger complains that the phrase "natural values" is confusing and unhelpful. His work on the kinship between humans and nature expresses similar values to those that Daniel communicates in "Remembering the Sacred Family," but the abstract, quasi-social-science vocabulary of the questionnaire leaves him cold. This suggests that even professional authors who routinely—and perhaps obsessively—explore the meaning of their experiences with nature tend to recoil from direct, explicit values-elicitation processes. Sometimes, as in the case of William Kittredge, the authors simply allowed themselves to be prompted by the questionnaire and then took off in their own directions. Many of Berger's responses suggest that the language of social science (natural values) and even the language of literary scholarship (narrative) were baffling and almost offensive. Had we simply asked him to tell a few stories about important experiences in nature, he surely would have had no difficulty at all—in fact, he could have simply pointed us to examples of his previous work, such as "The Mysterious Brotherhood" and "Heat."

One of the important points Berger makes in his questionnaire responses is the importance of "telling it slant," a phrase made famous by the poet Emily Dickinson. Both of his writing samples included here do just that—particularly the short essay "Heat." This is a celebration of the pleasure of intense—almost painful—temperatures. It is an indirect rhapsody about desert heat, suffered through at times and passionately missed after the author moves to the cooler mountains. Most of the essay simply offers images of heat and then a single narrative of extreme Sonoran desert heat. It shows that the author values the phenomenon of desert heat (a phenomenon many desert newcomers strive mightily to avoid, with air conditioners and swimming pools) mainly by offering an enthusiastic story, not by abstractly and directly expressing his appreciation. This is what's meant by "telling it slant." And this is often, in fact, how values are communicated through narrative.

♦

QUESTIONNAIRE RESPONSES FROM BRUCE BERGER

Bruce Berger prepared these responses to the narrative-values questionnaire at his home in Aspen, Colorado, and returned them to us by mail.

Q1: Why do you think you became a nature writer?

Berger: I don't think of myself as a nature writer per se; nature is an element in my writing. I've always been interested in nature and in language, so the combination was inevitable.

Q2: Do you see your work as an attempt to articulate the value(s) of nature?

Berger: From our standpoint as human beings, a wildly atypical species, we can only observe the rest of life, which we call nature. Under such a scheme, we look on as outsiders. The values of nature that we can make out are the drive toward survival and a tendency toward complexity and diversity. But from the way the phrase "values of nature/natural values" is used in the rest of the questions, I suspect that something else is intended, something more like its value for human beings, our stake in it, values that are opposed to civilization—the lack of knowing what is meant by this phrase makes many of the questions hard to answer.

Q3: Which statement is closer to the truth in your case, or are both true?

A. You write in order to express your sense of nature's value.

B. You derive a sense of nature's value from the process of writing.

Berger: As I understand the phrase, I can't express "nature's values." The importance of nature to me as an individual is implicit in my choice of subjects and expressed attitudes; writing about nature makes me look at it more closely, which gives it more value to me (and maybe readers).

Q4: What mode(s) of expression work(s) best for you in articulating the values of nature: Exposition? Argument? Description? Narrative? A combination? Please explain.

Berger: The essayist Philip Lopate was preparing an essay anthology a few years ago and asked me what nature writing to look at and mainly to explain why most of it was so boring. I think what he objected to was the constant description and "appreciation." All of the methods mentioned have their place and the selection or combination that works best varies from piece to piece. The one that doesn't work, except in very short pieces, is unalloyed description.

Q5: Why is this mode the most successful? How does it appeal to/elicit understanding in the reader or listener?
Berger: Answered in 4.

Q6: Do you feel that a responsive reader learns natural values from your work, or that your work alerts the reader to values already held?
Berger: Readers already interested in, or sensitive to, nature are the ones who usually read about it, so one generally writes to the converted. One can always open new areas to them or fire them up, and there's always the chance that someone previously uninterested in nature will have a conversion experience.

Q7: What do you see as the strengths and limitations of narrative as a carrier/elicitor of natural values?
Berger: Another terminology problem; I'm not sure what is meant by "narrative." It's generally a story that unfolds through time, a plot, but I don't know whether this is about fiction, nonfiction, both—and I don't know what is meant by "natural values"—so I can't get a grip on this question.

Q8: Has your sense of the importance of narrative changed over the course of your writing life to date? If so, how? If you didn't begin as a writer of narrative, how did it happen that you became one?
Berger: Another blank wall, so I'll digress. I began writing because I was inspired by writers I admired, particularly Conrad, Faulkner, and Durrell as they conjured place. The first experience that life gave me to apply this to in a major way was a trip through the already doomed Glen Canyon, so I suppose the account of that trip counts as a narrative. I actually began as a writer of lyric poetry, which contains narrative elements but isn't usually considered "narrative."

Q9: Are there values that can *only* be told in and learned from narrative?
Berger: Again, I'm not sure what's being asked.

Q10: Can natural values be fully and accurately expressed in purely rational terms, or is there inevitably an emotive content?

Berger: I'll have to write around my ignorance of "natural values." An antagonism can be set up between the most abstract ideas, so that there is tension between them that engages the right reader. People with an investment in those ideas will feel emotion. Also, there is no predicting what strange association an individual may have in the most abstract reference.

Q11: Is there inevitably an ethical or moral content to these values?

Berger: "These values," to me, haven't been established, so I can't answer. Ethics, to me, involves behavior concerned with interests beyond one's own; in nature, that would be the welfare of other species. The Leopold quotation in Question 22 speaks to this.

Q12: Why are these values difficult for many people to express?

Berger: Assuming that "these values" means concern for nature, a root problem is the vast gulf between the natural world and the technological surroundings we grow up in. People have no idea where their food comes from, what keeps their water pure, what produces the oxygen they breathe. Nature has become background and decoration rather than the limb we're sitting on.

Q13: In your opinion or experience, what would be the best ways to elicit these values and identify them in people who may harbor them but find them difficult to articulate?

Berger: One has to come in obliquely, to "tell it slant," as Emily Dickinson advised. People can relate to the importance of nature if they can attach to particulars—to individual animals or plants, or species, or ecosystems. People can become involved through stories about the particulars—and if that's narrative, fine.

Q14: In your opinion, are these values "held," so to speak, or are they more closely integrated with one's being? Are they learned or are they innate?

Berger: This will vary greatly between people. Some people are born feeling connected to nature, a feeling they retain; others relate purely to the interactions within our species. Most of this seems to me genetically hardwired within the individual, but culture can also mediate in one direction or the other.

Q15: Do you believe that environmentally responsible behavior flows from having a conscious sense of the values of nature? From an unconscious sense? Or is there no reliable causal relationship between values and behavior?

Berger: Those terms again. Values certainly influence behavior, but given the human capacity for self-deception, it is only one factor. An unconscious sense of nature's worth surely results in the more responsible behavior, but ethics must be instilled consciously.

Q16: Has your own sense of the values of nature changed over time? If so, how? Can you identify particular experiences that contributed to the change(s)?

Berger: Radically. For instance, as a small child I felt instinctively that plants had feelings. My mother tried to enlist my help in weeding the vegetable garden. I felt that weeds had as much right to live as beans and that weeding was murder and held back until my mother said, "It's all right—they don't have feelings, you know." Such is parental authority that in that moment the vegetable world, as fellowship, died. Nature has always remained vivid and important, but on a different level, and I think at this point we all undergo a similar civilizing experience, a gradual alienation. Wordsworth has limned the whole cycle in his "Intimations" ode, a poem I feel close to. Another crucial experience was to have seen Glen Canyon just before it was lost, to have discovered the Utah canyons for the first time in that stricken moment.

Q17: Do you consider beauty a value of nature? If so, please hazard a definition of natural beauty.

Berger: Beauty is a human construct, not something inherent in nature. Within human beings it can be a congruence of something in the natural world with what we already consider idyllic—but that doesn't allow for surprise, for beauty in unexpected forms. Books can be written on this subject, and have; I wouldn't trust a short definition.

Q18: Do you find more value (non-utilitarian) in some things and creatures of nature than you do in others? If so, what do you think accounts for the difference?

Berger: I prefer dogs to cats, like snakes and spiders, dislike slugs. Freud, Jung, and others have written tomes on those reactions, most of them now discredited; they are givens of personality, rolls of the genetic dice.

Q19: Do rocks have rights? Trees? Whales? Planets? Is there a concept other than "rights" by which you prefer to identify the worthiness of natural things and creatures?

Berger: I like the idea of Justice Douglas that trees have "standing" and especially Schweitzer's touchstone, "respect for life," but we must also recognize that we are born into a food chain, which sustains us. To whatever extent possible, we should extend rights to other creatures, what I mentioned earlier as my concept of ethics.

Q20: Does wilderness have a value in and of itself? To what extent is wilderness an objectively identifiable thing, and to what extent is it a category of mind projected onto natural surroundings?

Berger: Concepts of wilderness are constantly changing, and today it is academically chic in some circles to find wilderness "man's most artificial construct." This is nonsense, of course, but we are learning that man has changed the landscape more than previously recognized—much of what we now consider wilderness was constantly changed by aboriginal peoples through fires, "primitive" man may have caused the extinction of the larger mammals, etc. For me, it is enough to call something "wilderness" if it can be allowed to heal its wounds and start to regenerate, starting now.

Q21: How important is direct sensory experience of nature to having a sense of natural values and being conscious of those values?

Berger: This is a major problem, alluded to earlier, that we grow up with no contact with or understanding of our origins in and dependence upon nature. We will never value what we have never known and virtual chipmunks won't help. I'm currently working on an extended essay on how everything, especially nature, is turning into a theme park of itself, thus losing its reality and importance for us.

Q22: Aldo Leopold wrote: "A thing is right when it tends to preserve the integrity, stability, and beauty of the biotic community. It is wrong when it tends otherwise." Do you agree? How would you modify his definition to better reflect your own view?

Berger: I agree wholeheartedly when I take the statement in a general way. When I look at it closely, aspects break down. Integrity, yes. Stability, yes if it is defined as adaptability to changing conditions—nature must keep adapting to its own changing conditions, not just our ozone holes and global warming. Beauty is a human concept, projected on the world, and too subjective as a criterion for biotic health without some rigorous definition (which I can't imagine).

Q23: Leopold wrote of the land community, by which he meant the entire biota in a place. Is community in some sense a natural value of your own? How so?

Berger: Living within an ongoing biotic community that we don't wreck is important to me. Again, that phrase "natural value" makes this a question I'm not sure I get.

Q24: What is the most important value of nature, if you believe there is one?

Berger: Value for us? It keeps us alive! Beyond that, it enhances our lives, connects us with our origins, makes us brothers of creatures who are here at the same time we are. Value to itself? To survive, healthily.

Q25: What is the least understood or appreciated value of nature? Why is it poorly understood or appreciated?

Berger: The value of other creatures for their own sake, rather than ours; what Schweitzer called "respect for life."

Q26: Do you believe that we have made progress toward a generally held land ethic—an ethical sense that values the things and creatures and systems of nature—since Leopold called for one in the 1940s? What do you see as the chief obstacles to such an ethic? How optimistic or pessimistic are you about our chances of realizing a land ethic?

Berger: The conservation movement itself is much stronger and immensely more sophisticated; we have passed impressive laws to restrain ourselves and protect the environment; our knowledge itself of the natural world is increasing exponentially. Also increasing exponentially is human population and unrestrained technology that, as far as I can see, are really overwhelming everything. Wilderness areas—nature inside a protective fence—don't keep out contaminated air and water. Good land ethics are already out there, but compared to the urge of an exploding population to keep multiplying and wielding ever more potent and destructive machinery on a finite planet, I see the goal of bringing ourselves in balance with nature to be constantly receding. So, yes, I'm pessimistic. But I also don't see that we have any choice but to keep trying to turn things around.

Q27: Is it a land ethic in Leopold's sense that we most need, or is it something else?

Berger: It is a base from which to expand with education, changes of heart, restorative technology, new laws on a global level, whatever it takes.

Q28: What piece of your work best expresses your sense of the value of nature?

Berger: The most direct expression, in the sense of a sermon, is "Time and the Exxon Valdez" from *Season of Dead Waters,* a collection of writers' responses to the Prince William Sound oil spill. As I mentioned, I prefer coming in slant, so I personally prefer an essay like "The Mysterious Brotherhood," in which we and nature (represented here by cactus) are linked by our common mortality; I would also point to the extended piece on Glen Canyon in *There Was a River,* and my book about thirty years of observation of Baja California.

This is a fascinating questionnaire, but as you could tell from some of the responses, I also found it quite a wrestle. One problem is its ambiguous vocabulary: I recommend finding some substitute for "natural values" (if it means values that come naturally, it could include power and greed; are they values for nature or human beings?—it also resembles the kind of phrase that will show up on a loaf of whole-grain broad). "Narrative" is another word that needs definition in context. The other problem is that some of the questions are huge. Defining major categories or abstractions like beauty and ethics can consume volumes. Anyway, if I can question the questionnaire, I would recommend focusing it. It was, nonetheless, interesting to think through.

♦

Heat[1]

—unlike cold—is one of those pleasures most keenly relished on the threshold of pain. It is oddly comforting to feel noon pouring down, to bake from beneath over bedrock, to find your marrow vaguely radiating. The best midsummer lunch is to gorge on enchiladas blazing with chiles, return to the car you have left in the sun with the windows rolled up, lock yourself in to steep in your own tears and sweat, then step out to find the heat wave has turned delicious. It is invigorating to walk over simmering gravel, feeling your soles come alive as they toughen, and baths are most relaxing when they resemble the first stages of missionary stew. Perhaps it is a desire to return to the womb, where we began for nine months at 98.6, that makes the warmth of alcohol so seductive, and one can comprehend—if not envy—the uncomforted who go through life sucking the eighty proof tit.

To test my heat tolerance I once went into the desert when daytime temperatures were easing off around 107 degrees, to see what might transpire. I expected an escort of insects, lizards, snakes, scorpions and chuckawallas, all the cold-blooded predators warmed like me for action, but the cactus stood in stunned silence. The afternoon lay like a ruin through which I seemed the only moving thing. My eyes ran with salt, my thirst became pathological, and I fled homeward to chug two beers nonstop before I could explain myself. But did I dream of cool mountains, as I did in childhood? No. It is as an adult, exiled to cool mountains, that I dream of the desert.

♦

The Mysterious Brotherhood[2]

It was a custom in medieval times for saints and scholars to keep a human skull around to remind them of their mortality. That practice seems morbid as we plunge, youth-obsessed, toward the twenty-first century, and the great bonescapes of Georgia O'Keeffe, their elegant folds of calcium and sky, remind us less of death than the deep cleanliness beneath the flesh. To see finality as a kind of radiance, one can turn to the desert not just for the melodramatic bones—which, despite cartoons, are few and far between—but for the quieter revelations of the vegetable world. Those unlikely green lives, each stranded in its claim to water, shed their skins to reveal still deeper miracles.

Cactus are among our most treasured species, yet only cholla has attained posthumous notoriety. The cuddly looking shrubs—actually great fountains of barbed grenades which, in certain varieties, nearly leap out for affection—strew in death the sections of their hollow stems, lattices of holes strung together by a woody fiber like asbestos. The delicacy of the recurrent patterns, the modulations of their holes, their rich patina make them sought after, and they grace the kinds of coffee tables where manhattans are served, find their way into flower arrangements, are positioned as a foil for foliage. They have been strung into lamps, hung up as hat racks, woven into macrame, tricked out as toy covered wagons. They have been stood on end and hollowed with ovals for the insertion of Heidi vignettes in isinglass, seashells and mother of pearl. They have in fact been conscripted for so many forms of kitsch, schlock and inventive bad taste that they seem some Sonoran revenge on deer antlers, abalone shells and Japanese fishing balls.

But it would be too bad to let their abuse obscure one of the desert's most moving cycles. Even as the cholla grows it drops its extremities, and if the pieces are not dispersed by wind, water, the flanks of animals or your pierced skin, they mass themselves under the plant like a field of charcoal. As the plant ages, the trunk turns black, the needles become brittle and the skin begins to peel. The cholla may simply crumble, strewing bits of its stem among the decayed pieces, or tip intact into a small jungle gym. But if it remains on its feet, stripped to its fretted skeleton, it leaves a shape refined as sculpture, lord of its clearing, elegant by day and a spidery presence beneath the moon.

The prickly pear, less noble than the cholla, simply runs out of strength and lays its pads on the ground. If it is noticed at all, it seems a vaguely repellent grey heap. Trodden upon it answers crisply to the shoe, a sensuous crunch like a bite of water chestnut or the slow dismemberment of a champagne cork. The serenity of its depths can call up visions of snakes napping in the cool, scorpions at rest, tarantulas digesting their friends. Menacingly pale, it is most comfortably crossed after making a fair noise, in a state of high alertness. "Here we go round the prickly pear," said T. S. Eliot, and one can see why.

But reach down and examine a pad. The skin, turned sulphurous brown, peels off like cracked cardboard, to reveal a mesh of fibrous sheets, each stamped with a similar pattern like a netting of veins and arteries, laminated sheet onto sheet. Each layer is a faint variation on the last as the holes rework their shapes throughout the pad. Fat green health hides the complexity of the prickly pear, and its disclosure is one of death's small rewards.

The smaller the cactus, the denser its spines, until one reaches the pincushion, one to three inches high, a white thimble usually nestled beneath some larger plant. The pincushion reverses the process by dying inside out, the flesh collapsing to leave a standing cup of barbed lace. Seldom recognized, the spent pincushion is a strange jewel, a crucible of woven stars each sprouting a hook like a talon, delicate as a doll's negligee.

Death on the desert: its forms are extravagant as the species themselves—the barrel's great mashed thumb, the organ pipe's burnt candelabra, the staghorn still more like antlers when stripped of its flesh. But for sheer pageantry the saguaro remains supreme. Largest of the cactus except for its Mexican cousin, the *cardón*, the saguaro reveals itself by painful degrees, breathtakingly. "What will become of . . . the huge and delicate saguaro?"

asks Richard Shelton in his moving poem, "Requiem for Sonora," but delicacy would not seem a prime characteristic of this stout colossus, one of whose arms, even as I watch in a suburban backyard, has been severed for months, is dangling by a thread, and is blooming furiously. The saguaro can be killed, *is* being killed by destruction of habitat, but the individual, capable of storing up to ten tons of water, taking fifteen years to grow the first foot, surviving a half century before it blooms and attaining a height of sixty feet, seems resilient to an inspiring degree.

We know when an animal like ourselves dies: it is the moment when the heart stops beating. But when does a plant die? When it turns brown? When it falls? When the shape is finally obliterated? The saguaro begins to die even as it grows. King of its habitat, it is home to entire species of woodpeckers and flickers, which riddle it with holes for many other varieties of birds. The injured pulp secretes a thick shell, a petrified leather that offers a comfortable cave for the nesting bird while protecting the cactus, a hole that actually survives the plant in a collectible object called a desert boot. Branches routinely meet with calamity, suffer injury or fall off, to shrivel like crocodiles in the sun, yet the plant grows on, oblivious. The more grotesque its deformities, the more humanly it seems to express itself. By maturity the plant is pocked, gouged, may be missing or trailing branches, or gored to its bare ribs as if it were being eaten by darkness. Remorselessly it thrives. By the time it is actually ready to die, at the age of one hundred fifty or two hundred years, the saguaro may seem the butt of assaults past imagining.

At last letting go, the energy-collecting green skin turns sallow: the plant's least attractive phase. After preliminary jaundice the outer skin deepens, hardens, begins to crinkle, and finally attains a kind of rich parchment. It extrudes a shiny black substance sticky to the eye, glassy as obsidian to the touch, as if it were being caramelized. Peeling skin reveals the inner pulp turning black, a burnt coral brittle to probing fingers. When tapped the skin now gives a report like a primitive drum, and could almost be played like a xylophone. Itself in sepia, the entire saguaro appears to be burning from inside.

At last the flesh is fallen, the skin strewn like old vellum, and the saguaro stands revealed: a white idea. If the specimen has many branches, or the ribs extend too far, the extremities will sheer off, leaving stumps in a variety of crosses and elemental shapes. Occasionally a cactus boot, former home of some flicker or owl, will catch in the ribs, a hole become substance, revealed as if in a structural model. Tough skin at the bottom may hold the freed ribs like poles in an umbrella stand, an immense rattle when shook. But at last the saguaro will fall. It is now only a confusion of hard skin, spines and crumpled flesh, with perhaps a stray boot, though even now the flung ribs may parody its shape in split bamboo.

Object of beauty, toy, curiosity, decoration, cheap firewood, musical instrument, home for scorpions, motive for metaphor—even a dead cactus has its uses. But a taste for the desert is a taste for ultimates, and death is the backdrop against which all we know comes to brilliance. Cactus tell us nothing of what's ahead, any more than the death of a close friend: all they reveal is process, but process which retains, even in human terms, immeasurable beauty. Their odd green lives, if nothing else, bring to consciousness our complicity in a mystery that becomes, even as we reject it, our own:

> Saguaros brave putrefaction like tough meat.
> Chollas strew black fruit while a skinful of char
> Peels into moonlight bleaching on its feet.
> The ocotillo collapses into a star.
> A mesh of fiber loosened by your nail
> Separates into bones of the prickly pear.
> Or lay your hands on a lung. Resemblances fail.
> Death is a common bond we never share.

12

THRIVING ON AMBIGUITY: LATENCY, INDIRECTION, AND NARRATIVE

Gary Paul Nabhan was born in Gary, Indiana, in 1952. Despite being raised in the industrial Midwest, Nabhan is a scientist and literary artist whose work is associated through and through with the desert Southwest. He has what some might call the perfect background, the perfect sensibility, for a naturalist. Already as a teenager, he felt that proper learning should happen out of doors—during high school his truant meanderings along the shores of Lake Michigan led to his dropping out of school. A few years later, Gary made his way to Prescott College, in Arizona, where he completed a B.A. in 1974 with an emphasis in environmental biology and Western American literature. During the next decade, he earned master's and doctoral degrees in plant science and desert ecology at the University of Arizona, developing a scientific specialty in arid lands ethnobotany and agricultural ecology with a focus on the Tohono O'odham people of southern Arizona. His scientific work for the past two and a half decades has involved a combination of agricultural science, ecology, botany, physiology, anthropology, and linguistics.

But the literary impulse has always been present, too. Even as he was completing his Ph.D. in Arizona's Arid Lands Resources Program (in 1983), he published his first book of nonfiction ethnobotanical nature writing, *The Desert Smells Like Rain*, in 1982. A year later, he helped to start the nonprofit organization Native Seeds/SEARCH, which aimed to conserve traditional crops, seeds, and farming practices of native people in the American Southwest and northern Mexico. His second book, *Gathering the Desert*, appeared in 1985 and received the John Burroughs Medal for outstanding natural-history writing the following year. While developing his reputation as a literary nature writer, Nabhan has maintained simultaneous scientific research and publishing—he has published more than sixty-five technical journal articles in fields ranging from geography and nutritional ecology to linguistics and regional studies. He has also published books on environmental topics for general audiences, such as *Enduring Seeds: Native American Agriculture and Wild Plant Conservation* (1989) and, with co-author Steven Buchmann, *The Forgotten Pollinators* (1996). A journey to northern Italy in September 1990 resulted in a foray into travel writing and autobiography, which appeared in 1993 under the title *Songbirds, Truffles, and Wolves: An American Naturalist in Italy*. Also in 1993, he edited a collection of writings called *Counting Sheep: Twenty Ways of Seeing Desert Bighorn Sheep*. Nabhan and Utah nature writer Stephen Trimble co-authored a braided collection of essays on their own childhood experiences and on experiencing the world with their children—*The Geography of Childhood: Why Children Need Wild Places* came out in 1994. *Desert Legends: Re-storying the Sonoran Borderlands*, another collaboration—this one incorporating Gary's essays with distinguished Arizona photographer Mark Klett's visual work—also was published in 1994. Nabhan's playful, multicultural, transdisciplinary, and engagingly narrative essays were collected again in the 1997 volume *Cultures of Habitat: On Nature, Culture, and Story*. In 2002, he published *Coming Home to Eat: The Pleasures and Politics of Local Foods*, followed by *Singing the Turtles to Sea: The Comcáac (Seri) Art and Science of Reptiles* a year later. *Cross-Pollinations: The Marriage of Science and Poetry* appeared in Milkweed Editions' Credo Series in 2004.

Gary was honored in 1990 with both a Pew Scholarship for Conservation and the Environment and a five-year MacArthur Fellowship. More recently, in 1999, he received a Lannan Literary Award. After spending a number of years as the director of conservation science at the Arizona–Sonora Desert Museum in Tucson, Gary moved to Flagstaff in 2000 to become the first director of the Center for Sustainable Environments at Northern Arizona University.

Like Alison Hawthorne Deming and Robert Michael Pyle, Nabhan emphasized in his comments during the narrative-values interview the relationship between scientific thinking and language and literary expression. Even when speaking of story, he tended to sound like a biologist, noting that one of the values of narrative language is how it "encode[s] messages of adaptive worth in a way that we may not always consciously understand, but that stick with us and deeply motivate us"—how it is a style of language that touches readers and listeners, impressing them with practical urgency and insight in a way that expository, straightforward, analytical language often does not. Scientists and others of rationalist intellectual bent are just as capable of creating and understanding stories as other people, Nabhan argues. In fact, he makes the point that scientists today need to be able to communicate with the general public, not just with other specialists in narrow fields.

He states, "Science needs to be communicated in a variety of genres to a variety of audiences. A good scientist these days has to be able to blend scientific expertise with other disciplines." This claim forcefully corroborates the ideas gathered from reading the interviews with and sample writings of Deming and Pyle—the belief that there are important intellectual and political reasons for merging the "two cultures" of science and the arts, of empirical observation/quantitive measurement and story/image/beauty. One of the reasons scientists, economists, resource managers, and legislators may be uncomfortable with narrative discourse is that story tends to function as a "zone of tension," a place of ambiguity and uncertainty, of exploration rather than fixed truth. Nabhan suggests that we often encounter situations in the world where there is no simple, fixed resolution, where we must tolerate ambiguity and retain a multi-perspective view: "I think that those tensions can't necessarily be explained entirely by linear, expository logic. A story can keep a multi-sided domain intact in our minds."

Nabhan's writing sample in this volume is the essay "Hornworm's Home Ground: Conserving Interactions," from his 1997 collection of essays, *Cultures of Habitat.* This essay is closely related to the idea of keeping "a multi-sided domain intact in our minds," for it addresses on several levels the significance of "conserving interactions," interactions between moths and flowers (and pollinators and plants in general) and between scientists, linguists, and local people (indigenous and not). From interactions representing contact among multiple organisms (multiple perspectives) comes a healthy community. Interactions do not always facilitate neatness and order, clean and unanimous political decisions. "Hornworm's Home Ground" consists of multiple stories of interactions among different kinds of scientists (naturalists, linguists, O'odham Indian people), expressing the value of these interactions in enabling necessary knowledge ("messages of adaptive worth") to be retained and communicated. When Nabhan concludes his essay by echoing ecologist Daniel Janzen's warning about the "extinction of interactions" and by expressing his hope to "learn the songs" that will keep the hornworm's home ground "vibrant," he is thinking about how language contributes to ecological health. The message is often in the medium. This seems to be an idea that many of the writers participating in this study would agree with.

♦

A Conversation with Gary Paul Nabhan

Terre Satterfield and Scott Slovic conducted this interview at Gary Nabhan's home in the desert west of Tucson, Arizona. Nabhan has since moved and now lives near Flagstaff.

Satterfield: If we have a starting point for this project, it is the conviction that nature writing is a form of storytelling, and that storytelling is relevant to how we think about value or values, particularly environmental values. So perhaps we should just begin here, with this question: Do you see your work as an attempt to explore the value or values of nature?

Nabhan: Well, in a sort of sideways glance at my own work, I would say yes. I would say my more expository writing, for example, an essay about nature services or the forgotten pollinators, is really trying to crack open those arguments. For example, with *The Forgotten Pollinators*, I explicitly collaborated with Steve Buchmann because I felt that the issues surrounding the Endangered Species Act were not being articulated very well. I felt that there really were a lot of ways to talk to farmers, fishermen, beekeepers, a variety of people who make their livelihoods from interactions with the natural world about just how one interaction with the system could damage a system's services, a decline that would affect them directly. It was a way to not merely offer a utilitarian argument for protecting endangered species, but to say that all of us are dependent on these free services and that we all benefit from these services every day.

We introduced other ways to value pollinators besides the dollar loss to consumers with rising food prices all the while trying to come into the discussion about utilitarian versus non-economic uses. A lot of people have said to me: "I never thought about the value of these things to me before." And "If you had hit me with aesthetic arguments at the same time I was being barraged by either the logging industry or other people, it wouldn't really have had the impact that it did." So that's explicitly expository writing about nature's services that about twenty of us collaborated on simply to say, "Here are some ways to value ecological services in a non-monetary way that are nevertheless ones that we all benefit from."

Satterfield: How fully aware are you, when writing, that one of your goals is to illuminate the values or services intrinsic to a natural system or object?

Nabhan: The more image-based or story-driven the essay is, the less likely I am to immediately or consciously know how I'm talking about values. I can see it afterwards, with hindsight, but I seldom know about it in advance.

Satterfield: Would you say you then use storytelling or the narrative process as a way to get yourself there, to sort of clarify your thinking about values?

Nabhan: Yes, exactly. For instance, in *Cultures of Habitat*, I knew there were some inherent parallels between cultural diversity and biological diversity. So I basically said, "I'm going to try to immerse myself in the tensions between those two and see what new insights emerge." So I don't necessarily predict where an essay is going to go, or, for that matter, where a book is going to go in advance. I don't outline it in advance, but I do put together pieces to see what juxtapositions are fruitful, and then I pursue those.

Slovic: You've sometimes referred to narrative space as a "tension zone." What is it about narrative that it creates these tensions when other vehicles of expression don't?

Nabhan: Well, I think that those tensions can't necessarily be explained entirely by linear, expository logic. Oftentimes, I'll look at, say, the essays in *Gathering the Desert* as a mosaic or set of vignettes where the image in one vignette plays off the previous one. A story can keep a multi-sided domain intact in our minds. Yesterday, I was thinking about a scholar in Maryland who looked at what people remembered of a didactic expository text about some science topic, as opposed to a narrative sort of feature story with the people embedded in it and a sense of the place. And not only was there a stronger staying power of the topical material when it was embedded in a story, but people were also more motivated to action. It was a story about someone's life being disrupted by toxins. People felt motivated by the story to care and do something about that. If it was simply told in an analytical way, there was far less motivation to take action.

One element of the biophilia hypothesis that I really like is the idea that stories have been with us for a long time; they have staying power in part because they encode messages of adaptive worth in a way that we may not always consciously understand, but that stick with us and deeply motivate us. There are certain kinds of archetypal stories that loosen the tensions that we all face in our life—such as the many "anti-tragedy of the commons stories" where consuming for our own benefit is side-stepped in such a way that equity within a group is preserved.

Slovic: To me, "tension" also implies a kind of persistent ambiguity. And so I'm interested in how ambiguity corresponds to the presentation of a message, the encoding of some kind of valuable advice. In one sense, you would think that an ambiguous, indirect statement would be difficult to process and transfer into some sort of advice or code to live by, wouldn't you?

Nabhan: Well, I think there are two parts to that. With stories, each reader is enacting the drama of solving a problem for herself or himself. This is consistent with the theory of psychodrama or the idea that we really have to bodily live that dilemma if we're going to solve it. We can't really take up the seven principles of wisdom of the Tang Dynasty, embody them in our own life, unless we take their journey with them. Stories allow us to take the journey rather than trying to live via a distilled set of bald principles. This only gives the false impression that context doesn't matter, that you can be wise in any kind of context. The people I know who are wise are wise because they've made contextual sense of something. It doesn't take a literary critic or an ethicist to tell us that—most people don't get what *Moby Dick* is about by reading the Cliff's Notes version.

Slovic: Yes, but much of our culture gravitates to Cliff's Notes or the equivalent. They want the boiled-down version. My students are often frustrated with literary texts that are ambiguous—they want to get right to the meaning of the text.

Nabhan: Well, you're right. The best-selling environmental book in the twentieth century is *50 Things You Can Do to Save the Earth*. I mean, I would never look at it. I don't know if either of you have ever looked at it. Similar tendencies run in our society—the belief that fast food or quick sex is satisfying. Yet, most people aren't very satisfied.

Satterfield: And yet you, a scientist by training, resist the "quick list" tendency. Why is this, aside from your desire to write?

Nabhan: Well, my storytelling self comes in very handy in biology courses and in work with biology students. The contemporary reality is that scientists face increasingly complex social and technical communication problems. Consider an organization like The Nature Conservancy here in the Southwest. Because of the tense circumstances between resource users and others, only messages in a certain range are allowable. The Conservancy is trying to set up collaborations with ranchers, and with the Mexican government, that are non-confrontational. This takes a tremendous amount of tact and negotiating skills. People who have come out of the strict evolutionary biology training, a major conservation science program, except for a few remarkable exceptions, have no skills and no predilection for the rhetorical complexity of these situations—they're frightened.

Science needs to be communicated in a variety of genres to a variety of audiences. A good scientist these days has to be able to blend scientific expertise with other disciplines.

Slovic: There could be a branch of literature—artistic writing—relevant to almost any branch of science, including molecular biology, chemistry, and so forth.

Nabhan: I would say two things. Some of the most exciting experiments on campuses today are for return people. UC–Santa Cruz's "Science Communication Program" is offering a program for journalists who've been given a science beat and want to come back to get some science training. Or, vice versa, scientists who say, "I am terrible at this writing. I don't know how to do this." Most of the natural-history magazines I know brought some of the Santa Cruz students on as interns and kept them on as staffers.

The discussion going on in biology following Michael Soulé and Gary Lease's book, *Reinventing Nature*, is a case in point. I don't think that collection works very well, but I think biologists finally grasped the possibility that we're constructing a view of the natural world, too. And it's not necessarily consistent with other ones around us. I really think they always did think that they were "accumulating truth" and that everyone else was doing constructs or something. It's like something Richard Nelson said recently: "I grew up in Wisconsin where we were always surprised to hear how everyone else from other regions had accents."

That kind of statement is endemic of biologists at this point. There's this glimmer of the notion that they have a theoretical construct of what the natural world is and that biases what they study.

Satterfield: How do you think they've come around to this realization? For years that was a distant notion at best. Has literature, has story, changed that? Or is it the deconstructionists talking about science who have changed that?

Nabhan: No. They're not hearing the deconstructionists directly. But I would say two things. In the last twenty years, a tremendous number of students from foreign countries have entered the United States to study. Some of them practiced science for years. And when they talked about what they'd done to American scientists, there were these huge differences—about how they think about experiments, and about science generally. The effect is to have science, to some extent, become de-Westernized. It's like classical music and all of its permutations all over the world.

Slovic: Can you provide us with an example?

Nabhan: My moment of insight occurred while I was helping a group of desert scientists in Lubbock, Texas. There was a Chinese scientist who had done one year at Harvard and had been called back in 1948 or '49 to China. He had all his American books burned during the Cultural Revolution. There was a Russian scientist, an Egyptian scientist, and a couple of Texans and me. The Russian scientist came out and said, "So what is this plant community? What are these plants here doing for the common good?" And the Chinese scientist said, "I'm wondering which two plants you put together in herbal mixtures that have a greater effect together than they do by themselves." And the Egyptian said: "What plants here are good oil producers?" And then we'd start talking about the plant community. And an American, Tony Burgess, would say, "Well, all of these plants here are competing for scarce resources." And the Russian would say, "But how about the cooperative principles between the plants, what are they?"

Satterfield: Beautifully said.

Nabhan: I mean, all of sudden, "Oh, my God!" We're not even talking the same language. And so I think where it's happened is in arguments about the nature of the plant community. Whether it's individual plant species moving independently through space and time or random parts that are thrown together. They understand that there are historical and philosophical and even political differences in issues like that. Lewontin fighting with E. O. Wilson about sociobiology and adaptation is the other example. Most biologists get that in their training now. You know, they're thinking, "Jesus, these guys are on the same faculty at Harvard!" How did Harvard let guys with such divergent views on the same faculty together? You know, these guys hate each other, but on top of that, one's a flaming Marxist and the other's a flaming capitalist.

Satterfield: What are the implications of this multiplicity of perspective for land management or policy purposes?

Nabhan: I would say that as a result, the prevailing paradigm has shifted, even for politicians. They understand that their task is, at some level, to make very different constituencies feel like they're in service toward them, and that they're being listened to and that they need to find consensus. Any on-the-street politician who goes to public hearings must absorb very divergent views, must realize that the situation does not allow for a simple, one-sided solution.

I'm thinking of situations that you know a lot better than I do—salmon fishermen talking about the impacts of logging on their livelihood. It's not always environmentalists against loggers or people with a utilitarian view. It's that different user groups have to resolve their differences with one another. If we log watersheds and silt up streams, it affects the production of some other user group. So I really think that there is recognition that most communities in the United States now are now multicultural.

What I'm proposing is not necessarily true of science; there may not yet exist the same kind of pluralism. I still see a lot of debates boiling down to genetic versus environmental determinism.

Slovic: Gary, I'd like to link your thoughts just now about science and our earlier conversation about values. I'm curious to know how your own sense of the values of nature has changed through time, and what is the relationship between your personal sense of nature's value and your scientific valuing or knowledge of nature.

Nabhan: I would say that the general ethical framework of popular natural history writing is very, very deeply ingrained in how I think about the world. And that a lot of my values come from other nature writers—from listening to their stories, being deeply moved by them. That's not merely a rational experience, but an affective one, too. At the same time, I am constantly challenged by scientists' hypotheses about how things work. So, when I read the statement that is basic to the Land Ethic, the idea that "the highest good is that which is best for the larger biotic community," I also find myself thinking about the work of some very fine scientists who would argue that "communities aren't as cohesive as what we once thought they were." My pack-rat midden research shows that even though we say that saguaros are completely dependent on paloverdes and mesquites as nurse plants, saguaros actually got here three thousand years before mesquites and paloverdes. That dependency, as we currently see it, has not been structured this way through all time. These are semi-independent players. I'm challenged by the fact that scientists still throw out alternative hypotheses and that good scientists will say, "I've devoted my whole career to this topic and I think my research supports hypothesis X, but if new information emerges that contradicts that, I'm willing to shift my view." I think there's a really wonderful freshness and intellectual honesty to the scientist who does that.

And so at one level in my values system, I completely and deeply support Aldo Leopold's credo, the Land Ethic. Yet I see that my allegiance to it will shift through time as the notions of biotic communities shift. And, again, I like that tension, that contingency and impermanence.

The way I accommodate this is by saying: Well, how can we use language in a dynamic way to come to some new understanding of what this revised view of a community is that doesn't have philosophical and emotional and political biases? How can we explain what this new concept of a community is in a way that still informs ethical decisions rather than taking a nihilistic approach that all is random action out there in nature? I live daily with an ambiguity or tension between scientists in their best "doubting Thomas" mode, their hypotheses and theories, and a deeper desire to see us act on protecting what order has been revealed in the natural world. That order, whatever order there is out there, is likely much more complex than what our simplistic scientific models express today. This is the healthy side of chaos theory infecting biological research. But at another level, even chaos theory is responding to some prevailing political and social trends in our society. So, I'm constantly asking myself, "Am I willing to modify my own beliefs as new information about how the world works comes in and registers in the scientific community?" And that's a pretty difficult tension to deal with.

Satterfield: When you say "modify your beliefs," you're not just talking about theoretical beliefs but beliefs in some more fundamental sense?

Nabhan: Yes. I mean for thirty years, the whole scientific sense of relationship between diversity and stability has gone up and then crashed and then gone back up again and crashed as people study it, applying different scales and different tools, and so on. If you ask me a really basic question: Do you think we should be preserving biological diversity because it makes our world a safer and healthier place to live in, despite knowing all the controversies and gray areas and permutations in that argument, I would say, at this point in time, *yes*. I would still say we need that diversity. And again, I'm really interested in the issue of whether we need cultural diversity in the same sense.

So at one level if you're asking me, "Do we need a strong endangered-species act as well as other kinds of legislation to protect biodiversity and how do we explain it to people?" I would say we use a whole range of values that scientists have related to biodiversity to convince different constituencies that it's in their interest to do it. If someone believes that plants are worth saving only because they are a potential cancer cure, we provide them with that information as well as saying, "You know, there are other scientifically elucidated reasons for protecting that diversity, besides its impact on human health." But if that's the way to engage someone in a discussion, it's a good first step.

Slovic: So engagement, here, is not really about narrative per se, but about the richness or diversity of values brought to bear in the discussion?

Nabhan: Well, it's just that I think that appealing to one set of values or arguments might help to open up the discussion in the first place but thereafter a broader picture is essential. A Native American might be concerned about seeing a place protected because it's a sacred mountain, yet be oblivious to arguments about biodiversity in that same place, or watershed stability, or whatever. I think the point is to listen and to engage such people in a discussion by first hearing their concerns about the sacredness of that place and then building into a broader discussion from there. One of the nice things about nature writing is that it usually presents a multifaceted discussion. Maybe in the early seventies we could rely exclusively on aesthetic arguments or deep-ecology arguments for protecting other species or landscapes, but I think there are really a lot of ideas emerging out of natural history literature now that have broadened arguments tremendously.

Slovic: Do you think environmental writing is speaking to a broad audience? Or is it primarily a kind of closed circle?

Nabhan: I think there are a couple of different ways to walk into that one. Pragmatically, I must admit at the outset that Richard Nelson or David Quammen, or even Terry Tempest Williams, might sell fifty to a hundred thousand copies of their books and 90 percent of that is preaching to the saved. But their books are having a tremendous effect on people like Barbara Kingsolver, who might sell several million copies of one of her books. Barbara is teaching writers' workshops with these other writers and is embedding all those same values into her books. My mother reads *Animal Dreams* and she gets it, whereas the most polite thing she can say about my books is, "I finally finished one of your books." Barbara Kingsolver and Peter Matthiessen and others have huge audiences, who really don't give a shit whether the writers know anything about ecology—they're good storytellers. And so I think the cumulative impact of the natural-history writing community goes way beyond the group of people who call themselves "environmentalists." I think there's even, you know, trickle-out from there. I loved it when Dave Foreman said in *Wild Earth* that a movie like "The Emerald Forest" was basically an allegory for tropical rain-forest stuff—and it appealed to millions of people in a deep ecological way. It's not simply that the whole ripple effect ends with Barbara Kingsolver or with Dan Janzen or one of the tropical writers who has a relatively large audience. I think it continues out from there, so that a dozen playwrights may be moved by the way Barbara Kingsolver structures the debate in one of her books, and so on.

Satterfield: What do you consider "good" evidence in the larger public world for environmental values, the values you imagine the environmentalist reader holding dear?

Nabhan: Well, I really liked what the anthropologist Willett Kempton had to say about environmental values. If you look at what a dry-cleaning worker in L.A. says about his basic values and you look at what an Earth First!er has to say, their perspectives are much closer than most Americans would believe. Most Americans still believe in the greater good, that we've been gifted with living in a great land and that we should take care of it for future generations. And that there is still something exciting about being in a beautiful and wonderful place. I mean even the working guys talk, where you don't bring these things up, but you do say: "Whatcha doing this weekend? Oh, going hunting, trying to get away from the old lady." The guy isn't out to get away from the old lady—he's trying to get an excuse to have some contact with something other than the human world. Speaking about the confines of his household in a pejorative way, or in a sexist way, is male shorthand for "I need some contact with the nonhuman world."

Satterfield: Assuming you're right, this hesitancy to be forthcoming about needing, for instance, contact with the nonhuman world is a problem for those who study values. The values that people hold most deeply, particularly those that we are unwilling to state directly, may not be those we're able to put words to or offer up as rationalizations for the interested researchers. I wonder if this is where narrative comes in, that storytelling can provide a comfort zone, a comfortable way in which to discuss or disclose those more intimate or affectively resonant concerns. Can a story get that point across without having to make it quite so direct, approach it in a way that's safe?

Nabhan: Yes, I mean Cormac McCarthy is writing about wolves in a much more comfortable way for most people than the way they're covered in *High Country News*, the wars over wolf re-introduction programs. You feel in reading his book that there is something great about the Mexican borderlands as one of the last surviving places that something as wild as a wolf has lived. You want to hang on to that. He doesn't have to beat you over the head with proselytizing to get that across. Instead, you feel at such a deep current emotionally what the kid growing up on a ranch already knows. Still, it's a pretty tough story. It's a story with a lot of ugliness. But what struck me was that it's about people trying to deal with the end of the frontier in a very real way. Despite forty years of Western literature on the subject, it isn't a solved issue and it's no surprise that McCarthy's books are extremely popular in Australia, for example.

Slovic: I noticed that while we were talking you made a marginal note beside the question [on the questionnaire, provided before the interview]: Do you find more value in some creatures of nature than others and if so what accounts for that difference? You've got a "yes" here. I'm curious to know what that's about.

Nabhan: Well, the fact is most of us are never going to put much value on bacteria, viruses, or nematodes. Yet, these are the little things that make the world work. We're never going to notice them unless perhaps we have a great biology teacher who gives us a glimpse of them through a microscope that manages to leave an impression on us. I also like the weirdness of a guy who has devoted his whole life to nematodes, and I like to be reminded that I'm likely disturbing and maybe damaging those organisms every day. At an intellectual level, and maybe at an emotional level, the way I value those organisms might lead me to being a lot more careful.

But, of course, the contradictions remain: That awareness doesn't keep me from driving an hour and a half across town to see Barbara Kingsolver, even though I know that I might be running over a bunch of those little guys with my tires. I think, inherently, that we value things that we can see or emotionally relate to on a daily or weekly or yearly basis, much more so than those organisms that are out of sight, beyond our immediate awareness.

Satterfield: Environmental ethicists often use the phrase "charismatic megafauna" to denote species that garner considerable attention—a grizzly bear or spotted owl. But you seem to be asking the question: Is there wisdom there?

Nabhan: Well, it's sort of the flagship species idea, the notion that if we protect ironwood, we protect a big chunk of the ecosystem that's associated with that species. However, I'm less likely to believe in that possibility than I was ten years ago. I don't necessarily think there will be a trickle-down effect to rarer and more problematic species.

Slovic: How important is direct sensory experience to awareness of the kind of biological minutiae that you're talking about?

Nabhan: It's critically important. Let's see. I went to Italy recently in search of local understandings of plant life. I realized that most Italians eat more wild fruits and have more contact with wild species than do most Native

Americans or Anglo Americans. Why this has persisted in both rural and urban Italian societies is because they are, to put it bluntly, hedonists. They indulge the sensory pleasures of having three hundred mushrooms in a marketplace. One of my Italian friends says that the real crux of this situation is that most outsiders think Italians are very materialistic. But I think they're the opposite of that because they value the quality of each element in the material world for its own specific uniqueness. That's the opposite of materialism. The food in Assisi is distinct from the food in Gubbio. You can't commodify them both by slam dunking them into a chain restaurant. True hedonism resists commodification of the material world. It's manifest in people who delight in the sensory pleasures of hearing the mockingbird vespers in the spring evenings in Tucson, as opposed to what mockingbirds sound like in some other part of the world or what a generalized mockingbird might sound like. It is about protecting the elements that really need to be protected and not just the generalities.

Slovic: So where does story play into this?

Nabhan: Story reminds of us of that detail. The writer Naomi Nye said that she considers her writing about the ordinary details and pleasures of daily life to be a profoundly political act. Her stories all revolve around giving dignity back to the things that are closest to home. It's about loving the weirdness of our backyards and not the backyards in *Sunset Magazine* or whatever is trendy. The values that I have that make me want what is right here, what is distinct from anywhere else in the world. I've gotten them not from scientists, but from writers like Bill Stafford and Naomi Nye and Charles Simic and people who celebrate the littlest treasures around us.

Slovic: Given the kind of local intimacy that you're speaking of, I wonder whether or not you see nature writing as a way of accessing a wilderness experience or as a substitute in some sense for experience.

Nabhan: Let's see. I'm disinclined to read reflective impressions of the soul, or on being human in the wilderness. I tend to tune out that category of wilderness writing.

Satterfield: Is it that you fear literature becoming a surrogate for the real thing?

Nabhan: I regularly face this prospect at the museum. Just yesterday, a friend asked me if I worry that people who are inclined to come to the aviary don't bother to listen to birds in the desert. If the museum is good at making exhibits feel like natural habitats, they produce what Jack Turner refers to in *Abstract Wild.* I think that's definitely, definitely true. Nature films are even more dangerous. Museums are dangerous. But I would say that nature writing is the least dangerous in the group in that it spins people back to their own experience quickly rather than manufacturing another reality.

Satterfield: Is that because there's a greater capacity for reflection in the act of reading than in watching? Or why, why is that true?

Slovic: Or is it because the difference between reading a book and watching a nature video has a lot to do with time and how much time it takes to process what one has experienced in the text? You can control the pace of reading.

Nabhan: The amazing thing for me with *The Geography of Childhood*, more than any book I've been involved in, was that so many people took it as an inroad to their own childhoods, their own experience. So many people said to me: I can't remember what childhood experience you wrote about, but when I was reading one of your chapters, I kept on thinking about what happened to me when I was four when I got lost on the beach and so on. The readers move into their own experiences so quickly—they just flipped over into bodily remembering something of their own experience, their own reverie. That adds value to your own life—it goes beyond merely gaining pleasure from the other person's story. Your own imagination is actively in play. The most imaginative and satisfying experiences are those in which we're given a minimal cue, and we build on that with our own imaginations.

Slovic: Can you think of any particular techniques of storytelling that might help to elicit the imaginative response from the reader, rather than providing that entire response?

Nabhan: What I know I've learned from poets: the preciseness of the imagery. I mean, it seems to me, how my mind or imagination works is that once I connect with a particular image that has some emotional content, it's like shooting off into hyperspace. I'm completely into that story for a while. Often there's a very quick intuitive trigger that must trick me—it must be a surprise; it must startle me in a bold way, take me out of my sensibility. It's the art of setting up a dialogue or a dialectic between your own experience and something that someone is putting before you. All of us have felt the euphoria of being in a dialogue like that.

Satterfield: I can't help noticing that you keep coming back to ideas about emotion or emotional content as the partial basis for engagement in a story. Is the narrative form particularly good at permitting that emotional content to come into play, particularly in reference to the way in which we think about and value nature? Any thoughts on that?

Nabhan: Well, my immediate thought is that fewer and fewer people have the tangible currency of imagery, have daily knowledge of nature that carries with it any emotional content. When someone during the Tang Dynasty would write about a particular tree's leaves shimmering and dropping in the breeze, that would work as a feeling of sadness and loss in a Tang Dynasty poem because everyone knew that that was what the last spurt of greenness at the end of the summer meant. We live in a very different age. And our storytellers, when they try to communicate their environmental values, have different challenges for that reason.

♦

Hornworm's Home Ground: Conserving Interactions[1]

> The character of the individual fruit tree simply cannot be understood without reference to others of its species, to the insects that fertilize it and to the animals that consume its fruit and disperse its seeds.
>
> David Abram, *The Spell of the Sensuous*

Have you ever imagined a hornworm procession: tens of thousands of pinstriped, multicolored larvae gathering together for a desert promenade? I had been dreaming of them for weeks but had hardly seen a "worm" all summer. The spring drought had been so prolonged that not a single green-and-yellow larva had flashed before my eyes, nor had I spotted any of their metamorphosed white-lined sphinx moths. I longed to see even one moth hover before a blossom of the rare plants I had been monitoring since early May. Such night-flying hawk-moths are needed to pollinate certain desert flowers if these floras are to form plump, seed-rich fruit. The absence of hawkmoths meant that nearly all the flowers had withered and aborted, leaving little hope for the ripened fruit this year.

Week after week, my Desert Alert work crews had meandered up and down desert slopes, searching for moths, their eggs, or their larvae, but we had had no success in finding them through late July. It looked as though some of the rarest plants in Arizona would not be pollinated sufficiently to produce any progeny at all this season. There were a few more flower buds that could still develop into blooms, but I doubted that a hawkmoth would arrive in time even if they were to blossom.

Night after night, I had been entirely preoccupied by the fate of these flowers. I was sorely in need of a time-out to clear my mind or at least to muddle over something different. I decided to drive out to see some old

O'odham Indian friends living in the heart of the desert fifty miles west of my home.

I was hardly five miles from my front door when I noticed something wriggling across the road. I dismissed it at first. No hornworm in its right mind would venture onto burning black asphalt on a midsummer's desert day. The pavement would be wavering around 160 degrees, which was hot enough to fry any low-riding pilgrim.

Then I caught sight of a second wriggler. It looked like nothing more than a greenish noodle when seen at sixty miles an hour, but I tried to steer away from hitting it nonetheless; I would feel awful it my tires flattened one of the few hornworms seen all summer.

Fortunately, I spotted another. And another. I must have splattered the green guts of the fourth sitting on the pavement in the path of my front right tire, despite another valiant attempt to swerve in time to miss it. I began to count every one that I passed on my way to Hot Fields Village. By the time I slowed to a stop in front of the Cruz family adobe, I had tallied 463 hornworms on the march, enough to share with friends.

"I brought you something for dinner," I hollered to Margie Cruz, who groaned when she opened the cardboard box I had filled with hornworms.

"Ohhhh!" She grimaced in mock horror, peering down into the box, shaking her head. "I thought we told you already that we don't eat no worms anymoooore. The kids especially—they won't eat them."

"But can't you fix them up so the kids wouldn't know what we're having?" I pleaded. Then, I whispered, "Just hide them under some spaghetti sauce and no one will notice until they crawl on top of a meatball. . . ."

"You got to squeeze out their entrails before you cook them up," her husband Remedio interjected. "We don't treat them like noodles, we roast them in lard in a frying pan so that they taste like popcorn. Or sometimes we put them on a stick over a campfire, then string the cooked ones up like a necklace. Old ladies used to wear strings of them around their necks and snack on them like candy."

Marge and Remedio were still amusing themselves by peering into the box and groaning when their grandchildren ran into the kitchen. They peeked over Marge's shoulder and saw that my take-out food was alive and squirming. They all shrieked in unison and tore back out of the kitchen toward the TV room. There, they turned up the volume of some monster film, as if to blast away any memory of the creepy-crawlies close to home.

"*Makkum*," Remedio repeated over and over, like a murmur. "*Makkum*."

This is the O'odham name for this kind of larvae, a widespread sphingid species called *Hyles lineata* by scientists.

"Where do they come from, Mr. Cruz? I've been waiting for them all summer long, but I hadn't seen any until today."

Remedio Cruz glanced up at me, then back down at the floor. "I don't know for suu-ure," he sighed, as he always did just before making an astute observation, "but I think they came out with that rain about two weeks ago."

I realized that he was probably right—the larvae looked as though they were in the third or fourth larval stage, maybe as much as the fifth. They could have hatched from eggs soon after the one modest rain we had received, for it had probably been wet enough to send them on their way toward metamorphosis into moth-hood.

"But all of a sudden they're crawling around out there in the desert," I said. Remedio blinked his eyes; I wasn't sure if his hearing had begun to fail him or if he was still trying to figure out what I was talking about. I scratched my head, then tried tentatively to phrase my observation in his native tongue: *"Hegam mamakkum o oimed gnhu g tohono jewed-c-ed."*

Remedio smiled knowingly. He had seen the hornworm emigrations many times over his seventy-some years of living in the desert. He sometimes forgot that I had only been a desert dweller for two decades and that what was commonplace to him was often some special event to me.

"They come from the *makkum ha-jewed,*" Remedio explained to me, referring to the name of a summer wildflower that he had once shown me in his fields. It was a sticky-leafed, low-growing herb that I had identified as *Boerhaavia coccinea,* one of several related plants collectively called "spiderlings" in English. But *makkum ha-jewed* referred to only two of the stickier species of local spiderlings. This name means "the hornworm's home ground," although in another Piman dialect the same plant is called "the hornworm's mother."

These native names cryptically encode the notion of a plant that moths require for their early life stages. Lepidopterists have encoded the same notion in their technical jargon, using the term "larval host plant." Both *makkum ha-jewed* and *larval host plant* speak to a pattern of relationships between a particular moth species and the flora that nurtures it.

"Once those worms eat all the leaves on the *makkum ha-jewed*, they all start to wander around just like you said. They must be looking for something special, because sometimes they don't stop to eat other plants. They all come marching out of my backyard one morning, going over there toward the fields." He nodded toward the old fields for which the village was named.

"Then they crawl onto my devil's claw plants or onto the chiles and tomatoes I've been hand-watering, and they eat them all up. Then they wander back through the yard before the sun goes down. I never have figured out where they go to sleep. Sometimes if it rains real hard at night, though, it will knock them out. A lot of them will drown."

"I wish I could figure out when they will be turning into *hohokimal,*" I said, referring to the moths that had yet to be found visiting the now-withered flowers in my field plots. I wondered whether there would be time for any moths to metamorphose before the last floral buds broke open that summer.

"I think that maybe there's a chance you could be seeing some of those night butterflies soon," predicted Remedio, failing to remember the English word *moth.* I couldn't be sure that he knew which moths the green-and-yellow larvae turned into. He did, however, know when the moths would begin a sequence of events with which he was intimately familiar: "About this time after a good summer rain, those little night butterflies start to swarm around our porch lights."

I had gone out to Hot Fields to get my mind off moths and plants, but they had shown up anyway. Within a week, the larval densities in the desert began to soar just as Remedio had suggested they might. They continued to do so for another month. I watched the march of larvae day after day for a fortnight.

Finally, on the last flowering night of the season for the rarest of plants I was tracking, white-lined sphinx moths arrived to hover before the blossoms, reaching their tongues into the deep, sweet nectar pools and getting their faces and wings plastered with pollen. The next morning, the delicate scales of moth wings had been left like calling cards in a few of the blossoms, and pollen had been sprinkled onto their receptive stigmas. Where some of these blossoms had been, bulbous red fruit would emerge, and they would be chock full of shiny black seeds.

If the moths had not arrived in time, the rare plants would not have reproduced at all, even though they were just "protected" within a couple of national parks and wildlife refuges near my home. All the legal protection in the world would not ensure their survival if the moths failed to arrive to bless them and transfer their pollen from one blossom to the next. When and where this might happen, I realized, was something that grade-school-educated Remedio Cruz could predict far better than I. Despite my Ph.D. studies in desert ecology, I was a novice in observing the life histories of local moths—species that Remedio and Marge had lived among all of their lives.

I had been learning native plant and animal names from Remedio for nearly twenty years when I finally realized that he also had considerable knowledge of the ecological interactions among particular plants and animals. I had hardly ever stopped to ask him about nature's relationships, for I presumed they were unnamed and therefore unknown. I was not the first conservation biologist to have downplayed the importance of such knowledge in being a good steward of the natural world. Ecologist John Thompson has recently commented, "The diversity of life has resulted from the diversification of both species and the interactions among them. . . . Nevertheless, the focus of studies on the conservation of biodiversity has often been primarily on species rather than interactions."

Many desert ecologists and conservation biologists remain unaware of the rich oral commentaries on ancient relationships between plants and their coevolved animal dispersers, foragers, and pollinators. A few years ago, a graduate student studying the history of ecology mentioned to me that he had read of a curious "discovery" made by biologists at the University of Texas three decades before. Vern and Karen Grant described how hawkmoths visiting sacred datura blossoms often exhibited "intoxicated behavior" for a while after having drunk nectar from this hallucinogenic plant. Floral chemists have described a complex chemical brew in sacred datura nectar, including aromatics, amino acids, fatty acids, and terpenoids. But no one had verified that the psychotropic alkaloids atropine and scopolamine found in datura seeds and leaves were also present in the nectar, especially in quantities sufficient to induce intoxication. Nevertheless, the Grants hypothesized, something was making the nocturnal *Manduca* moths get dizzy and trip the night fantastic. They inferred that sacred datura nectar provided enough psychotropic rewards to these moths to lure them away from other flowers that were blooming simultaneously.

Around that time, I stumbled on an ancient datura "hunting song" recorded by Pima Indian José Luis Brennan from an elderly neighbor Virsak Vali, around 1900. It was a prayer to ensure the successful capture of deer, but it was also used to cure the psychosomatic "staying sicknesses" from which Pima individuals who had broken taboos occasionally suffered. I could tell from reading the Piman text that a clumsy translation had obscured a rich ecological message. While the text was certainly alluding to nocturnal hawkmoths visiting sacred datura flowers, Brennan's collaborator Frank Russell had used the English term *butterfly,* and the ceremonial plant had been reduced to being "a weed." After hours of consulting Piman-speaking friends and language texts, I worked up a new translation, which I hoped would be closer in spirit and biological precision to the native text:

> Stopping for a while in the white of dawn,
> stopping for a while in the white of dawn,
> rising to move through the valley
> where the blue evening flies away,
> rising to move through the valley.
>
> Sacred datura leaves, sacred datura leaves,
> eating your greens intoxicates me,
> making me stagger, dizzily leap.
> Datura blossoms, datura blossoms,
> drinking your nectar intoxicates me,
> making me stagger, dizzily leap.
>
> Leaving the ground, the winged one overtakes me,
> his bow looms large as he shoots to wound me;
> my horns are severed, strewn hither and yon.
> Leaving the ground, the winged one overtakes me,
> his arrows loom large as he shoots to wound me,
> my foldings, shot open, strewn hither and yon.
>
> As flying insects, insects aflight, we are crazily set ablaze,
> we drop to the ground, drop off to sleep as our wings flap still,
> our last gasp, our last chance to fly back from way over there.
> As drunken hawkmoths, hawkmoths drinking, we are set ablaze,
> wings pressing shut, then spreading again,
> fluttering, fluttering, way over there.

It is clear from this song that the same kind of psychotropic "trips" that medicine men associate with ingesting datura are attributed to both the leaf-feeding hornworm larvae and the nectar-drinking nocturnal moths. Decades before the Grants' scientific "discovery," the oral tradition of indigenous desert people evocatively celebrated the same alkaloid-mediated relationship between animal and plant.

Indigenous desert dwellers do not name the entire spectrum of insects found within their home territories, nor are they necessarily aware of most interactions between the plants and animals there. But they do know about interactions between animals and the major food plants that fill their larders, even when these interactions might seem obscure to the outsider.

One such interaction seems especially obscure to most desert dwellers today. Mesquite pods were, up until this century, the most important food in the Sonoran Desert region. But these pods were easily infested with minuscule bruchid beetles if they were left to sit under a mesquite tree after they fell. Female bruchids would lay eggs in the seeds, and the hatchlings would bore their way out by eating enough of the seeds to make them inviable. Remedio Cruz and his kin call these tiny beetles *kui kai mamad,* "mesquite bean babies." Once they have infested a bunch of mesquite pods, its value as food plummets.

The Seri Indian neighbors of the O'odham had an unusual way of finding pods that had been removed from the bruchid-dense desert floor beneath mesquite trees. Long after most mesquite pods had fallen from the trees, the Seri would search for piles of them in pack-rat middens. I once went out into the desert with Angelita Torres, who used a long stick to pry open the messy mounds of desert plant matter collected by these furry desert archivists. Angelita said that she could recover several pounds of edible mesquite pods in a matter of minutes. She was, in a sense, short circuiting the food chain. Rather than gaining one-tenth of the food value of pods by eating the pack rat—as she occasionally did—she and her family ingested all of the nutritional value that the pack rats would have consumed.

The Seri were particularly observant of such interactions between native plants and animals, perhaps because their families depended on such knowledge in order to survive times of famine and drought. One out of every ten of their names for plants refers in some way to an animal, and at least half of those names accurately encode knowledge about native plant-animal interactions.

As important as it was for the Seri to understand such ecological associations in order to feed themselves, some of the interactions they describe had little utilitarian value. Why, for instance, would Seri hunters pay particular attention to the kinds of wildflowers that desert tortoises eat, when the wildflowers themselves are not considered edible for the Seri nor are they the best indicators of where to look for *ziij hehet coquij,* "The live thing that hides in bushes"? What do they "gain" by giving three very different-looking plants (from different families) the same name, *hap oacajam,* simply because mule deer stags scrape the velvet of their new antlers off on the branches of widely scattered individuals of these plants? While such information may have helped Seri men decide where to hunt, I have noticed that the Seri also delight in being sensually and intellectually aware of these ecological relationships for "knowledge's sake" alone.

While sitting on a beach talking to Seri turtle hunter Jesús Rojo about his people's names that allude to plants and their animal associates, I could see that the terms were more than mere words; they were also prompts to images that were like scenes out of a story. We were talking, for instance, about a red algae found on the backs of sea turtles, and Jesús reminded me that only one kind of sea turtle is adorned by *moosni yazj*, "the green sea turtle's covering." It is found only on a rare population of green sea turtles that does not emigrate away from the Seri's coastal waters in the wintertime but instead goes dormant, sleeping on bottoms of shoals that are laden with red algae and that lie between the Sonoran coast and Tiburon Island. Jesús and other Seri men who formerly made their living as turtle hunters treat this rare population as though it were its own species; in fact, biologists have speculated that it may indeed be a distinctive breeding pool of sea turtles.

As Jesús talked of this sea turtle and its algae, he began to sing a song about them, and as he sang the song, he motioned with his hands how the sea turtle would rise from the channel bottom and come up for air. Then he sang another song about an equally distinctive population of sea turtles, and he mimed the act of harpooning one of them. Each name gave rise to an image, the image to a song, and the song to a larger drama, enacted with gesture, voice, and eye movements. Each was an ancient story, one in which turtle, alga, and harpooner danced to the same music.

Only now are we beginning to see the conservation value of such local knowledge—now that these sea turtles and other rare critters have been decimated through the spread of modern hunting technologies. Although most Seri alive today have never seen even a single Sonoran pronghorn antelope—an endangered subspecies now limited to fewer than 500 individuals—they still remember a winter herb that it once ate. The Seri name for a wild mitten-leaved bean is *haamoja ihaap*, "the pronghorn's bean food"; the name comes from a now-moribund dialect spoken by a band of Seri that once wandered into the southern reaches of the pronghorn's range. Even in the core of its range 200 miles to the north of the Seri, the pronghorn has been exceedingly rare for nearly a century, as a result of being gunned down by the first recreational trophy hunters to venture into the region. *Haamoja* is such an archaic word that contemporary Seri have coined another, more descriptive term to describe this animal when they are shown pictures or photos of it by biologists. Yet many of them still use its ancient name as part of the term for the lentil-like bean that grows on the silty flats that the pronghorn frequented. The plant had escaped the notice of wildlife biologists charged with inventorying the remaining pronghorn population's diet, but once the biologists heard of the Seri "lore" about this plant, they conceded that it deserved to be added to the roster of potential nutritional resources required to sustain this endangered animal.

Is such linguistically encoded knowledge about ecological relationships disappearing? Among the Seri, the younger generation can still name 70% of the native animals in photographs we provided, but their elders have an average score of 90%. Janice Rosenberg, who interviewed more than 50 Seri individuals about traditional ecological knowledge, found that the children were unaware of many local interactions involving insects and reptiles in particular—ecological relationships that their grandparents could discuss in detail. Seri youth were even less familiar with the traditional songs and rituals about floral and faunal relationships that their elders still held dear.

Ethnobotanist Kay Fowler has already witnessed dramatic changes in both cultures and environments over three decades of research in the Great Basin. But as she has conceded, "even by the time we started collecting traditional knowledge about plants and animals associated with them, we were . . . getting less than half of the traditional knowledge [that] once existed." She had the good fortune to be out with traditional foragers when *Pandanus* moth larvae appeared in abundance one year, and the Owens Valley Paiute had a field day collecting them off desert plants to eat. But such harvests are few and far between these days.

In other regions, the survival of indigenous knowledge of plant-animal interactions may be in even greater doubt. Nancy Turner reports that the Salish people of the coastal rain forests of Washington have used banana slugs as a poultice for cuts and wounds because these slugs consume a certain set of plants that collectively have medicinal value. But there are fewer than ten Salish speakers left in this world; the details of which medicinal plants the slugs love are passing out of local knowledge. Richard Ford reports that the same is true in the Rio Grande pueblos, communities where, twenty years ago, speakers of the Tewa language distinguished dozens of kinds of trees and wildflowers from one another; today, young children use the old word for "firewood" for most trees and the old word for "weed" for most herbaceous plants. Should such a collapse of all names for flowering herbs into one catchall term come to the Seri, their community might lose track of which wild bean the endangered pronghorn antelope ate or which bush the desert tortoise hid under. And if that happens, what will become of the images, the gestures, songs, and stories once conjured up by native names?

It has been more than two decades since I first heard the ominous warning given by field ecologist Daniel Janzen, that "what escapes the eye is the most insidious kind of extinction—the extinction of interactions." That prophetic phrase—and the sound of Jesús Rojo singing his sea turtle songs—echoed through my head as I drove back through the night from the hornworm's home ground. My hope is that I can keep the images of that home ground alive in my mind's eye and eventually learn the songs that keep it vibrant.

13

A CONCLUDING CONVERSATION

What is it that we can say to conclude this highly unconventional volume of interviews, based as it is on important research concerns about representing values in simplified metrics—be they as dollars, rankings, or the descriptive statistics born of survey research? Put simply, *What's Nature Worth?* is a project that we can describe with complete candor only as a "guilty pleasure"—the pleasure of thinking beyond these conventional metrics. Its contributions lie in the deeply thoughtful and wide-ranging perspectives that each of the authors has put forth on why he or she writes in various literary forms to articulate the difficult-to-articulate dimensions of value. Further, while the book is driven by an important academic and practical problem, as an outcome it does not easily conform to the rules of procedure, representation of "data," or argument for any one discipline or set of disciplines. Had we conformed to disciplinary conventions, we might never have finished the book. We agreed, from beginning to end, on the importance of narrative for articulating value, but thereafter we often parted ways. Scott, at times, found Terre's preoccupations with narrative as a powerful means for processing information or for challenging practices widely upheld in policy venues to be unfruitful and sometimes even confusing. Terre couldn't always follow Scott's interests in rhetoric or the precise crafting of an image that a particular author had employed. Moreover, Terre initially worried that she would find nature writers a frustratingly romantic group, too far removed from the gritty realities of everyday life. This, of course, was not the case. Rather, as Richard Shelton and many others state so well, they have little patience on this point and are quick to contradict such naive assumptions about this literary genre.

It thus seems only appropriate to conclude this book with some final informal thoughts on our mutual experiences with the project and to reflect briefly on the collective insights of the contributing authors concerning their implications for future work in the field. We have done so by way of a conversation. In order of writing, Scott first offers his own thoughts on the collaboration and its relevance for questions that fuel his work as a literary scholar. Terre then follows with her own.

Terre Satterfield
Scott Slovic
June 2003

Concluding Thoughts: Scott Slovic

In the final pages of my 1992 book, *Seeking Awareness in American Nature Writing*, I tried to pull together several of the overarching questions I had been probing throughout my study of the phenomenon of consciousness (its expression and elicitation) in American writing about nature since the mid-nineteenth century. As a literary critic, I had been concerned in that project with the aesthetics of literary style; and as an environmentally concerned citizen, I had felt compelled to examine the statements of personal environmental consciousness and tactics for prodding readers' consciousness evident in the work of writers ranging from Henry David Thoreau to Barry Lopez. In conclusion, I asked: "How does nature writing . . . influence people's attitudes and behavior? Is there any discernable and empirically verifiable influence?" (1992, 181).

Since 1992, other literary critics have directly or indirectly responded to these questions, aiming essentially to answer the submerged, self-justifying query: Does nature writing—or, more broadly, "environmental literature"—matter? As we mentioned in the introduction to this current volume, Daniel G. Payne addresses the political ramifications of environmental writing, particularly from the nineteenth century up through the 1980s, in his 1996 book, *Voices in the Wilderness: American Nature Writing and Environmental Politics*. He finds that

> Nature writers today are less likely to be the immediate force behind the creation of environmental advocacy groups, the passage of legislation, or other reforms than was once the case, and more likely to play the part of political gadfly. The polemical function of nature writers has been diminished as television, radio, and the direct mail of advocacy groups has come to play a greater role in environmental politics. (Payne 1996, 168–69)

The development of new technologies and the evolution of new processes of social change have altered the role of the written word—of literature—in American culture and in similar societies around the world in recent years. As Sven Birkerts puts it in *The Gutenberg Elegies: The Fate of Reading in an*

Electronic Age, "The stable hierarchies of the printed page—one of the defining norms of [the familiar, slower] world—are being superseded by the rush of impulses through freshly minted circuits" (1994, 3). During the early years of the twenty-first century, many of us who have long been devoted to books, journals, magazines, and newspapers have found ourselves daily engaged in communicating by e-mail and gathering information from the web. But whether we communicate and receive ideas from traditional sources or from electronic media, our need to understand the subtleties of language has not changed at all since the days of Emerson and Thoreau. Regardless of the technology of transmittal, the medium of expression and elicitation remains language. As Payne puts it, thinking of the social role that writers play in influencing public opinion, "There is a continued need for nature writers with the skill to reach and influence the public, and earlier writers such as those discussed in this study [including John Muir, Aldo Leopold, and Rachel Carson] provide us with a number of important lessons in rhetoric and advocacy that are still relevant today" (1996, 174). Other new studies, such as Daniel J. Philippon's 2004 book *Conserving Words: How American Nature Writers Shaped the Environmental Movement*, extend and refocus Payne's analysis, illustrating the historical efficacy of environmental writing and attempting to extrapolate from the past to understand the continuing importance of this literary tradition.

So, when Terre Satterfield first asked if I would be interested in collaborating with her on a study of narrative expressions of environmental values, my position was as a specialist in the literary representation of nature (poetry, fiction, and nonfiction), interested in the psychological and rhetorical implications of this literature. My perspective was similar to the scholarly angles of Payne and Philippon, although I was perhaps even more rooted (isolated?) in the aesthetics of literary expression. I was—and am—primarily a scholar of American literature, but I have long been interested in international literature and by the mid-1990s had experienced year-long study grants in Germany and Japan (more recently I have spent time in Australia and Central America, gaining familiarity with additional traditions of environmental writing). I saw the collaboration with Terre as a unique opportunity for me to increase my knowledge of the philosophy of environmental values, practical procedures of environmental valuation, and cutting-edge linkages between new evaluation strategies and government policy. I also viewed this project as an opportunity to benefit from the special eloquence and wisdom of contemporary American environmental writers—a uniquely gifted and generous subculture. At a time in world history when the United States is becoming notorious for its support of corporate colonization in the name of "globalization" (and particularly at a moment when the American government and its corporate colleagues are continuing their colonization of Iraq), it seems important to turn to our wisest artists and scholars for guidance.

In certain ways, Terre and I are mirror images of each other. We approach similar topics from opposite scholarly angles. She is an anthropologist with a strong interest in psychology, environmental conflicts, and discourse. I am a literary historian and critic with an interest in—some would say "obsession" for—the psychological and rhetorical aspects of environmental literature. When Terre first contacted me about this project, she had recently completed a Ph.D. dissertation examining the conflict between logging communities and environmentalists in the Pacific Northwest, with a particular focus on identity and agency and the forms of language used by all parties involved in the debate over timber harvesting. This fascinating study has now been published as *Anatomy of a Conflict: Identity, Knowledge, and Emotion in Old-Growth Forests* (2002). I had recently completed a rhetorical study titled "Embedded Rhetoric and Discrete Rhetoric: Epistemology and Politics in American Nature Writing" (1996) and was in the midst of preparing an overview of environmental literature, titled "Giving Expression to Nature: Voices of Environmental Literature," to be published in a 1999 issue of *Environment* magazine for an audience of environmental scientists and environmental policy specialists. Terre and I found ourselves united in our shared concern for contemporary North American social conflicts (particularly in the environmental arena) and our shared appreciation of the language of story. She is an anthropologist with a love for literature and art, and I am a literary scholar with a fascination for the social sciences. When we launched this collaboration, we knew we had common intellectual ground, but we didn't exactly know where we were headed. Perhaps the most important aspect of our initial collaboration was our respect for each other's expertise in a neighboring discipline, our sense of humor and goodwill in inviting each other to dabble in a new field, and our willingness to risk displaying naiveté by venturing beyond our realms of intellectual comfort.

Terre had conducted numerous interviews, with ordinary citizens and with activists and experts, while completing the research for *Anatomy of a Conflict*, and she was familiar with the theoretical aspect of ethnographic fieldwork as a result of her training in anthropology. I, on the other hand, had had no formal training in interview strategies as a graduate student in English, but I have long had a wide circle of friends in the community of environmental writers, and I was confident that I could help Terre to engage in a pertinent and challenging series of discussions with this articulate, thoughtful group of people. I had conducted one extended, formal interview with nature writer Rick Bass in the early 1990s (published first in the journal *Weber Studies* and later reprinted in the 2001 collection *The Literary Art and Activism of Rick Bass*), so I had a sense of how the interview, transcription, and revision process would occur. Before we actually began scheduling our meetings with individual writers, we enlisted my friend John Daniel to draft a set of fundamental questions about story (narrative discourse) and environmental values that he thought would be accessible and interesting for writers like himself. We plied him with a copy of the National Science Foundation proposal (the set of ideas that funded this and related work), knowing full well that as a distinguished poet and environmental essayist, John would appreciate the importance of making the leap from literary art to public policy. We ended up using John's questionnaire in lieu of face-to-face interviews in three cases (with Bruce Berger, William Kittredge, and Richard Shelton), and although the respondents sometimes disputed the phrasing of the questionnaire, we find the responses very helpful in clarifying the goals of contemporary environmental literature and some of the strategies for composing statements of values used by leading practitioners of environmental narrative. Terre and I conducted most of the actual interviews during a series of trips to Tucson, Arizona, and Salt Lake City, Utah, the latter to visit with Terry Tempest Williams (shortly before she and her husband moved to southern Utah) and with Stephen Trimble. We then traveled together to Tucson, where we stayed at the University of Arizona's Poetry Center (thanks to the kindness of Alison Deming) and spent a few days interviewing Deming, Gregory McNamee, Gary Paul Nabhan, Simon J. Ortiz, and Ofelia Zepeda. Over the course of the next few years, Terre and I interviewed John Daniel (not using his questionnaire, except as a general template) at the offices of Decision Research in Eugene, Oregon, and Robert Michael Pyle at his home in Gray's River, Washington. I interviewed author and photographer Stephen Trimble by myself at his home in Salt Lake City.

Perhaps it is the nature of interview documents to lack the precise, argumentative focus of formal essays. As such, the questionnaire responses and interview transcripts included in this volume tend to offer stabs at insight rather than full, extended articulations of strategies, beliefs, and experiences. Sometimes the interview transcripts meander and digress, despite the fact that we have edited the original documents down to less than half of their original length in most cases, seeking focus and coherence. At times, we found that our ways of asking questions or raising topics seemed to baffle or annoy the writers we were interviewing. I'm afraid that some of this may simply be the result of my ineptitude as an interviewer, or my tendency to use academic-sounding jargon even when I'm trying to speak plainly. But in a way, that's the very purpose of doing this project, as far as I'm concerned. Although I believe in the importance of talking about our lives and our hopes and fears in vivid, visceral language—in the language of story and image—I don't feel that I'm particularly skilled at doing so. I find that I lapse into abstractions, into technical/professional language. And I believe this hampers the effectiveness of my attempts to communicate what I value about life, about nature, about community. From my perspective, every one of the people Terre and I interviewed is a masterful practitioner of evocative language. Every one of these writers has demonstrated that he or she can take the most abstract or complex philosophical or scientific concept and state it in a way that makes my heart stop, makes tears come to my eyes. I deeply admire (even envy) the splendid communication skills of these writers and dozens of other contemporary environmental authors. This book represents, from my perspective, an effort to learn from these masters a little bit about why they care so much about the language of story and how they employ story in their own lives and their own work.

While working on this project, I became aware of innovative efforts among federal agencies to solicit public commentary when I received a copy of the "Visions Kit" prepared by the Bureau of Land Management as part of the process of developing a management plan for the proposed Grand Staircase–Escalante National Monument in southern Utah. The Visions Kit contained a map and descriptions of the landscapes within the monument, a statement of the monument's "guiding principles," a copy of President Clinton's proclamation establishing the monument, and a worksheet with questions designed to help citizens "think creatively about the future of the Monument." The three-page worksheet is divided into four sections: 1) Values; 2) Purposes and Management; 3) Community; and 4) Other Concerns. There are between six and eleven lines available for each of these categories of response. Under the values category, the worksheet states: "People value the Monument for a variety of reasons. *What do you value about the Grand Staircase–Escalante National Monument, and why?*" There is no particular guidance or restriction offered in the worksheet for how members of the public should offer suggestions to BLM officials, except for the suggestion that "specific comments are most helpful." I'm sure many people, keen to communicate their perspectives to "the people in charge," simply pulled their thoughts into words without worrying terribly about stylistic elegance or rhetorical weight. I'm sure there were some respondents, though, who found themselves at a loss for words and expressive structures as they scrambled to state their views succinctly by the appointed deadline for public comment. I imagine this book as a potential source of advice and encouragement for people hoping to contribute to future planning efforts for national monuments and various other environmental management projects.

Likewise, in addition to what literary and policy scholars might glean from the insights of the dozen authors queried in these pages, I hope that BLM officials and representatives of other management agencies might find useful tips here for interpreting the commentary of experts and laypeople as well as arguments in support of the legitimacy of non-economic, non-quantitative expressions of environmental values and other social values. In the fall of 2002, nature writer David Strohmaier came to Reno to read from his recent book *The Seasons of Fire: Reflections on Fire in the West*. During his visit, I spoke with Dave about his "day job" as a public comment analyst for the U.S. Forest Service, the leader of a "Content Analysis Team" based in Missoula, Montana. He explained to me that he and his colleagues carefully read and "code" the letters sent to the Forest Service—and other federal and state agencies and sometimes municipalities—from citizens commenting on various management issues, collecting information about public values and specific suggestions for management strategies. The least valuable letters, from his perspective, are those that simply follow a pre-formulated pro/con format, advocating a particular management policy or its opposite. Trained in religious studies and philosophy, and a skilled essayist in his own right, Dave reads these public testimonials with an eye for nuance and individual expression—and in his reports to agency officials, he says, "our primary goal is not to capture how many people said x, but rather to capture what x is and why some respondent is advocating x." He goes on to explain: "As it now stands, neither NEPA [the National Environmental Policy Act] nor our analysis process treats public comment as a vote. It doesn't matter if one person articulates a concern or 10,000 people submit postcards that say the same thing—in our report it is displayed as one public concern. That concern then stands or falls on the merits of its argument: this could be an argument based on law or policy, or an informal argument bound up in a narrative account of having camped at a particular spot for the last 25 years" (personal correspondence). From his perspective as a government employee responsible for interpreting public comment, Dave acknowledges the legitimacy of multiple modes of discourse, from the language of law and policy to the language of story. He resonates to the essential premise of *What's Nature*

Worth?, to the argument that the meaning of the world, the value of the world and our experience of it, cannot be encapsulated merely in dollars and cents, or in the formalities of law and policy, but must sometimes be expressed in the form of stories built from our daily lives.

The headnotes to the individual interviews and questionnaire responses mention the insights that Terre and I found particularly salient in the comments of each of the participating authors. My purpose in this concluding statement has been to offer an overarching view of my own experience of participating in this project and my sense of how it might contribute to future work in the areas of environmental policy, environmental management, and the study of environmental literature. I don't know that we have managed yet to *prove* the influence of environmental writing on public attitudes or on management policies of government officials, in response to the questions posed at the end of my 1992 book. But I believe we have given the twelve authors featured here opportunities to demonstrate again and again their *belief* in the efficacy of narrative discourse and the importance of such language to the pursuit of healthy communities and just relationships between humans and the natural world. I am inspired to continue refining my own storytelling skills, seeking to meld story and analysis into usable forms of "narrative scholarship."

I find myself thinking of my visit to British Columbia several years ago to spend the weekend working with Terre on this project. In particular, I recall waking up early in the morning, before sunrise, to run in Vancouver's Stanley Park, while Terre and my son Jacinto rode bikes through the darkness, in the driving winter rain. I could scarcely see where I was going, glimpsing the path just far enough ahead to avoid careening into the lush undergrowth. Occasionally a distant street lamp lit the path and provided a guiding beacon, but more often I could not see where I planted my feet. My work on this project—like many of my other scholarly efforts—has progressed somewhat like that rainy morning run. It has been an act of faith in the worth of transdisciplinary, transnational, transcultural projects. An act of faith in the value of finding the right scholarly, literary, and personal words, even as children succumb to drugs, forests fall to the axe, and bombs drop on the other side of the planet so that an American president can pursue a personal vendetta. Sometimes the best we can do is to take one step at a time, through the darkness and rain, looking forward to friendship and community when we return home. Sometimes the best we can do is to experiment with new scholarly angles and directions, hoping to build new connections across disciplines or to illuminate pre-existing connections that have been under-appreciated.

Concluding Thoughts: Terre Satterfield

I was drawn to this project, as Scott rightly notes, following a long stint working in the field as an ethnographer tracking the cultural conflict between loggers and environmentalists (among others) over the fate of Oregon's old-growth forests. In that period—whether I found myself at a gathering of activists occupying land that was to be logged or bounding along back roads in a logger's worn-out pickup truck—I invariably listened to the richly textured and morally dense stories that both parties had to tell. At times, this might involve a logger's story of how he (and it was nearly always he) had suffered a crushing injury on the job only to be vilified in public life for the work he performed and the good he provided, be that paper or wood. On other occasions, I recorded with great care an environmental activist's grief at the loss of a beloved watershed or an immense stand of 500-year-old fir and cedar trees. On each occasion, it was palpably clear that embedded in these stories were the "environmental values" that social scientists sought to know, describe, and understand. Values, in this sense, struck me as, yes, a profoundly normative impulse about appropriate or inappropriate behavior, but also as something accessible only via the detailed and contextually dense narrative field in which they live and are articulated.

My point is not that all policy studies aimed at capturing and representing how we "value" nature should be field studies. Most policy studies are confined by time—the anthropologist's inclination toward in-depth fieldwork or "deep hanging out" over sustained periods is not often an option.[1] It is, nonetheless, necessary to mimic this effort in some fashion, however abbreviated. It is imperative that we develop better value-elicitation opportunities, frames, or contexts that resist the tendency to fit the articulation of values into economistic expressions, that seek alternatives to direct question-answer formats, and/or that denude value expressions of relevant moral or affective content. I have explored this possibility elsewhere (Satterfield 2001; Satterfield et al. 2000). Overall, it seems patently clear that most of us are delightfully articulate about a wide variety of noncost and nonutilitarian values when the opportunity to articulate our values encompasses, rather than avoids, affective, imagistic, storied, or morally meaningful content.

In this book, our purpose was and is rather different. It seeks evidence, from those most skilled at articulating environmental values in narrative form, as to why this form works. What is it that becomes possible with narrative but also literary exposition or poetry that is not possible in some other form? There is no clear, single answer to these questions, yet perusing the final edited interviews does reveal a few distinct patterns or consistent trains of thought across this diverse group of authors. Further, a few of these author-inspired observations are fundamentally important to scholarship on environmental values—its purpose, future, weaknesses, and strengths. It is to these points that I now turn: namely, the importance of indirect expressions of value, the problems of narrative as value evidence, the idea of narrative as a medium for delivery of value content, and the notion of narrative as a basis for articulacy and for incorporating the emotional dimensions of value.

On the necessity of allowing for opportunities to approach our thinking and language-driven expressions of value indirectly

The first observation is that most of the authors reject (as missing the point) efforts to isolate, define, or pinpoint precise, even didactic, value statements. Put differently, there is resounding support for the claim that many of our most important values are nearly impossible to express directly—as definitive statements of belief, as claims or goals, and so on. Greg McNamee makes one of the more unique points on this when he uses the analogy of searching for a "land racist." No one is going to say, and I paraphrase here, "I value those who rape the land" or even "I don't care about the land." The answers, he notes, are more subtle than that—the devil is in the details. What McNamee refers to as the "wrinkles" are the subtle ways in which language allows us to elaborate, hide from, insert nuance and illustration into the values that steer our lives. Avoiding a fully didactic approach is also a form of assigning respect, even deference, to that which we hold dear. John Daniel speaks of shifting in his career from a more didactic approach to environmental values to narrative in part because he felt that "preaching . . . can activate an automatic resistance," while "telling a story without an overt didactic burden does not." Stephen Trimble says something quite similar when commenting on the experience of writing for the edited collection *Testimony*, a volume aimed at members of Congress: "The essay I wrote for *Testimony* has a very specific purpose. I want to move the readers and change the way [members of Congress] think about wild country in Utah. . . . And yet I wanted to do it in a way that wasn't didactic and obnoxious." Simon Ortiz also champions the utility of narratives as an anti-didactic or indirect approach to values when he defines story as a vehicle for advice and counsel. A more direct approach, he finds, might be both quickly forgotten (without the story to anchor in our memory) or simply rejected.

For Terry Tempest Williams, indirect expressions of value are understood as that opportunity to "enter in through the back door" or approach gently the difficult and strongly felt. The "back door" metaphor reminds us that stories provide an opportunity for articulating that which is so taken for granted that it's not obvious or conscious. We might even begin sorting out our value-laden ethical investments by beginning with a story, using it as a basis for initial reflection. This might also be what Williams means when she follows the "back door" reference with "We don't even know what we're saying in a story. I really believe that. It just helps us think and begin to talk to others." Certainly, and finally, Gary Nabhan and Bruce Berger both find themselves negotiating their way through value-like ideas (that is, bringing them to consciousness) in the act of writing. For Nabhan: "The more image-based or story-driven the essay is, the less likely I am to immediately or consciously know how I'm talking about values. I can see it afterwards, with hindsight, but I seldom know about it in advance." For Berger, it is that thickening of expression, the indirect articulation of value, that occurs in the act of narrating a story. "I can't express 'nature's values.' The importance of nature to me as an individual is implicit in my choice of subjects and expressed attitudes; writing about nature makes me look at it more closely, which gives it more value to me (and maybe readers)."

On narrated experience, value, and emotion

There are, in the end, a large number of common points of view that these authors have put forth. But rising to the fore among them are the many points about the emotional qualities of values that story allows one to articulate. I particularly appreciated Alison Deming's phrase "emotional hue." The very idea that stories have such a hue and that this is the basis of our engagement in narrative in the first place cheers me enormously. She even posits narratives as a kind of antidote to conventional cost-benefit analysis as a means for determining value: "I can only hope that in the midst of the meeting about cost-benefit analysis, some writer is triggering an emotional response in people. If they remember their emotional response to the land, people will remember their passion for the issue. If nothing else, literature can replenish the energy that is depleted by the coldness of the cost-benefit arguments."

Going back to the point about "emotional hue," I've always thought something rather similar about values, by which I mean it seems nearly impossible to be strongly attached to a principle without that manifesting equally as a strong emotional attachment. There is a growing academic literature that says just this. It's never been my point to suggest that public discussions of value should become emotional fests of some sort. But it doesn't seem reasonable to assume that the strong affective dimensions of value should be silenced either—they may in fact be an important window into understanding why and how fully some things matter to some people. I am reminded of the work a few years back of the anthropologist Catherine Lutz (1988). In an ethnography of a Pacific Island community in Micronesia, she finds that emotions are the central communicative medium through which the rules for moral and ethical practice—particularly about how the human self should behave toward the rest of society—are conveyed. Describing to another the emotional experience of losing a job or giving birth is a way of conveying an intimate subjective perspective, but such communications can also assert how one *ought* to behave given a job loss or major life event. Similarly, to say "I am angry about a certain person's behavior" is to assign value to one mode of behavior (the implied desired behavior) and disvalue to the behavior that is rejected (the behavior that produced anger).

When we asked John Daniel point-blank whether it is possible to have a value without having an emotional investment in it, he quickly responded, "If it's a value, it's worth something. And if it's worth something, you're going to have an emotional sense of that. I'm not sure even understanding is possible without an emotional content, an emotional excitation of some kind." William Kittredge finds, similarly, that some combination of narrative and emotion provides the vehicle through which values become less cognitive or rationalized, more fully lived, realized, or internalized. Values, he tells us, "can usually be intellectually understood. But narrative helps readers internalize values, make them their own, emotionally, as necessary to life rather than simply interesting or distracting, as platforms from which to act."

Bob Pyle has, perhaps, more to say on the subject of emotion than any of us. As a trained scientist and an author who works in multiple literary genres, he understands precisely the role of emotion and reason as manifest across different literary expressions of knowledge. No stranger to the enlightenment premise that emotional dimensions of experience are regarded as extraneous, he nonetheless supports their necessity and even suggests the possibility that scientists have simply conveniently ignored the affective realm. During our conversation with him on these points, he goes so far as to call for something of a hybridization of literature and science through narrative, stating that scientists believe that things progress by means visible to the scientific method but he believes that literature is also valid. "The differentiation of the factual and emotional, or just the nonfactual (I'm not wedded to the term 'emotional'), can be completely subverted in essays or narrative nonfiction. I believe that if you are able to approach both sides of experience, the emotional and the observational-factual, in the same piece of writing, which is then read seriously, you have a chance to convince with both artfulness and fact."

At the very least, if I take my lead from these authors and from my own sensibilities, I can say with some confidence that diminished attention to emotion might lead only to a naive or ill-elaborated portrait of value.

On narrative as a medium for delivery of value content

Perhaps more than any other theme, it was narrative as a medium for delivery of value content that drove this book (whether delivered to or received from people participating in value-elicitation exercises). The authors' comparisons of poetry versus essay form versus narrative are too many to list here. But at the very least, I cannot help but draw some attention to the resounding support for the idea of narrative expressions of value in principle and practice. I particularly enjoyed the conviction on the part of many herein that narratives remain an important basis for value reflection. It takes time and effort in any conversation, be it group-based or one-on-one, to develop a candid dialogue on something as personal as one's values. What matters to us most is not always readily available. Trimble, Kittredge, Williams, Daniel, and Pyle all talk about narrative as a stimulus or basis for value deliberation as well as a spark to help elicit the reader's own narratives of purpose and intention. Steve Trimble opens his interview with Scott by retelling the story of listening to Wallace Stegner's *Crossing to Safety* on tape—an act that led him to his own thoughts: "When you do listen to a story, pretty soon you drift into all kinds of other places in your world and in your life. Something in the story will make you think of one of your own stories. And something in a character's personality will make you think of your kid or your wife or your mother." Speaking of the purpose of narrative forms, Bill Kittredge makes the same point when he refers to stories as "mirrors" into our own imaginations: "[Narrative] form leads readers into emotional participation in the processes of coming to understand. The storytelling invites readers to make up stories of their own, to use the story they're being told as a mirror in which to view their own responses to their own concerns."

In the end, we can champion narrative expressions of value ad infinitum. But it remains the case that we are not adept at just what to do with such expressions once collected. There are a number of possibilities here. Values scholar Robin Gregory (2000) regards the elicitation of values as a fundamental first step upon which all else depends, namely, the subsequent need to understand what a decision that realized those values might look like (including the trade-offs they imply and the alternatives they support or reject). Scott writes above, in his concluding thoughts, of Dave Strohmaier, a writer who works for the Forest Service, analyzing the value content of public-comment documents. The point for the Forest Service is not to "count votes" but to seek clarity and quality of argument—something captured more fully in narrative or prose forms than in, say, a survey. We noted, too, in the Introduction that narratives can be successfully used to present technical information in an easily consumable form. Bob Pyle defers to this possibility when he speaks of hybrid value-scientific-literary forms; Alison Deming is a master of just this form. (See, particularly, her book *Science and Other Poems,* which is first introduced in the biographic note that begins her chapter.) And Gary Nabhan finds that in an increasingly complex world, his talents (I would say, immense talents) as a biologist and a storyteller reciprocally enhance one another:

> My storytelling self comes in very handy in biology courses and in work with biology students. The contemporary reality is that scientists face increasingly complex social and technical communication problems. Consider an organization like The Nature Conservancy here in the Southwest. Because of the tense circumstances between resource users and others, only messages in a certain range are allowable. The Conservancy is trying to set up collaborations with ranchers, and with the Mexican government, that are non-confrontational. This takes a tremendous amount of tact and negotiating skills. People who have come out of the strict evolutionary biology training, a major conservation science program, except for a few remarkable exceptions, have no skills and no predilection for the rhetorical complexity of these situations—they're frightened. Science needs to be communicated in a variety of genres to a variety of audiences. A good scientist these days has to be able to blend scientific expertise with other disciplines.

Particularly thorny is the very idea of narrative as evidence. In the current period, this problem is faced often by the courts in aboriginal land-claims cases wherein narrated oral history is a typical basis for validating a claim in the first place. Ofelia Zepeda cuts to the quick on this evidentiary problem when she speaks of the difficulty First Nation peoples have had in this regard: "In the instances where tribes, especially small tribes, are trying to get federal recognition and they don't have enough documentation to prove their existence, they have tried to use things like story to, in some way, document their own native existence or whatever." Fortunately there are some very positive signs to this end. In a recent land-claims-related decision in British Columbia, Canada's supreme court (Delgamuukw v. B.C.), hereditary chiefs from the Gitksan and Wet'suwet'en First Nations presented their legal arguments in narrative form in deference to long-standing oral traditions. They did so in a manner that followed the necessary legal arguments at stake; and yet also enacted "narratives, songs and dances that had formerly been performed only within a community context, presenting these as statements linking history . . . and land" (Cruikshank 1998, 63–64).

This seems a happily positive note on which to end. I can close only by noting that this book has been a most rewarding experience. I hope that Scott and I carry on, that we and others manage, as he so modestly puts it, to see our way through the winter rain. Only good can come of the effort to bring together the policy problems that fuel much social science and the literature we all turn to for full expression of the forces that drive our lives and read to "replenish" the weary, as Alison Deming might say.

NOTES

Notes to Introduction

1. See, for instance, Satterfield 2001, "In Search of Value Literacy," Sagoff's 1998 study "Aggregation and Deliberation in Valuing Public Goods," Gregory's 1999 literature review, "Identifying Environmental Values," and Thomas Brown's 1984 ground-breaking article "The Concept of Value in Resource Allocation."

2. Much recent economic valuation work has augmented WTP methods with those focused on choice processes and the costing of observable (or revealed) behavior, such as the travel costs one invests to get to a wilderness area, national park, recreation facility, and so on.

3. This notion is well articulated in Baruch Fischhoff's "Value Elicitation: Is There Anything Out There?" (1991) and Paul Slovic's "The Construction of Preference" (1995).

Chapter 1, William Kittredge

1. From *Who Owns the West?* (1996), 11–13.

2. Ibid., 104–6. The version reprinted here was originally published in *Outside* (September 1991), 72–73.

Chapter 2, Simon J. Ortiz

1. Ortiz is referring to Joy Harjo's poem "Rainy Dawn," which was printed on a broadside hanging on the wall in the University of Arizona Poetry Center's guest cottage while we talked. "Rainy Dawn" was also published in Harjo's book *In Mad Love and War*.

2. From *Men on the Moon: Collected Short Stories by Simon J. Ortiz* (1999), 3–14.

3. From *Woven Stone* (1992), 137.

Chapter 3, Terry Tempest Williams

1. From *Red: Passion and Patience in the Desert* (2001), 72–78.
2. Ibid., 79–81.

Chapter 4, Gregory McNamee

1. Review of *Consuming Desires: Consumption, Culture, and the Pursuit of Happiness*, edited by Roger Rosenblatt, in *Tucson Weekly*, 30 August 1999. Available online at http://weeklywire.com.
2. From "Yaak and the Unknowable World," in *The Roadless Yaak*, edited by Rick Bass (2002), 43–44.

Chapter 5, Alison Hawthorne Deming

1. From *Writing the Sacred into the Real*, 51–72. The version reprinted here was originally published in *The Georgia Review* (Summer 2000), 259–71.
2. Tony Davis, *High Country News* 3, no. 1 (18 January 1999), 10.
3. Ibid.
4. Siobhan LaPiana, "An Interview with Visiting Artist Bei Dao," *The Journal of the International Institute* 2, no. 1 (Fall 1994), 5.
5. From *The Monarchs: A Poem Sequence* (1997), 1–4.

Chapter 6, Ofelia Zepeda

1. From *Jewed 'I-hoi / Earth Movements* (1997), 18–19.
2. From *Ocean Power: Poems from the Desert* (1995), 68.
3. Ibid., 69–70.

Chapter 7, Richard Shelton

1. From *Of All the Dirty Words* (1972), 75–76.
2. From *You Can't Have Everything* (1975), 41.

Chapter 8, John Daniel

1. From *The Trail Home: Nature, Imagination, and the American West* (1992), 159–76.
2. From *Common Ground* (1988), 62.

CHAPTER 9, STEPHEN TRIMBLE

1. From *Weber Studies: An Interdisciplinary Humanities Journal* 11:3 (Fall 1994), 79–83.
2. From *The Sagebrush Ocean: A Natural History of the Great Basin* (1989), 219–21.

CHAPTER 10, ROBERT MICHAEL PYLE

1. From *The Thunder Tree: Lessons from an Urban Wildland* (1993), 140–52.
2. From *Orion Afield* 5, no. 2 (Spring 2001), 8.

CHAPTER 11, BRUCE BERGER

1. From *The Telling Distance: Conversations with the American Desert* (1990), 46.
2. Ibid., 157–61.

CHAPTER 12, GARY PAUL NABHAN

1. From *Cultures of Habitat: On Nature, Culture, and Story* (1997), 249–59.

CHAPTER 13, A CONCLUDING CONVERSATION

1. This phrase is borrowed from Rosaldo, quoted in Clifford 1997, 56.

BIBLIOGRAPHY

Abbey, Edward. 1968; reprinted 1990. *Desert solitaire: A season in the wilderness.* New York: Ballantine.

Anderson, Lorraine, Scott Slovic, and John P. O'Grady, eds. 1999. *Literature and the environment: A reader on nature and culture.* New York: Addison Wesley Longman.

Armour, Audrey. 1995. The Citizens' Jury Model of Public Participation. In *Fairness and competence in citizen participation*, edited by Ortwin Renn, Thomas Webler, and Peter Wiedemann, 175–87. Boston: Kluwer Academic.

Armstrong, Susan J., and Richard J. Botzler. 1993. *Environmental ethics: Divergence and convergence.* New York: McGraw-Hill.

Atran, Scott, and Douglas Medin. 1997. Knowledge and action: Cultural models of nature and resource management in Mesoamerica. In *Environment, ethics and behavior*, edited by Max H. Bazerman, David M. Messick, Ann E. Tenbrunsel, and Kimberly A. Wade-Benzoni, 171–208. San Francisco: New Lexington.

Axelrod, Lawrence. 1994. Balancing personal needs with environmental preservation: Identifying the values that guide decisions in ecological dilemmas. *Journal of Social Issues* 50 (3): 85–104.

Baron, Jonathan, and Sarah Leshner. 2000. How serious are expressions of protected values? *Journal of Experimental Psychology* 6: 183–94.

Baron, Jonathan, and Mark Spranca. 1997. Protected values. *Organizational Behavior and Human Decision Processes* 70: 1–16.

Bass, Rick. 1991. *Winter: Notes from Montana.* Boston: Houghton Mifflin.

———, ed. 2002. *The Roadless Yaak: Reflections and Observations About One of Our Last Great Wild Places.* New York: The Lyons Press.

Bazerman, Max H., David M. Messick, and Ann E. Tenbrunsel. 1997. *Environment, ethics, and behavior.* San Francisco: New Lexington.

Berger, Bruce. 1979; expanded edition 1994. *There was a river: Essays on the southwest.* Tucson: University of Arizona Press.

———. 1980. *Hangin' on: Gordon Snidow portrays the cowboy heritage*. Flagstaff, AZ: Northland.

———. 1987. *Notes of a half-Aspenite*. Denver, CO: Graphic Impressions.

———. 1989. *A dazzle of hummingbirds*. San Luis Obisbo, CA: Blake Publishing.

———. 1990; reprinted 1991. *The telling distance: Conversations with the American desert*. New York: Doubleday.

———. 1995. *Facing the music*. Lewiston, ID: Confluence Press.

———. 1998. *Almost an island: Travels in Baja California*. Tucson: University of Arizona Press.

Birkerts, Sven. 1994. *The Gutenberg elegies: The fate of reading in an electronic age.* Winchester, MA: Faber and Faber.

Brosius, J. Peter. 1999. Analyses and interventions: anthropological engagements with environmentalism. *Current Anthropology* 40, no. 3: 277–309.

Brown, Thomas. 1984. The concept of value in resource allocation. *Land Economics* 60: 231–46.

Bruner, Jerome. 1986. *Actual minds, possible worlds*. Cambridge, MA: Harvard University Press.

Buell, Lawrence. 2001. *Writing for an endangered world: Literature, culture, and environment in the U.S. and beyond.* Cambridge: Harvard University Press.

Bureau of Land Management, Grand Staircase–Escalante National Monument. 1997. *Visions kit.* Cedar City, UT: Author. Retrieved June 24, 2003, from http://www.ut.blm.gov/monument/Monument_Management/Initial%20Planning/planning_process/Visions_Kit/visions_kit.html.

Callicott, J. Baird. 1984. Non-anthropocentric value theory and environmental ethics. *American Philosophical Quarterly* 21: 299–309.

———. 1986. On the intrinsic value of nonhuman species. In *The Preservation of the species*, edited by B. G. Norton, 138–72. Princeton, NJ: Princeton University Press.

———. 1995. Environmental ethics: Overview. In *The Preservation of Species,* edited by W. T. Reich, 138–72. Princeton, NJ: Princeton University Press.

Clifford, J. 1997. *Routes: Travel and translation in the late twentieth century.* Cambridge, MA: Harvard University Press.

Cohan, Steven, and Linda M. Shires. 1988. *Telling Stories: A Theoretical Analysis of Narrative Fiction*. New York: Routledge.

Costanza, Robert, Ralph D'Arge, Rudolf de Groot, Stephen Farber, Monica Grasso, Bruce Hannon, Karin Limburg, Shahid Naeem, Robert V. O'Neill, Jose Paruelo, Robert G. Raskin, Paul Sutton, and Marjan van den Belt. 1998. The value of the world's ecosystem services and natural capital. *Ecological Economics* 25: 3–15.

Crosby, Ned. 1995. Citizen juries: One solution for difficult environmental questions. In *Fairness and competence in citizen participation: Evaluating models for environmental discourse*, edited by Ortwin Renn, Thomas Webler, and Peter M. Wiedemann, 157–74. Dordrecht, The Netherlands: Kluwer Academic.

Cruikshank, Julie. 1998. *The social life of stories.* Vancouver: UBC Press.

Damasio, Antonio. 1994. *Descartes' error: Emotion, reason, and the human brain.* New York: Putnam.

Daniel, John. 1988. *Common ground.* Lewiston, ID: Confluence Press.

———. 1992. *The trail home.* New York: Pantheon.

———. 1994. *All things touched by wind.* Anchorage, AK: Salmon Run Press.

———. 1996. *Looking after: A son's memoir.* Washington, D.C.: Counterpoint.

———. 1997. *Oregon rivers.* Photographs by Larry N. Olson. Englewood, CO: Westcliffe Publishers.

———. 2002. *Winter creek: One writer's natural history.* Minneapolis: Milkweed Editions.

———, ed. 1998. *Wild song: Poems of the natural world.* Athens: University of Georgia Press.

Deming, Alison Hawthorne. 1994a. *Science and other poems* (reprinted ed.). Baton Rouge: Louisiana State University Press.

———. 1994b. *Temporary homelands.* San Francisco: Mercury House.

———. 1997. *The monarchs: A poem sequence.* Baton Rouge: Louisiana State University Press.

———. 1998. *The edges of the civilized world.* New York: St. Martin's/Picador USA.

———. 1999. Science and poetry: A view from the divide. In *A view from the divide: Creative nonfiction on health and science*, edited by Lee Gutkind, 11–29. Pittsburgh: University of Pittsburgh Press.

———. 2001. *Writing the sacred into the real.* Minneapolis: Milkweed Editions.

Deming, Alison Hawthorne, and Lauret E. Savoy, eds. 2002. *The colors of nature: Culture, identity, and the natural world.* Minneapolis: Milkweed Editions.

Dickson, Barnabas. 2000. The ethicist's conception of environmental problems. *Environmental Values* 9: 127–52.

Dillard, Annie. *Pilgrim at Tinker Creek.* New York: Harper and Row.

Dunlap, Riley E., and Rik Scarce. 1991. The polls—Poll trends: Environmental problems and protection. *Public Opinion Quarterly* 55: 713–34.

Dunlap, Riley E., and Kent D. Van Liere. 1978. The "new environmental paradigm." *Journal of Environmental Education* 9: 10–19.

Dunlap, Riley E., Kent D. Van Liere, Angela G. Mertig, and Robert Emmet Jones. 2000. Measuring endorsement of the new ecological paradigm: A revised NEP scale. *Journal of Social Issues* 56 (Fall): 425–42.

Earle, Timothy, and George T. Cvetkovich. 1995. *Social trust: toward a cosmopolitan society*. Westport, CT: Praeger.

Epstein, Seymour. 1994. Integration of cognitive and psychodynamic unconscious. *American Psychologist* 49: 709–24.

Finucane, Melissa L., Ali Alhakami, Paul Slovic, and Stephen M. Johnson. 2000. The affect heuristic in judgments of risks and benefits. *Journal of Behavioral Decision Making* 13: 1–17.

Fischhoff, Baruch. 1991. Value elicitation: Is there anything out there? *American Psychologist* 46: 835–47.

Fiske, Alan Page, and Phillip E. Tetlock. 1997. Taboo tradeoffs: Reactions to transactions that transgress spheres of justice. *Political Psychology* 18: 255–97.

Foster, John M., ed. 1997. *Valuing nature? Ethics, economics, and the environment*. London: Routledge.

Franzosi, Roberto. 1998. Narrative analysis—or why (and how) sociologists should be interested in narrative. *Annual Review of Sociology* 24: 517–54.

Frazier, Charles. 1997. *Cold mountain*. New York: Atlantic Monthly Press.

Freeman, A. Myrick. 1993. *The measurement of environmental and resource values: Theory and methods*. Washington, DC: Resources for the Future.

Geertz, C. 1973. *The interpretation of culture*. New York: Basic Books.

Gregory, Robin. 1999. Identifying environmental values. In *Tools to aid environmental decision making*, edited by Virginia H. Dale and Mary R. English, 32–58. New York: Springer-Verlag.

———. 2000. Valuing environmental policy options: A case study comparison of multiattribute and contingent valuation survey methods. *Land Economics* 76, no. 2: 151–73.

Gregory, Robin, James Flynn, Stephen M. Johnson, Theresa A. Satterfield, Paul Slovic, and Robert Wagner. 1997. Decision pathway surveys: A tool for resource managers. *Land Economics* 73, no. 2: 240–54.

Gregory, Robin, Sarah Lichtenstein, and Paul Slovic. 1993. Valuing environmental resources: A constructive approach. *Journal of Risk and Uncertainty* 7: 177–97.

Gregory, Robin, Donald G. MacGregor, and Sarah Lichtenstein. 1992. Assessing the quality of expressed preference measures of value. *Journal of Economic Behavior and Organization* 17: 277–92.

Gregory, Robin, and Paul Slovic. 1997. A constructive approach to environmental valuation. *Ecological Economics* 21: 175–81.

Gregory, Robin, and Katharine Wellman. 2001. Bringing stakeholder values into environmental policy choices: A community-based estuary case study. *Ecological Economics* 39: 37–52.

Habermas, Jürgen. 1979. *Communication and the evolution of society.* Translation and introduction by Thomas McCarthy. Boston: Beacon Press.

Harjo, Joy. 1990. *In Mad Love and War.* Hanover, NH: Wesleyan University Press.

Hepworth, James, and Gregory McNamee, eds. 1985. *Resist much, obey Little: Notes on Edward Abbey*. Salt Lake City: Dream Garden Press.

Herndl, Carl G., and Stuart C. Brown. 1996. *Green culture: Rhetorical analyses of environmental discourse.* Madison: University of Wisconsin Press.

Inglehart, Ronald. 1995. Public support for environmental protection: Objective problems and subjective values. *PS Political Science and Politics* 28: 57–71.

Kahneman, Daniel, and Jack L. Knetsch. 1992. Valuing public goods: The purchase of moral satisfaction. *Journal of Environmental Economics and Management* 22: 57–70.

Kahneman, Daniel, Paul Slovic, and Amos Tversky. 1982. *Judgment under uncertainty: Heuristics and biases.* New York: Cambridge University Press.

Kahneman, Daniel, and Jackie Snell. 1990. Predicting utility. In *Insights in decision making: A tribute to Hillel J. Einhorn*, edited by Robin M. Hogarth, 295–310. Chicago: University of Chicago Press.

Kates, Robert W. 1999. Part and apart [Editorial]. *Environment* 41, no. 2.

Kearney, Anne R. 1994. Understanding global change: A cognitive perspective on communicating through stories. *Climate Change* 27: 419–41.

Keeney, R. L. 1992. *Value-focused thinking: A path to creative decisionmaking.* Cambridge: Harvard University Press.

Kellert, Stephen R. 1993. Attitudes, knowledge, and behavior toward wildlife among the industrial superpowers: United States, Japan, and Germany. *Journal of Social Issues* 49, no. 1: 53–69.

———. 1996. *The value of life: biological diversity and human society*. Washington, DC: Island Press.

Kempton, Willett, James S. Boster, and Jennifer Hartley. 1995. *Environmental values in American culture.* Cambridge, MA: MIT Press.

Kida, T., and J. F. Smith. 1995. The encoding and retrieval of numerical data for decision making in accounting contexts: Model development. *Accounting, Organizations, and Society* 20: 585–610.

Kittredge, William. 1978. *The Van Gogh field and other stories.* Columbia: University of Missouri Press.

———. 1984. *We are not in this together.* St. Paul: Graywolf Press.

———. 1987. *Owning it all.* St. Paul: Graywolf Press.

———. 1992. *Hole in the sky.* New York: Knopf.

———. 1996. *Who owns the west?* San Francisco: Mercury House.

———. 1999. *Taking care: Thoughts on storytelling and belief.* Minneapolis: Milkweed Editions.

———. 2000. *The nature of generosity.* New York: Knopf.

Kittredge, William, and Steven M. Krauzer [Owen Rountree, pseud.]. 1982. *Cord.* New York: Ballantine Books.

———. 1983a. *Cord: Black Hills duel.* New York: Ballantine Books.

———. 1983b. *Cord: Gunman Winter.* New York: Ballantine Books.

———. 1983c. *Cord: The Nevada war.* New York: Ballantine Books.

———. 1984a. *Cord: Hunt the man down.* New York: Ballantine Books.

———. 1984b. *Cord: Kin of Colorado.* New York: Ballantine Books.

———. 1985. *Cord: Gunsmoke River.* New York: Ballantine Books.

———. 1986a. *Cord: Brimstone Valley.* New York: Ballantine Books.

———. 1986b. *Cord: Paradise Valley.* New York: Ballantine Books.

Kittredge, William, and Steven M. Krauzer, eds. 1977. *Great action stories.* New York: New American Library.

———. 1978. *The great American detective.* New York: New American Library.

———. 1979. *Fiction to film.* New York: New American Library.

Kraus, S. 1995. Attitudes and prediction of behavior: A meta-analysis of the empirical literature. *Personality and Social Psychology Bulletin* 21, no. 1: 58–75.

Ladd, E. C., and K. H. Bowman. 1995. *Attitudes toward the environment: Twenty-five years after earth day.* Washington, DC: AEI Press.

Lamberton, Ken. 2000. *Wilderness and razorwire: A naturalist's observations from prison.* San Francisco: Mercury House.

Leopold, A. 1966. *A Sand County almanac: With essays from Round River.* New York: Ballantine.

Lockwood, M. 1999. Humans valuing nature: Synthesizing insights from philosophy, psychology, and economics. *Environmental Values* 8: 381–401.

Lopez, Barry. 1986. Natural history: An annotated booklist. *Antaeus* 57 (Autumn): 283–97.

Lueders, Edward. 1989. *Writing natural history: Dialogues with authors.* Salt Lake City: University of Utah Press.

Lutz, C. 1988. *Unnatural emotions.* Chicago: University of Chicago Press.

Lyon, Thomas J., and Terry Tempest Williams, eds. 1995. *A great and peculiar beauty: A Utah reader.* Salt Lake City: Gibbs Smith Publisher.

McCarty, Teresa L., and Ofelia Zepeda, eds. 1995. *Bilingual Research Journal* 19, no. 1 (Winter). Special issue on Native American languages.

McNamee, Gregory. 1990a. *Inconstant history: Poems and translations.* Seattle: Broken Moon Press.

———. 1990b. *The return of Richard Nixon.* Boulder, CO: Harbinger House.

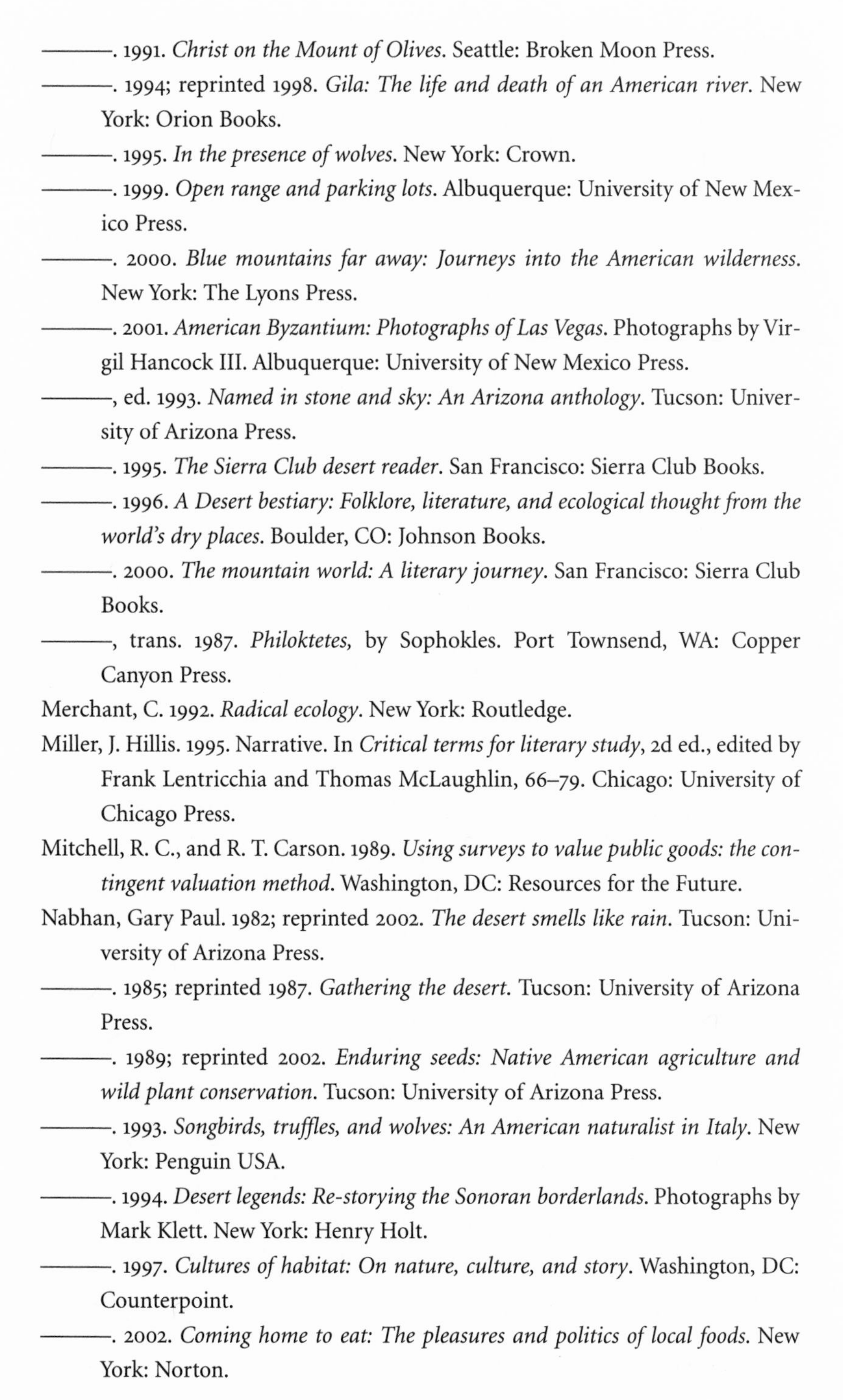

———. 1991. *Christ on the Mount of Olives*. Seattle: Broken Moon Press.

———. 1994; reprinted 1998. *Gila: The life and death of an American river*. New York: Orion Books.

———. 1995. *In the presence of wolves*. New York: Crown.

———. 1999. *Open range and parking lots*. Albuquerque: University of New Mexico Press.

———. 2000. *Blue mountains far away: Journeys into the American wilderness*. New York: The Lyons Press.

———. 2001. *American Byzantium: Photographs of Las Vegas*. Photographs by Virgil Hancock III. Albuquerque: University of New Mexico Press.

———, ed. 1993. *Named in stone and sky: An Arizona anthology*. Tucson: University of Arizona Press.

———. 1995. *The Sierra Club desert reader*. San Francisco: Sierra Club Books.

———. 1996. *A Desert bestiary: Folklore, literature, and ecological thought from the world's dry places*. Boulder, CO: Johnson Books.

———. 2000. *The mountain world: A literary journey*. San Francisco: Sierra Club Books.

———, trans. 1987. *Philoktetes,* by Sophokles. Port Townsend, WA: Copper Canyon Press.

Merchant, C. 1992. *Radical ecology*. New York: Routledge.

Miller, J. Hillis. 1995. Narrative. In *Critical terms for literary study*, 2d ed., edited by Frank Lentricchia and Thomas McLaughlin, 66–79. Chicago: University of Chicago Press.

Mitchell, R. C., and R. T. Carson. 1989. *Using surveys to value public goods: the contingent valuation method*. Washington, DC: Resources for the Future.

Nabhan, Gary Paul. 1982; reprinted 2002. *The desert smells like rain*. Tucson: University of Arizona Press.

———. 1985; reprinted 1987. *Gathering the desert*. Tucson: University of Arizona Press.

———. 1989; reprinted 2002. *Enduring seeds: Native American agriculture and wild plant conservation*. Tucson: University of Arizona Press.

———. 1993. *Songbirds, truffles, and wolves: An American naturalist in Italy*. New York: Penguin USA.

———. 1994. *Desert legends: Re-storying the Sonoran borderlands*. Photographs by Mark Klett. New York: Henry Holt.

———. 1997. *Cultures of habitat: On nature, culture, and story*. Washington, DC: Counterpoint.

———. 2002. *Coming home to eat: The pleasures and politics of local foods*. New York: Norton.

———. 2003. *Singing the turtles to sea: the Comcáac (Seri) art and science of reptiles.* Berkeley: University of California Press.

———. 2004. *Cross-Pollinations: The marriage of science and poetry.* Minneapolis: Milkweed Editions.

———, ed. 1993. *Counting sheep: 20 ways of seeing desert bighorn.* Tucson: University of Arizona Press.

Nabhan, Gary Paul, and Steven L. Buchmann. 1996. *The forgotten pollinators.* Washington, DC: Island Press.

Nabhan, Gary Paul, and Stephen Trimble. 1994. *The geography of childhood: Why children need wild places.* Boston: Beacon Press.

Nash, Roderick F. 1989. *The rights of nature.* Madison: University of Wisconsin Press.

Nelson, Richard. 1997. *Heart and blood: Living with deer in America.* New York: Knopf.

Norton, Bryan G. 1986. *The Preservation of species: The value of biological diversity.* Princeton, NJ: Princeton University Press.

———. 1991. Thoreau's insect analogies: Or, why environmentalists hate mainstream economists. *Environmental Ethics* 13: 235–51.

Oatley, Keith. 1994. A taxonomy of the emotions of literary response and a theory of identification in fictional narrative. *Poetics* 23: 53–74.

O'Riordan, Timothy. 1995. Frameworks for choice: Core beliefs and the environment. *Environment* 37, no. 8: 4–9.

Ortiz, Simon J. 1971. *Naked in the wind.* Pembroke, NC: Quetzal-Vihio Press.

———. 1976a. *Going for the rain: Poems.* New York: Harper and Row.

———. 1976b. *Howbah Indians.* Tucson: Blue Moon Press.

———. 1977; reprinted 1984. *A good journey.* Reprint, Tucson: University of Arizona Press.

———. 1980. *Fight back: For the sake of the people, for the sake of the land.* Albuquerque: Institute for Native American Development, University of New Mexico.

———. 1981a. *A poem is a journey.* Bourbonnais, IL: Pternandon Press.

———. 1981b. *From Sand Creek: Rising in this heart which is our America.* New York: Thunder's Mouth Press.

———. 1983. *Fightin': New and collected stories.* New York: Thunder's Mouth Press.

———. 1992. *Woven stone.* Tucson: University of Arizona Press.

———. 1994. *After and before the lightning.* Tucson: University of Arizona Press.

———. 1999. *Men on the moon: Collected short stories.* Tucson: University of Arizona Press.

———. 2002. *Out there somewhere.* Tucson: University of Arizona Press.

Payne, Daniel G. 1996. *Voices in the wilderness: American nature writing and environmental politics.* Hanover and London: University Press of New England.

Payne, John W., J. Bettman, and E. Johnson. 1992. Behavioral decision research: A constructive processing perspective. *Annual Review of Psychology* 43: 87–132.

Payne, J. W., J. R. Bettman, and D. A. Schkade. 1999. Measuring constructed preferences: Towards a building code. *Journal of Risk and Uncertainty* 19, no. 1: 243–70.

Peacock, Doug. 1990. *Grizzly years: In search of the American wilderness.* New York: Henry Holt.

Pennington, N., and R. Hastie. 1993. A theory of explanation-based decision making. In *Decision making in action: Models and methods*, edited by G. Klein et al., 188–204. Norwood, NJ: Ablex.

Philippon, Daniel J. 2004. *Conserving words: How American nature writers shaped the environmental movement.* Athens: University of Georgia Press.

Proctor, J. 1996. Whose nature? The contested moral terrain of ancient forests. In *Uncommon ground: Rethinking the human place in nature*, edited by W. Cronon, 269–97. New York: W. W. Norton and Co.

Pyle, Robert Michael. 1974. *Watching Washington butterflies.* Seattle: Seattle Audubon Society.

———. 1981. *The Audubon Society field guide to North American butterflies.* New York: Knopf.

———. 1986; reprinted 1995. *Wintergreen.* Boston: Houghton Mifflin.

———. 1993; reprinted 1998. *The thunder tree: Lessons from an urban wildland.* New York: The Lyons Press.

———. 1995. *Where Bigfoot walks: Crossing the dark divide.* Boston: Houghton Mifflin.

———. 1999. *Chasing monarchs: Migrating with the butterflies of passage.* Boston: Houghton Mifflin.

———. 2000. *Walking the high ridge: Life as field trip.* Minneapolis: Milkweed Editions.

Renn, O., T. Webler, and P. Wiedemann. 1995. *Fairness and competence in citizen participation.* Dordrecht, The Netherlands: Kluwer.

Rimmon-Kenan, Shlomith. 1983. *Narrative fiction: Contemporary poetics.* London: Methuen.

Ritov, Ilana, and Daniel Kahneman. 1997. How people value the environment: Attitudes versus economic values. In *Environment, ethics and behavior*, edited by M. Bazerman, D. Messick, and A. Tenbrunsel, 33–51. San Francisco: New Lexington.

Rokeach, H. 1973. *The nature of human values.* New York: Free Press.

Rolston, Holmes, III. 1988. *Environmental Ethics.* Philadelphia: Temple University Press.

———. 1994. *Conserving natural value.* New York: Columbia University Press.

———. 1999. Ethics and the environment. In *Ethics applied*, edited by E. Baker and M. Richardson, 407–37. New York: Simon and Schuster.

Ronald, Ann. 1995. *Earthtones: A Nevada Album.* Photographs by Stephen Trimble. Reno: University of Nevada Press.

Sagoff, Mark. 1988. *The economy of the earth.* New York: Cambridge University Press.

———. 1991. Zuckerman's dilemma: A plea for environmental ethics. *Hastings Center Report* 21, no. 5: 32–40.

———. 1998. Aggregation and deliberation in valuing public goods: A look beyond contingent pricing. *Ecological Economics* 24: 213–30.

Sanfey, Alan, and Reid Hastie. 1998. Does evidence presentation format affect judgment? An experimental valuation of displays of data for judgments. *Psychological Science* 9, no. 2: 99–103.

Satterfield, Terre. 1999. *New methods to elicit and identify environmental values.* Paper presented at the American Academy for the Advancement of Science Annual Meeting, Los Angeles.

———. 2001. In search of value literacy: Suggestions for the elicitation of environmental values. *Environmental Values* 10: 331–59.

———. 2002. *Anatomy of a conflict: Identity, knowledge, and emotion in old-growth forests.* Vancouver: University of British Columbia Press.

Satterfield, Terre, and Robin Gregory. 1998. Reconciling environmental values and pragmatic choices. *Society and Natural Resources* 11: 629–47.

Satterfield, Terre, Paul Slovic, and Robin Gregory. 2000. Narrative valuation in a policy judgment context. *Ecological Economics* 34, no. 3: 315–31.

Schkade, David A., and John W. Payne. 1994. How people respond to contingent valuation questions: A verbal protocol analysis of willingness to pay for an environmental regulation. *Journal of Environmental Economics and Management* 26: 88–109.

Shanahan, L., L. Pelstring, and K. McComas. 1999. Using narratives to think about environmental attitude and behavior: An exploratory study. *Society and Natural Resources* 12, no. 5: 409–19.

Shelton, Richard. 1971. *The tattooed desert.* Pittsburgh: University of Pittsburgh Press.

———. 1972. *Of all the dirty words.* Pittsburgh: University of Pittsburgh Press.

———. 1975. *You can't have everything.* Pittsburgh: University of Pittsburgh Press.

———. 1978. *The bus to Veracruz.* Pittsburgh: University of Pittsburgh Press.

———. 1982. *Selected poems: 1969–1981.* Pittsburgh: University of Pittsburgh Press.

———. 1987. *The other side of the story.* Lewiston, ID: Confluence Press.

———. 1992. *Going back to Bisbee.* Tucson: University of Arizona Press.

———. 1993. *Hohokam.* Tucson: SUN/gemini Press

Slovic, Paul. 1995. The construction of preference. *American Psychologist* 50: 364–71.

Slovic, P., J. Monahan, and D. G. MacGregor. 2000. Violence risk assessment and risk communication: The effects of using actual cases, providing instructions, and employing probability vs. frequency formats. *Law and Human Behavior* 24, no. 3: 271–96.

Slovic, Scott. 1992. *Seeking awareness in American nature writing: Henry Thoreau, Annie Dillard, Edward Abbey, Wendell Berry, Barry Lopez.* Salt Lake City: University of Utah Press.

———. 1996. Embedded rhetoric and discrete rhetoric: Epistemology and politics in American nature writing. In *Green culture: Rhetorical analyses of environmental discourse*, edited by Stuart C. Brown and Carl G. Herndl, 82–110. Madison: University of Wisconsin Press.

———. 1999. Giving expression to nature: Voices of environmental literature. *Environment* (March): 6–11, 25–32.

———. 2001. A paint brush in one hand and a bucket of water in the other: Nature writing and the politics of wilderness. Reprinted with a new introductory note in *The literary art and activism of Rick Bass*, edited by O. Alan Welzien, 24–45. Salt Lake City: University of Utah Press.

Smart, William B., Gibbs M. Smith, and Terry Tempest Williams, eds. 1998. *The new genesis: Mormons writing on the environment.* Salt Lake City: Gibbs Smith Publisher.

Soulé, Michael, and Gary Lease. 1995. *Reinventing nature: Responses to postmodern deconstruction.* Washington, DC: Island Press.

Steel, Brent S., Peter List, and Bruce Shindler. 1994. Conflicting values about federal forests: A comparison of national and Oregon publics. *Society and Natural Resources* 7: 137–53.

Stern, Paul, and Thomas Dietz. 1994. The value basis of environmental concern. *Journal of Social Issues* 50, no. 3: 65–84.

Stocker, Michael, and Elizabeth Hegeman. 1996. *Valuing emotions.* New York: Cambridge University Press.

Stone, C. 1987. *Earth and other ethics.* New York: Harper and Row.

Strohmaier, David J. 2001. *The seasons of fire: Reflections on fire in the west* (Environmental Arts and Humanities Series). Reno: University of Nevada Press.

Suter, G. W. I. 1993. *Ecological risk assessment.* Boca Raton, FL.: Lewis.

Trimble, Stephen. 1975. *Great sand dunes: The shape of the wind.* Tucson: Southwest Parks and Monuments Association.

———. 1987. *Navajo Pottery: Traditions and Innovations.* Flagstaff, AZ: Northland.

———. 1989. *The sagebrush ocean: A natural history of the Great Basin.* Reno: University of Nevada Press.

———. 1993. *The people: Indians of the American Southwest.* Santa Fe, NM: School of American Research Press.

———, ed. 1988; expanded edition 1995. *Words from the land: Encounters with natural history writing.* Reno: University of Nevada Press.

Trimble, Stephen, and Terry Tempest Williams, eds. 1995; reprinted 1996. *Testimony: Writers of the West speak on behalf of Utah wilderness.* Minneapolis: Milkweed Editions.

Turner, Jack. 1996. *The abstract wild.* Tucson: University of Arizona Press.

Tversky, Amos, and Daniel Kahneman. 1981. The framing of decision and the psychology of choice. *Science* 211: 453–58.

Wilkinson, Charles. 1992. *The eagle bird: Mapping a new west.* New York: Pantheon.

Williams, Terry Tempest. 1984. *Pieces of white shell: A journey to Navajoland.* Albuquerque: University of New Mexico Press.

———. 1989. *Coyote's canyon.* Salt Lake City: Peregrine Smith Books.

———. 1991. *Refuge: An unnatural history of family and place.* New York: Vintage.

———. 1994. *An unspoken hunger: Stories from the field.* New York: Pantheon.

———. 1995a. *Desert quartet.* New York: Pantheon.

———. 1995b. The erotic landscape. *Northern Lights* (Winter): 20–21.

———. 2000. *Leap.* New York: Pantheon.

———. 2001. *Red: Passion and patience in the desert.* New York: Pantheon.

Zepeda, Ofelia. 1995. *Ocean power: Poems from the desert.* Tucson: University of Arizona Press.

———. 1997. *Jewed 'I-hoi / Earth movements.* Tucson: Kore Press.

Zepeda, Ofelia, and Teresa McCarty, eds. 1998. *International Journal of the Sociology of Language* 132. Special issue on Indigenous Language Use and Change in the Americas.

Zwinger, Ann. 1984. *Run, river, run: A naturalist's journey down rivers of the American west.* New York: Harper and Row.

ABOUT THE EDITORS

Theresa (Terre) Satterfield is assistant professor of culture, risk, and the environment at the University of British Columbia's Institute for Resources and the Environment. She is also a research scientist with Decision Research in Eugene, Oregon. An anthropologist by training, she focuses her work on sustainable thinking and action as manifest in the context of specific environmental controversies. Her research has been funded by the Social Science and Humanities Research Council of Canada, the U.S. National Science Foundation, the U.S. Department of Energy, the World Health Organization, and the Getty Conservation Institute. Her work has been published in edited collections and in such journals as *Society and Natural Resources, Ecological Economics, Environmental Values, Journal of Social Issues, Journal of Anthropological Research, Human Ecology Review,* and *Risk Analysis.* The University of British Columbia Press published her book *Anatomy of a Conflict* in 2002.

Scott Slovic is professor of literature and environment and chair of the Graduate Program in Literature and Environment at the University of Nevada, Reno. The founding president of the Association for the Study of Literature and Environment (ASLE), and the current editor of the journal *ISLE: Interdisciplinary Studies in Literature and Environment,* he has published more than fifty articles on environmental literature and has authored, edited, or co-edited nine books, including *Seeking Awareness in American Nature Writing* (1992) and, more recently, *Getting Over the Color Green: Contemporary Environmental Literature of the Southwest* (2001) and *The ISLE Reader: Ecocriticism, 1993–2003* (2003).

CREDITS

"Heat" and "The Mysterious Brotherhood" from *The Telling Distance,* by Bruce Berger. Copyright 1990 by Bruce Berger. Reprinted by permission of Ted Macri Associates.

"Ourselves" is reprinted with the permission of Confluence Press from *Common Ground.* Copyright 1988 by John Daniel.

"Remembering the Sacred Family" from *The Trail Home,* by John Daniel. Copyright 1992 by John Daniel. Reprinted by permission of the author.

Alison Hawthorne Deming, *Writing the Sacred into the Real* (Minneapolis: Milkweed Editions, 2001). Copyright 2001 by Alison Hawthorne Deming. "Tucson" is reprinted by permission of Milkweed Editions.

Three poems reprinted by permission of Louisiana State University Press from *The Monarchs: A Poem Sequence* by Alison Hawthorne Deming. Copyright 1997 by Alison Hawthorne Deming.

Pages 11–13 and 104–6 from *Who Owns the West?* Copyright 1996 by William Kittredge. Published by Mercury House, San Francisco, CA, and reprinted by permission. Please visit www.mercuryhouse.org/kittredge.html

First published, in different form, as "The Unknowable Wild" in *The Sierra Club Wilderness Calendar 1997* and reprinted as part of the essay "Yaak and the Unknowable Wild" in Gregory McNamee's collection *Blue Mountains Far Away: Journeys into the American Wilderness* (Lyons Press, 2000). Reprinted by permission of the author.

Review of Roger Rosenblatt's *Consuming Desires.* Copyright 1999 by Gregory McNamee. Reprinted by permission of the author.

"Hornworm's Home Ground: Conserving Interactions" from *Cultures of Habitat* by Gary Paul Nabhan. Copyright 1997 by Gary Paul Nabhan. Reprinted by permission of Counterpoint Press, a member of Perseus Books, L.L.C.

"Men on the Moon" from *Men on the Moon,* by Simon Ortiz. Copyright 1999 by Simon J. Ortiz. Reprinted by permission of the University of Arizona Press.

"Yuusthiwa" from *Woven Stone,* by Simon Ortiz. Copyright 1992 by Simon J. Ortiz. Reprinted by permission of the author.

"Spark-infested Waters," by Robert Michael Pyle. This article originally appeared in *Orion Afield,* 187 Main Street, Great Barrington, MA 01230, www.oriononline.org. Reprinted by permission of the author.

"The Extinction of Experience" from *The Thunder Tree,* by Robert Michael Pyle. Copyright 1993 by Robert Michael Pyle. Reprinted by permission of The Globe Pequot Press.

"Requiem for Sonora" and "Sonora for Sale" from *Selected Poems: 1969–1981* (University of Pittsburgh Press), by Richard Shelton. Copyright 1982 by Richard Shelton. Reprinted by permission of the author.

Selection from *The Sagebrush Ocean,* by Stephen Trimble. Copyright 1989 by Stephen Trimble. Reprinted by permission of the University of Nevada Press.

"A Wilderness Photographer in Marlboro Country," by Stephen Trimble, from the Fall 1996 issue of *Weber Studies.* Reprinted by permission of the author.

"Statement Before the Senate Subcommittee on Forest & Public Lands Management Regarding the Utah Public Lands Management Act of 1995, Washington, D.C., July 13, 1995." From *Red: Passion and Patience in the Desert,* by Terry Tempest Williams. Pantheon Books. Copyright 2001 by Terry Tempest Williams. Reprinted by permission of Brandt & Hochman Literary Agents, Inc.

"Bloodlines." From *Red: Passion and Patience in the Desert,* by Terry Tempest Williams. Pantheon Books. Originally published in *Testimony: Writers of the*